Past and Present

Disputes and

Past and Present Publications

General Editor: T. H. ASTON, *Corpus Christi College, Oxford*

Past and Present Publications comprise books similar in character to the articles in the journal *Past and Present*. Whether the volumes in the series are collections of essays – some previously published, others new studies – or monographs, they encompass a wide variety of scholarly and original works primarily concerned with social, economic and cultural changes, and their causes and consequences. They will appeal to both specialists and non-specialists and will endeavour to communicate the results of historical and allied research in readable and lively form. This series continues and expands in its aims the volumes previously published elsewhere.

For a list of titles in Past and Present Publications, see end of book.

Disputes and Settlements

Law and Human Relations in the West

Edited by

JOHN BOSSY
Professor of History, University of York

DAMAGED

CAMBRIDGE UNIVERSITY PRESS

Cambridge
London   New York   New Rochelle
Melbourne   Sydney

PUBLISHED BY THE PRESS SYNDICATE OF THE UNIVERSITY OF CAMBRIDGE
The Pitt Building, Trumpington Street, Cambridge, United Kingdom

CAMBRIDGE UNIVERSITY PRESS
The Edinburgh Building, Cambridge CB2 2RU, UK
40 West 20th Street, New York NY 10011–4211, USA
477 Williamstown Road, Port Melbourne, VIC 3207, Australia
Ruiz de Alarcón 13, 28014 Madrid, Spain
Dock House, The Waterfront, Cape Town 8001, South Africa

http://www.cambridge.org

First published 1983
First paperback edition 2003

A catalogue record for this book is available from the British Library

Library of Congress catalogue card number: 83–2010

ISBN 0 521 25283 0 hardback
ISBN 0 521 53445 3 paperback

Contents

Contributors

JOHN BOSSY was born in London in 1933, and is a graduate and Ph.D. of Cambridge. From 1966 to 1978 he taught at Queen's University, Belfast, and is now Professor of History at York. His work has been in the history of English Catholicism, on which he published *The English Catholic Community, 1570–1850* in 1976; and on the social history of western Christianity both before and after the Reformation.

JAMES CASEY is the author of *The Kingdom of Valencia in the Seventeenth Century* (1979). He teaches European history at the University of East Anglia. His current research is on family structure and social networks in Andalusia in the early modern period. He was born in Belfast in 1944, and is married with two children.

NICOLE CASTAN, whose background is in law and history, is a Professor at the University of Toulouse II. Her work has been concerned with the analysis of social regulation and judicial practice in Languedoc during the later eighteenth century: a watershed in the history both of crime and of its resolution, which was then still to a considerable extent achieved by mediation.

MICHAEL CLANCHY is Reader in Medieval History at the University of Glasgow. He has edited legal texts for the Selden Society and the Wiltshire Record Society and is the author of *From Memory to Written Record: England 1066–1307* (1979), which relates legal records to the growth of literacy. His most recent book is *England and its Rulers 1066–1272* (1983).

JOHN GILLIS holds degrees from Amherst College and Stanford University. He is the author of *Youth and History* (1974) and *The Development of European Society, 1770–1870* (1977). His most recent research on the history of working class marriage in England and Wales, 1600 to the present, will be published in 1985. He has taught at Stanford and Princeton, and is now Professor at Rutgers University.

DIANE OWEN HUGHES received her Ph.D. at Yale, has taught at Toronto and is at present at Amherst College. Her work has been on medieval urban and family history, and she is engaged on a comparative study of the cities of Genoa, Marseilles and Barcelona.

EDWARD JAMES is a member of the Department of History at the University of York. He has published a number of studies of Frankish history and archaeology, including *The Merovingian Archaeology of South-West Gaul* (1977) and *The Origins of France* (1982). Among other works in progress is a translation of some of the hagiographical works of Gregory of Tours.

RICHARD L. KAGAN received his Ph.D. at Cambridge in 1968. He has taught at Indiana University and the Johns Hopkins University, where he has been a Professor of History since 1979. His publications include *Students and Society in Early Modern Spain* (1974) and *Lawsuits and Litigants in Castile, 1500–1700* (1981). He is writing a book on *The Toledo of El Greco*.

SIMON ROBERTS was born at Micheldever, Hampshire in 1941. He read law at the London School of Economics, then taught at the School of Law in Malawi, where he became interested in legal anthropology; he later did two years' field research in Botswana. His publications include *Law and the Family in Africa* (ed., 1977), *Order and Dispute* (1979) and (with John L. Comaroff) *Rules and Processes* (1981). He is at present Reader in Law at L.S.E.

J. A. SHARPE is a B.A. and D.Phil. of Oxford and, after holding temporary posts at Durham and Exeter, has lectured in history at the University of York since 1973. He is the author of several articles on crime in early modern England, and of *Crime in Seventeenth-Century England: a County Study* (1983).

JENNY WORMALD is a graduate of Glasgow, a Lecturer in Scottish History there, and at present British Academy Reader in the Humanities. As Jennifer M. Brown she edited and contributed to *Scottish Society in the Fifteenth Century* (1977); she is general editor of the *New History of Scotland* (Arnold), and author of volume 4, *Court, Kirk and Community: Scotland, 1470–1625* (1981). She is writing a book on James VI and I.

Editor's Note

Six of the chapters in this volume (1, 3, 4, 6, 7 and 10) were, in their original form, contributions to the Past and Present Conference on Law and Human Relations, held in July 1980. All of them are here published for the first time, with the following three exceptions: chapter 5, by Jenny Wormald, appeared in *Past and Present*, no. 87 (May 1980); parts of chapter 6, by Richard Kagan, appeared in his *Lawsuits and Litigants in Castile, 1500–1700*, published by the University of North Carolina Press, Chapel Hill, 1981; chapter 9, by Nicole Castan, is a translated version of chapter 1 of her *Justice et répression en Languedoc à l'époque des Lumières*, published by Flammarion in their Collection 'Science', Paris, 1980. The editor and the Past and Present Society are extremely grateful to the authors of all three, and to the publishers of the last two, for allowing their contributions to appear in this volume.

1. The Study of Dispute: Anthropological Perspectives

SIMON ROBERTS

For a long time anthropologists who studied disputes in other cultures showed most interest in institutions and processes within small, local groups; many paid little attention to the larger units within which these groups had been incorporated by the time they came to observe them. Often there was, for reasons discussed later, even a conscious effort to stop thinking about people like kings and governors, or such features as centrally organized sanctions. But the picture has changed, and anthropologists are now showing greater interest in relations between the centre and the localities, especially at those moments when government is being consolidated and expanded. Many are looking directly at the points where institutions of central government and those of local communities come into contact, at the efforts of rulers to establish themselves, and at the effects which such efforts have upon those at the periphery. This shift of focus leads to a close community of interest with those social historians whose work John Bossy has collected here, as the concerns I have mentioned show themselves repeatedly in the chapters which follow.

I begin by outlining the directions which anthropological studies of order have taken. Social historians will perhaps recognize some of the debates as having counterparts within their own discipline. They should certainly feel sympathy with the struggles of anthropologists to prevent domestic preconceptions upsetting the picture obtained of other people's arrangements, and with their concern to see action through the eyes of those involved in it. They will probably be perplexed by the extent to which 'rule' and 'action' somehow got separated, and by the difficulties which have been experienced in putting them together again. If they explore the literature they may also be surprised by the strong 'private law' flavour of many studies, concerned primarily with family, property and inheritance disputes, and with wrongs which appear only as the

1

affair of those immediately involved. For social historians the 'public' aspect, control from the centre, and therefore the question of the criminal law, must nearly always have appeared important. Before considering some of the special problems which legal proceedings and their records may present, I say something about the efforts which anthropologists have made to distinguish different kinds of dispute processes, and particularly the different forms of third-party intervention. Here it is essential to recognize the considerable diversity of forms which recent studies have revealed; we can no longer identify all informal processes under the general head of 'arbitration'. As the contributors show, there are a number of different ways in which it is possible to intervene in a quarrel, and the attempt to distinguish between them must be made if we are to see where power is located and how it is exercised in different cultural contexts.

I. DIRECTIONS IN LEGAL ANTHROPOLOGY

If we look at anthropological studies of order from a distance, three more or less distinct phases may be identified. The first began with Maine in England and some distinguished contemporaries on the Continent and in America.[1] They worked within a broad comparative, evolutionary framework upon the development of social organization, government and law. This tradition continued in the writings of scholars like Vinogradoff and Hobhouse roughly until the First World War.[2] The arrival of the second phase was secured in publications of Radcliffe-Brown and Malinowski during the 1920s, though its beginnings may be traced back earlier than that. In this work interest in larger questions to do with change and historical development receded to be replaced by a much less ambitious programme which centred on very detailed studies of particular cultures, even individual communities, deliberately cut off from their surroundings and viewed as working wholes. Only now, over the last decade, have anthropologists drawn back from

---

[1] Alongside H. S. Maine's writings we should note particularly J. Bachofen's *Das Mutterrecht* (Basle, 1861); and L. H. Morgan's *Ancient Society* (New York, 1877).

[2] In America the tradition proved much more durable, with continuing interest being shown in legal-evolutionary themes: see, for example, E. A. Hoebel, *The Law of Primitive Man* (Cambridge, Mass., 1954); M. H. Fried, *The Evolution of Political Society* (New York, 1967); and latterly, R. Cohen and E. R. Service (eds.), *Origins of the State* (Philadelphia, 1978).

these minute studies, and begun to examine the relationship between these small groups and the larger states within which they are now encapsulated. Armed with more extensive ethnographic material, they are also returning to those large questions which preoccupied scholars in the nineteenth century.

The retreat to more painstaking and detailed studies which followed the exciting start under Maine was closely linked to a new research technique. Instead of relying on accounts prepared by missionaries, traders and administrators, or at best the brief and severe cross-examination of a few 'native' informants, anthropologists went into the field to see for themselves what other societies were like; and stayed there for sustained periods. This new style of work was epitomized by Malinowski pitching his tent in a Trobriand fishing village and observing closely over a period of months what was going on around him. Thereafter, participant observation rapidly became the accepted, indeed the obligatory, starting-point of anthropological work. In this way researchers came to look in great detail, and in isolation, at those small-scale, relatively simple cultures with which their discipline has come to be associated. Outside influences, such as agents of the colonizing power or contact with adjacent indigenous groups, tended to be ignored or blocked out as contaminating the purity of the sample. The view obtained was thus typically of one culture at a particular moment, leading to a rather flat, ahistorical account, strong on the here and now but weak on change. It is understandable that under these circumstances the comparative and historical concerns which had been central in the earlier period should have fallen away. But beyond that there was an explicit reaction against trying to understand particular features of the culture under observation as survivals from some earlier 'stage'.

Initially, much of this new work had a straightforward, functionalist character, with a central focus upon institutions. Social life was seen as a matter of compliance with rule; normal behaviour was rule-governed behaviour, and settlement institutions were there to put things right if temporary malfunction in the form of a dispute developed. This was a view of order which owed much to Durkheim, but was also close to that underlying the dominant tradition in western jurisprudence. It is not surprising that many anthropologists relied explicitly on legal theory. Even where they did not do so, legal categories and ways of thinking often dominated their work.[3] Radcliffe-Brown identified 'law' as one of the principal compartments into which anthropological study should be divided up; and in his important essay 'On Social Structure' (1940) law appears as a separate and privileged element in the proposed 'social physiology'.[4]

Despite the initial vigour and confidence of these 'rule-centred' studies they soon began to face competition from work with a transactional flavour. The new emphasis was already visible in some of Malinowski's work of the 1920s,[5] but gathered strength in the 1950s and 1960s. This movement involved a shift of interest away from rules and structure towards the actions and strategies of real people, and was founded on an assumption that order could be understood through the study of processes in which living men and women were involved. In these studies human behaviour came to be seen as constrained by the relationships within which individual actors became enmeshed, rather than by rules. Instead of being rule-governed, men were seen as self-seeking, co-operating with each other only out of enlightened self-interest. Disputes, far from being pathological, were normal and inevitable as people struggled to secure their objectives; and order was the product of the *ad hoc* accommodations and adjustments which ensued. In short for those within this tradition social order came to be seen as the changing product of conflicting interests, constantly renegotiated, 'made up' as life went on.

In contrast to the rival tradition, these studies owed little to legal theory. In some it was disregarded; in others it was explicitly rejected as positively hampering the understanding of other cultures. Looking back, this emphasis on 'interest' and 'process' seems an inevitable development, given the research strategy which has already been referred to. Out there in his village, the ethnographer was bound to lose himself in the activities, plotting and talk which were going on around him. Furthermore, public quarrels, just because they were readily accessible, were bound to become the show-pieces of his work.

The achievements and limitations of work done during this

---

[3] Among the classic monographs in this tradition is I. Schapera's *A Handbook of Tswana Law and Custom* (London, 1938).
[4] *Journal of the Royal Anthropological Institute*, lxx (1940), pp. 1–12.
[5] E.g. *Argonauts of the Western Pacific* (London, 1922); *Crime and Custom in Savage Society* (London, 1926).

second phase speak for themselves. In terms of political theory, numerous studies of small-scale, relatively egalitarian societies without rulers decisively undermined the idea, stretching back at least as far as Hobbes, that social order is only conceivable in the context of some form of central government. It is not the fault of anthropologists if the lessons of these studies, clear as they are, have yet to be absorbed by some legal and political theorists. Empirically, as accounts of 'what other societies are like', the best legal ethnographies of the period are also very impressive, both in the quality and depth of detail presented, and in the level of analysis. But this strength is in one respect deceptive; mesmerized by the life and bustle of a small face-to-face community, some lost sight of the wider picture. The progress of longer-term change and the effects of 'contact' with larger external groupings both tended to recede in the struggle to understand immediate surroundings in the present. But they were a part of that 'present', so even the picture of the moment was impaired when they were neglected. Damaging also was the opposition between 'rule-centred' and 'processual' approaches which I have already outlined.[6] In some studies functionalist and transactional assumptions were found together in an uneasy blend; but in general the separate development of these two traditions seriously hampered understanding as the normative element in social life tended to appear dominant in one set of studies while conflict and the pursuit of interest assumed too much importance in the other.

Over the last couple of decades or so, legal anthropologists have extended increasingly their interests beyond the small groups with which they are traditionally associated to consider the relationship of these groups with those larger units within which they are now all incorporated. As I noted at the beginning, a focus upon the relationship between the state and partially autonomous local groups within it is also a major feature of several contributions to this book. Interesting parallels appear between these cases from the European past and the contemporary results of nineteenth- and twentieth-century colonial expansion at present being studied by anthropologists: in both we find rulers struggling to establish, consolidate and expand control in peripheral areas; in both the rulers present themselves as judges of local disputes, and we see

[6] See pp. 3–4 above.

those on the periphery seeking to exploit or avoid these agencies. In anthropological studies this shift of interest has led to a much greater emphasis on 'change' and 'development', and there are signs of a return to those large questions which preoccupied scholars in the nineteenth century. Work drawing on Marxist theory is prominent here,[7] but this is not the only direction which renewed comparative and historical concerns have taken.[8] A revival of these concerns must lead us to re-examine the conditions under which different institutional forms and dispute processes are likely to be found; to consider the critical differences between dispute processes in small, acephalous groups and those of the state; and even to postulate sequential stages for the growth of legal systems. Again, there are clear signs of similar interests in these contributions, notably in Castan's chapter.

Other contemporary work represents a less radical break with earlier studies, and can be seen as an attempt to 'put rules and action back together'. Sensitive to the harm done by any rigid opposition between 'rule-centred' and 'processual' approaches, it recognizes that the concerns reflected in both represent necessary and complementary areas of inquiry. Only by contemplating structure and process together, it is argued, can we confront fundamental questions to do with social order.[9]

[7] E.g., M. Godelier, *Perspectives in Marxist Anthropology* (Cambridge, 1977); C. Meillassoux, *Maidens, Meal and Money* (Cambridge, 1981); P. Fitzpatrick, *Law and State in Papua-New Guinea* (London, 1980); F. G. Snyder, *Capitalism and Legal Change* (New York, 1981).

[8] Note, for example, the efforts of members of the Chicago School to establish an underlying economic rationality in the organizational forms of 'primitive' society. See e.g. R. A. Posner, 'A Theory of Primitive Society, with special reference to Primitive Law', *The Journal of Law and Economics*, xxii (1980) no. 1, p. 53.

[9] Following M. Barkun's approach in *Law Without Sanctions* (New Haven, 1968), a number of recent ethnographic studies of dispute settlement processes in small-scale cultures have treated 'rules' as comprising a series of reference points, a kind of symbolic grammar out of which reality may continually be constructed and re-constructed. On this view there is neither discontinuity nor opposition between norm and behaviour; the two exist in a dialectical relationship, reacting on each other as time goes on – the normative repertoire providing the conceptual elements out of which this interaction is rendered meaningful and negotiable. From this angle, it is possible to observe how changes in the repertoire come about, as individual rules are utilized and reformulated in the course of exchanges between parties to a dispute in the light of the objectives of the disputants. Thus, as the system is experienced, changes take place in the content of the rule base which will themselves have consequences for future behaviour as people develop their strategies in the light of the reformulated rule. See e.g. J. L. Comaroff, 'Rules and Rulers: Political Processes in a Tswana Chiefdom', *Man*, n.s., xiii (1978), pp.

2. THE STUDY OF DISPUTES

Anthropologists have been widely criticized for their failure to conceptualize 'dispute' in such a way that this sphere can be marked off from other forms of conflict.[10] Here one difficulty, as we have already seen, is that those working within 'rule-centred' and 'processual' paradigms have tended to regard conflict rather differently: the former, as an abnormal feature associated with breaches of rule; the latter, as part of the normal flow of life and inherent in the pursuit of interest. On another level, even when the element of distortion which polarization of these rival positions can produce in fieldwork is allowed for, empirical studies show that 'folk' views of conflict differ sharply from one culture to another. In some, any confrontation or controversy is strongly disapproved, and peace and quiet valued above anything. Elsewhere, loud, aggressive behaviour is perfectly acceptable, and people may openly relish a quarrel.

One possible approach is to identify as 'disputes' only those confrontations which follow from an actor's perception that some harm he has suffered or anticipates flows from another's departure from accepted criteria of association. The existence of any human group must imply *some* understanding among the members as to how the activities of everyday life should be arranged, and as to what forms of conduct are to be acceptable or unacceptable in a given context. How far these understandings are translated in explicit, articulate normative terms has been shown to vary considerably from one culture to another; but some shared idea of recognized interest, some conception of 'wrong', constitutes a necessary basis of association. From that position, we could treat as disputes those occasions where one feels he has suffered an injury, sees another as to blame and confronts him with responsibility.

1–20; S. A. Roberts, 'The Kgatla Marriage: Concepts of Validity' in Roberts (ed.), *Law and the Family in Africa* (The Hague, 1977); J. L. Comaroff and S. A. Roberts, *Rules and Processes: The Cultural Logic of Dispute in an African Context* (Chicago, 1981); see, generally, A. L. Strauss, *Negotiations: Varieties, Contexts, Processes and Social Order* (San Francisco, 1978) and P. H. Gulliver's concluding remarks in *Disputes and Negotiations: A Cross-Cultural Perspective* (New York, 1979), pp. 274–5.

[10] See, for example, M. Cain and K. Kulcsar, 'Thinking Disputes: an Essay on the Origins of the Dispute Industry', *Law and Society Review*, xvi (1981–2), pp. 375–402.

That would enable us to distinguish such cases from those where one suffers a reverse or another secures an advantage without any departure from approved patterns of behaviour. Examples of the latter occasion are provided by any form of 'competition' in which two struggle for a resource which one will attain and the other inevitably lose even though both may adhere to mutually acceptable standards of conduct throughout: obvious instances of this kind are struggles for political ascendancy, or rival efforts to capture the market for a particular product. While the distinction suggested here may still seem too loose or vague, the advantage of such an approach is that it gets away from the intractable difficulties inherent in attempting to define an area of 'political' conflict, and avoids probably fruitless attempts to distinguish 'political' and 'legal' spheres.

Even if a conception of dispute along these lines is agreed on, it can still be objected that the occasions falling within the field mapped out are far too varied to be treated as a single category. Here, for example, much anthropological work can be criticized as tending to present all disputes as confrontations between equals; the implications of stratification, the presence of control from the centre (and thus the question of 'crime') have frequently been ignored. This emphasis can be explained as a consequence of the kind of society which anthropologists have typically studied; but as soon as we move away from small-scale, relatively egalitarian cultures at least three broad categories of dispute have to be distinguished:

1. disputes between parties in relationships of relative equality;
2. disputes which cross lines of stratification (e.g. confrontations between lord and villein; between employer and employee);
3. disputes which arise directly out of a ruler's efforts to govern and in which the ruler himself or his agents will be directly involved.

Dispute processes within each category may be expected to take a different shape; and variations in institutional structure may be observable, as in the criteria invoked by the disputants and those attempting to achieve an outcome.

When we look at the manner in which quarrels are pursued a general distinction between fighting and talking characterizes much of the discussion in this book. In this connection, two quite durable ideas about dispute processes are challenged in anthropological studies of order. One is the notion that fighting somehow precedes talking in evolutionary terms and then gives way to talking at an identifiable point in social development. The other asserts that while processes of settlement-directed talking tend to be rule-governed, fighting is not. Recent research has yielded a number of careful studies of small, stateless groups in which a high level of inter-personal violence is observable and in which fighting is seen by the members as the proper way to deal with a quarrel. Equally, other studies reveal similar groups in which violence hardly features at all and in which any form of fighting is strongly disapproved. Elsewhere, fighting and talking are found side by side in a complex relationship within the same culture. Furthermore, the scale and form of fighting in these cultures seem infinitely varied, sometimes limited to private acts of retaliatory violence, sometimes involving protracted exchanges between rival segments, even extending to cyclical warfare between adjacent groups of different ethnic affiliations. But satisfactory predictions as to the conditions under which fighting is likely to be encountered and as to why quarrels involve fighting in some groups but not in others remain elusive.

It is clear from these papers that social historians require no introduction to the ways in which anthropologists have seen the particular institution of the feud; and anthropologists should find very interesting what the former have to say here about the treatment of feud where central government has been established. On the whole anthropologists have assumed that fighting is seldom an approved mode of handling disputes under central government. Rulers tend to object strongly to sustained fighting among their subjects, to present themselves as authoritative agents of dispute settlement and to do their best to make sure that they are treated as such. Where significant resort to retaliatory violence and fighting between groups has been found in association with central government, this has been taken as an indication of the uncertain extent to which government is established. I am not sure how far this view is challenged by Wormald's account of the incorporation and regulation of the feud in early modern Scotland. For any ruler struggling to establish or extend his authority an alternative to attempting direct suppression must be to associate himself closely with indigenous institutions in the first instance and gradually subject them to regulation.[11]

---

[11] See the example provided by the growth of the Merina Kingdom outlined by M. Bloch, 'Decision-Making in Councils among the Merina of Madagascar' in A. Richards and A. Kuper (eds.), *Councils in Action* (Cambridge, 1971).

If it is the case that where fighting does survive under strongly established central government it is likely to be subject to close normative control, often taking on a ritual form, fighting in stateless groups tends to be closely rule-governed also. Bohannan's terse reflection that there are 'basically two forms of conflict resolution: administered rules and fighting, Law and War',[12] is misleading. The picture emerges clearly from recent studies that where fighting is found in small, acephalous groups it almost invariably takes an institutionalized form.[13]

When social historians turn to those dispute processes which depend in the first instance upon talking as opposed to fighting, they are free of two constricting assumptions which it took anthropologists a long time to throw off. We no longer see the presence of central government agencies as essential to social order; and we now recognize that third parties who intervene in disputes do not necessarily do so as judges. In *Ancient Law* and in subsequent writings, Maine treated adjudication as the basic means of dispute settlement from the very onset of social life. From the senior male agnate right through to the Victorian high court judge he saw the mode of resolution as one of third-party decision. In tantalizing asides he expanded upon this position slightly to suggest that this process began as arbitration and only gave way to adjudication later on. But it was a matter of 'judging' from first to last; the only differences being that, as successive stages of 'civilization' were reached, different kinds of people did the judging and new criteria underpinned their judgements. Underlying this view, as I have already noted, was a long-standing assumption that order is only conceivable if there are strong men in positions of authority ready to tell others what to do. Non-lawyers were slow to challenge this position,[14] which was still subscribed to by a few anthropologists working within a 'rule-centred' paradigm as late as the 1950s,[15] but at least from the publication of Malinowski's field studies in the 1920s[16] the majority of anthropologists began to accept the

---

[12] *Law and Warfare* (New York, 1967), p. xiii.
[13] See, for example, R. Rappaport, *Pigs for the Ancestors: Ritual in the Ecology of a New Guinea Mountain People* (New Haven, 1967).
[14] Both E. Durkheim and M. Weber certainly appear to have assumed a necessary link between social order and some form of central control.
[15] See, for example, L. Pospisil, *Kapauku Papuans and their Law* (New Haven, 1958).
[16] Notably the volumes referred to in footnote 5 above.

possibility of social order in the absence of central government. If this all seems obvious today, we should not underestimate the importance of the liberation thus achieved. Once we are freed from the *necessity* of the King and the Judge, though in the West still expecting to find them somewhere in the picture, it becomes possible to examine the range of dispute institutions in a far less restricted way.

At this point we must note that the 'rule-centred' and 'processual' traditions offer different and complementary perspectives in looking at disputes. Work associated with the former approach has had an institutional focus, dwelling on structural differences between settlement institutions; while processual work, with a strong transactional bias, has examined disputes from the standpoint of the disputants themselves and of intervening third parties, revealing how objectives are pursued through the recruitment of support, choice of forum and the development of strategy.

With regard to institutional forms, a number of tentative typologies of dispute institutions were put forward on the basis of field research carried out in the 1960s. These emphasized various features, such as the presence or absence of third-party intervention, or the form which such intervention might take in those cases where it was to be found.[17] A measure of agreement also began to emerge as to the essential range of variation which empirical studies disclosed.[18] Most typologies revolve around three basic forms which settlement-directed discourse may take: the disputants may feel their way towards a settlement through bilateral negotiation; they may try to resolve the matter with the help of a neutral mediator; or they may submit the quarrel to an umpire for decision.

Bilateral negotiation represents the least complex form of settlement process. Here the rival disputants approach each other without the intervention of third parties and try to bring the dispute to an end through discussion. No intermediaries or supporters are involved; the achievement of communication and the subsequent process of settlement lie in the hands of the two disputants alone. A

---

[17] See, for example, P. H. Gulliver, *Social Control in an African Society* (London, 1963); T. Eckhoff, 'The Mediator, the Judge and the Administrator in Conflict-Resolution', *Acta Sociologica*, x, p. 158; M. Gluckman, *Politics, Law and Ritual in Tribal Society* (London, 1965), pp. 183–96; K. F. Koch, *War and Peace in Jalemo* (New Haven, 1974).

[18] The following account is abstracted from S. Roberts, *Order and Dispute* (Harmondsworth, 1979), pp. 69–71.

variation of this mode of settlement is present where partisans align themselves in support of one or other of the disputants; but while the 'strength' of the respective sides may be altered by this procedure, the structural form of the encounter remains unchanged.

In each of the remaining modes of settlement this bilateral element is removed by the intervention of third parties in some intermediate position. Where this role is mediatory, the third party helps the disputants towards their own solution rather than imposing a solution upon them. The most limited form of mediation arises where the third party acts as a 'go-between'. His role is passive in the sense that while he operates as a bridge or a conduit pipe between the two disputants, he does no more than carry messages backwards and forwards between them. Through this means of communication the disputants themselves reach some kind of settlement. The go-between has not actively contributed to this settlement by giving his opinion, making value judgements, tendering advice or urging particular avenues of conduct; but he has enabled the disputants to communicate with each other. This form of mediation may be contrasted with a more active one in which the third party takes a positive part in promoting a settlement. His intervention may take the form of advice, suggested solutions, reasoned pleas, or even emotional cajoling, threats and bullying. Unlike the go-between, he actively pursues a settlement, while remaining ostensibly neutral and without seeking to impose an outcome.

Under the third mode of settlement the neutral party seeks to resolve the dispute by making a decision, rather than assisting the disputants towards their own solution. Within this broad category we can distinguish two types of umpire, whom I shall label the arbitrator and the adjudicator. The arbitrator derives his authority to decide the dispute from the invitation of the disputants themselves, who have voluntarily submitted to his decision; while the adjudicator, who derives his authority from some office in the community, intervenes to impose a decision by virtue of that office rather than by the invitation of the disputants. In some respects this last distinction is of limited importance, as in both cases authority to resolve a dispute in the face of competing claims by imposing a decision is present. None the less, the distinct sources from which this authority is derived may (as we shall see later in this section) be of critical importance.

This typology underlines some important variables which attend these different processes: the achievement of a solution by negotiated agreement or imposed decision; the presence of third-party involvement; the nature of the intervener as partisan or neutral; and the derivation of authority in decision-making. But it fails to lay sufficient emphasis upon what may be considered the crucial feature of any dispute process, the location of power to decide the outcome. The hallmark of both arbitration and adjudication, if we choose to distinguish them, is that the power of decision is transferred from the disputants to the arbitrator or adjudicator. In bilateral processes, and those in which third parties intervene as mediators, the power to decide remains with the disputants themselves. Gulliver has treated this as the critical variable in dispute processes, and the importance he attaches to it underlies the division which he has proposed between processes of negotiation and those of adjudication.[19] Processes of negotiation are seen essentially as bargaining procedures in which the parties try to feel their way towards an agreement while retaining control over the outcome, whether or not they may be assisted by supporters and/or mediating third parties; in adjudicatory processes the power to decide is surrendered to some third party.

If we do accept Gulliver's simple distinction between adjudication and negotiation, with a view to laying stress on the importance of identifying the locus of decision in dispute processes, we must not let this conceal other important variables which may cut across these two institutional forms. We should begin from the point that procedural formality, the invocation of rules in decision-making and the operation of particular forms of sanction need not necessarily be linked together, or associated with one type of process or the other. For example, it appears in these contributions that adjudication and formality of procedure are not invariably associated; we see cases where the power of decision is transferred to a third party and yet the process remains speedy and informal. Similarly the anthropological literature provides many examples of negotiatory processes hedged about with all sorts of formal constraints; indeed formality of procedure may assume a special importance where there are no agencies of central government to enforce an agreement once it has been reached, and the full burden

---

[19] *Social Control in an African Society*, pp. 296–9.

of enforcement may be carried in the ceremonial and ritual sphere. A similar point may be made about the use of rules in decision-making. In negotiatory processes, as in those of adjudication, disputants and third parties organize their arguments around normative propositions. These may be more or less explicit and clear-cut, and are unlikely rigidly to determine an outcome; but they will inform the arguments and play some part in the outcome that is reached. We must not assume that the clarity with which rules are invoked, or the stress which is laid on them as guiding the decision, necessarily point towards either adjudication or negotiation. Judgement may be *ad hoc* and the negotiated outcome presented in the idiom of rule. The relationship between sanction and settlement process must also be left open. Adjudicators very often have coercive sanctions behind them to make their decisions stick; but this is not invariably the case. Again, while one mediator may be a well-meaning neighbour another may be a hectoring feudal superior. In the same way we should not take for granted that compliance with the negotiated outcome is left to the good will of the parties themselves.

If we are to distinguish adequately between different institutional forms and have any success in establishing a systematic relationship between internal variations of process and the wider context in which they are found, we must remain open to the range of combinations in which these internal features may be clustered together.[20] It is perhaps easy to slip from a constructive distinction between adjudication and negotiation into a misleading opposition of a wholly different kind: between the formal, judicial processes of the state, yielding rule-based decisions to be imposed by force; and private, informal processes of negotiation which move through mutual accommodation towards agreed resolution, secured by harmonious acceptance. We must avoid the ethnocentric assumption of a link between government sponsored adjudication, procedural formality, rules as the dominant criteria in decision-making and coercive sanctions; this grouping represents no more than a caricature of our own arrangements and could anyway be found only where 'law' takes on a specialized, differentiated character largely absent in the times and places these contributions are concerned with. There is another reason for rejecting this

[20] R. L. Abel, 'A Comparative Theory of Dispute Institutions in Society', *Law and Society Review*, viii (1973), pp. 217–347.

beguiling opposition, which I come back to later:[21] the picture of negotiation is on the whole too beautiful; we cannot necessarily present negotiation and adjudication as law and love respectively.

A further point must be made hastily. In the form in which they appear here, these processes appear distinct; but we must recognize what I have sketched so far as models only, cut away from any historical or cultural context. Processes observed in operation will not always be crisply distinguished and in practice may shade off into one another. Even the broad distinction between bilateral negotiation and processes involving third-party intervention may break down where mediators emerge from the groups of supporters aligned behind each party. Similarly, where there is unanimity among the members of the respective support groups as to an appropriate settlement, the disputants may be in much the same position as they would be in the face of a decision by an adjudicator. They have no alternative but to comply with the proposed settlement, as failure to do so will imperil the future co-operation of their supporters. In many situations where third parties intervene in a bridging position between two disputants there may be a lack of clarity as to whether the part being played is of a mediatory or umpiring character. The mediator and the adjudicator are perhaps best represented as polar cases at different ends of a continuum along which these analytically distinct functions merge into one another in practice.

It is only worth the trouble it takes to classify the internal characteristics of dispute institutions if we can move on to speculate as to the conditions under which analytically distinct forms are likely to be found and then try to locate them in specific socio-cultural contexts. Here anthropological research offers disappointingly few clues as to the way different institutional forms are related to each other and the conditions in which we should expect to find them. The principal conclusion, perhaps a lame and predictable one, is that judges are creatures of the state. The ethnographic evidence suggests pretty strongly, in sharp contrast to Maine's early speculations, that adjudicatory decision-making as opposed to mediatory activity is almost exclusively linked to the presence of central government. This conclusion may be supported from a wide variety of sources; but it is most strikingly demons-

[21] See p. 19 below.

trated by Mair in her careful review of the East African ethnography.[22] However, we should be cautious of taking for granted the idea that as adjudication becomes established other modes of intervention fall away. Rather, we should expect to find a range of structurally different processes, including those of a mediatory nature, even in the context of the state. Without challenging in any way the point which Castan makes in the context of Languedoc in the eighteenth century, we should therefore be cautious about generalizing upon her view of mediation as 'the index of an uncompleted state' and that 'the more the state extended its action, the more mediation decayed'.[23] Which agencies, present as the state becomes established, manage to survive that development must depend upon a range of circumstances. Certainly we should see mediation under threat if those who have traditionally mediated are seen by the ruler as competitors for power. We must also recognize that mediatory processes may grow up subsequently 'in the shadow of adjudication'.[24]

On the other hand, settlements reached through negotiated agreement, in some cases achieved with the help of mediation, are widely reported from stateless groups as well as being found to coexist with adjudicatory processes under central government. Reports from East Africa also indicate those organizational features which must be present in an acephalous group if mediatory procedures are to be established. 'Neutrals' must be available who can distance themselves from either side.[25] Certain types of kinship system do not yield such figures; people who might otherwise have been mediators may have fixed obligations of support towards one side or the other, determined by their relative positions in the kinship structure. But even where this is the case, the respective groups of supporters lined up behind each disputant often seem to operate in the same way as mediators in co-operating to push the respective parties whom they support towards a mutually acceptable solution. Gulliver's account of the Arusha (1963) provides an interesting illustration of such processes.

Anthropological work offers little support for the idea suggested

---

[22] *Primitive Government* (Harmondsworth, 1962).   [23] See p. 258 below.
[24] R. H. Mnookin and L. Kornhauser, 'Bargaining in the Shadow of the Law: the Case of Divorce', *Yale Law Journal*, lxxxviii (1979), p. 950.
[25] Gulliver, *Social Control in an African Society; Neighbours and Networks* (Berkeley, 1971).

tentatively by Maine in *Ancient Law* and in *Early Law and Custom*,[26] and subsequently quite widely held, that there may be a general shift from arbitration to adjudication. There are very few reports indeed from stateless groupings which describe disputants taking their disputes voluntarily before third parties for decision as opposed to mediation; but three instances should be mentioned. Barth describes Pathan 'saints' as sometimes being called upon to arbitrate in disputes.[27] Gellner and Lewis also hold that a similar role is performed by religious specialists in Berber[28] and Somali[29] communities. However, it is not absolutely clear in these cases that the role is one of decision-making, rather than mediating.[30] Assuming there is a decision-making role here, in each case the arbitrator is a figure standing somewhat 'outside' the system, and this marginal situation is in each instance supplemented by a state of grace or privileged access to supernatural agencies. It is clear from the contributors to this book that these meagre suggestions could be valuably supplemented through a careful review of the role in disputes played by the clergy in Christian Europe. There is limited evidence that arbitration may develop once the state is in the process of being established, as people who want to be rulers try to impose themselves in private disputes between people they are trying to rule.[31] But there is much more support for the suggestion that arbitration generally grows up in the shadow of adjudication, rather than the other way round. Disputants who do not wish to involve themselves with agents of the state take their quarrel to a chosen third party for decision. In some cases, the state itself has encouraged arbitration at the lower levels as a substitute for adjudicatory processes.[32]

Overall there is much more work to be done before we can offer detailed speculation as to the conditions which are likely to yield different forms of dispute process. The present contributions offer many suggestive hints; making it clear that we have to look to differences in social and governmental organization, to productive

[26] At pp. 220 (1917 edn) and 170 (1883 edn) respectively.
[27] *Political Leadership among the Swat Pathans* (London, 1959).
[28] *Saints of the Atlas* (London, 1969).
[29] *A Pastoral Democracy* (London, 1961).
[30] See J. Black-Michaud, *Cohesive Force: Feud in the Mediterranean and the Middle East* (London, 1975), p. 11, n. 2.   [31] See M. Bloch, note 11 above.
[32] This was certainly the case during the period of indirect rule in some of the former British African possessions.

processes and settlement patterns, and overall to the ways in which actors in different cultures view their worlds.

Work within the 'processual' paradigm inevitably yielded a different, if complementary, view of disputes. As quarrels were seen as normal and inevitable, rather than signs that something had gone wrong which needed to be put right, the emphasis on institutions as 'settling' disputes and securing a return to the proper state of things fell away. But beyond that there was a shift of interest away from institutions altogether, towards living men and women, people who were constructing their lives as they went along rather than following rules. Thus if disputes were to be 'made sense' of this had to be in terms of the actors' objectives. If rivalry and dispute represented normal moments in the intersecting biographies of actors' behaviour, their respective circumstances, goals, strategies and actions determined the nature of the interaction between them. The decision whether, or in what manner, to precipitate a confrontation was predicated upon these factors. If the form and content of dispute processes were to be explained, therefore, attention had to be given to the disputants' ostensible motives in pursuing a quarrel, how they recruited support, their strategic efforts to influence the procedural course of events, and so on. At the same time rules were recognized as themselves the objects of negotiation, as resources to be managed to advantage.

Some of the more extreme forms of 'transactional analysis' do not perhaps help us explain much at all; but the very directing of attention towards the litigant and his attempts to exercise choice was constructive in that it led scholars to ask why one agency rather than another was chosen by a disputant once the dispute was before it. These are important questions and, as we can see from several of the contributions here, they may lead to answers which in themselves bring into question the nature of litigation and the manner in which its objectives are conventionally viewed.

There was another important gain in the move away from concern for structure and institution. The attention given to the objectives and strategies of individual disputants naturally led to a close study of their oratory, and thus to another important means through which they struggled to control one another.[33] Finally,

---

[33] See M. Bloch (ed.), *Political Language and Oratory in Traditional Society* (London, 1975).

there was perhaps a necessary corrective in the emphasis of 'processual' work upon pursuit of interest over compliance with rule, and this applies to our view of third parties who intervene in disputes as well as to those in dispute. In connection with the former, Wormald is clearly right to warn us that rulers who judge their subjects do so as powerful men pursuing their interests.[34] So far as the disputants themselves are concerned, that point brings us back to the question of law and love. However the outcomes may be presented by disputants or mediators, we should be cautious of accepting uncritically a romantic view of negotiatory processes as means whereby, in the absence of coercive adjudication, disputants achieve a compromise in the interests of, and readily acceptable to, both parties. Those in dispute in any society are generally out to secure their interests, among which only one possibility is represented by return to idyllic harmony. Consequently the disputant with superior bargaining power, whether of a political or economic nature, is likely to be able to coerce the other notwithstanding the operation of some normative constraint. We should not necessarily perceive the outcomes of negotiatory or mediatory processes as inherently 'fairer' and more beautiful than those achieved by adjudication. That leaves open the question of Christianity, absent entirely from many of the cultures studied by anthropologists, present everywhere in these contributions. What part did charity play in local level dispute processes in Europe? How far did the normative framework provided by Christianity restrain stronger parties from imposing themselves when negotiation took place?

3. THE RECORD OF DISPUTE

For anthropologists and for social historians occasions of conflict must offer privileged access to a *range* of material which will not be rivalled in any other source. They will find talk about everyday life, about what disputants and other people have done, and about the physical surroundings to their lives. Alongside these kinds of information will appear various kinds of normative proposition; statements in which rules, beliefs and values are either explicitly articulated or emerge by implication. Here we can obtain the

---

[34] See p. 126 below.

disputants' view of the normal and the abnormal through their claims as to what people should or should not have done. At the same time, as soon as we move outside the smallest, relatively egalitarian societies studied by anthropologists, we shall also have the utterances of the specialists handling the dispute (whether as mediators or decision-makers). Thus, from these occasions we can build up a picture of rules and structure *and* of people interacting in the context of conflict. At the same time, if we are not directly interested in conflict at all, we can use them to reconstruct at least a partial picture of the beliefs and everyday lives of those involved. Le Roy Ladurie's *Montaillou* is, of course, an amazing example of this latter use of legal records.

When we consider the quality of the information available to anthropologists and social historians, and the demands they will respectively make upon their sources, a considerable disparity is obvious. For the anthropologist, the record of dispute is likely to be an account which he has prepared for himself from his own observations, and with his own purposes in mind. He will similarly have had ample opportunity to fill in for himself the general cultural background against which the dispute has taken place. If he does use an official record prepared by someone else, this will almost certainly represent a subsidiary source. There will be no question of his having to recreate some aspect of the culture from records of dispute alone. For the social historian, on the other hand, the records available to him will have been prepared long ago by someone else, probably an ecclesiastical or legal specialist, for very different purposes. Furthermore, these records may constitute virtually his only source, both about disputes and about the context within which they took place. From these materials, often ample in quantity but invariably limited in perspective, he will be trying to write not only about conflict but probably about other aspects of everyday life in the culture concerned.

Here an insoluble problem is posed wherever legal records represent the principal source. Disputes are specific to particular cultures and can only be understood in the wider context within which they take place. So we need to know about the surroundings if we are to make full use of the record, yet the record is all we have got to tell us about the dispute and the context. There are more superficial problems of omission. The legal or clerical specialist making the record knows what material is necessary for his purposes, and omits the rest. I remember reading some Tswana customary court records, made during the colonial and immediate post-colonial periods, before I went into the field. These terse, factual accounts were a disappointment, because I knew from earlier anthropological studies how vividly the Tswana could talk about their rules, yet nothing of this appeared at all. However, I was reassured when I began to listen to disputes directly and heard the richness of the language through which normative material was presented. It soon became clear that court clerks simply 'shut off' when these important but highly formalized parts of a speech were arrived at, leaving a crucial dimension of Tswana legal oratory totally unrecorded. A view of Tswana disputes built up on records alone would have conveyed a 'fact-mindedness' totally uncharacteristic of these processes. Although the selectivity of legal records is in itself interesting and revealing it inevitably hampers research, and their shape must not be allowed to dictate the view we form of the culture under observation.

There is a related hazard in drawing general conclusions as to social conditions from the profile of court business. During 1968, the first year I did work in the Kgatleng, nearly 60 per cent of the disputes heard in the traditional ruler's *kgotla* (the only local court keeping records at that time) were cases of assault and stealing; and earlier records showed that this figure was exceeded in some years of the previous decade. Dominating the business in this court, these cases presented a horrifying picture of theft and violence hard to square with the overall picture I formed of life in the Kgatleng. What in fact was happening was that cases of theft and assault from a very wide area were concentrated in this single court while other kinds of business were spread around a variety of agencies.

There is another temptation in the tantalizingly incomplete picture yielded by court records. They will invariably leave us knowing too little about who the disputants were and what made them behave as they did in court. Often, for example, an anthropologist knows something of the relationship of the parties, but nothing of why particular alignments of opposition or support existed. Inevitably we shall speculate about these matters on the basis of what contextual matter is available and what we know of the overall cultural background. But we must be very cautious of accounting for such alignments with glib authority in spurious structural terms. (For example 'X supported Y because he was his mother's brother,' and so on.)

In any culture we must also expect some disparity between the form in which a dispute appears in court and the 'real' substance of the quarrel which gives rise to it. Even in the absence of the specialization which characterizes the courts of contemporary legal systems, there is likely to be some gap between the way in which the parties conceive of their quarrel and the manner in which it is seen by interveners. The disputants will probably know this and thus present the matter in such a way that the court will be prepared to hear it. Repeatedly during fieldwork I came across records which revealed enormous disparities between what I knew of the quarrel from external evidence and the manner in which it appeared in court. Examples included a dispute which was ostensibly about damage to cooking pots but in fact concerned the relative seniority of co-wives; similarly, an apparently trivial quarrel over the misdeeds of a billy goat turned out to be a serious issue between agnates over succession to high political office. The record of law may therefore provide an uncertain guide to the nature of social tensions.

This disparity must inevitably increase in a 'plural' context where agencies of central government deal with disputes from communities which have been lately or uncertainly incorporated in the state, or which lie near the margin of the jurisdiction. This will be so even where, as in medieval and early modern Europe, sharply differentiated legal systems were not present. Here the categories of wrong, concepts of relevance and notions of proof entertained by agents of government may be remote from those current in the localities. If a disputant wants his case tried at the centre he must formulate his cause in such a way that the courts will be prepared to listen, probably transforming the original quarrel in doing so. It is clear from some of the contributions that these disparities were sometimes so great that specialists such as the clergy or the *seigneur* had to interpret the working of the system to the litigant as well as present his case for him. Where such specialist intermediaries are involved, they will reconstitute the quarrel according to the appropriate conventions in such a way that it may be virtually unrecognizable to the litigant. The social historian who wishes to feel his way back to real life from the court record must therefore know a lot about the way in which a court recruited and organized its business before he can feel sure what the trouble really was. Similar problems surround the interpretation of observed changes in the pattern of litigation. These may be attributable to reorganization of the legal machinery as well as to variation in litigant demand. Thus a rash of defamation disputes, for example, appearing suddenly in the records of a given agency may well have more to do with shifts within the legal bureaucracy than with changes in attitudes towards the management of honour in the society outside.

Something which appears very clearly in these chapters is the relatively undifferentiated nature of government in Europe across virtually the whole period covered by the contributors. Everywhere we see political, administrative and judicial powers intermingled, even in the face of a growing division between the public and the private sphere. The close links and vague divisions between the secular and the ecclesiastical in the field of government are also a consistent part of the picture. There is an interesting contrast here with the formal specialization and differentiation which characterizes legal systems in the West today.

This general lack of specialization should make us very cautious in forming views as to the nature of apparently court-like institutions, and in reaching conclusions about the purposes for which parties approach them. Here we must not allow the idea of 'dispute settlement' to mislead. People go to court-like agencies for a wide variety of purposes: for reasons of honour, to publicize some established position which requires no court ruling, or just to make things difficult for an enemy. The very notion of 'dispute' may not be apposite if the court is just being used as a platform from which to tell people something. In cases of this sort, the objective may not lie in terms of judgement at all. In this connection, the observation of Kagan, Casey and Castan that a high proportion of suits before the agencies they examined were discontinued is significant; so is Casey's conclusion that many 'proceedings, before both the *chancillería* of Granada in civil suits and the church courts in marriage litigation, were not lawsuits in our sense at all'.[35]

These accounts of government being established and extended, like those of later colonial enterprises now studied by anthropo-

[35] See p. 212 below.

logists, must invite speculation about general directions of legal development. But we see here, as in anthropological writings, how generalization is hampered by the diversity of the local institutions which lay in the path of government, the varied responses of government (suppression here, incorporation or regulation there), and the unpredictable approach of litigants to new and surviving institutions. Even so the amount and quality of the material available make such speculation a serious possibility, which it was not in Maine's day. Some will see John Bossy's introduction of 'the West' into his title as a direct challenge in this respect.

2. 'Beati pacifici': Bishops and the Law in Sixth-Century Gaul

EDWARD JAMES

In 585 a dispute arose in Touraine. The servant of a priest went to deliver an invitation, and was killed. Sichar, a friend of the priest, started a fight with Austregisel, a friend of the murderer. A pitched battle between their supporters was ended by a number of clerics, and Sichar fled to his country estate. Austregisel attacked the priest's house, where Sichar had left some servants and valuables; he killed the servants and made off with the property. A local court declared Austregisel guilty. But a few days later Sichar attacked those who were looking after his stolen property, and killed them and their servants. The count of Tours and the local bishop, Gregory, together ordered the principal participants to appear before them. Gregory begged them to make peace, so that they might be worthy of the Kingdom of Heaven: 'as He Himself has said, "*Beati pacifici, quoniam filii Dei vocabuntur* – Blessed are the peacemakers, for they shall be called the sons of God" (Matthew v. 9). And if he who is judged guilty does not have the money to pay the fine, then the fine shall be paid by the Church, in order to save his soul' (*LH* VII. 47).[1] Gregory did indeed offer money but the supporters of Chramnesind, whose father, uncle and brother had all been killed by Sichar, refused to accept compensation. Not long afterwards Sichar was attacked, his property pillaged and some of his slaves killed. The culprit, Chramnesind, was ordered to forfeit half the compensation awarded to him – 'and this was done against the law, so that peace might be reached' – and Sichar ordered to pay the other half, which he did with financial assistance from Bishop

[1] In what follows *LH* stands for the *Decem Libri Historiarum* by Gregory of Tours. His other works are *GM* (*Liber in Gloria Martyrum*), *VSJ* (*Liber de Virtutibus S. Iuliani*), *VSM* (*Libri de Virtutibus S. Martini*), *VP* (*Liber Vitae Patrum*) and *GC* (*Liber in Gloria Confessorum*). The edition used is that of B. Krusch, in *Monumenta Germaniae Historica, Scriptores Rerum Merovingicarum*, i: in my quotations from *LH* I have usually followed L. Thorpe's translation (Harmondsworth, 1974).

25

Gregory. The feud was settled, although only temporarily: two years later Chramnesind killed Sichar, who was then twenty years old, feeling that public opinion would despise him if he did not avenge his relatives.

The story is well known to those interested in the history of the blood feud (largely because such cases are so very rarely described in detail),[2] but is also of considerable relevance to the study of the role of the early medieval church in the settlement of disputes. The clergy intervened at an early stage to end the violence; the bishop was given a formal role in the legal proceedings; and he used his position to mediate between the law, in the person of the count, and the parties in the dispute, to produce what it was hoped would be an acceptable compromise. He even pledged money from the episcopal coffers: if a settlement was not reached, then a man's soul was in danger. Gregory's action, therefore, and his expenditure, were justified on theological grounds, a point which he emphasized by quoting from the Sermon on the Mount. Bishops took their role as agents of love and peace seriously in the sixth century, just as they took seriously the task of protecting and assisting the poor and the weak.[3] There are indeed texts written by clerics which proclaim, in terms which would have been familiar to the late medieval lawyers discussed by Michael Clanchy in this volume, the dominance of love over law: a letter from Theophilus of Alexandria to St Jerome opposes law and charity, and truth and mercy, while a Gallic text from the last quarter of the fifth century says that it is the duty of a bishop 'to exhort disputing brothers, whether clerics or lay people, to peace rather than to judgement'.[4]

It is the purpose of this chapter to inquire how bishops set about

[2] In particular G. Monod, 'Les aventures de Sichaire', *Revue Historique*, xxxi (1886), pp. 259–90 and J. M. Wallace-Hadrill, 'The Bloodfeud of the Franks', in his *The Long-Haired Kings* (London, 1962), pp. 121–47.

[3] See above all W. Ullmann, 'Public Welfare and Social Legislation in the Early Medieval Councils', *Studies in Church History*, vii (1971), pp. 1–39. For more detail, see S. M. MacGonagle, *The Poor in Gregory of Tours* (New York, 1936); H. G. J. Beck, *The Pastoral Care of Souls in South-East France during the Sixth Century* (Rome, 1950), esp. pp. 317–44; and M. Rouche, 'La matricule des pauvres', in M. Mollat (ed.), *Etudes sur l'histoire de la pauvreté* (Paris, 1974), pp. 83–110.

[4] See Jerome, Epist. 96. 20 (J.-P. Migne (ed.), *Patrologia Latina*, xxii. 789), cited by J. Gaudemet, *L'Eglise dans l'Empire romain IVe–Ve siècles* (*Histoire du droit et des institutions de l'Eglise en Occident*, iii) (Paris, 1958), p. 237; and *Statuta Ecclesiae Antiqua*, 54, in C. Munier (ed.), *Concilia Galliae, A.314–A.506* (Corpus Christianorum, Ser. Lat. cxlviii) (Turnholt, 1963), p. 175.

the business of peace-making in practice. Our major source, inevitably, will be the historical and hagiographical writings of Gregory of Tours himself. Informative as Gregory is, there are of course problems in relying upon the work of an active bishop who was eager to put across a very positive idea of the role of a bishop in the community. At times we may be getting a clearer picture of what Gregory would have liked to have happened than an accurate reflection of the political realities: but this in itself is important historical information. Taken together with the ecclesiastical and secular sources which provide us with the legislative framework, the writings of Gregory give us our best chance of understanding the actions of the Merovingian clergy as well as their aspirations.

Bishops had no doubt played an informal role in settling disputes within the early Christian communities; within a few years of the last persecution they were given a formal legal position. In 318 Constantine enacted that a judge should not object if a case was brought before an episcopal court, and that if 'any person should desire him to transfer his case to the jurisdiction of the Christian law and to observe that kind of court, he shall be heard, even though the action has been instituted before the judge, and whatever may be adjudged by them shall be held as sacred' (*CT* 1. 27. 1).⁵ In intention this may have been more to protect Christians from pagan judges than to exalt bishops. It was certainly not always welcomed by the latter, and both Hilary of Poitiers and Augustine of Hippo complained that it involved them in much unpleasantness: apart from taking up their time it must also have involved them deeply in the internal feuds of their diocese and jeopardized their position as impartial leaders of the community.⁶ And indeed in Augustine's day imperial legislation was already beginning to whittle down the powers of the bishop's court, the *audientia episcopalis*. In secular cases the bishop was to act as no more than an arbiter, as any citizen could 'since private persons can hear those persons who have given their consent, even without the knowledge of the judge' (AD 408: *CT* 1. 27. 2). The most important formal legal function left to the bishop was in relation to offences of a religious nature, and offences

⁵ In what follows *CT* and *SC* stands for Theodosian Code and Sirmondian Constitutions. I have followed the translation of Clyde Pharr, *The Theodosian Code and Novels and the Sirmondian Constitutions* (Princeton, 1952).
⁶ See K. Baus *et al.*, *The Imperial Church from Constantine to the Early Middle Ages* (*History of the Church*, ii) (London, 1980), p. 285; the whole question is discussed by Gaudemet, *L'Eglise dans l'Empire romain*, pp. 230ff.

committed by the clergy. Even this privilege was revoked in the case of ordinary crimes by Valentinian III, although the claims of the clergy to the *privilegium fori* seem often to have been accepted by the barbarian kings of the West.[7]

The formal judgements of bishops naturally occur most often in the pages of Gregory in cases involving bishops and priests. Perhaps the most notorious episcopal criminals were Bishop Salonius of Embrun and Bishop Sagittarius of Gap, brothers who apparently indulged in most secular and ecclesiastical crimes. The bishops of Guntram's kingdom met at Chalon in 579 to settle this long-standing problem, and interestingly the restrictions of ecclesiastical practice presented them with some difficulties. Adultery and murder were among the charges, but peccadilloes of that sort could be purged by penance, and in order to make sure of their deposition the bishops had to accuse them of being guilty of *lèse-majesté* and treason – *rei maestatis et patria proditores (LH* V. 27). Bishop Praetextatus of Rouen was also accused of treason, although falsely in Gregory's view. A sentence of exile in this case was only reached after Chilperic had put pressure on the bishops, tricked Praetextatus into a confession and forged some canons which declared that a bishop guilty of murder, adultery or perjury should be expelled from his diocese. Chilperic complained bitterly of the professional solidarity of the bishops, quoting an old Latin proverb, 'corvus oculum corvi non eruit', 'a crow does not peck out the eye of another crow' (*LH* V. 18). That solidarity certainly seems to have been at work in the case of the flagrantly political bishop of Rheims, Egidius. Even after he had confessed to treason, the bishops hoped that they could produce something by which to exculpate him; they did indeed save his life, but agreed to his removal from the priesthood and exile (*LH* X. 19). Gregory of Tours himself was tried by the bishops for a secular crime: that of an alleged slander against Chilperic and Queen Fredegund. The bishops agreed unanimously that 'the word of an inferior can not be believed above that of a bishop', and charged Gregory to clear himself by swearing an oath to his innocence – a procedure which was uncanonical, said Gregory, but with which he complied in order not to upset the king

---

[7] See Pharr, *The Theodosian Code*, pp. 545–9: Novel 35 of Valentinian III. A. H. M. Jones, *The Later Roman Empire* (Oxford, 1964), p. 491, suggests that 'some later emperor must have restored the privileges of the clergy'. On the *privilegium fori*, see Gaudemet, *L'Eglise dans l'Empire romain*, pp. 241ff.

(*LH* V. 49). The power of a bishop's oath is recognized as early as the time of Constantine: 'The testimony given by a bishop, even though he may be the only witness, shall be unhesitatingly accepted by every judge' (*SC* 1). Gregory's own brother Peter, a priest accused of killing a man by magic, also cleared himself by an oath at a court made up of both bishops and laymen, presided over by Bishop Nicetius of Lyons – his own great-uncle (*LH* V. 5). The privileges of the clergy were considerable: the right to settle their own disputes, the ability to use an unsupported oath as a defence, and the freedom from the death penalty – for ecclesiastics could not impose that on any convicted person. Those lay judges who dared lay hands on clerics are shown in Gregory's pages to have come to unfortunate ends. Count Palladius of Javols, who accused Bishop Parthenius unjustly at the king's court, was punished by the vengeance of God: he committed suicide and received a suicide's burial (*LH* IV. 39). Archdeacon Vigilius of Marseilles, whose men had stolen wine-jars from ships in the harbour, was arrested by Albinus, governor of Provence, while conducting Mass on Christmas Day: Albinus was eventually forced to pay the massive fine of sixteen thousand gold coins (*LH* IV. 43). When Guntram Boso arrested Bishop Theodore of Marseilles a great globe of light appeared in his prison-cell and remained above the bishop's head for two hours, in the sight of the terrified duke (*LH* VI. 24); when Duke Rathar was at a later date sent by King Childebert to arrest the same Theodore, he pillaged the goods of the church, and his servants and his own son died (*LH* VIII. 11). The only case of a cleric in Gregory's works tried by a secular court with Gregory's own apparent approval was the subdeacon Riculf – condemned to death for plotting the deposition of Gregory himself: even then Gregory used his influence to save Riculf from the death penalty (*LH* V. 49).

The legal role of the bishop was not however restricted to the settlement of disputes within the ranks of the clergy, or those created by the actions of clergy. There were certain types of case reserved for ecclesiastical courts: disputes involving marriage, sexual misdemeanours, religious belief and, above all, the property and other rights of the church, and also disputes involving certain categories of people – widows, orphans, freedmen and the *pauperes* (the poor and defenceless). There are a number of stories in Gregory confirming such episcopal involvement. A feud arose in the church of St Denis between the family of a woman accused of adultery and the family of the husband: it was settled by the church at the request of King Chilperic (*LH* V. 32), involving as it did both sacrilege and adultery. When Pelagius, a well known criminal from Tours , stole from the church, it was Gregory who tried him, not the count. Initially Gregory excommunicated him, more as a cure than a punishment, he wrote. Then Pelagius found twelve men prepared to swear to his innocence, and after some argument Gregory agreed to readmit him to the sacrament. But he repeated his crime, and died soon afterwards (*LH* VIII. 40). The case of Tetradia and Count Eulalius of Clermont was settled by a council of bishops, perhaps because of the nature of the case, although also perhaps because of the eminence of the parties involved and the reluctance of the king to make any judgement. Eulalius, who had once been suspected of matricide, had married Tetradia. He neglected her, and then killed her lover. Tetradia then married Duke Desiderius. The bishops decreed that Tetradia should repay Eulalius fourfold for the property she had taken with her when she married the duke, and that her children by Desiderius were to be regarded as illegitimate (*LH* X. 8).

There are a number of occasions when bishops and lay judges might sit together in court, as when Gregory of Tours and the count arbitrated in the case of Sichar and Chramnesind. The Council of Mâcon in 585, which claimed for the church exclusive jurisdiction over freedmen, also required lay judges, under pain of excommunication, to hear cases involving widows and orphans only in the presence of a church official.[8] Gregory describes Count Leudast of Tours sitting in court together with senior laymen and clerics (*LH* V. 48); Badegisil, bishop of Le Mans, used to argue about legal cases with the judges every day (although Gregory certainly did not approve of this) (*LH* VIII. 39).[9] There is only one reference in Gregory to suggest that a bishop might have a court which could act as a rival to that of the count, a tantalizing and incidental reference in a story designed to show the forgiving nature of Nicetius, bishop of Lyons (*VP* 8. 3). Nicetius sent his priest Basil to tell Count

---

[8] Mâcon, c. 12: C. de Clercq (ed.), *Concilia Galliae, A. 511–A. 695* (Corpus Christianorum, Ser. Lat. cxlviii A) (Turnholt, 1963), pp. 244–5.

[9] See Beck, *The Pastoral Care of Souls*, pp. 327–8: but we may doubt that these joint tribunals of clergy and laymen 'seem to have become the normal procedure by the last third of the century'.

Armentarius that the bishop had settled a particular legal case and did not want it reopened. Armentarius replied that there were higher courts than those of the bishop, and Nicetius refused to offer Basil his blessing for having passed on to him these words spoken in anger. Nicetius whispered to his great-nephew Gregory, then a deacon, who was sitting at the bishop's left hand, to stand up and speak on behalf of Basil: Gregory did so, and the priest was pardoned. Clearly this was a legal case which fell within the competence of both the bishop and the count; clearly too there were possibilities available to litigants to prolong proceedings by appealing to another court. The fact that bishops could only offer ecclesiastical penalties, and had no way of enforcing their judgements, might also have encouraged an appeal to the secular court.[10]

Armentarius had argued that there were higher courts than those of bishops. Presumably he meant that the count's court, held in the presence of a representative of the king and thus in effect a royal court, was a higher court. Bishops such as Nicetius might well have disagreed. The fount of justice was not the king, but God. Bishops as judges and arbitrators derived their authority and prestige from God and the saints; this is a message which Gregory of Tours constantly puts before his readers and hearers. When the Merovingian pretender Gundovald is betrayed by his own supporters he cries out to the only higher court to which he could appeal:

> Eternal judge and true avenger of the innocent, God, from Whom all justice proceeds, Whom no lie pleases, in Whom there is no trickery or cunning, I commend my case to you, and ask that You should bring quick vengeance on those who have betrayed me, an innocent person, into the hands of my enemies. (*LH* VII. 38)

Mummolus and Bishop Sagittarius, the principal betrayers, were killed not long after Gundovald's own death, in accordance with the pretender's wish. God will intervene to protect the innocent, as when He saved a woman falsely accused of adultery from being drowned in the Saône (*GM* 69). And He will act in support of the

[10] The powerlessness of bishops to enforce their judgements is emphasized by I. N. Wood in his discussion of the position of Avitus of Vienne: 'The overwhelming impression is one of a bishop who was uncertain of his position and was frequently on the defensive before the king, his congregation and the clergy': see I. N. Wood, 'Avitus of Vienne: Religion and Culture in the Auvergne and the Rhône Valley, 470–530' (unpublished D.Phil. thesis, Oxford, 1980), p. 135.

legal decisions of bishops and of the rights of the church. St Germanus of Paris excommunicated King Charibert and his new wife, who was the sister of his other wife; they paid no attention, and were both struck by the judgement of God, and died (*LH* IV. 26). A wicked merchant of Lyons lost all his wealth, by the judgement of God (*GC* 110). King Guntram told his nephew Childebert that his uncles had agreed not to enter Paris without the permission of the others, and had nominated St Polyeuctos, St Hilary and St Martin to judge the circumstances and punish the offender: both Sigibert and Chilperic had entered Paris without permission, and both were assassinated not long afterwards. 'They both suffered the judgement of God and the maledictions specified in the pact' (*LH* VII. 6). Nantinus, count of Angoulême, believed that the bishop was involved in the death of his predecessor, Bishop Marachar, Nantinus' uncle, and took the law into his own hands rather than putting the matter to the bishops. He attacked the property of the church, killed a priest, and died in agony. 'Everyone ought to be amazed at these things, and fear lest they offend the bishops, since the Lord will avenge those of his servants who put their trust in Him' (*LH* V. 36).[11]

The phrase *iudicium Dei*, 'judgement of God', had of course a very specific sense in later sources: it meant the ordeal. The origins of the ordeal are uncertain. It is mentioned in the earliest Burgundian and Frankish legislation, from the sixth century, but it is also mentioned, although in odd circumstances, by Gregory of Tours. The ordeal of the cauldron, picking out a ring from a cauldron of boiling water, solves a dispute between an Arian and a Catholic (*GM* 80); another such dispute was settled by an ordeal of fire (*GC* 14). The roots of the developed legal institution of the ordeal are already present in the sixth century; Gregory's belief in the active interest of God in the pursuit of justice and the settlement of disputes would by the Carolingian period have its own liturgy and its own position in the legal process, underlined by Charlemagne himself, in one of his capitularies, when he declared that 'all men should believe in the judgement of God without any doubts'.[12] But

---

[11] Gregory was not so much uttering an accepted opinion as trying to persuade his contemporaries of the necessity for *reverentia*: see P. Brown, *Relics and Social Status in the Age of Gregory of Tours* (Reading, 1977), now reprinted in Brown, *Society and the Holy in Late Antiquity* (London, 1982), pp. 222–50. See esp. pp. 233–5.

[12] *Monumenta Germaniae Historica, Capitularia*, i, p. 150. See my comments in E.

there was another way in which beliefs fostered by the church were already by Gregory's day having a significant influence upon the way in which the legal process was organized and disputes settled: the use of the oath taken upon an altar or upon relics. Those who perjured themselves or who went back on their word would suffer the judgement of God, or the indignation of the saint in whose church the oath was sworn. Solemn oaths were taken in more than one church, as when the pretender Gundovald made Guntram Boso swear in twelve churches that he would be safe when he returned to Gaul (*LH* VII. 36). Certain churches were known to Gregory for their particular efficacy in punishing perjury, such as St Pancras in Rome (*GM* 38) or St Julian at Joué in the diocese of Tours (*VSJ* 40). There, when the Devil persuades a man to perjure himself, divine vengeance immediately follows, bringing disasters such as the loss of relatives, or consumption. Even barbarians dare not perjure themselves there, claims Gregory. And scattered throughout his hagiographical works (the two stories at *LH* VIII. 16 are the only examples I can find in his *History*) are moral tales of the vengeance of God upon perjurors. Perjurors are paralysed, their right hand raised in the oath, in the church itself (*GM* 52, 57), they contract gangrene in the offending hand, leading to amputation of the arm and death (*GC* 67), they are struck dumb (*VSJ* 19), or they die almost on the spot (*VSM* I. 31). Such tales reinforced the message which Gregory of Tours and other early medieval churchmen were attempting to convey: that God and the saints were prepared to intervene to bring to earth some measure of the justice and peace which reigned in Heaven.

The intervention of God not only saved the innocent and punished the wicked: it also helped to soften the rigours of the law and to protect the criminal from death by execution. Sometimes this intervention took a miraculous form. A slave was arrested and condemned to death for theft; he prayed to St Martin and fell free and alive from the gallows (*VSM* III. 53). A hardened criminal who had done penance for his crimes was nevertheless arrested and condemned by the judge; he prayed to Martin, the ropes broke and he too fell to the ground alive. The judge tried to hang him again, but the abbot of a neighbouring monastery pleaded for the man and

James, *The Origins of France* (London, 1982), pp. 88–90, which was written in ignorance of P. Brown, 'Society and the Supernatural: a Medieval Change', *Daedalus*, civ (1975), pp. 133–51, now in Brown, *Society and the Holy*, pp. 302–32.

the count freed him (also *VSM* III. 53). We can clearly see here an opposition of views; in the eyes of Gregory a man who had gone through penance, or even someone who was repentant, should not be punished by death, and perhaps should not be punished at all. It was not necessarily a popular view. In another story Gregory tells of a habitual criminal, a robber and a murderer, who was led off to be hanged. Eparchius, a recluse of Angoulême, sent a monk to beg the count to spare the man's life. But there appears to have been a demonstration by a furious mob, who demanded that no pardon should be given. The criminal was therefore tortured and hanged; but Eparchius prayed, the gallows collapsed, and the man was saved (*LH* VI. 8). Afterwards the count (who told the story to Gregory of Tours) excused himself to Eparchius claiming that had he not been afraid of the mob he would indeed have let the man go: it was only then that Eparchius revealed, to the count's stupefaction, that the criminal was still alive. According to Gregory, Eparchius performed a similar miracle even after his death (*GC* 99).

F. X. Graus, in his important study of the hagiographical topos of the freed prisoner,[13] relates such stories of freeing from the gallows[14] – his Type III, of which he lists nineteen examples from Merovingian sources – to the literary traditions of Gallic hagiography. But they clearly ought also to be seen in the light both of legislation and of examples of clerical intervention in Gregory's *History* which have no miraculous content. Churchmen in the fourth and fifth centuries regarded it as the duty of clerics to intercede for condemned prisoners: it did not even matter, explained Augustine to a puzzled Macedonius, whether the prisoner was guilty or not, for time would at least be given to the guilty to make peace with God.[15] Some of the abuses were attacked

---

[13] 'Die Gewalt bei den Anfängen des Feudalismus und die "Gefangenenbefreiungen" der merowingischen Hagiographie', *Jahrbuch für Wirtschaftsgeschichte* (1961), pp. 61–156. This topos is placed in a much broader context in the same author's *Volk, Herrscher und Heilige im Reich der Merowinger* (Prague 1965).

[14] On these *Galgenwunder*, see also H. Brunner, *Deutsche Rechtsgeschichte*, ii, ed. C. von Schwerin (Berlin, 1928), p. 602, and two articles by B. de Gaiffier, 'Un thème hagiographique: le pendu miraculeusement sauvé', *Rev. Belge d'Archéologie et d'Histoire de l'Art*, xiii (1943), pp. 123–48 and 'Liberatus a suspendio: à propos d'un thème hagiographique', in *Mélanges de linguistique et de littérature romanes offerts à Mario Roques*, ii (Paris, 1953), pp. 93–7.

[15] Epist. 152 and 153: trans. by Sr W. Parsons, *St Augustine: Letters*, iii (New York, 1953), pp. 279–303 – a fascinating statement of the Christian position on crime.

in 398, when clerics were allowed their right of *intercessio*, but only for recent cases and only in order to find out whether any injustice had been done, through error or corruption. In particular clerics and monks were forbidden to take and hold by force those who had been convicted (*CT* 9. 40. 16). Is the hagiographical topos a way of justifying the right of *intercessio* in all cases, contrary to the wishes of the secular authorities? It is perhaps relevant that in a number of tales the cleric alone was the witness to the miraculous loosing of the bonds or collapse of the gallows. But it is also clear from Gregory that it could be perfectly acceptable for clerics to intervene to secure a pardon. Thus Leudovald, bishop of Bayeux, interceded for Baddo, accused of high treason, and the man was released (*LH* IX. 13); a bishop, perhaps Gregory himself, saved Berulf and Arnegisel from execution at the orders of King Childebert (*LH* VIII. 26). Gregory of Tours brought Garachar and Bladast, two important Frankish aristocrats implicated in the revolt of Gundovald, before King Guntram to beg for their pardon. At first Gregory had no success. But then he told the king that he had been sent by his master to ask for the pardon – his master being St Martin (*LH* VIII. 6). Guntram relented and restored the two to his favour and to their property. When King Chilperic ordered men who had stolen from St Martin's church to be brought to him, Gregory 'was afraid that these men might be put to death because of the very saint who, while he was on earth, had so often begged for the life of condemned criminals'; and so he sent a letter to the king, 'beseeching him not to have them executed, and saying that he who must make the charge proposed not to do so' (*LH* VI. 10). The first instinct of some criminals and others who feared for their lives was indeed to flee to the nearest bishop. When Parthenius, an over-efficient tax-collector, feared a lynching by the mob, he asked two bishops to protect him and to quell the mob by their sermons; in the end they hid him in a chest of vestments, but to no avail (*LH* III. 36). Guntram Boso sought sanctuary in Verdun cathedral, confident that he could obtain pardon through his godfather Bishop Ageric, who had also sponsored King Childebert at his baptism. And indeed the king allowed Guntram Boso to stay under Ageric's protection until his trial. When the trial came, Ageric was not there: 'it had been decided that Guntram Boso should not have anyone to defend him, so that if the king were to decree that he should be executed, no plea for pardon could be advanced' (*LH* IX. 10): the implication is that it would have been very difficult to refuse a bishop's plea, or at least that that was the message which Gregory intended to imply. In Ageric's absence it was agreed that Guntram Boso should die. But he fled to Magneric, bishop of Trier, and tried to force him to intercede. The bishop's house was broken into, and Guntram Boso seized and killed. A fellow Austrasian plotter, Berthefried, was sought at the same time, and he too took refuge with Bishop Ageric. Soldiers tore off the roof-tiles from the bishop's house, and succeeded in killing Berthefried and three of his men; Bishop Ageric was so depressed by his failure to save the lives of these two aristocrats that he gave up eating, and died (*LH* IX. 12).

Appeal to bishops was clearly a recognized means of obtaining a pardon, or at least of preserving one's life. And it was normally done, not by going directly to the bishop, but by seeking sanctuary in a church. The rebel Mummolus was persuaded to leave the safety of St-Bertrand-de-Comminges; if he did not immediately obtain a pardon from the king he could take sanctuary in some church, 'so that he might escape the punishment of death' (*LH* VII. 38). Sanctuary thus fulfilled a double function: it could delay arrest, in order to allow matters to calm down and allow the arbitration of kin and the pleas of the clergy, and it could also allow the criminal, or the accused person, to repent and, possibly, to escape the death penalty.

Sanctuary has a long history in the Mediterranean world, predating the Christian period;[16] an echo of pre-Christian practice is preserved in the Theodosian Code, in a mandate which allowed people to take refuge by the statues of Emperors (*CT* 9. 44). Sanctuary seems to have caught on rapidly in the new Christian Empire, and imperial legislation was more concerned to detail restrictions on the right to sanctuary than to spread the custom: those categories of people not allowed to avail themselves of the privilege included debtors, Jews, slaves, procurators, collectors of

---

[16] See A. Wenger, 'Asylrecht', in *Reallexicon für Antike und Christentum*, i (Stuttgart, 1950) pp. 836–44; Brunner, *Deutsche Rechtsgeschichte*, pp. 792–3; Gaudemet, *L'Eglise dans l'Empire romain*, pp. 282–7; etc. There are parallels in many other cultures: e.g. the Leopard Skin Chief among the Nuer (E. E. Evans-Pritchard, *The Nuer* (Oxford, 1940), pp. 163ff.), the Giver-of-Life councillor among the Barotse (M. Gluckman, *The Ideas in Barotse Jurisprudence* (Manchester, 1972), pp. 39–41), and among the Cheyenne, the Lozi and others (M. Gluckman, *Politics, Law and Ritual in Tribal Society* (Oxford, 1965), p. 216).

public dye-fish and anyone involved in public or private accounts (*CT* 9. 45. 1, 2, 3). A later decree permitted slaves to take sanctuary, for one day only, and significantly required the slave-owner then to grant pardon to the slave for his wrongs (*CT* 9. 45. 5). Those who entered sanctuary could not carry arms of any kind, and could not eat or sleep actually within the church; the space around the church (for fifty paces beyond the church doors) was to be counted as part of the sanctuary area (*SC* 13). Those who carried arms could be taken from the church forcibly without consulting the bishop or the judges (*CT* 9. 45. 4). Not long after the publication of the Theodosian Code, we have the first mentions of sanctuary in Gallic church councils, and it is obvious that the church is claiming much more general rights of sanctuary. The Council of Orange (441) demands that the sanctity of the church be recognized by all, and forbids anyone to recover someone who has sought sanctuary: there was no time limit, no distinction between armed and unarmed and no mention of excluded categories. The bishops at Orange did not allow for the restitution of a slave in sanctuary to his master, and offered excommunication to those who seized the slaves of the church as restitution for slaves in sanctuary.[17] The conflict of opinion apparent here was still present in the sixth century, as can be seen from the writings of Gregory of Tours. Gregory constitutes the first and best glimpse of how the late Roman institution of sanctuary worked in practice; there are over thirty references to sanctuary in his works, and considerable detail in the case of some of those who took sanctuary in St Martin's church at Tours.

Gregory supports the institution of sanctuary by telling stories of the fate which awaited those who violated its laws, above all in his books of miracles, which teach such lessons rather more conveniently than history. Sanctuary is not so much seeking the protection of the church as putting oneself under the protection of a saint, who was perfectly prepared to defend those who sought his help (as Duke Rauching's wife knew when she fled to St Medard's: *LH* IX. 9). When Duke Austrapius wanted to escape Chramn, King Chlothar's son, he came to St Martin's, and Chramn ordered him so

---

[17] Orange (441), c. 5 and 6: Munier, *Concilia Galliae*, p. 79. There are a number of canons relating to sanctuary in sixth-century councils: Orleans (511) c. 1, 2, 3; Epaon (517), c. 39; Orleans (538), c. 14; Orleans (541), c. 21, 24, 30; Orleans (549), c. 22 and Mâcon (585), c. 8.

closely watched that no one could even offer him food or drink. When someone did get through with some water the judge poured the water on the ground. God and St Martin acted, and the judge was dead before midnight that same day (*LH* IV. 18). A man who tried to break down the doors of St Julian's in Brioude to get at his enemy was struck down with a great pain (*VSJ* 5). A man who had lost an eye in a fight tried to take his enemy from the basilica, and lost the sight of his other eye. 'I deserve to be judged without mercy, for I did not know how to pardon my enemy' (*VSJ* 10): again sanctuary is portrayed as a means of obtaining pardon. The slave of a certain Maurus took refuge in the church of St Lupus at Troyes. Maurus came to take him away (as he was entitled to do, by Roman law), and as he did so he cursed the saint. His tongue ceased to work, and he wandered around the church making animal-like noises. Despite the gifts his wife made to the church he died on the third day; the wife immediately took back what she had given, but the slave stayed free (*GC* 66). Another slave, belonging to Faretrus, took refuge in the oratory of Abbot Venantius; Faretrus took away the slave while the abbot was absent, and killed him. He himself caught a fever and died almost immediately (*VP* 16. 3).

Such stories can of course be taken together with all those which portray the vengeance of God or the saint being taken on those who violate the property or other rights of the Church. King Charibert died shortly after seizing property belonging to St Martin (*VSM* I. 29); the troop of men who massacred the monks of Latte all died, except for the man who had rebuked them for their action (*LH* IV. 48); the man who stole the metal from the windows of a church was struck down by an awful disease each year on the anniversary of his theft (*GM* 58); the troops of King Guntram who broke into the church of St Vincent at Agen in order to steal the treasure left there for safe keeping were subsequently struck down by fatal quarrels, demoniac possession and spontaneous combustion (*LH* VII. 35; cf. *VSJ* 13 and *GM* 104); the soldier who came to St Denis and stood on the tomb in order to detach the holy dove suspended above it, his feet one on each side of the sharply sloping roof of the tomb, slipped, crushed his testicles and pierced his side with a javelin – no one could doubt, said Gregory, that it was no accident, but the judgement of God (*GM* 71).

In the miracle stories Gregory stresses the punishments of those who infringe the rights of the church and of sanctuary; in his *History* he shows us that in most cases the law and custom of sanctuary were respected. When Roccolen is sent by King Chilperic to force Gregory of Tours to expel Guntram Boso from sanctuary, he does not dare to violate the sanctuary itself: when he is struck by God with a fatal bout of jaundice it is not for breaking sanctuary, but for destroying a house belonging to the church in his frustration at being thwarted, and for the sin of eating rabbits during Lent (*LH* V. 4). Most of those who reach sanctuary and whose fates are described by Gregory in fact emerge to resume their normal lives, a crisis having been weathered or a pardon obtained. When Childeric the Saxon came to St Martin's, Gregory of Tours not only persuaded King Guntram to let his wife join him, but also persuaded him to allow both of them to leave sanctuary in peace (*LH* VIII. 18). The commanders of the disastrous expedition to Septimania in 585 sought sanctuary in the church of St Symphorian in Autun on their return; Guntram visited the church on the saint's feast day, spoke to them, and later allowed them to go free (*LH* VIII. 30). Several of those implicated in the palace conspiracy against Childebert in 589 fled to various churches. The king went to them and said (according to Gregory):

> Come out and stand trial! It seems to me that you would never have sought sanctuary in church unless your conscience had been pricking you. All the same, you have my promise that your lives will be saved, even if you are proved guilty. I am a Christian, and I deem it wrong to punish people convicted of a crime if I have to drag them out of a church to do so. (*LH* IX. 38)

Even so, Childebert was not pleased when they pleaded not guilty; it took another flight into sanctuary and pleading by bishops before they were allowed to go free. Their only punishment seems to have been the removal of the property bestowed on them by the king; they were allowed to keep the rest of their property.

One recourse of the forces of law and order was to try to prevent persons reaching sanctuary. Guntram's chamberlain Chundo made a dash for a church after his champion in a trial by battle had been killed; the king had him chased, and he was stoned to death before he reached the church (*LH* X. 10). When King Chilperic heard a rumour that his rebellious son Merovech was trying to reach St Martin's, he had the church closely guarded and all approaches blocked, leaving just one door free for the clergy to go in and out (*LH* V. 18). Otherwise all that could be done was to hope that some transgression might take place which would make the breaking of sanctuary possible. Gregory did not shed too many tears over the forcible removal of Eberulf from St Martin's, particularly as the man actually sent by Guntram to remove Eberulf died in the attempt (*LH* VII. 21–2). Eberulf had committed manslaughter in the church, got drunk, attacked a priest, forced Gregory to leave the church, and threatened to kill the bishop if any attempt was made to remove him. Moreover, and this is perhaps still more important, Eberulf was not under St Martin's protection, since he had not prayed to the saint with contrite heart (*LH* VII. 29). Some years earlier Count Leudast of Tours had similarly abused the privilege of sanctuary in St Hilary's at Poitiers, occasionally emerging from the church to plunder the homes of Poitevins and committing adultery in the porticus of the church itself: Queen Fredegund ordered him to be expelled and he was driven into hiding in Berry (*LH* V. 49). Fredegund herself, after her husband Chilperic's assassination, sought sanctuary in the cathedral at Paris, and proved to be no more contrite than Leudast: 'she had no fear of God, in whose house she had sought sanctuary, and was the prime mover in many outrages' (*LH* VII. 15). It must have been very difficult for bishops like Ragnemod of Paris and Gregory of Tours to cope with distinguished refugees, for whom the privilege of sanctuary had hardly been designed. For the great aristocrats it was often no more than a temporary haven during a time of political crisis; some, like Guntram Boso, even used sanctuary as a means of keeping their womenfolk safe while they were active elsewhere in Gaul (*LH* V. 24). Such people came with their family, servants and dependants, and do not seem to have been scrupulous observers of the ban on weapons in sanctuary; they must have been a most unwelcome addition to a bishop's problems.[18]

Claiming sanctuary, therefore, was a way of calling in the bishop or another cleric to act as peace-maker; by doing this the malefactor increased his chances of a pardon, but also did much to ensure the preservation of his life. Churchmen could not be responsible for the shedding of blood, or even have anything to do with it: a Merovingian council forbade clerics from being present at the examination (that is, torture) of accused people, or at an

---

[18] Particularly annoying in the case of the priest Willichar who, with his wife, took refuge in St Martin's: through their *ludibria* (wantonness) the church was set on fire (*LH* IV. 20).

execution.[19] Moreover there was a strong current of opinion within the church which was hostile to the shedding of blood by the state; this is part of the explanation for the zeal of churchmen in protecting criminals. This zeal extended to the assistance of those already arrested and imprisoned. We have already seen how bishops, dead or alive, could effect miraculous release from prison, and F. X. Graus has skilfully related these stories to a literary tradition which looked back to the Acts of the Apostles.[20] But the stories also need to be related to the legislative texts and to actual historical conditions. Fourth-century Roman legislation gave priests the right to enter prisons on missions of compassion, 'to heal the sick, to feed the poor and to console the innocent; when he has investigated thoroughly and has learned the case of each person, according to law he shall direct his intervention before the competent judge' (*SC* 13). Later imperial edicts formalized the system. In 409 bishops were given authority to make sure that judges were looking after their prisoners in a proper manner: judges were to examine prisoners as to their treatment and ensure proper nourishment (*CT* 9. 3. 7). Later still the duty of inspecting prisons was given to the bishops themselves: each Wednesday or Friday they should visit the prisoners, find out whether they were slaves or freemen, and whether they had been detained for debt, for murder or for some other cause.[21] In Gaul the task of visiting prisons, each Sunday, was assigned to the archdeacon or praepositus.[22] One must assume that their duty was to watch for any injustices and, if they felt it appropriate, to sue for pardon for a particular prisoner. There is no doubt that obtaining the release of a prisoner was regarded as a pious deed, like the ransoming of prisoners-of-war or the manumission of slaves.[23] Even in the Roman period the mass

[19] Mâcon (585), c. 19: de Clercq, *Concilia Galliae*, p. 247.

[20] See above, note 13.

[21] Codex Justinianus 1. 4. 22: text translated and commented on by P. R. Coleman-Norton, *Roman State and Christian Church* (London, 1966), pp. 1029–31.

[22] Orleans (549), c. 20: de Clercq, *Concilia Galliae*, p. 155.

[23] On the former, see Beck, *The Pastoral Care of Souls*, pp. 338–41 and K. Weber, 'Kulturgeschichtliche Probleme der Merowingerzeit im Spiegel frühmittel-alterlicher Heiligenleben', *Studien und Mitteilungen zur Geschichte des Benediktinerordens und seiner Zweige*, xlviii (1930), pp. 347–403, esp. pp. 395ff. Her comments on the possible future of released captives, as dependants of the saint or monks in his monastery, are interesting. Sometimes slaves cured by a saint seem to have obtained their freedom by that act: e.g. *GM* 77. Miraculous cures and

release of prisoners could be proclaimed as a religious gesture. There are a number of texts in the Theodosian Code which refer to such mass pardons: 'On account of the Day of Easter, which we celebrate in the depths of our hearts, We release from confinement all those persons who are bound by criminal charges or who are confined in prison' (*CT* 9. 38. 3: cf. 9. 38. 4, 6, 7 and 8, and *SC* 7), or, in the more colourful language of the Sirmondian Constitutions, 'We lay aside the chains and properly abolish the occasion for uncombed hair in the prison that is dark with filth. We snatch all persons from the death penalty except those who cannot properly be assisted because of the magnitude of their crimes' – that is, those convicted of treason, sacrilege, sorcery, adultery, rape or homicide (*SC* 8). The tradition survived into the Merovingian period: Chilperic ordered all prisoners freed and all fines owing to the treasury cancelled in order to celebrate the birth of a son and heir in 582/3 (*LH* VI. 23). The symbolism of the release of prisoners on the anniversary of Christ's resurrection is an obvious and intentional one; equally obvious is the symbolism in the stories of prisoners being miraculously released at Easter (*VSM* II. 16), on the feast day of a saint (*VSM* III. 41, IV. 26 and IV. 41) or on the passing of the relics of a saint on the occasion of a funeral or a translation (*VP* 8. 3 and 4; *LH* IV. 19 and V. 8).[24] Miracle stories should not be dismissed from the purview of all but the literary historian, as Graus tends to do; such stories not only reflect the moral principles and concerns of their author, or their age, but may also be an embellishment or echo of non-miraculous events. Did bishops prevail upon counts to release prisoners at Easter, as emperors had done, or on saints' days? Do some miracle-stories relate to the inquiry of bishops into the conditions and circumstances of prisoners, as required by Roman law, as in the case of the 'miraculous' release of men refused food and drink by their guards (*VSM* II. 35 and III. 47), or of those imprisoned unjustly (*VSM* II. 41 and IV. 35)? Are they stories intended to show to the authorities that requests for release in such cases have the sanction of God and His saints?

In the last book of the *History*, Gregory told how Avitus of

releases may both be seen as symbolic of the restoration of the individual into the full Christian community.

[24] For the symbolism of the chains themselves, see Graus, 'Die Gewalt bei den Anfängen des Feudalismus' pp. 135–6.

Clermont successfully pleaded for the release of prisoners; but he placed the plea after the chains had snapped miraculously, as if made of glass (*LH* X. 6); is this merely a literary device to underline the authority of the bishop? The frequency of miracle-stories of this type testifies to the accepted role of the bishop as a freer of prisoners; the supernatural element could only be heightened for the faithful when they witnessed the piles of chains and fetters left at the tombs of saints by grateful ex-prisoners.

At Medard's holy tomb [in Soissons] I myself have seen the chains and shackles of prisoners burst asunder and lie broken on the ground; and to this day they are preserved there as a proof of his miraculous power. (*LH* IV. 19) The town of Châlons has for its special patron the holy Memmius, who, when he was still in his mortal body, it is said, raised a dead man. We have often seen at his tomb the broken chains and fetters of the wretched, and we have moreover made ourselves the proof of his power. (*GC* 65)

When Gregory's deacon Aigulf visited the shrine of Nicetius of Lyons he examined the register of miraculous cures which was placed in the church, and saw the broken chains and shattered leg- and neck-irons of criminals and captives:

if one wants to know how many prisoners the saint has freed, how many chains he has broken, one has only to look at that mass of irons which is lying in his church. Recently in the presence of King Guntram, I heard Syagrius, bishop of Autun, tell how in one night the holy man appeared in seven towns to prisoners, whom he delivered from their prisons and to whom the judge had after that not dared to do anything. (*VP* 8. 6)

The acquiescence of the king or the judge in the saint's action, made public by the issuing of a pardon, is several times mentioned by Gregory.[25]

A number of years ago, Katherine Weber remarked on the link between reality and miracle:

Ordinary people simply transferred the sanctuary rights of the church on to the saint. In the proximity of the saint, everything was free; when he approached, locks sprang open, chains fell off and prisons opened themselves. Whether the freed man deserved freedom was never discussed: one spoke always of

---

[25] *VSM* IV. 26 and IV. 37; *GC* 88: see Weber, 'Kulturgeschichtliche Probleme', p. 399.

Barmherzigkeit (charity, compassion), never of *Recht* (justice, law).[26]

The opposition of 'law and love' appears indeed as one of the main ideas underlying the passages of Gregory of Tours cited above, and the legislation of the bishops of sixth-century Gaul. Early Merovingian bishops were heirs to the values of an earlier age, in which a persecuted Christian minority had created the image of an inimical secular state, against which they strove to set their own ethical system, by example and by preaching. The incompatibility between 'church' and 'state' was still a lively theme of Merovingian hagiography, thanks very largely to the success of Sulpicius Severus' *Life of St Martin*. But someone like Gregory of Tours would have been well aware that this dramatic confrontation was not just a useful literary topos: there were very real differences of opinion on moral and legal issues between churchmen and laymen. Sometimes the Merovingian church was in opposition to the Germanic Franks. The ideas of the church on the permanence of marriage and the impossibility of marrying within certain relationships came into conflict with some very basic Germanic customs. Their propagation of the idea of the inalienability of church land and the desirability of the donation of land to churches and monasteries struck at the core of Germanic society, at their notions of family property rights and inheritance.[27] Canon 1 of the first Merovingian church council, held at Orleans in 511, which said that a fugitive could only be taken from sanctuary if the injured party and his kin swore not to take revenge on him, was itself an attack on 'ancient and very entrenched Teutonic principles' concerning the duty of blood feud.[28]

The conflict between ecclesiastical and secular notions of morality was not a conflict between a largely Gallo-Roman church and a Germanic monarchy and aristocracy; the attitude of Merovingian churchmen towards law and justice was at variance with Roman ways too. The most obvious divergence was in the attitude towards the poor. It was a principle of Roman law that the rich and powerful, the *honestiores*, were punished more leniently

---

[26] See Weber, 'Kulturgeschichtliche Probleme', p. 398.
[27] Some of these ideas have been discussed by James, *The Origins of France*, pp. 78ff; see also M. Rouche, *L'Aquitaine des Wisigoths aux Arabes* (Paris, 1978), pp. 169–74.
[28] Ullmann, 'Public Welfare and Social Legislation', p. 15.

than the poor and weak, the *humiliores*; the church proclaimed that mercy should be reserved above all for the humble.[29] The poor, for whom scarcely a single Roman law pays any regard save in terms of the preservation of law and order, were a particular concern for the Merovingian episcopate. The very first Merovingian council decreed that the poor who were unable to work should be provided with food and clothing; every episcopal town had its scores or hundreds of poor, registered on the *matricula*, whose daily sustenance was provided by the church.[30] In particular the church felt that it was its duty to protect the poor at law; the Council of Tours threatened any judges or *potentes* with excommunication if they oppressed the poor.[31] It is interesting to compare the Merovingian record on legislation for the poor with that of the Visigoths, who were on the whole faithful heirs of the Romans. It is perhaps relevant that the ordeal, that instrument by which, so the Merovingian clergy taught, God could manifest his will as the protector of the innocent and the fount of justice, only appeared in one late Visigothic law: rather than showing 'the declining standards of the kingdom as it neared the end',[32] it could be seen as a demonstration of the lack of impact that the new and socially radical Christian ideas had upon the privilege-obsessed and hidebound descendants of Roman lawyers in Spain.

In the end, of course, with the decline of conciliar legislation in the seventh century, the secularization of the episcopate and then the reform of the church in the eighth and ninth centuries under the firm hand of the Carolingians, the particular concept of peace and justice that the early Merovingian clergy had maintained was almost forgotten, although elements of it reappeared at the time of the early Capetians with the Peace of God movement.[33] That movement too was concerned with peace at various levels. It campaigned for the limitation of warfare, just as Gregory's bishops had done: Gregory himself wrote emotionally about the evils of civil war in the preface to Book V of his *History*, and he told moral stories of how God and the saints encouraged kings to make peace

---

[29] See, for example, Jerome in Migne, *Patrologia Latina*, XXV. 157 and 732.
[30] Orleans (511), c. 16: de Clercq, *Concilia Galliae*, p. 9. On the *matricula*, see Rouche, 'La matricule des pauvres' in note 3.
[31] Tours (567), c. 7: de Clercq, *Concilia Galliae*, p. 194.
[32] P. D. King, *Law and Society in the Visigothic Kingdom* (Cambridge, 1972), p. 121.
[33] For some comments on the weakening of sanctuary laws, see Ullmann, 'Public Welfare and Social Legislation', pp. 15–16.

(*LH* IV. 49), or punished those who refused to do so (*LH* IV. 51).[34] But *pax* had other meanings: it meant the security of sanctuary, the settlement of a dispute by compromise, the absence of violence of any kind. Violence, whether offered by criminals or by the political system, endangered the soul of the unrepentant criminal or judge. The concern of the bishop with the well-being, both spiritual and physical, of his flock, led him to think of justice in terms of repentance and reconciliation rather than punishment and retribution. Bishops, the spiritual leaders of their *civitates*, were the natural peace-makers, guiding their flock away from evil and violence towards peace and love. *Arbiter* and *compositor*, meaning mediator or peace-maker, were words used in their praise in contemporary epitaphs;[35] they achieved peace not by imposing rules but by bringing both parties to an agreed settlement. The ideal, though no one stated it, was to replace the rule-based justice of kings with the ultimate justice of God. Such an ideal, of course, took no account of the realities of power and authority; the ideal as stated by bishops in councils or in the calm of their studies was not necessarily what they put into practice, in the daily intrigues of the *civitas* and faced by rival obligations to class and kin. But it was sustained by two factors: the pressure upon the bishop to assert his position and the need for a consensus within society which avoided loss of face because it depended upon supernatural sanctions.[36] And, if we are to believe Gregory of Tours, it had not an insignificant part to play in the history of social relations in sixth-century Gaul.[37]

---

[34] For general comments on peace, see F.-L. Ganshof, 'La paix au très haut Moyen Age', *Recueil de la Société Jean Bodin*, xiv (1962), pp. 397–413; G. Fasoli, 'Pace e Guerra nell'alto medioevo', *Settimane di Studio del Centro Italiano di Studi sull'Alto Medioevo*, xv (Spoleto, 1968), pp. 15–47; and J. M. Wallace-Hadrill, 'War and Peace in the Early Middle Ages', in his *Early Medieval History* (Oxford, 1975), pp. 19–38. The ambiguities and difficulties inherent in the church's attitude to war are dealt with in intriguing fashion in F. Prinz, *Klerus und Krieg im frühen Mittelalter* (Stuttgart, 1971).

[35] See M. Heinzelmann, *Bischofsherrschaft in Gallien* (*Beihefte der Francia*, v) (Munich, 1976), p. 180; pp. 179–83 form a useful excursus on the *episcopalis audientia*.

[36] I echo P. Brown, *Society and the Holy in Late Antiquity* (London, 1982), p. 323, although I think he is mistaken in suggesting a dramatic shift from consensus to authority in the twelfth century.

[37] I am most grateful for the comments of Ian Wood upon this chapter.

3. Law and Love in the Middle Ages

MICHAEL CLANCHY

Pactum legem vincit et amor iudicium (Agreement prevails over law and love over judgement)

I want to use this proposition from the *Leges Henrici Primi* as a standpoint from which to view the place of law in medieval human relations.[1] The *Leges* is the compilation of a Frenchman writing in England early in the twelfth century. It is a long and muddling work, but it has the merit of including wide-ranging general principles like the one above. Other statements in the *Leges* confirm the contrast it makes between ways of resolving disputes: either by agreement and love or by law and judgement. Disputants are 'brought together by love or separated by judgement'.[2] An accused person chooses either to proceed by formal pleading (*de placito*) or to make peace; wise men avoid 'the utterly uncertain dice of pleas'.[3] Agreement (*pactum*) or peace (*pax*) is good and even better is 'to proceed by love (*per amorem*), if the parties wish to have the perfect freedom of friends to come and go'.[4] Love in such a context does not mean something gratuitous or sentimental. Rather it is a bond of affection, established by public undertakings before witnesses and upheld by social pressure. A modern example

---

[1] L. J. Downer (ed.) (Oxford, 1972), p. 164, ch. 49, 5a. I sometimes differ from Downer in my translation, but I am much indebted to his work. I have mentioned this proposition from the *Leges* before, with reference to the court rolls of Highworth hundred, Wilts., in an unpublished talk given at the Cambridge Legal History Conference in 1975. S. D. White, 'The Settlement of Disputes by Compromise in 11th Century France', *American Journal of Legal History*, xxii (1978), p. 308, also refers to it, as does R. C. Van Caenegem (ed.), *Royal Writs in England from the Conquest to Glanvill* (Selden Soc., lxxvii, 1959), p. 45, n. 4.

[2] 'Vel amore congreget vel sequestret iudicio', *Leges Henrici Primi*, p. 100, ch. 7, 3a. Downer translates 'sequestret iudicio' as 'let a judgment stand in settlement between them'. But 'sequestrare' in English medieval usage means to 'cut off' or 'excommunicate' and not to 'mediate' as in classical Latin. 'Congreget' and 'sequestret' are used as antitheses here and at *ibid.*, p. 176, ch. 57, 1a.

[3] 'De placito vel de pace', *ibid.*, p. 156, ch. 46, 4; 'incerta penitus alea placitorum', *ibid.*, p. 98, ch. 6, 6.

[4] *Ibid.*, p. 240, ch. 76, 5b.

of such a bond is the marriage contract and the most characteristically medieval one is the link between lord and vassal. As the compiler of the *Leges* observes, 'we offer love only to those whom we cannot do without'[5] – whether they be kinsmen, feudal lords, or reconciled enemies. It was in this spirit that the duke of Norfolk, Shakespeare's 'Jockey of Norfolk' in *Richard III*, asked John Paston immediately before the battle of Bosworth to bring along a company of tall men and signed himself 'Your lover, J. Norfolk'.[6] It was in this spirit too that lords addressed their men in charters as their 'lovers (*amantes*)' or 'friends (*amici*)' and demanded from their peasants 'love boons' and 'love silver'.[7] On the estates of St Albans abbey to make love meant to do an extra piece of work for the lord: thus various serfs in 1332 'faciet xlii opera et i *love*'.[8] Love became 'routinized' in medieval society rather in the way that charisma becomes 'routinized' (in Max Weber's description) after the original voluntary appeal of a leader has disappeared.

Because love alone brings freedom and security it is seen in the stateless conditions of the early Middle Ages as being more powerful than law, which it 'prevails over' or 'conquers (*vincit*)'. The exact origins of this idea are difficult to trace. Neither of the successive editors of the *Leges Henrici Primi*, F. Liebermann and L. J. Downer, cites any precedent in Roman or canon law for the proposition 'pactum legem vincit et amor iudicium'. Possibly it recalls Virgil:

Omnia vincit amor et nos cedamus amori.
(Love conquers all and we must yield to love.)[9]

Medieval familiarity with that is suggested by Chaucer's prioress wearing a brooch bearing the motto *Amor vincit omnia*.[10] The idea of yielding to love would be appropriate in the context of the *Leges*,

[5] *Ibid.*, p. 98, ch. 6, 5.
[6] *Paston Letters and Papers of the 15th Century*, ed. N. Davis (Oxford, 1971–6), ii, p. 444, no. 801.
[7] Downer, *Leges Henrici Primi*, pp. 437–9, discusses meanings of *amicus*. See also J. Riley-Smith, 'Crusading as an Act of Love', *History*, lxv (1980), p. 190. J. A. Sharpe (see below p. 176) cites a Yorkshire witness in the late sixteenth century speaking of 'lovers and frendes' in a reconciliation.
[8] A. E. Levett, *Studies in Manorial History* (Oxford, 1938), p. 343.
[9] *Eclogues*, x, line 69. Cf. *Proverbia Sententiaeque Latinitatis Medii Aevi*, ed. H. Walther, 5 vols. (Göttingen, 1963), i, pp. 116–17.
[10] 'The Canterbury Tales, General Prologue', line 162, *The Works of Geoffrey Chaucer*, ed. F. N. Robinson, 2nd edn (Oxford, 1974), p. 18.

as parties to litigation have to yield to a compromise: 'where someone has the option through a judge of friendship (*amicitia*) or law (*laga*) and chooses friendship, this is to stand as firm as a judgment itself'.[11] Put in this form, the text of the *Leges* recalls Anglo-Saxon law: a thane has two choices, *lufu* (love) or *lagu* (law), and he that chooses *lufu* is as much bound by that as he would be by a judgement.[12] Somewhere behind this idea of love overriding law there must lie the influence of the New Testament and of such texts as 'Judge not, that ye be not judged' and 'He that loveth another hath fulfilled the law.'[13] The clergy were enjoined not to let the sun go down upon the anger of their flock and one statement from thirteenth-century English canons approaches the proposition of the *Leges*: the duty of prelates is to 'coerce those in discord, whether they be clerics or laymen, much more to peace (*pacem*) than to judgement (*iudicium*)'.[14]

As an explicit principle the proposition of the *Leges* seems to be confined to England, where there are precedents for it in Anglo-Saxon law and subsequent examples of it being applied in practice. The treatise called Glanvill (written towards the end of the twelfth century) states that 'it is generally true that agreement prevails over law (*generaliter verum est quod conventio legem vincit*)'.[15] Although this statement substitutes the word *conventio* for the *pactum* and *amor* of the *Leges*, the idea that agreement 'prevails (*vincit*)' is explicit. In thirteenth-century England evidence from some local court rolls suggests that the proposition of the *Leges* was well understood and even commonplace. One example from a roll of the manor of Sevenhampton will illustrate this for the time being.[16] A certain William le Despencer was summoned on 26 May 1282 to 'make law (*facere legem*)'. This meant that he was to produce oath helpers to swear to his innocence in accordance with the custom of 'wager of law'. However, a note in the margin against this

---

[11] *Leges Henrici Primi*, p. 172, ch. 54, 3. Downer translates 'per iustitiam' here as 'in accordance with justice', whereas I prefer 'through a judge'.

[12] *The Laws of the Kings of England from Edmund to Henry I*, ed. A. J. Robertson (Cambridge, 1925), p. 70, Aethelred no. iii, ch. 13, 3.

[13] Matthew vii. 1. Luke vi. 37. Romans xiii. 8. Cf. the assize sermon on Romans xiii. 8, cited by J. A. Sharpe, below, p. 169.

[14] J. W. Bennett, 'The Medieval Loveday', *Speculum*, xxxiii (1958), p. 358, n. 41.

[15] *The Treatise on the Laws and Customs of the Realm of England Commonly Called Glanvill*, bk. x, ch. 14, ed. G. D. G. Hall (London, 1965), p. 129.

[16] *Court Rolls of the Wiltshire Manors of Adam de Stratton*, ed. R. B. Pugh (Wilts. Record Soc., Devizes. xxiv, 1970), pp. 71–2.

enrolment states that William 'may wage an out-of-court settlement (*vadiet finem extra curiam*)'. At a subsequent meeting of the court on 16 July it was noted in the margin of the roll that the case concerning William 'was waged in love (*vadiata fuit in amore*)' and was therefore concluded. These laconic marginal notes suggest that this enrolling clerk was familiar with the idea that law (*lex*) is a process duly done in court, whereas love (*amor*) involves an agreement out of court.

Unlike the enrolling clerk of Sevenhampton, historians of law have not made their readers familiar with love as a foil to law and a 'routinized' method of settling disputes. In the classic surveys of English medieval law, Pollock and Maitland's *History* and Plucknett's *Concise History*, the words 'agreement', 'arbitration', 'concord' and 'love' do not appear in the indexes and are scarcely discussed.[17] Even the 'loveday', a day for reconciling disputants like William le Despencer of Sevenhampton, which was a commonplace of village life, is missing.[18] In a way Maitland and Plucknett were right to exclude the medieval idea of love from their purview because it prevails over law and is therefore above their terms of reference. Nevertheless beneath the exclusion of love from the mainstream of medieval legal history there lies, I think, a fundamental presupposition which needs examining.

Legal historians have tended to see 'law and order' as something imposed by authorities from above through codes of rules, rather than something which grew from below by the extension and reinforcement of bonds of affection beyond the immediate family. In other words they are proponents of what Simon Roberts in his chapter calls the 'rule-centred' paradigm as opposed to the 'processual' one. In the former 'normal behaviour was rule-governed behaviour, and settlement institutions were there to put things right if temporary malfunction in the form of a dispute developed'.[19] The 'processual' paradigm by contrast implies an entirely different approach to conflict: 'disputes, far from being pathological, were normal and inevitable as people struggled to secure their objectives'.[20] Legal historians usually look at past societies from above – and in the process unconsciously opt for the

[17] F. Pollock and F. W. Maitland, *The History of English Law before the Time of Edward I*, 2nd edn (Cambridge, 1898); T. F. T. Plucknett, *A Concise History of the Common Law*, 5th edn (London, 1956).   [18] See notes 36–9 below.
[19] Roberts, p. 3 above.   [20] *Ibid.*, p. 4.

'rule-centred' paradigm – because of the nature of their sources. Rulers leave the most impressive monuments for posterity, whether we think of the pyramids or of the hundreds of thousands of parchments in the Public Record Office. Because of the latter, historians of medieval England in particular have tended to be the 'king's friends'.[21] As Simon Roberts points out, the 'rule-centred' paradigm is not necessarily wrong and the 'processual' one correct: 'the concerns reflected in both represent *necessary* and *complementary* areas of inquiry'.[22] It is in this spirit that I want to use the proposition from the *Leges Henrici Primi* as an insight into attitudes to law and human relations extending beyond medieval England where the proposition found explicit expression. *Lex* and *amor* in the words of the *Leges*, or 'rule-centred' and 'processual' paradigms in anthropological terms, are complementary ways of settling disputes, each of which is necessary in certain contexts.

In some medieval societies law was indeed reduced to a code of rules and order was imposed from above, and there were good precedents for this in the Old Testament and in the majestic *Corpus Iuris Civilis* of Roman jurisprudence. But there were other societies where good neighbourliness and custom – welling up from below – were more trusted than a code, and the precedents for this were equally strong: in the New Testament and in the barbarians' victory over the Romans. Augustine argued in the *City of God*, as he surveyed the ruins of the Roman empire, that there could be no justice on earth but only a kind of peace. One persistent medieval tradition rejected written law: in England 'law comes from nothing written', Bracton stated at the beginning of his treatise, and at about the same time the French nobility asserted that their kingdom had been won from the Romans 'not by *ius scriptum*, nor by the arrogance of clerks, but by the sweat of war'.[23] The knights ruled in the Middle Ages, although their rivals the clergy had the best of the argument in the end because they did the writing for posterity.

[21] M. T. Clanchy, 'Law, Government and Society in Medieval England', *History*, lix (1974), p. 74, citing K. B. McFarlane. For an example of the arguments of the 'King's Friends' see my comments at notes 44–50 below.

[22] Roberts, p. 6 above, my emphasis.

[23] 'Ex non scripto ius venit', *De Legibus et Consuetudinibus Angliae*, ed. G. E. Woodbine, rev. S. E. Thorne, 4 vols. (Cambridge, Mass., 1968), ii, p. 19; Matthew Paris, *Chronica Majora*, ed. H. R. Luard, 7 vols. (Rolls ser., lvii, 1872–84), iv, p. 593.

Impressive as the records of the clerks are – the glossed and gilded folios of the law professors of Bologna and Paris, the discursive chronicles of the monks, the elegant title-deeds and wills of the scriveners and notaries, the masses of writs emanating from chanceries – all this parchment provides only a partial record of the actual disputes of medieval people or of their ways of settling them, a record that is 'partial' in both senses of that word.

Law (standing for learning and the application of rules) and love (standing for common sense and bonds of affection) can be seen as contrasting styles in the settlement of disputes in the Middle Ages. The contrast is simply illustrated by comparing the Emperor Frederick II (1215–50) '*Stupor Mundi*' with Louis IX (1226–70), 'St Louis'. Take Louis first. His approach to disputes is described by his biographer, Joinville, in a passage familiar to all medievalists, although it has never been satisfactorily explained.[24] The atmosphere is relaxed: the king sits at the foot of his bed, or in summer with his back against an oak in the Bois de Vincennes, or on a carpet in the Jardin de Paris without any head covering other than a cap of white peacock's feathers. Litigants came forward without formality and the king himself asks them, 'Why don't you take what our people offer you?' When they reply that the offers are too little, the king does everything he can to 'put them on a right and sensible course'. Plaintiffs are not obstructed by a court usher; the king himself asks, 'Is there anyone here who has a suit to bring?' and when the litigants stand up, he says, 'Keep quiet, all of you, and your business will be dispatched (*deliverra*) one by one.' Joinville's use of the verb *delivrer* (literally 'deliver') for the method of settling a case is significant. The king asks his counsellors whether there is anyone who cannot be 'delivered' without his personal intervention; he goes to the Jardin de Paris 'to deliver his people (*pour delivrer sa gent*)'. The verb *delivrer* emphasizes how the method of adjudication is one of 'delivering' the litigants from their toils through discussion and bargaining. The king does not say, 'Why don't you acknowledge the ruling of our judges?' but 'Why don't you take what our people offer you?' Instead of officers

---

[24] 'Histoire de St. Louis', ch. 12, *Oeuvres de Jean Sire de Joinville*, ed. N. de Wailly (Paris, 1867), pp. 38–43. Cf. *La vie de St Louis: Texte du XIVe siècle*, ed. N. L. Corbett (Quebec, 1977), p. 95. Recent introductions are: E. Pognon, 'Les arbitrages de St Louis', *Le siècle de St Louis* (Paris, 1970), pp. 221–7 and W. C. Jordan, *Louis IX and the Challenge of the Crusade* (Princeton, 1979), p. 143.

administering justice, Joinville describes people making bargains. All this suggests that Louis IX is typical of the 'processual' rather than the 'rule-centred' paradigm.

The difficulty with Joinville's description is that Louis was the most powerful ruler in Europe. He had clerks hearing petitions, ushers at his court of *parlement*, and bailiffs governing through royal ordinances. He could not have controlled France by sitting back and asking anyone who had a problem to come forward. If Louis had allowed free access to his person and at the same time been so good at settling disputes, he would have been overwhelmed by demands for his services. On the other hand Joinville's testimony cannot be ignored as he wrote as an eyewitness, indeed as one of the counsellors who sat at ease around their king at the foot of his bed or by the carpet in the garden. A solution to this difficulty is to appreciate the tradition in which Joinville lived and wrote. He sat in aristocratic ease with his king at the centre of France, the only place perhaps where turbulence ceased. In his touchingly simple description of Louis Joinville was not being untruthful or naïve. Rather, he was evoking and reinforcing an ideal of kingship which was fast disappearing in the face of bureaucracy. Among the barbarians justice had traditionally been administered under trees (weather permitting).[25] In the *Chanson de Roland* Charlemagne is first depicted sitting in an orchard under a pine tree surrounded by his vassals on white carpets.[26] The lack of stress, the assumption that problems are resolvable by compromise, and that there is room for all men of good will under the greenwood tree were likewise French royal traditions. Almost a century earlier Walter Map had spoken in Paris with Louis VII about the wealth and display of contemporary rulers like Henry II of England and had noted as a true and appropriate dictum that Louis said: 'We in France have nothing – except bread and wine and joy.'[27] These of course were all that man required according to the troubadours and medieval wandering scholars.

By contrast Frederick II said he had everything. As his *Liber Augustalis* proclaimed in 1231, he was 'Caesar' and 'Augustus' and

---

[25] H. S. Bennett, *Life on the English Manor* (Cambridge, 1937), p. 203 has a few references; there are many more.

[26] F. Whitehead (ed.), 2nd edn (Oxford, 1946), laisse 8, p. 4.

[27] 'De Nugis Curialium', distinctio 5, ch. 5, *Anecdota Oxoniensa*, ed. M. R. James (Medieval and Modern ser. xiv, 1914), p. 225, lines 24–5; R. W. Southern, *Medieval Humanism* (Oxford, 1970), p. 147.

much more. The *Liber Augustalis* is the apotheosis of law-making in the Middle Ages. Justifying its elaborate provisions is the premise that:

Man, whom God created upright and simple, did not hesitate to mix himself up in wrangles; and so by this compelling necessity of things, and no less at the instigation of divine providence, the princes of nations were created by whom criminal licence can be coerced, for they are judges of life and death among the nations.[28]

The differences between Frederick II's approach to justice and Louis IX's – in their public images at least – are profound. Frederick is not relaxed; fallen man has to be coerced and made subject. Nor are the surroundings open and informal; Frederick and his judges ape the panoply of Roman and oriental despotism. The function of Frederick's justiciars is not to arbitrate between disputants but to hand down infallible judgements. For the parties to reach agreement among themselves in a criminal case is contempt of court, penalized by a large fine; moreover the court may not accept the agreement.[29] Such rules are the reverse of the principle that 'pactum legem vincit et amor iudicium'.

My purpose is not to decide whether Louis' or Frederick's was the better way to settle disputes, but to highlight the contrasts between them. Frederick's way, with its emphasis on coercion, looks forward in time to Hobbes' *Leviathan* and back to the Old Testament and Roman law. Man's redeemer is not the Christ of the Gospel, who conquers all by love, but Caesar Augustus 'victor ac triumphator' in his present embodiment as Frederick II. Frederick is in the mainstream of academic jurisprudence: law is something written down in books, expounded by professors (at his university of Naples), and applied by a hierarchy of judges (headed by the Ciceronian rhetorician, Piero della Vinea). Shortly after promulgating the *Liber Augustalis* Frederick built a triumphal gate at Capua which gave visual expression to his concept of authority.

---

[28] 'Liber Augustalis', proemium, *Historia Diplomatica Friderici Secundi*, ed. J. L. A. Huillard-Bréholles, 6 vols. (Paris, 1854–60), iv, pp. 3–4. There is an English translation of the *Liber Augustalis* by J. M. Powell (New York, 1971) and a recent introduction to his jurisprudence is H. M. Schaller, 'Die Kaiseridee Friedrichs II', in J. Fleckenstein (ed.), *Probleme um Friedrich II* (Sigmaringen, 1974), pp. 109–34.

[29] Plaintiff and defendant may reach agreement before joinder of issue but if they compromise thereafter, they will have to pay 24 *augustales* to the treasury, 'Liber Augustalis', bk. ii, title 16, iv, pp. 88–9.

Above the gate at the top sat a statue of Frederick himself, with an inscription in Latin verse at his feet, and beneath this was a bust of 'Justice' dressed as a classical maiden with two judges like ancient Romans to her left and right.[30] Although this structure is now in ruins, it was described by various observers, the earliest being Andrew of Hungary who saw it in 1266. He was impressed by the threatening effect of the statue of Frederick and of the verse at his feet, 'as if the puffed-out mouth was intoning the lines of menace to the terror of passers-by'.[31] The verse begins:

> Cesaris imperio regni custodia fio
> Quam miseros facio quos variare scio
>
> (By Caesar's command the kingdom's guard is me,
> How wretched I make those I know to disagree).

Although Andrew thought this verse was to be said by Frederick himself, it makes better sense if it is voiced 'by Caesar's command' by the figure of 'Justice' at Frederick's feet. On either interpretation the gate at Capua is consistent with the *Liber Augustalis* in presenting justice as essentially coercive and threatening to deviants. Frederick's style of ruling has some resemblances to the 'new monarchies' of early modern Europe and even to fascism, as has often been pointed out. Nevertheless it was explicitly backward-looking rather than modern, as it evoked the authority of the Old Testament and of the Roman emperors. Louis' way on the other hand was – from a medieval point of view – more modern. It drew on the New Testament rather than the Old and it reflected not the awesome Romanesque figure of Christ in Majesty judging mankind, and still less a pagan impersonation of 'Justice', but the Gothic Christ, the teacher who presents a human face. The nearest to an authentic image of Louis, the wooden statue from the *Sainte Chapelle*, presents him as calm, open and beautiful, and the stance is that of Christ the Teacher of Chartres (south portal) or the *Beau Dieu* of Amiens.[32] Unlike Frederick, Louis required no menacing verse to impress his authority on bystanders. In reconciling

---

[30] T. C. Van Cleve, *The Emperor Frederick II of Hohenstaufen* (Oxford, 1972), pp. 339–43 and plates 9–12. I owe this reference to Dr Robert Bartlett.

[31] *Monumenta Germaniae Historica: Scriptores*, xxvi (1882), p. 571.

[32] The wooden statue, now in the Musée de Cluny, is illustrated by Joan Evans as frontispiece to her translation of Joinville (Oxford, 1938). The more commonly illustrated stone statue of Louis (from the church of Mainneville), which has similar features, dates from the early fourteenth century. The one significant

disputants Louis followed the example of the new Christ, St Francis; it was Franciscan friars whom he chose as his *enquêteurs*. Louis' style had its roots not only in the New Testament but in the traditions of the Franks: in their apartness from the Romans, in their memories of Charlemagne, and above all in their feudal loyalties. Frederick had subjects terrified into obedience by coercion. Louis had vassals bound to him by willing service.

Of course the realities of government were not as clear cut as these models. Louis promoted the inquisition and persecuted Jews, while Frederick was seen by the popes as a dangerous anarchist. I, on the other hand, have made Frederick and Louis into *exempla* of law and love respectively. But that requires no apology, because it is as ideals that the *Liber Augustalis* and Joinville present them. Too little survives of the day-to-day records of either Frederick or Louis to establish what really went on. Only one medieval monarchy, England, has left records of its daily business from so early a date. Like Louis IX, Henry II of England listened to complaints. But Walter Map's picture of the scene differs from Joinville's and differs also from Walter's image of Louis VII, who was content to have nothing 'except bread and wine and joy'. There was no peace and contentment with Henry II: he was constantly on the move and was jostled and shouted at by crowds of suitors whenever he went out in public.[33]

In response to this overwhelming demand for redress – or so runs the theory – Henry II devised an automated system of justice emphasizing speed and decisiveness.[34] The plaintiff obtained a writ in standardized form (novel disseisin for example) instructing a jury to be summoned, the jury gave a verdict of 'Yes' or 'No', and judgement and execution then followed. The system stopped people rambling on about their grievances by compelling them to

difference in stance between figures of Christ and those of Louis is that, where Christ has his right hand raised in blessing, Louis' right hand is intended to hold a sceptre.

[33] 'De Nugis Curialium', distinctio 5, ch. 6, ed. James, p. 241, lines 27–31; W. L. Warren, *Henry II* (London, 1973), p. 210.

[34] What follows derives from my *Civil Pleas of the Wiltshire Eyre, 1249* (Wiltshire Record Soc., xxvi, 1971), pp. 10–12. This account is abbreviated and simplified. Fuller introductions will be found in D. M. Stenton, *English Justice between the Norman Conquest and the Great Charter* (London, 1965), pp. 22–53; A. Harding, *The Law Courts of Medieval England* (London, 1973), pp. 49–63; R. C. Van Caenegem, *The Birth of the English Common Law* (Cambridge, 1973), *passim*.

confine their statements within prescribed forms. There is no record like Ladurie's *Montaillou* in English common law, because the judges were not inquisitors meticulously searching out the truth but operators of a slot machine intended to produce decisions every few minutes. Like Frederick II's system, the common law penalized people for making agreements. To compromise with the defendant was to insult the king, whose aid had been given to the plaintiff to prosecute a wrongdoer. In practice, however, compromises were numerous and were paid for by fines and oblations which profited the crown. The truth was often too complex to encapsulate in a standardized writ of complaint or in a jury verdict of 'Yes' or 'No'. Nor did neighbours in a village community, who had to live with each other for years to come, invariably share the king's court's enthusiasm for snap judgements in which the winner took all.

At least one source, the *Liber Memorandorum* of Barnwell priory, demonstrates discrepancies between official records and actual events. In one instance the final outcome of a case was the reverse of the official record. In 1286 Henry Tuillet of Cambridge won the action of novel disseisin for rent brought against him by the prior of Barnwell, according to the plea roll, that is (which is still extant in the Public Record Office), and that was the end of the matter.[35] Nevertheless the Barnwell *Liber* shows that this was only the beginning. The case is worth dwelling on because, thanks to the Barnwell *Liber* and not to the plea roll, it illustrates the shortcomings of the common law system. The prior claimed that Henry had deprived him of the rent due on a house by walling up the door to prevent the prior's bailiffs from entering and distraining Henry's goods; Henry meanwhile was able to go in and out of the house over a piece of property not belonging to the prior. The prior therefore brought an action of novel disseisin against him. Henry denied the disseisin, saying that it was not he but his father, William, who had walled up the door. The jury in their verdict confirmed this and so judgement was given against the prior. Within the terms of reference of an action of novel disseisin this judgement was correct, as that action required the actual author of a disseisin

[35] *Liber Memorandorum Ecclesie de Bernewelle*, ed. J. Willis Clark (Cambridge, 1907), pp. 158–9. M. T. Clanchy, 'A Medieval Realist: Interpreting the Rules at Barnwell Priory, Cambridge', in A. Attwooll (ed.), *Perspectives in Jurisprudence* (Glasgow, 1977), case D, pp. 189, 191–2. For the law on this point see D. W. Sutherland, *The Assize of Novel Disseisin* (Oxford, 1973).

to be sued. But the prior could not sue William because he was dead: he had sued Henry instead on the common-sense grounds that Henry actually lived in the house and benefited from the fraud. The prior might have been better advised to have proceeded by an action of 'entry sur disseisin' which prosecuted the beneficiary of a disseisin, but there was a difficulty with that too as Henry had not entered the house after the disseisin, as he had been living in it when the wall was built at his father's expense.

The Barnwell *Liber* reveals that the prior, caught in these technicalities, resorted to intimidation though still within the confines of legality. He threatened to 'attaint' the jury, that is, to accuse them of bringing in a false verdict. This frightened the jurors very much and it frightened Henry even more so that he 'came weeping to the prior and sought his grace on bended knee'. Through the mediation of a justice's clerk a compromise was worked out: the prior pardoned Henry half his arrears of rent and Henry swore on the Gospels not to obstruct the rent collectors in future. Because it was made out of court, there is no record of this arrangement on the plea roll. Moreover, its terms go back in spirit behind Henry II's automated system of justice to the principle of the *Leges Henrici Primi* that 'pactum legem vincit et amor iudicium'. Like a repentant lover, Henry came to the prior weeping and on bended knee. The dispute was resolved not by the judgement in the king's court, which Henry seems to have used as a bargaining point, but by a more ancient and hallowed procedure, an oath on the Gospels. The fact that the clerk writing the plea roll made no mention of this agreement is not a mistake on his part. The agreement had prevailed over the law and it was therefore none of his business. The plea roll correctly recorded what took place in court; its purpose was not to record the full facts about a case but the law.

Henry Tuillet and the prior of Barnwell had had a 'loveday', although the records did not call it that. In some village courts, which were less touched by the king's majesty and had fewer powers of coercion, the 'loveday' was a common event. One procedure for it is described in *The Court Baron* dating from *c.* 1265, which gives instruction (in French) in the form of hypothetical court-room scenes. For example, Thomas Lorimer complains that Stephen Glover owes him 40 shillings.[36] Stephen prays the steward of the

---

[36] F. W. Maitland and W. P. Baildon (eds.) (Selden Soc., iv, 1890), pp. 47, 57.

court for a *jour d'amour* with Thomas. 'We grant it you', replies the steward, 'so that you be at one between now and the next court.' At the next court the steward asks: 'Thomas Lorimer and you Stephen Glover, how has the business gone between you? Are you at one?' Thomas answers, 'Yes, sir'; and that is the end of the matter, apart from a payment to the court. A 'loveday' (*jour d'amour* in French or *dies amoris* in Latin) is therefore a day of reconciliation between disputants. The court does not adjudicate this reconciliation, nor does it inquire what its terms are; the court's only function is to fix a time limit within which agreement is to be reached. The court's lack of responsibility is explained by the principle that 'pactum legem vincit et amor iudicium'. The request to the steward for a day of reconciliation supersedes the law and the subsequent bond of love between Thomas and Stephen eliminates further action by the court. The steward asks them, 'Are you at one?', which is literally translated as 'Are you one people or kindred (*une gent* or *une genz*)?' The loveday makes the contending parties into *une genz* just as the marriage ceremony does. Like marriage, a loveday should be sealed by a kiss (the kiss of peace), blessed by a priest, and witnessed by mutual friends and kinsmen. One English writer, Thomas Usk, describes the Redemption itself as a loveday between God and mankind, with Mary as umpire to put the quarrel at an end.[37]

Nevertheless it is difficult to find out much about lovedays from legal sources beyond the basic procedure. The only discussion of them in Bracton's large treatise on English law (revised in the 1230s) is a note that the plaintiff should make clear that he takes a loveday under protest, so that 'if love does not take him' he still has recourse to his plea.[38] Bracton seems here to be aware of the principle 'pactum legem vincit et amor iudicium' and he tries to protect the plaintiff from its implications, since in the king's court love does not override the law. The best evidence about the frequency of lovedays might be expected to come from manorial and other court rolls, which start in the latter half of the thirteenth century. This evidence is perplexing, however, as the summary of it appended to

[37] 'The Testament of Love', bk. i, ch. 2 in W. W. Skeat (ed.), *Chaucerian and Other Pieces* (Oxford, 1897), p. 11, line 95.
[38] 'Diem amoris capiat sub tali protestatione, quod si amor se non capit', *De Legibus*, iv, p. 160. At *De Legibus*, iv, p. 129, Bracton says similarly that the plaintiff runs the risk of losing his action if he takes a loveday with the defendant.

this chapter (pp. 66–7 below) shows. Some rolls (Bec, Chalgrave, Ramsey) contain no references to lovedays, whereas in others (Adam of Stratton, Halesowen part iii, Highworth) references are quite frequent, though brief; the rolls of Wakefield, which extend over a long period, contain proportionately more lovedays in the thirteenth century than in the fourteenth. How are such discrepancies to be explained? Sometimes the editor is at fault in not providing an index of subjects (Alrewas, Durham) or in indexing incompetently (Halesowen part i). Sometimes too the rolls are incomplete or the editor has made a selection from them which may unwittingly exclude lovedays. Nevertheless editorial shortcomings do not explain the lack of lovedays in the rolls of Chalgrave and Ramsey in particular. Sometimes the loveday may be called something else by the enrolling clerk; thus the rolls of Halesowen (part iii) and of St Ives make it clear from their marginal notes that a *dies amoris* and a *dies concordandi* are synonymous. The practice of enrolment seems to have differed from one court to another. Some courts kept no record of lovedays at all, others described them by different names, and others again noted them in passing. Even the rolls which note lovedays (like Adam of Stratton's) merely record the granting of the recess; they do not record the terms of the agreement reached at the loveday. This is because the principle of 'pactum legem vincit et amor iudicium' put the loveday itself outside the purview of the court. Like the plea rolls of the king's court, local court rolls confined themselves to the law, that is, to what officially took place in court.

Although legal records cannot provide consistent evidence about lovedays because they were, strictly speaking, outside their terms of reference, literary and miscellaneous vernacular sources suggest that the loveday was commonplace in the fourteenth and fifteenth centuries. The principal sources have been discussed by J. W. Bennett and there is no need to repeat them here.[39] It is worth emphasizing, however, that love was not necessarily better than law in the opinion of the great fourteenth-century writers. According to Langland lovedays are a corrupt inducement of Lady Meed

---

[39] 'The Medieval Loveday' (note 14 above). T. J. Heffernan, 'A Middle English Poem on Lovedays', *The Chaucer Review*, x (1975–6), pp. 172–85, prints a poem of 216 lines which was noted by J. W. Bennett. This poem does no more than exhort lords holding lovedays to be fair and not to betray their trust 'for love or lordship, for silver or for gold' (p. 177, line 23).

(Bribery) to settle out of court, when the litigant's best interest is to prosecute:

> And doth men lese thorw hire loue – that lawe myghte wynne.
> (And men lose through love of her what law might win them.)[40]

Thus in Langland's view law should win, since true love has been prostituted by Lady Meed. Chaucer too contrasts law and love in the lines:

> Mo love-dayes and acordes
> Then on instrumentes be cordes.[41]

The distinction here is between oral 'accords' or agreements on the one hand and written legal 'instruments', to which seals are attached by 'cords', on the other. Although Chaucer compliments lovedays here, in so far as there are more lovedays than the vast number of seals weighing down legal instruments, he points to the 'discords' and 'dissimulations' of love a few lines earlier.[42] Wyclif is the severest critic of lovedays: they are abused by lords so 'that right and law may not run their course'; priests at lovedays 'bear down truth and poor men in their right by colour of lords kneeling in chapel'.[43] In the later Middle Ages procedure by love seems to have become as embroiled in faction as the ordinary processes of law.

I have not intended to suggest that love was in reality more effective than law, but to point out that in one persistent line of medieval thought law and love are seen as opposite ways of settling disputes. It was a common medieval way of thinking to see things as pairs of opposites. The resolution of opposites – Abelard's *Sic et Non* and Gratian's *Concordia Discordantium Canonum* – was the basis of the scholastic method. Pairing law and love was peculiarly suited to oral transmission in English because of the alliteration: the Anglo-Saxon *lufu* and *lagu* become Langland's *loue* and *lawe*. Medieval

---

[40] *The Vision of William concerning Piers the Plowman*, ed. W. W. Skeat, 2 vols. (Oxford, 1886), i, p. 76, B text, Passus iii, line 158. Bennett, 'The Medieval Loveday', p. 364. The C text of *Piers the Plowman*, p. 77, Passus iv, line 197, reads: 'Thoruh which loueday ys lost that *leaute* myghte wynne'; it therefore substitutes 'loyalty' for the 'law' of the B text.

[41] 'The House of Fame', lines 695–6, *The Works of Geoffrey Chaucer*, p. 288; Bennett, 'The Medieval Loveday', p. 352.

[42] 'The House of Fame,' lines 685–6.

[43] Bennett, 'The Medieval Loveday', p. 364, n. 70 and p. 359, n. 48.

historians on the other hand have not looked at law and love together, and still less at the notion that love may prevail over law. They have been beguiled by the size, elegance and order of 'rule-centred' medieval records like Frederick II's *Liber Augustalis* or the English plea rolls into accepting them at their face value, whereas the provisions of the *Liber Augustalis* cannot be checked against day-to-day practice and the English plea rolls demonstrably mislead those who think they record the facts rather than the law of a case. In English medieval historiography in particular the assumption has been that disputes were best resolved not by compromise but by strong kings, like Henry II and Edward I, imposing 'law and order' from above. The remarkable growth in the volume of recorded litigation between the reigns of Henry II and Edward I is seen as proof that disputants sought out the king's court because it provided better justice. 'The success of the system was remarkable, the enthusiasm of the plaintiffs evident.'[44] Nevertheless a sufficient explanation for this growth is that plaintiffs had no choice. Pessimistically interpreted, Henry II's reforms had the long-term effect of weakening and straining the bonds of affection existing in feudal lordship and kindred loyalties and putting nothing as adequate in their place.[45] As S. F. C. Milsom concludes in his study of this formative period:

> The great mass of land litigation in the thirteenth century may largely have been generated by these changes; it is not that disputes which would have arisen anyway are brought to a preferred jurisdiction [that of the king's court]; they are the miserable products of uncertainty, of the ending of that conclusive seignorial title.[46]

Even if 'seignorial title' and the bonds of feudalism were not as conclusive as Milsom suggests, Henry II's automated system of law made it easier – and more necessary – for neighbours to sue each other in the king's court. Yet justice remained as elusive as ever.

---

[44] Van Caenegem, *Birth of the Common Law*, p. 61.

[45] This interpretation likewise contrasts with Van Caenegem, *Royal Writs* (Selden Soc.), p. 46, who writes of 'the sweeping advances made by the royal courts in the 12th century . . . with their adequate, practical, swift, firm and straightforward procedure'. By contrast the old law is described as 'a ghost-like institution, sapped at the roots and ready to give way entirely as soon as some satisfactory substitute appeared', *ibid.*, p. 46.

[46] S. F. C. Milsom, *The Legal Framework of English Feudalism* (Cambridge, 1976), pp. 185–6.

The alleged success of Henry II's system, in R. C. Van Caenegem's statement of the traditional argument,

resulted from the quality of the professional royal justices: compare the intellectual level and technical standard (only slightly influenced by the revival of Roman law) of Glanvill's treatise with some of the helpless compilations of the earlier years of the century; it was also due to the coherence of the system, clearly understood as such in Glanvill, encompassing all free men in the same royal solicitude, and to the combination of royal efficiency with judicial guarantees.[47]

This statement does indeed accurately reflect the opinions of the author of Glanvill. The judges are paragons: 'his highness's court is so impartial that no judge there is so shameless or audacious as to presume to turn aside at all from the path of justice'.[48] Glanvill's treatise is certainly more coherent and technically competent, from an academic lawyer's point of view, than the muddles of the *Leges Henrici Primi* whose author apologizes for his incompetence: 'Although I may carry out this task less adequately because of the great diversity of relevant matters, at least I offer a universal expression of good will.'[49] Likewise according to Glanvill the king's court does show solicitude: 'for there indeed a poor man is not oppressed by the power of his adversary, nor does favour or partiality drive any man away from the threshold of judgment'.[50] The difficulty with Glanvill's point of view is that it was not shared by other contemporaries. John of Salisbury, Walter Map and Peter of Blois all wrote in vituperative terms of the corruption of Henry II's judges.[51] The author of the *Chronicle of Battle Abbey* described in circumstantial detail how success in litigation depended on Henry II's moods and current politics.[52] Furthermore favour in lawsuits can be demonstrated in practice by tracing the fees paid to individual judges by litigants through the thirteenth and fourteenth centuries. There was nothing unusual or secretive about this. Judges expected to make money and 'a supplicant's influence on the

---

[47] Van Caenegem, *Birth of the Common Law*, p. 61.
[48] *Glanvill*, prologue, p. 2. [49] *Leges*, p. 105, ch. 8, 7. [50] *Glanvill*, p. 2.
[51] The best introduction to this theme in general is J. A. Yunck, *The Lineage of Lady Meed* (Notre Dame, 1963), ch. iv, and for England in particular see R. V. Turner, 'The Reputation of Royal Judges under the Angevin Kings', *Albion*, xi (1979), pp. 301–16, which has a more balanced view than mine.
[52] Ed. E. Searle (Oxford, 1980). See my review in the *American Journal of Legal History*, xxv (1981), pp. 252–3.

crown's servants was largely determined by the usual constituents of political power: wealth, landed authority and favour at court'.[53] The author of the Barnwell *Liber* is explicit about the methods used. He explains how the prior gave such abundant gifts to the judges that he was not fined for losing against Henry Tuillet and 'by the end all the justices, as well as the clerks, serjeants and solicitors returned prolific thanks, and they and theirs were under an obligation to the prior'.[54] The most fundamental of all bonds in medieval society was that of mutual obligation. This is what had given the principle that love prevails over law whatever strength it had. But now Langland's Lady Meed had prostituted true love and created overriding obligations to her instead. The love of Lady Meed gives an ironical twist to 'pactum legem vincit et amor iudicium': haggling (*pactum*) and favouritism (*amor*) prevail over legality (*legem*) and justice (*iudicium*).

Because law officers were corrupt, enforcement could make things worse. 'It might even be argued that royal power contributed to disorder and the judicial authority of the crown was a public nuisance.'[55] Since I published that opinion in 1974 some research on fourteenth-century judicial commissions by R. W. Kaeuper and B. W. McLane has tended to confirm it.[56] J. B. Given in his study of homicide in England in the thirteenth century goes so far as to say that 'the most effective means of settling disputes were informal; the mediation of friends, relatives and neighbours was undoubtedly far more effective than the activities of royal and manorial courts'.[57]

[53] J. R. Maddicott, *Law and Lordship: Royal Justices as Retainers in 13th and 14th Century England* (Past and Present Supplements, no. 4, 1978), p. 1. See also B. A. Hanawalt, *Crime and Conflict in English Communities 1300–1348* (Cambridge, Mass., 1979), pp. 46–51.

[54] *Liber Memorandorum*, p. 171. Cf. note 35 above.

[55] Clanchy, 'Law, Government and Society', p. 78. A mine of new evidence about law enforcement, which can be interpreted according to taste, is provided in *Medieval Legal Records Edited in Memory of C. A. F. Meekings*, ed. R. F. Hunnisett and J. B. Post (London, 1978).

[56] Kaeuper, 'Law and Order in 14th Century England: the Evidence of Special Commissions of Oyer and Terminer', *Speculum*, liv (1979), pp. 734–84; McLane, 'The Royal Courts and the Problem of Disorder in Lincolnshire, 1290–1341' (University of Rochester Ph.D. thesis, 1979). I am indebted also to Dr McLane's unpublished paper, 'Rule Makes Misrule: the Royal Administration as a Source of Disorder in early 14th Century England'.

[57] *Society and Homicide in 13th Century England* (Stanford, 1977), p. 201. Three papers on arbitration in later medieval England have appeared since the composition of mine in 1980: C. Rawcliffe, 'The great lord as peacemaker: arbitration by English noblemen and their councils', to be published in the

It would be pleasant to agree with that and to conclude that love was 'undoubtedly far more effective' than law. However, as Given is aware, informal means of settling disputes cannot be accurately weighed against the activities of the courts because the latter are usually on record whereas the former are not. Whether law or love prevailed on average over medieval disputes as a whole is matter for speculation only. The 'rule-centred' and 'processual' paradigms are complementary (as Simon Roberts points out). Both were subject in medieval conditions to Lady Meed.

'Pactum legem vincit et amor iudicium' contains a number of lessons for historians of law. It cannot be interpreted sentimentally to mean that there really was a golden age on earth in the Middle Ages when peace and love prevailed. Christian doctrine taught that such a state of perfection existed only in the past, in the garden of paradise, and in the future, at the second coming of Christ. Nevertheless because love was the message of the New Testament and the essential foundation of kindred and feudal loyalty, it is appropriate that it should have been accorded a place of honour as victor over law and judgement. The idea that love prevails over law stands also as a useful warning to users of legal records. These are not as informative as they appear at first sight precisely because they restrict themselves to law. Law – the great weight of treatises, statutes, plea rolls and the like – is easier to study than love and has traditionally been considered a more appropriate subject for a historian; it gives him *gravitas* and esoteric knowledge. If love does prevail over law it usually leaves no record, whereas litigation amasses more documents, those 'miserable products of uncertainty' (in Milsom's phrase), the longer a dispute continues. Understandably enough, historians of law have concentrated on elucidating this mass of material. The occupational hazard of doing so is to lose a sense of proportion and to see things from too lawyer-like and anachronistic a point of view. For much of the thousand years of the Middle Ages the most important things were probably not written down at all. The peace was kept, in so far as it was kept, by whatever means were at hand: sometimes by royal authorities and lawcodes; at other times by the moral and social pressures of kindred groups

proceedings of the 5th British Legal History Conference, ed. H. Beale and J. Guy; I. Rowney, 'Arbitration in gentry disputes', *History*, lxvii (1982), pp. 367–76; E. Powell, 'Arbitration and the law', *Transactions of the Royal Historical Society* (1983), forthcoming.

and feudal loyalties reinforced by the sanctions of the church. How successful these bonds of affection were is impossible to establish, as they are not well documented apart from their basic existence and elementary procedural rules. Polarization between law and love, which I have exemplified in the differences between Frederick II and Louis IX and the differences between the king's court in England and the village tradition of lovedays, clarifies attitudes to the resolution of disputes in the Middle Ages. But it also makes the historian's task more difficult because the spirit of love – including the love of Lady Meed – is harder to trace than the letter of the law.

APPENDIX

Lovedays in local court rolls

Listed below are the principal printed editions of local court rolls starting before 1300. Rolls in manuscript or those printed in extracts only are excluded from the list.

Rolls with indexed references to lovedays:
Adam of Stratton: *Court Rolls of the Wiltshire Manors of Adam Stratton* (1275–88), ed. R. B. Pugh (Wilts. Record Soc., xxiv, 1970). The occurrences are analysed by the editor (pp. 14, 18), whose impression is that 'manor courts of the 13th century often assigned lovedays' (p. 18).

Halesowen: *Court Rolls of the Manor of Hales, 1270–1307*, parts i and ii, ed. J. Amphlett (Worcs. Historical Soc., 1910 and 1912), part iii, ed. R. A. Wilson (1933). Parts i and ii have only one indexed occurrence (p. 24), but there are others (e.g. pp. 62, 73, 83). Part iii, containing addenda, has a number of references: those at pp. 43, 74, 79, 83, 113, 121, make it clear that a *dies amoris* is synonymous with a *dies concordandi* or *dies ad concordandum*. However, the editor of part iii confuses *dies amoris* meaning a boon day (pp. xxii, 168) with *dies amoris* meaning a day of reconciliation.

Highworth: *The Rolls of Highworth Hundred, 1275–87*, ed. B. Farr (Wilts. Record Soc., xxxi and xxxii, 1966 and 1968). The index of subjects reads: 'loveday, *passim*'. Occurrences are in fact rather rare.

St Ives: *Select Cases Concerning the Law Merchant: Local Courts* (Fair Court of St Ives, 1270–1324), ed. C. Gross (Selden Soc., xxiii, 1908). There are references to *dies amoris* by that name and to *dies ad concordandum* glossed by *amor* in the margin of the roll (pp. 3, 18), as noted by J. W. Bennett, 'The Medieval Loveday', *Speculum*, xxxiii (1958), p. 355.

Wakefield: *Court Rolls of the Manor of Wakefield, 1274–1309*, ed. W. P. Baildon (Yorks. Archaeological Soc., xxix and xxxvi, 1901 and 1906),

1313–17, ed. J. Lister (lvii and lxxviii, 1917 and 1930), *1322–31*, ed. J. W. Walker (cix, 1945). This series of rolls, which is still in the process of publication, suggests that recorded lovedays become less frequent over time. The first editor, Baildon, comments on their frequency (xxxvi, p. 9) and indexes fifty-nine occurrences, whereas Lister indexes fifteen occurrences for the years 1313–16 (he supplies no index of subjects for the years 1315–17), and Walker indexes only two occurrences for the years 1322–31.

Rolls with no indexed references to lovedays:
Alrewas: *Alrewas Court Rolls, 1259–61, 1266–69, 1272–73*, ed. W. N. Landor (William Salt Archaeological Soc., new series x, 1907 and 3rd series, i, 1910). There are no indexes of subjects to these texts.

Bec et cetera: *Select Pleas in Manorial and Other Seignorial Courts* (1246–1303), ed. F. W. Maitland (Selden Soc., ii, 1888).

Chalgrave: *Court Roll of Chalgrave Manor, 1278–1313*, ed. M. K. Dale (Beds. Record Soc., xxviii, 1950).

Durham: *Halmota Prioratus Dunelmensis, 1296–1384*, ed. W. H. Longstaffe and J. Booth (Surtees Soc., lxxxii, 1889). There is no index of subjects to this volume.

Ramsey: *Court Rolls of the Abbey of Ramsey and the Honour of Clare*, ed. W. O. Ault (Yale Historical Publications, ix, 1928).

4. *Sumptuary Law and Social Relations in Renaissance Italy*

DIANE OWEN HUGHES

History has proved that all sumptuary laws have been everywhere, after a brief time, abolished, evaded or ignored. Vanity will always invent more ways of distinguishing itself than the laws are able to forbid.[1]

Voltaire's dismissal, written when sumptuary laws were on the wane in his own country, prompts the question, why, then, were they enacted? We do not have to wait until the eighteenth century to find reference to their futility. The concept of legislating against consumption was ridiculed almost from its inception, often by those who favoured controlling it. Franco Sacchetti, writing in Florence during the first century of its legislative activity against consumption, went further even than Voltaire to suggest that the law itself promoted what it sought to control. As the defeated enforcement officer in one of his *Trecentonovelle* explains to his superiors, legal insistence on restraint bred linguistic and stylistic invention:

My lords, all the days of my life have I studied to learn the rules of the law, and now, when I did believe myself to know somewhat, I find that I know nothing. For when, obeying the orders that you gave me, I went out to seek the forbidden ornaments of your women, they met me with arguments the like of which are not to be found in any book of laws; and some of these I will repeat to you. There comes a woman with the peak of her hood fringed out and twisted round her head. My notary says, 'Tell me your name, for you have a peak with fringes'. The the good woman takes this peak, which is fastened round her head with a pin, and, holding it in her hand, she declares that it is a wreath. Then going further, he finds one wearing many buttons in front of her dress, and he says to her, 'You are not allowed to wear these buttons.' But she answers, 'Yes, Messer, but I may, for these are not buttons but studs, and if you do not believe me, look, they have no loops, and

[1] Quoted by Etienne Giraudias, *Etude historique sur les lois somptuaires* (Poitiers, 1910), pp. 103–4.

moreover there are no buttonholes.' Then the notary goes to another who is wearing ermine and says, 'Now what can she say to this? You are wearing ermine.' And he prepares to write down her name. But the woman answers, 'Do not write me down, for this is not ermine, it is the fur of a suckling.' Says the notary, 'What is this suckling?' and the woman replies, 'It is an animal.'[2] The laws themselves tried to respond to this inventiveness of language and style: by the fifteenth century, the outlawing of expensive buttons involved the listing of *bottoni*, *maspilli* and *pianetti*; of headdresses, *berretti*, *cuffie*, *balzi*, *cappuci* and *selli*; of head ornaments, *cerchielli*, *ghirlande*, *corone*, *fruscoli*, *guazzeroni*, *frenelli* and *vespaii*. When the Venetian Senate in 1443 forbade women to wear dresses cut from cloth of gold or silver, they and their tailors began to use it to line sleeves, which were slashed or lengthened to let it show. This practice was outlawed in 1472; and finally in 1488 the Venetian legislators instructed their enforcement officers to report all changes in fashion.[3] The Genoese, a century later, required the Tailors' Guild to register new designs for approval by the censors, the so-called *Ufficio delle Virtù*.[4]

If legislators recognized a certain defeat in their innumerable preambles lamenting that their statutes were not observed,[5] their usual solution was not to abandon but to increase their legislative activity. The repeal in 1339 by the *Maggior Consiglio* of the voluminous Venetian sumptuary regulations of 1334 on the grounds that 'they lead to confusion and civic impediment, as is clear to all and as even the officials constituted for this assert', is a rare example of a drawing back. And it had taken Zer Ziani Baduario, who proposed the repeal, three years to gather sufficient votes to push it through.[6] He certainly had later followers. Five citizens of Padua, two of whom were knights, accused the sumptuary law of 1504 of infringing liberty, damaging the city, and destroying marriage and lineage. But its supporters, who carried the day, argued that far

---

[2] Novella 137.

[3] Margaret M. Newett, 'The Sumptuary Laws of Venice in the Fourteenth and Fifteenth Centuries', in T. F. Tout and James Tait (eds.), *Historical Essays by Members of the Owen's College, Manchester* (London, 1902), p. 275; G. Bistort, *Il Magistrato alle Pompe nella Repubblica di Venezia* (Venice, 1912), p. 372.

[4] L. T. Belgrano, *Della vita privata dei Genovesi*, 2nd edn (Genoa, 1875), p. 265.

[5] E.g. Siena, 1433, ed. Eugenio Casanova, 'La donna senese nel Quattrocento nella vita privata', *Bullettino senese di storia patria*, vii (1901), p. 79.

[6] Archivio di Stato, Venice (A.S.V.), Maggior Consiglio, Delib. spiritus, Reg. xxiv, 97; Newett, 'Sumptuary Laws of Venice', p. 276.

from removing true liberty the law merely tried to restrain feminine licence, and that if it had not been passed a more drastic one would have been required.[7] Both in Padua and in Venice, cities which have preserved records of the votes on sumptuary legislation, such arguments in its favour seem heavily to have outweighed its recognized defects.

Most cities turned their sporadic medieval legislation into formal Renaissance codes, which were endlessly amended in response to criticism and fashion. It has been calculated that the Italian cities produced eighty-three substantial sumptuary laws in the fifteenth century and more than double that number in each of the following two centuries.[8] Both Venice and Genoa produced at least eight pieces of extensive sumptuary legislation between 1450 and 1500, and other cities did not lag far behind. The Venetian Senate, in particularly productive sessions of 15 October 1562, issued four separate pieces of sumptuary law, one of which it modified only a month later. Turkish inactivity in 1562, which one observer claimed had given Venice the time to dedicate itself to luxury and display, may arguably also have given senators the time to turn from military affairs to matters of morality, but this certainly had not been the case in 1512 during the crisis of the League of Cambrai, when the Senate also enacted a major sumptuary code. As Venice's enemies gathered for the attack, the Senate debated dress materials, the size and design of sleeves, fringes and ornaments, belts and head-dresses, shoes and slippers, home furnishings and bed linens.[9]

What provoked such legislative zeal? It may well have been the shock of losing so much of its *terrafirma* in 1509 that drove Venetians to 'placate the anger of our Lord' by establishing a permanent magistracy to control consumption in the city, guiding it back to its moral foundations. The linking of private extravagance, moral degeneration and political decline had been the theme of moralists from Isaiah to Savonarola, and it is hardly surprising that citizen legislators should have seized on it in their hours of need. Although one might argue that the organization of Venice's

[7] Antonio Bonardi, *Il lusso di altri tempi in Padova*, Miscellanea di storia veneta, ser. 3, ii (Venice, 1910), pp. 166–7.

[8] Rosita Levi Pisetzky, *Il costume e la moda nella societa italiana* (Turin, c. 1978), pp. 30–6.

[9] A.S.V., Senato, Terra, Reg. 18, 8 May 1512; Marino Sanudo, *Diarii*, ed. Federico Stefano, Guglielmo Berchet and Nicolo Barozzi, 58 vols. (Venice, 1879–1903), xiv (Venice, 1886), coll. 114–17.

Magistrato delle Pompe with offices at the Rialto and permanent boxes to receive anonymous accusations and the legislation of 1512, which its first magistrates guided through the Senate, fits into the city's psychology of loss during the crisis of the League of Cambrai,[10] such correspondence is rare. Padua had organized its magistracy before the beginning of the crisis;[11] other cities managed to conceive their long and repeatedly promulgated sumptuary laws without the guiding hand of special magistracies, just as Padua and Venice had done before the sixteenth century. And the laws themselves do not, on the whole, follow the curves of crisis. Most major cities, with the significant exceptions of Milan and Genoa, issued their first sumptuary laws before the Black Death, for example; nor did that plague or any other encourage particular legislative activity against extravagance. Nor is sumptuary legislation linked in a simple or satisfying way to contemporary economic opinion or conditions. Born in a climate of expansion, it was several centuries old before Italian decline had set in.

Historians have tended, with Voltaire, to mock sumptuary legislation and, by implication, its legislators. At the best their impulses are labelled paternalistic, a term for which it is hard to find a definition without pejorative overtones. This label does not do justice to the fanaticism of legislating zeal within Italian Renaissance cities, nor does it explain the developmental aspects of the legislation. Finally, it obscures the fundamental question of why some societies – but not others – develop a passion to legislate against consumption. These questions lie at the centre of this chapter.

I

The first Italian sumptuary law is probably that contained in Genoa's first law code, the so-called *Breve della Campagna* of 1157, which banned the use of rich furs; but this restriction was omitted in its re-issue in 1161.[12] During the law's short life, the citizens of Genoa may have had the distinction of being the first to suffer such

---

[10] As suggested by Felix Gilbert, 'Venice in the Crisis of the League of Cambrai', in J. R. Hale (ed.), *Renaissance Venice* (London, 1973), pp. 274–92.

[11] Bonardi, *Il lusso di altri tempi*, p. 82.

[12] F. Niccolai, *Contributo allo studio dei piu antichi brevi della campagna genovese* (Milan, 1939).

restrictions on dress since the days of the Carolingian empire. The aristocratic governments of other developing medieval cities do not seem to have issued sumptuary laws. They first appear, in the middle of the thirteenth century, in communes which had admitted the 'popolo' in at least a partial way into the government: Siena, whose government issued a law regulating trains on dresses in 1249, had admitted *popolani* to the government for almost a decade; Bologna's similar decree in 1260 was issued by a government in which non-nobles had sat for over a generation, and its more extensive laws of 1288 were the work of a government which would go on to issue severe restrictions on its aristocracy; Florence's first (now lost) sumptuary law of 1281 was part of a general legal code produced by a compromise government in which a popular presence is unmistakable.[13]

By this time sumptuary controls were being applied at various levels of European society. The Council of Montpellier had forbidden churchmen in 1195 slashings at the hems of their robes, and King Louis VIII had begun in 1229 to control the wardrobes of his nobles.[14] The character of the urban legislation, issued both in Italy and in southern France from the mid-thirteenth century, is significantly different from the royal: it does not regulate dress according to social hierarchy. Hierarchical considerations, absent from the Carolingian laws, have a place in Louis VIII's ordinance and are finely worked out in Philip the Fair's ordinance of 1294, which regulated the dress and furnishings (though not the food) of his subjects according to a system based on social rank and income. It has been argued that the restrictions were forced on the king by a nobility anxious to preserve its privilege in the face of royal advancement of the bourgeoisie.[15] If so, urban legislation seems to have found different advocates. None seems to be seriously concerned with hierarchy, and the Italian may show signs of an anti-aristocratic bias.

[13] Robert Davidsohn, *Geschichte von Florenz* (Berlin, 1927), iv, pt. 3, p. 67; Ludovico Fratri, *La vita privata in Bologna dal secolo XIII al XVII*, 2nd edn (Bologna, 1928), pp. 235–45; Hermann Kantorowicz and N. Denholm-Young, '*De Ornatu Mulierum*: A Consilium of Antonius de Rosellis with an Introduction on Fifteenth Century Sumptuary Legislation', in Helmut Coing and Gerhard Immel (eds.), *Rechtshistorische Schriften von Dr. Hermann Kantorowicz* (Karlsruhe, 1970), p. 357.

[14] Pierre Kraemer, *Le luxe et les lois somptuaires au moyen âge* (Paris, 1920), pp. 33–4.

[15] *Ibid.*, p. 89.

The limitation of numbers at weddings and funerals, if a form of sumptuary control, also served as a control on noble gatherings and a means, as Heers has suggested,[16] of weakening the power of those noble 'clans' that had dominated the cities' early political life. In Bologna, for example, a proclamation of 1276, repeated in the statutes of 1289, deprived mourning of its focus for manifestations of family power.[17] Weeping at or striking the doors of the dead was forbidden, bells might be rung only at the place and time of burial, and a death might not be announced through the city. Those in attendance were limited to ten men and eight priests and the mourners at home, to male relatives within the fifth degree and women within the third. If torches were forbidden, candles limited, and shrouds regulated, the proclamation as a whole seems less dedicated to sumptuary than to social control. Early clothing regulations also have an anti-aristocratic flavour. Siena's early reduction of trains on women's dresses, if it saved cloth, also censored an aristocratic style, one which by a later law of 1277 was completely forbidden to servants; and the outlawing of golden, jewel-bedecked crowns had similar overtones.[18]

They were laws designed less to keep down the upstart than to fetter the aristocrat. If it is true in Bologna from 1289 that knights and doctors of law might go to their graves in 'scarlet' and if in most of Tuscany certain exceptions were made for knights or members of the legal and medical professions, these seem to have been privileges exacted by those whose style of life was most directly challenged by the laws. Women certainly knew who was on their side. The intercessor who won for the women of Siena in December 1291 a few days' relaxation of the sumptuary law that forbade them crowns and garlands of gold and pearls was Count Robert of Arras; just as the annuller of a Florentine law of 1324 was the duke of Calabria.[19]

The sumptuary law, seen in this way as a curb on aristocratic display, becomes a symbol of republican virtue. Savonarola's reformed city comes to mind as perhaps the most fervent mating of sumptuary controls with republicanism; and the memory outlived a

[16] Jacques Heers, *Family Clans in the Middle Ages*, trans. by Barry Herbert (Amsterdam/New York, c. 1977), pp. 75–7.

[17] Fratri, *La vita privata in Bologna*, pp. 236–8.

[18] Curzio Mazzi, 'Alcune leggi suntuarie senesi del XIII', *Archivio storico italiano*, ser. 4, v (1880), pp. 133–44.

[19] *Ibid.*, p. 138; Davidsohn, *Geschichte von Florenz*, p. 352.

generation of Medici rule: one of the first acts of the re-established Florentine Republic in 1527 was the publication of a new sumptuary law.[20] Despots also sought to control consumption, of course, but with less enthusiasm. One of the least active cities in legislating against extravagance was Milan, whose first sumptuary code seems to have been that issued by Gian Galeazzo in 1396 after his assumption of the title of duke of Milan. The law was re-issued virtually untouched in its 1480 edition.[21] Within the duchy, the impulse to legislate was urban. The Sforza issued a sumptuary code in 1498, but not before the duke had received at least one petition urging such action from nineteen 'zealots of the city of Milan'; and those emanating from the viceroys of the Spanish king in the following century were meagre and largely devoted to proper behaviour in church.[22] City authorities finally countered aristocratic torpor in 1565 with the publication of a full and severe law; and it was citizens again who in 1581 petitioned the king to regulate excessive consumption and extravagance. Yet it took the virtual collapse of Milan's industrial economy in the seventeenth century to coax from the authorities some slender sumptuary codices.

The commissioners entrusted in 1581 with the promulgation of a new sumptuary law so designed 'that excess might be removed, but the decorum and proper splendour of the city still be maintained', solicited citizen opinion. One of the three extant replies recommended the sartorial humbling of the noble: it required nobles to dress modestly, leaving the others, especially prostitutes, free. The recommendation, written in the sceptical tones of a man experienced through his travels in the ways of the world, in laws and their evasions, was taken up again and received more sober attention a few months later in a pamphlet entitled 'A Way of Returning the People of Milan to Modest Dress'. Both were undoubtedly inspired by Diodorus Siculus' account of the solution (recently revived by Montaigne)[23] of Zaleucus, the law-giver of the Locri, who restricted the freeborn and gave licence to whores and pimps. The unwillingness of the great to stain their honour by

[20] Agostino Zanelli, 'Di alcune leggi suntuarie pistoiesi', *Archivio storico italiano*, ser. 5, xvi (1895), p. 210.

[21] Ettore Verga, 'Le leggi suntuarie milanesi', *Archivio storico lombardo*, xxv (1898), pp. 7–8.

[22] Ettore Verga, 'Le leggi suntuarie e la decadenza dell'industria in Milano, 1565–1750', *Archivio storico lombardo*, xxvii (1900), pp. 53–5.

[23] *Essais*, i, ch. 43.

copying the lowly and disreputable would keep them modest, and the desire of the others to appear noble and honourable would make them modest. The pamphlet's suggestion of black, unornamented clothes for the great and powerful anticipates later laws which clothed noble women in black.[24] But in its permission of one heron plume to mark nobility, it suggests a mocking of the aristocratic pretensions that the earliest sumptuary laws strove to contain. We may be surprised that the pamphlet's author was a citizen of Lucca; but the Milanese seem to have found it natural to seek advice from foreigners. Another reply to the commissioners argued that Milan, so little able or willing to restrain extravagance through legislation, should turn to the example of other cities, and especially to Venice, a republic whose sumptuary codes regulated everything. They would also, though the Milanese respondent could not have known it, continue to be issued and amended until the republic itself had ceased to exist.

One would also like to define the economic motives behind the sumptuary laws, but they are harder to discern. The early, medieval laws showed little awareness of the point made by the worldly Milanese who wickedly proposed imposing restrictions at the top – that it was not simply man's pride that defeated the law but the needs of artisans 'who seek their living in new inventions'. So great was the opposition of Florence's luxury crafts to its severe sumptuary law of 1330, that within three years the officer to enforce it had to be appointed not by the usual civic commission but by the bishop of Siena.[25] If it was believed that foreign markets could compensate for those lost at home, the laws nowhere stated this. And, in any case, citizens must have been aware that the sumptuary laws of others also limited their markets. In the fourteenth century, the *Maggior Consiglio* of Venice forbade its citizens the use of cloth of gold;[26] contemporary sumptuary law in Nuremberg denied its citizens 'silver cloth from Venice'.[27]

The earliest sumptuary laws offered no economic explanations. When, in the last half of the fourteenth century, the custom of preambles began, we find some differences of approach between the maritime trading cities and the more artisanal cities of the

[24] Verga, 'Le leggi suntuarie' (1900), pp. 64–6.
[25] Davidsohn, *Geschichte von Florenz*, p. 353.
[26] Newett, 'The Sumptuary Laws of Venice', p. 275.
[27] Kent Roberts Greenfield, *Sumptuary Law in Nürnberg* (Baltimore, 1918), p. 107.

interior. Both Venice and Genoa emphasized investment: 'our state has become less strong because money that should navigate and multiply . . . lies dead, converted into vanities', said a Venetian law of 1360;[28] 'a great quantity of money which is kept dead and wrapped up in clothing and jewels, converted into trade might bring great returns and profits', began the Genoese law of 1449.[29] The cities of the interior expressed the need for restraint in almost exclusively moral terms. The Bolognese laws of 1398 and 1401 were issued so 'that the state might be strengthened by good and honest customs and those pleasing to God'.[30] That of Siena in 1412 indicated a clearer sense that 'it is necessary to provide for a restraint of superfluous outlays from the purses of citizens, the rich as well as the poor, for the conservation and utility and honour of the Commune', but later preambles became even more general and moralistic.[31] The Pistoia legislation of 1558 also referred to the ruin of citizens, which led to urban decline, but the legislators were thinking in the personal and often strictly demographic terms that became common throughout Renaissance Italy.[32]

Economic protectionism can be detected in some laws from about the middle of the fifteenth century. The government of Siena began to back a local silk industry in 1438, and by 1440 the commune had decided to fine and brand anyone who removed a silkworker from the city.[33] While in its total banning of silk garments (except for one pair of sleeves) in 1433, the *Consiglio Generale* seems not to have considered the effects on Siena's *setaiuoli*, who were necessarily doing business with silk acquired elsewhere, its legislation of 1460 was protective of the new and still fragile industry. It allowed Sienese women a few silken garments as

---

[28] Bistort, *Il Magistrato alle Pompe*, p. 66, n. 2. The law is edited, without the preamble, by S. Romanin, *Storia documentata di Venezia*, 10 vols. (Venice, 1853–61), iii, pp. 386–9.

[29] Belgrano, *Della vita privata*, p. 394.

[30] Fratri, *La vita privata in Bologna*, p. 242; Umberto Dallari and Luigi Alberto Gandini, 'Lo statuto suntuario bolognese del 1401 e il registro delle vesti bollate', *Atti e memorie della R. Deputazione di Storia Patria per le Provincie di Romagna*, ser. 3, vii, p. 8.

[31] Mazzi, 'Alcune leggi suntuarie', p. 143.

[32] . . . onde aviene che assai giovani recusano amogliarsi, se gia excessiva dote et donera non si danno, a tale che bene spesso le dote superano la sostanza et patrimonio dei mariti, et le padri o fratelli delle fanciulle ne divengono poveri e nudi . . .', Zanelli, 'Di alcune leggi suntuarie', p. 214.

[33] Luciano Banchi, *L'arte della seta in Siena nei secoli XV e XVI. Statuti e documenti* (Siena, 1881).

long as they had been made from cloth manufactured in the city.[34] Milan began in the seventeenth century, after its prosperous silk industry had dramatically declined, to issue protectionist legislation.[35] Protectionist attempts are, however, both late and sporadic. They should not encourage us to believe that protectionism was generally an object or provocation of the law.

Nor do the sumptuary laws show a developed economic interest in bullion. Gold and silver, along with pearls and certain furs, form a privileged list of restricted items throughout the whole period of sumptuary control. The Sienese legislation of 1277–82 had allowed to women only one unadorned garland of silver for their heads, which was to weigh no more than two ounces. In Bologna in 1289 circlets for the head made of silver and gold were outlawed, as was almost every other ornament made of the precious metals. The fourteenth- and fifteenth-century allowance in many Italian cities of three gold rings became, like the single strand of pearls, a cliché of both law and contemporary portraiture. The restrictions were real, and the fines could be steep – in Siena £100 (or about one-half the average dowry of the period) for exceeding the two-ounce limit. But the level of concern seems to have borne no relation to the shifting price or availability of precious metals. In Venice where precious metal was regarded, at least by the beginning of the seventeenth century, as 'the sinews of all government . . . , the patron of all',[36] its regulation in sumptuary law remained remarkably regular in times of shortness and in times of relative plenty. A law of 1443 forbidding Venetian women all cloth of gold and silver and embroideries employing the two metals seems, if not unusually severe, at least unusually serious, for the penalty exacted from fathers or husbands whose daughters or wives disobeyed was a forced loan of £1,000 payable to the state. The law's explanatory preamble, while it may indicate a rising cost of gold and silver, does not suggest that the legislators' chief concern was the metal market. What disturbed them was at once more personal and more remote: the recent custom of a bridegroom's gift to the bride of a dress of cloth of gold had risen from 150 or 200 to 600 ducats, 'and every year

[34] Casanova, 'La donna senese', pp. 82–6, 89–93.

[35] Verga, 'Le leggi suntuarie' (1900), pp. 75–82.

[36] A Venetian senator, quoted by Fernand Braudel, *The Mediterranean and the Mediterranean World in the Age of Philip II*, trans. by Sian Reynolds, 2 vols. (New York, 1973), i, p. 462.

these expenses grow, so that [the custom] is a consumer of our citizens, and what is worse, provokes the wrath of our almighty Creator'.[37] In Genoa, where the fluctuations in the gold market were probably better understood than elsewhere, a law of 1449 allowing women up to £1,000 of gold and silver jewellery – far more than Siena and many other inland cities permitted their wives and daughters – was left essentially unchanged for more than half a century of increased availability of gold; and the new law of 1512 seems, without comment, to have reduced this allowance.[38] It is true that three merchants whose wives wore golden chains worth 25 florins apiece in contravention of the law were hauled before a magistrate in 1453, but they escaped conviction by arguing that since the jewellery had been hidden by their clothes, it had not set a bad example.[39] Public morality, not money, was the magistrate's concern.

II

The church came at sumptuary legislation through the same moralistic door. Suspicious of an economy whose health lay in expansion, dependent on the use and manipulation of money, churchmen worried not about the economic consequences of the withdrawal of wealth from productive enterprise, but about the personal and social consequences of the victory of *luxuria*. If civic governments spoke of public and private ruin, the church spoke of corruption. The friars, confessors of the medieval Italian cities, looked to sumptuary legislation as a weapon in the war against sin. Fra Paolino, in his *Government of the Family*, written in 1304, just five years after Venice had promulgated its first sumptuary law, recommended the law as perhaps the only protection against the pride of wives whose personal desire for extravagance was supported by prevailing custom and pandered to by husbands. He thought the matter should be 'regulated by laws after the manner of the Romans'.[40] It was the social aspects of the related sins of pride,

[37] A.S.V., Senato, Terra, Reg. 1, p. 91.
[38] Belgrano, *Della vita privata*, pp. 393–404; Archivio di Stato, Genoa (A.S.G.), Cod. Diversorum, x, 114, ann. 1511–12.
[39] A.S.G., Div. filze, no. 20, 23 Jan. 1453, cited by Jacques Heers, *Gênes au XVᵉ siècle* (Paris, 1969), p. 65, n. 5.
[40] Quoted in Cesare Foucard, *Lo statuto inedito delle nozze venetiane nel 1299* (Venice, 1858), Appendix.

avarice and *luxuria* that the friars stressed. St Thomas had allowed
that female display, even if it enhanced natural beauty, was usually
not a sin so long as it was employed in pursuit of a husband; it was,
in any case, venial, not mortal.[41] The Franciscan Orpheus de
Cancellariis rejected this argument. The sin was mortal, he argued,
not only because it was in contempt of God, but because, by
threatening to ruin the fathers or husbands who supplied the wherewithal for their finery, women were a peril to others. And when
their dress or habits were provocative; when, for example, they
bared their shoulders or even their breasts, they became a public
scandal. Orpheus admitted that the measure of extravagance was
tied to fortune and that a woman could wear rich clothes without
evil intention, but such expenses became a mortal sin if the clothes
were unsuited to her station or would impoverish her and hence
reverse her station.[42] San Bernardino of Siena went even further to
set the question of extravagant dress in the context of social charity,
condemning extravagant trousseaux as extracted from the blood of
the poor.[43]

The influence of the church in the promotion and direction of
sumptuary legislation was important. There was undoubtedly a
connection, for example, between the presence of the Franciscan
Cardinal Latino in Florence for the negotiations preliminary to the
establishment of a new government, and that government's
promulgation in 1281 of the city's first sumptuary regulations. The
cardinal, Salimbene tells us, had upset all women with a law
restricting the length of their trains.[44] Churchmen remained active
in encouraging sumptuary controls throughout the Italian penin-
sula. Florence had countered opposition to the sumptuary controls
of 1330 by bypassing citizen commissions and giving responsibility
for its enforcement to the bishop of Siena. So, too, under a military
threat from Milan, the Venetian Senate appealed in 1438 to the
patriarch Lorenzo Zustinian, who had the year before outlawed
silk, trains, long sleeves or sleeves ornamented with pearls and hair
adorned with gold, silver, pearls, or false tresses, threatening with
excommunication all who disobeyed.[45] The Senate wanted him to

---

[41] Summa Theologiae, Secunda Secundae, quaestio 169.
[42] Kantorowicz and Denholm-Young, '*De Ornatu Mulierum*', p. 355.
[43] *Le prediche volgari*, ed. L. Banchi (Siena, 1880), pp. 193–4.
[44] *Cronica*, in *Monumenta Germaniae Historica, Scriptores*, xxxii, p. 169.
[45] Newett, 'Sumptuary Laws of Venice', p. 259.

help *them* control extreme headdresses and excessive trains by the same ecclesiastical means. In neighbouring Padua, the Council, in 1460, sought from the bishop a definition of the length of trains the church would allow women, which they agreed to include and enforce as part of the sumptuary code they were then enacting.[46] The Council had, in any case, been goaded into action by the Franciscan Jacopo della Marca, whose influence on the city seems to be reflected in the record of the Council's votes. An attempt to limit the train of a woman's dress to one-quarter of a *brachia* had been passed in 1440 by 47 votes to 4; and a more general restriction on women's clothing in 1459, by 51 votes to 11.[47] These are fairly typical fifteenth-century figures; in the following century the number of votes cast was slightly higher, but the margin of victory somewhat narrower. In 1460, however, after Fra Jacopo had stirred the city, the long sumptuary code, voted in three sections, was passed by 114 to 0 (with three votes to amend), 121 to 6, 117 to 9.[48] The issue had risen to the level of popular concern.

Renewed episcopal activity under the influence of a strong papacy probably stimulated sumptuary legislation throughout Italy in this period. In some places, the church assumed full or substantial responsibility for the promulgation of the law. Citizens seem to have found episcopal legislation particularly hard to bear, both because of its severity and because of its penalty – excommunication. When Ginevra Sforza married Sante Bentivoglio in 1454, clothed with twelve attendants in gold brocade, a cloth the sumptuary law of Cardinal Bessarion had just denied to all Bolognese women, the church of San Petronio closed its doors to the bridal party. It went on to San Giacomo, where the friars married the couple, but some of the party suffered excommunication for flouting the law.[49] Everyone knew, of course, that the church also dispensed. The noble Venetian Cristina Corner managed in 1438 to secure from the pope for four and a half ducats, 'in honour of her parents and in respect of her own beauty', the right to contravene the sumptuary regulations of the patriarch.[50] In Perugia, where the bishop had taken over sumptuary concerns in

[46] Bonardi, *Il lusso di altri tempi*, p. 150.

[47] *Ibid.*, pp. 141–6.   [48] *Ibid.*, pp. 149–50.

[49] Fratri, *La vita privata in Bologna*, p. 35.

[50] Bistort, *Il Magistrato alle Pompe*, pp. 71–2 (and a similar petition of the same date, pp. 72–3).

the middle of the fifteenth century, the pope allowed, in 1468 and 1469, episcopal absolution of those who had incurred excommunication by flouting his legislation.[51] But the need for papal intervention is perhaps a measure of the effectiveness in this period of the combined force of mendicant preaching and episcopal legislation against extravagance.

It would be wrong to see sumptuary legislation as a simple response to ecclesiastical demands. Initially the aims of the church and those of city governments seem to have differed. Cardinal Latino, whose limitation of trains was in line with contemporary urban legislation, also ruled that women must cover their heads, an ordinance which, according to Salimbene – if no lover of women, an admirer of their abilities – encouraged the production of silken veils woven with gold, 'which all the more encouraged lust in the eye of the beholder'.[52] But this concern for female modesty did not find its way into contemporary civic codes, which on the contrary began to restrict first the sumptuousness of female head coverings and then the anonymity they might provide.[53] Yet ecclesiastical attempts to control seductiveness in female dress (and deportment) do seem to have made headway throughout Italy in the course of the fifteenth and sixteenth centuries. The Piacenzan chronicler De Mussis was commenting as early as 1388 on 'shameful dresses . . . called *ciprianae* . . . which . . . have such a large neck that the breasts show: and it looks as if the said breasts want to burst from the bosom'.[54] But only one commune, Perugia, whose legislation already reflected the influence of ecclesiastics, had acted (in 1342) to control *décolletage* 'beneath the collarbone'.[55] Milan, where the Dominican Galvano Fiamma had disapproved in the first half of the fourteenth century of the bare throats and necks of its women, seems to have waited for almost a century before legislating against such exposure, and then only in the mildest way: low-cut necklines

---

[51] Ariodante Fabretti, *Statuti e ordinamenti suntuarii . . . in Perugia dall'anno 1266 al 1536*, Memorie della R. Accademia de Scienze di Torino, ser. 2, xxxviii, pp. 137ff.

[52] *Cronica*, p. 170.

[53] Siena ruled against veils as early as 1342. They allowed the customary mantle, which might be held with the hands, but not fixed in some more permanent way; for a woman's face 'should be open and clear'. Casanova, 'La donna senese', pp. 71–2.

[54] *Placentinae urbis descriptio*, ed. Muratori, in *Rerum Italicarum Scriptores*, xvi, p. 579.

[55] Fabretti, *Statuti e ordinamenti suntuarii*, p. 95.

were allowed as long as the shoulder bones were covered in some other way.[56] The law encouraged women to resort to those shoulder covers of transparent silk mousseline (often embroidered with gold) which formed a part of many contemporary trousseaux.[57] It was only at the end of the fifteenth century that Milan, in legislation of 1498, outlawed necklines lower than one finger – placed sideways, as they took care to specify – from the collar-bone.[58]

By then a movement to cover female flesh was under way. Florence had already, in a law of 1456, forbidden any 'baring of the throat and neck' although in 1464 the government had relented and allowed a *décolletage* of about three centimetres from the collar-bone in front and twice that amount from the neckbone behind, measures which, as portraits of the period show, were not rigidly observed.[59] Savonarola, however, made of *décolletage* a major issue, insisting on a two-finger measure. Like the Franciscan Orpheus de Cancellariis, who reminded his readers that the baring of shoulders and breasts, by making the woman a public scandal, brought style to the level of mortal sin, Savonarola inquired whether such display was the sign of an honest woman.[60] By the sixteenth century, Venice and even Genoa, whose women had a reputation for daring display, had begun to regulate the amount of flesh they might expose. A Genoese law of 1506 insisted on lower hemlines, while one of 1511–12 decreed that women must cover completely their shoulders and the 'two bones before the throat', regulations that neighbouring Savona copied in 1531.[61] A Venetian law of 1562 ruled more liberally, and certainly more realistically, that camisoles or other coverings of the shoulder must be 'so closed in front that the breast is covered'.[62] Whatever the details of the legislation, they had become persuaded that such rules were necessary to ensure 'la honestà muliebre'.

The records of prosecution for contravention of the sumptuary laws clearly suggest that fellow citizens failed to accuse and the

---

[56] Verga, 'Le leggi suntuarie milanesi' (1898), p. 22.
[57] *Archivio storico lombardo*, ii, p. 65.
[58] Verga, 'Le leggi suntuarie milanesi' (1898), p. 50.
[59] E. Polidori Calamandrei, *Le vesti delle donne fiorentine nel Quattrocento* (Florence, 1924), pp. 64–6.
[60] Quoted by Pisetzky, *Il costume e la moda*, p. 39.
[61] Emilio Paniani, *Vita privata genovese nel Rinascimento*, Atti della Società Ligure di Storia Patria, xlvii (Genoa, 1915), pp. 154–63.
[62] Bistort, *Il Magistrato alle Pompe*, pp. 388–9.

authorities themselves were reluctant to pursue women who disobeyed such rules of modesty. In Venice and Padua, for example, records of prosecution and even conviction for extravagance exist for the sixteenth century; but there seems to be no mention of a woman cited for the plunge of her neckline.[63] This stands in clear contrast with prosecutions in Bern in the following century, where almost 65 per cent of the 133 cases of unlawful clothing in 1681 were concerned with exposure.[64]

The growing association in Italian cities of *décolletage* with shame should be seen in the context of a larger change in the direction of the law. Early sumptuary legislation can be divided fairly evenly into laws concerning clothes (often those of men as well as women), weddings and funerals. Although the expenses involved in the ceremonies and feasts accompanying marriage and burial rose steadily with their further elaboration and although new and extravagant customs surrounding parturition and baptism ate into household budgets, legislation directed against ceremony declined significantly in the fifteenth century in relation to that directed against clothing, particularly the clothing of women. (See Figure 1.) While some of this can be accounted for by legislators' attempts to counter rapid changes in style or evasions in the law, like those Sacchetti relates, that alone cannot explain the change, which the preambles to the laws enshrine. The preambles to the Venetian sumptuary laws of 22 May and 9 June 1334 locate in both sexes the extravagance they intend to attack, but that of 1360 mentions only 'vanities' which are directed towards 'brides and other women and ladies'.[65] Most fifteenth-century preambles state explicitly that women are the ruin of men.[66]

Both the rhetoric and the timing of the dramatic focus on women in the fifteenth century, when ecclesiastical sumptuary activity was at its height, point to the church's role. Although it sporadically regulated excesses in clerical dress, the church's interest in lay extravagance had a distinctly feminine focus. The code that Jacopo della Marca urged on the Paduan Council was designed to rectify the 'superfluous apparel and wanton expense surrounding the

---

[63] *Ibid.*, pp. 20–60; Bonardi, *Il lusso di altri tempi*, pp. 97ff.
[64] John Martin Vincent, *Costume and Conduct in the Laws of Basel, Bern, and Zurich, 1370–1800* (Baltimore, 1935), p. 104.
[65] Bistort, *Il Magistrato alle Pompe*, p. 66, n. 2: 329–52.
[66] E.g. Casanova, 'La donna senese', pp. 80–2 (Siena, 1426–7).

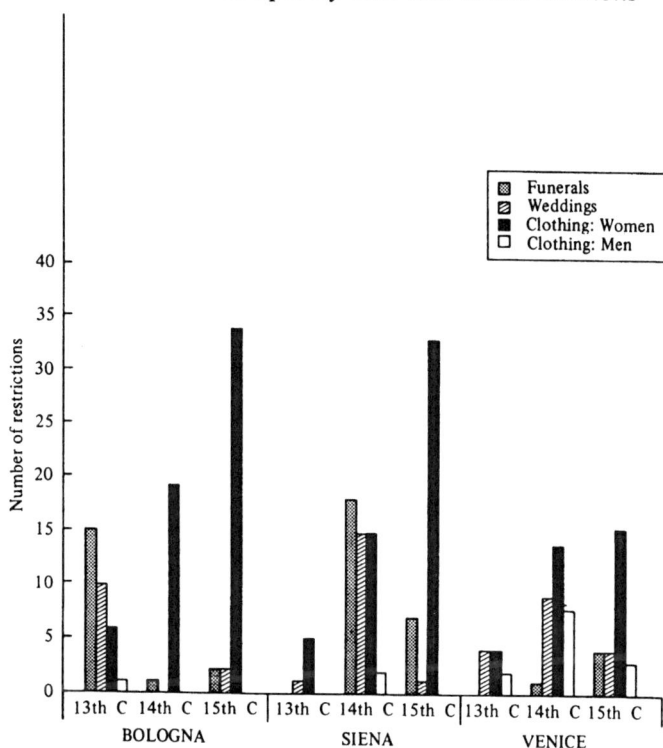

Figure 1 *A comparison of sumptuary restrictions in three cities*

women of the city and district', and all its clauses deal with this problem. So, too, the legislation of Cardinal Bessarion in Bologna in 1453 was devoted to feminine dress.[67] Even where the church role is less obvious, we often detect an association between ecclesiastical pressure and a narrowing of sumptuary interest to women. Bologna's laws of 1398 and 1401 were the first completely to exclude consideration of ceremonial extravagance and to focus on women; and while both were issued by urban authorities, their dating 'in the time of the pontificate of Boniface IX' suggests ecclesiastical guidance. Padua's first two sumptuary laws of 1277 and 1398 regulated ceremony – weddings, baptisms and funerals. All of the

[67] Bonardi, *Il lusso di altri tempi*, p. 147; Archivio di Stato, Bologna, Comune, Libro Novarum provisionum, f. 132.

fifteenth-century laws – issued in 1440, 1459, 1460, 1482 and 1488 – were devoted to female extravagance.[68]

But if the church's pressure both encouraged and directed sumptuary law in the fifteenth century, the legislation could count, as the votes in Padua show, on substantial popular support. Apart from generalities and clichés, it is hard to assess the response of women to their newly privileged sumptuary position. In Bologna, Cardinal Bessarion's law did provoke a female protest – from Sante Bentivoglio's learned and beautiful lover, Nicolosa Sanuti, whom Sabadino degli Arienti described on a hillside wearing a gown of purple silk and a rose-coloured cloak lined with the finest ermine.[69] She might have heard of events a year earlier in Siena, where the Emperor Frederick III had stopped with his fiancée Leonora of Portugal on the way to their coronation and marriage in Rome. Battista Petrucci, the daughter of a professor of rhetoric, had given a Latin recitation so appreciated by the couple that they asked her to select a reward. She chose release from all sumptuary regulations, a request which the city government reluctantly conceded.[70] Sanuti, however, argued not only for herself but for all the women of Bologna. Her elegant oration[71] reminded the cardinal that although Roman women had been limited in their use of gold and precious cloth during the rigours of the Second Punic War, freedom in finery was restored to them after the crisis had passed. That law, imposed by conditions of war, might be understandable, but it was hard to excuse the Bolognese restrictions, devised to feed the avarice of husbands who put money before dignity. They showed no concern for the domestic disruptions which would be a certain consequence of their restrictions, an argument that some Paduan nobles would use at the beginning of the next century in an attempt to defeat that city's sumptuary controls over women. The histories of women of the ancient world as well as the lives of many women of her own day proved, she argued, that feminine abilities could equal those of men: many resembled that 'Amesia, whom, since she bore a manly spirit beneath a female form, they called Androgynos'. Individual women of Bologna could rise, like some of

[68] The early laws are cited by Bonardi, *Il lusso di altri tempi*, pp. 9–11; the later, edited by him, pp. 141–54.
[69] Cecilia M. Ady, *The Bentivoglio of Bologna* (Oxford, 1936), pp. 141–54.
[70] Orlando Malavolti, *Historia . . . de' Fatti e Guerie de' Sanesi, cosi esterne come Civili* (Venice, 1599), parte 3, b. 38b.
[71] Ed. in Fratri, *La vita privata in Bologna*, pp. 251–62.

their Greek and Roman predecessors, to heroic action; and collectively, she reminded the cardinal, they had within them the power of the Sabines – to save a civilization from demographic ruin. Women deserved freedom of choice in clothes because it was to clothes that they had been reduced. If one conceded (as surely the cardinal would) that 'as patricians from the people, so should remarkable women differ from the obscure', then, she concluded, the sumptuary restrictions should be lifted.

Magistracies are not conceded to women; they do not strive for priesthoods, triumphs, the spoils of war, because these are considered the honours of men. Ornament and apparel, because they are our insignia of worth, we cannot suffer to be taken from us.

In a letter to her lover on the eve of his marriage to Ginevra Sforza, a despairing Nicolosa Sanuti recanted.[72] But she had been right. Clothes were women's insignia, and the legislators knew it. They knew, too, that men had become implicated in them: they designed and made them, their money bought them, their status was reflected in them. In 1343 the rich women of Florence lined up before a notary to register the clothes they owned which were in contravention of the recently promulgated sumptuary law, which allowed that such clothes might continue to be worn as long as they were taxed and marked with a special lead seal bearing the Florentine lily on one side and a cross on the other. The clothes, recorded in an extant register,[73] show that same restless variety as the laws designed to control them: dresses (usually of silk) take the form of sleeved and sleeveless underdresses and overdresses, often accompanied by cloaks and mantles, in various hues of red, blue and green, sometimes striped or pierced with white or contrasting colours, trimmed with fabric embroidered or woven with crowns, stars, rosettes, butterflies, birds and dragons. But from such sumptuous riot some order emerges. Lady Guerriera, the wife of Jacopo di Antonio de Albizis, and her sisters-in-law Nera and Piera all registered gowns and matching tunics of green samite (a heavy silk often interwoven with gold). The same Guerriera and Nera registered mantles of white cloth embroidered with vines and grapes of blood-red and lined in cloth of shimmering white. Their

---

[72] Ady, *Bentivoglio*, p. 57.
[73] Partly edited by Paolo d'Ancona, *Le vesti delle donne fiorentine nel secolo XIV* (Perugia, 1906).

clothes appear just after those of their mother-in-law Joanna, who distinguished herself from them in counterpoint: a cloak of purple to their white and blood-red; a dress of scarlet with silken crowns, which reflected the green of the gowns of her daughters-in-law only in its lining. Dinga, the daughter of Sandro Altovito, and Lisabetta, the daughter of Gentile Altovito, came together to register their identical and elaborate tunics, which were divided into two spheres of red, then checked with silk, and trimmed with yet another fabric. Relationships can be as easily guessed from the clothing lists as from the names. Nor are we dealing here with simple thrift – some cloth and a tailor for all the women of a household. Lady Ginevra, the wife of Agnolo di Giani de Albizis, probably a distant relative of Joanna and her daughters-in-law, who lived in another district of the city, had earlier registered the single piece of her clothing which was in contravention of the law and on which she chose to pay the tax – a mantle of white cloth embroidered with vines and blood-red grapes, lined in cloth of shimmering white. Those brilliant and distinctive cloaks must have become Albizi insignia. Even the limited view of wardrobe that this register of outlawed clothes gives us provides a glimpse of a society that described itself through clothes. Is it any wonder that the ordering of dress became for legislators a metaphorical way of talking about social distinction, a way of ordering human relations?

III

Fashion, in its delicate balancing of 'the desire for imitation and differentiation', signifies, as Simmel observed, 'the form of the social process'.[74] Unlike more hierarchical societies, whose rules repressed such a process, or poorer ones, whose poverty forbade it, the urban society of medieval Italy measured progress in terms of its dynamic. For Riccobaldo of Ferrara, looking back at the end of the thirteenth century on the times of Frederick II, the past was simple and static, lacking both splendour and social movement. Clothes were plain, ornaments few, meals frugal, and dowries small.[75] More censorious critics like Dante looked back on such simplicity with nostalgia; and Villani even hoped that the sumptuary laws would restore it. But sumptuary law of the thirteenth and fourteenth

[74] Georg Simmel, *Philosophie der Mode* (Berlin, 1914), pp. 8–9.
[75] *Historia Universalis*, in *Rerum Italicarum Scriptores*, ix, col. 128.

centuries sought to restrain, not to re-order. Pistoia's extant sumptuary law of 1332 seems to be based on the Florentine law of 1330 which Villani applauded in his chronicle.[76] Of its twenty-seven sumptuary provisions, only two were arguably more concerned with style than with excess, regulating the wearing of bi-coloured garments. Most of the others regulated yardage, material and ornament. If this reflected the realities of dress, which was of simple cut, depending for its effect on the quality and amount of material and on accompanying ornament, it also reflected a society more attuned to excess than disorder.

By the middle of the fifteenth century, however, as women's costume, with the extraordinary development of ruffs, bodices and detachable sleeves, became a series of interchangeable parts, fashion and change became a new target of the law.[77] It sought to regulate the rapidly shifting parts of an unstable whole, which even Cesare Vecellio, in his popular book on fashion, found hard to grasp.[78] In Venice on the eve of the crisis of the League of Cambrai the Senate debated fashions in sleeves. The debate had begun in 1503 when the legislators outlawed 'manege a comedo', those great leg-of-mutton sleeves which Lotto's subjects so favoured for their portraits and which the Senate found 'an ugly fashion' requiring three or more *brachia* of cloth of gold or silk for their execution.[79] By October 1504 the senators recognized that that 'dishonest fashion that is not appropriate to women' had been replaced by 'another fashion, larger and uglier than the first', and they decided to ban all sleeves wider than one third of a *brachia* at any point.[80] Within a year, they were outlawing 'certain fashions and new apparel, both offensive and dishonest, which were never before used in this city' – namely, sleeves cut of many pieces of fabric of diverse colours.[81] On 4 January 1507, the Senate complained that sleeves of the *investidure* had grown larger every time the matter had been legislated about. 'And if [women] are granted the right to put six *brachia* [into the sleeves], in a few months they will grow to an even larger size, so that they can be called not sleeves of the

---

[76] *Statuti suntuarii ricordati da Giovanni Villani . . . ordinati dal commune di Pistoia*, ed. Sebastiano Ciampi (Pisa, 1815).

[77] On these costume developments, see *Abbligliamento e costume nella pittura italiana*, i: *Rinascimento* (Rome, c. 1962), pp. 103ff.

[78] *Degli habiti antichi et moderni di diverse parte del mondo* (Venice, 1590), p. 141.

[79] A.S.V., Senato, Terra, reg. 14, f. 197.

[80] *Ibid.*, reg. 15, f. 37.   [81] *Ibid.*, f. 77.

investidure but sleeves of the gown itself and it will become necessary to concede more.'[82] They repeated the former limits and restricted the sleeves of the gown, the so-called 'manege ducali', to 32 *brachia* of silk or 28 of serge or another non-silken fabric. In the difficult summer of 1509, the doge spoke before the *Maggior Consiglio* and accounted for Venice's decline by the inordinate length of its sleeves.[83] The concern for expense is, of course, ever present: every extra *brachia* was a drain on the individual, and the point of the doge's speech was to encourage Venetian nobles to pay their state debts. But in the eyes of Renaissance legislators, fashion changes bred worse than excess or extravagance, they bred disorder. The *Consiglio Generale* of Siena spoke for more than that city when, in 1426, it announced that fuller and more inclusive sumptuary legislation was needed in the city since laws against previous extravagances had simply inspired worse ones.[84] The need to right the disorders of fashion seems to have extended beyond mere expense. Comments and laws on the disorder of clothes and the disruptiveness of fashion seem to have reflected a growing, if less easily expressible sense of social disorder. And the endless ordinances (*ordini*) to right the disorders (*desordini*) of dress seem to be ways of talking about a society which had lost its right order, a society in which (by Simmel's definition) differentiation had got out of hand.

Sumptuary law struck hardest at splendour and expense when they encouraged unacceptable differentiation and withdrawal from the social process. Sumptuary law was frequently lifted, on the other hand, to allow citizens properly to fulfil their civic (and highest social) function. Siena had allowed prohibited clothes to be worn for a short time in 1291 for the coming of Robert of Arras; and in 1459 the Venetian Senate, in order to welcome and impress the French ambassadors to the city, voted to require all women in attendance to appear in bright dresses and wear the jewels and ornament generally prohibited by the law.[85] Certain individual extravagance was actually encouraged when its effect was the fuller integration of the individual into the social fabric. Thus in Venice the Senate decided in 1433 to legislate in favour of more sumptuous

---

[82] *Ibid.*, f. 190. The *investidura* seems to have been a full dress that might in fact come with or without sleeves. See Bistort, *Il Magistrato alle Pompe*, p. 353, n. 4.
[83] Sanudo, *Diarii*, viii, col. 497.
[84] Casanova, 'La donna senese', p. 80.
[85] A.S.V., Senato, Terra, reg. 4, f. 126.

dress for councillors of the doge, who had adopted the unfortunate practice of wearing sombre robes except during their hours of government service. A century later the *Maggior Consiglio* addressed itself to the same problem and registered a decree forcing councillors to wear their scarlet robes, which they seem to have given up doing.[86] Useful splendour was one thing, fashion another. Under the rule of fashion, clothing lost both its real function and its emblematic significance. Shoes that impeded walking, robes and accessories that confused or concealed rather than expressed identity – such perversions were the sign of a profoundly disordered society. The Milanese friar Pietro Casola remarked on the similarity between the Chinese custom of binding women's feet to make them smaller and the Venetian one of wearing shoes on platforms so that 'they appear giants'.[87] If such shoes kept feet from the mire, the legislators knew that women really wore them because 'through the height of the shoes gowns can be made much longer'.[88] The resulting 'enormous and excessive expenses' were to be lamented, but the chief concern of the laws enacted against them was functional: these shoes, like bound feet, impeded walking to such an extent that, according to Casola, some women 'are only kept upright by the support of slaves'. Legislation against veils, which seems to have begun in Siena in 1343 and had little economic purpose, was concerned with the freedom from proper identification that such veils accorded their wearers. Officials of the commune were empowered to demand, on encountering a veiled woman, the name of her father and husband, her 'terzo', 'popolo' and 'contrada'.[89] This let them discover the names of those

---

[86] A. S. V., Misti, reg. 59, f. 12; Maggior Consiglio, Diana (33), f. 199; Newett, 'Sumptuary Laws of Venice', p. 249.

[87] He had visited Venice in 1494 on his way to and from the Holy Land. *Viaggio di Pietro Casola a Gerusalemme* (Milan, 1855), p. 14.

[88] A.S.V., Maggior Consiglio, Ursa, f. 81, 2 March 1430; and see Bistort, *Il Magistrato alle Pompe*, pp. 168–71. In Genoa, such shoes were not outlawed, but the length of the skirt was fixed in 1449 at one *palma* whether they were worn or not: Belgrano, *Della vita privata*, p. 398. The association of platform shoes with prostitutes is clear not only in Sienese law but in contemporary costume books like Vecellio's.

[89] Casanova, 'La donna senese', p. 70. In Venice in 1443 the Senate ruled that women could not cover their heads except to go to church, for veiling covered too many dishonourable acts: Terra, reg. 1, f. 105. A *crida* of the duke outlawed veils in Ferrara in 1476 for the same reason: Bernardino Zambotti, *Diario ferrarese dall'anno 1476 sino al 1504*, ed. Giuseppe Pardi, *Rerum Italicarum Scriptores*, 24–vii (Bologna, 1935), p. 6.

responsible for paying the fine if her clothing was in contravention of the sumptuary law but, more importantly, it restored an identity which clothes were meant to convey, not obscure. The perversion of purpose of the shoes and clothing perverted the wearer and society itself. Great platform shoes so impeded walking that 'pregnant women walking on the road with these shoes [which are] so high that they cannot hold themselves up, fall and in the event destroy or abort their children, to the perdition of their body and soul'.[90] Veils that masked perverted the function of normal headcoverings, which were commonly worn by women and had been endorsed by Cardinal Latino in the thirteenth century; their purpose was to protect the honour and modesty of the wearer. The mask, on the other hand, allowed a freedom akin to licence. In Siena, high platform shoes and veils fixed over the face to mask it were allowed only to one class of women – to prostitutes, women who lived outside the usual social categories.

The difference between *meretrix* and *matrona* stands at the heart of sumptuary distinction. Zaleucus' suggestion that only prostitutes be permitted rich dress as a means of shaming the virtuous into simplicity was taken up in the laws of some Italian cities: Siena allowed them not only platform shoes but also the dresses of cloth of gold and clothes painted or embroidered with trees, fruits, flowers and animals which it denied to other women; Brescia devised similar allowances.[91] In other cities, prostitutes were assigned more humiliating marks of distinction: in Venice, yellow scarves; in Milan, a cloak of common fustian, whose colour – white in the original law of 1412 – was changed to black in the new sumptuary code of 1498.[92] In most places prostitutes were increasingly segregated. In Genoa, for example, a city that did not identify them by either rich clothing or humiliating marks, a series of laws began at the end of the fourteenth century to confine prostitutes to a special district. This made it easier for communal officials to stand at the bordello door and collect the new tax imposed in 1418; but fiscal purposes were secondary.[93] Prostitutes were considered such

[90] A.S.V., Maggior Consiglio, Ursa, f. 81.

[91] Casanova, 'La donna senese', pp. 53, 59, 61–2; A. Cassa, *Funerali, pompe, conviti* (Brescia, 1887), p. 100.

[92] Bistort, *Il Magistrato alle Pompe*, pp. 264–6; Verga, 'Le leggi suntuarie milanesi' (1898), pp. 68–9.

[93] The tax was eventually transformed into a fixed monthly payment. Belgrano, *Della vita privata*, pp. 329–33.

outsiders in Ferrara by the end of the fifteenth century that responsibility for them was assigned to the same officials who collected the taxes on imported goods.[94]

Other women the sumptuary rules sought not to separate but to incorporate. Nicolosa Sanuti was right to notice that the legislation, by denying women clothing as an emblem of achievement, pushed them into a separate social category. And the legislators' frantic effort to deprive women of individual distinction or constant differentiation through fashion, certainly created for all women a kind of sumptuary ghetto. Nevertheless, at least part of the law's purpose was more positive than contemporary preaching and moralizing might seem to suggest. It sought to reconcile a woman's dual legal personality, as the daughter of one lineage and wife in another. The moment of reconciliation was marriage, when men's honour and position were most publicly displayed through their women, particularly through brides in whom the honour and position of the two houses merged. The bride, at that moment, dowered and arrayed in a trousseau, stood poised between the two sumptuary states – between childhood, when to a greater or lesser extent she might be indulged, and matronhood, when she would be struck by the full force of the sumptuary law.

Sumptuary restrictions in most cities were noticeably less severe for young, unmarried girls. In fourteenth-century Siena young women (*mulieres juvines*) were permitted a little additional jewellery, and in contemporary Lucca girls under the age of nine were allowed to wear more extravagant clothes.[95] Marriage signified almost everywhere the moment of passage from one sumptuary status to another: in Bologna in 1289, as in Lucca in 1337, that was when women lost the right to wear certain extravagant decorations.[96] The full refinement of the Genoese law of 1449[97] lets us explore the basis for such legal distinctions between children and married women. It explicitly established a period of sumptuary liminality which girls entered on the attainment of sexual maturity, or at least on becoming eligible to take a husband. At the age of twelve, the jewellery given them as children had to be

[94] Zambotti, *Diario ferrarese*, p. 209, where the author reports his activities in this office.
[95] Casanova, 'La donna senese', p. 61; *Bandi lucchesi del secolo decimoquarto*, ed. Salvatore Bongi (Bologna, 1863), pp. 49–50.
[96] Fratri, *La vita privata in Bologna*, p. 239; *Bandi lucchesi*, pp. 47–53.
[97] Ed. in Belgrano, *Della vita privata*, pp. 393–405.

put away. Although when she married, a trousseau pushed the Genoese bride towards sumptuary adulthood, the law demanded three further years of partial restraint when she could not receive from either her own family or her husband's any more than one silk dress, which could not, in any case, be dyed a fine red, and when all garments of silk pile were denied her. Three years from the day she crossed the threshold of her husband's house (the so-called *transductio*), she came of sumptuary age. Within this long period, the daughter was separated from her father's largesse, which was restored only on the day of her marriage, as trousseau; on this she had to live and dress while she was integrated into her new home. By the end of that period, it might well be understood that she would produce an heir and so move physically as well as legally from the status of *sponsa* to that of *matrona*. The period of greatest sumptuary restraint and special sumptuary status thus coincided with those years when her sexuality (and hence the honour of the man who was her legal guardian) was most at risk: when sexually mature, she had no husband; when married, she had borne no child.

No city found such distinctions totally satisfactory. By the beginning of the following century, Genoa had decided to allow girls to wear until they were taken into marriage golden headdresses that the law would deny them as wives.[98] The new approach may have been made necessary by the growing inability of fathers to arrange unaided the marriages of their daughters. Every city had come to feel by the fifteenth century that the institution of marriage itself had become a source of social disorder, from which fathers and daughters, not husbands, suffered most. The Venetian senator Giovanni Garzoni spoke in 1420 for more than himself or even his city, where dowries, trousseaux and other nuptial gifts had so increased that many nobles could not marry their daughters without ruining their heirs and estates; they were accordingly shut up in convents or kept at home unmarried.[99] The Senate's regulation of marital gifts and assigns was typical: a limit of 1,600 ducats for the dowry and trousseau, the latter set at no more than one-third of the whole. An attempt a few months later to repeal it was driven back, and the only exceptions eventually allowed were for the halt and the blind, the twisted and hunchbacked, whose deformities won them

[98] A.S.G., Cod. Diversorum X, 114, ann. 1511–12.
[99] A.S.V., Senato, Misti, reg. 53, f. 70.

larger dowries.[100] Yet throughout Italy dowries went up, and laws to restrain them multiplied. The cry was everywhere the same: 'our youth are no longer given to doing business in the city or at sea, or in other praiseworthy enterprise, placing all their hope in these excessive dowries';[101] 'so many young men refuse to marry if they are not first given excessive dowries and gifts, with the result that the price of dowries exceeds the substance and patrimony of husbands, and the fathers or brothers of the brides become poor and are stripped bare by them'.[102]

If demographic evidence suggests that men were marrying later and less frequently and that the convents were becoming fuller, the sumptuary evidence suggests that women who did marry were felt to have the whip hand over husbands whose livelihood seemed more and more to depend on their dowries. It is no wonder that such men lashed out at the changing fashions of their wives, which not only ate into the estate but also seemed to signify their loss of control. A series of new restrictions were passed overwhelmingly in Padua in 1555. Only one item was close: by a vote of 63 to 62 the Council barely agreed that the fines of 25 ducats would be paid by the fathers or husbands of the offenders.[103] Did they fear that by their inability to enforce the law at home, they would be called on publicly to pay up? It was certainly husbands who usually paid, since wives rather than daughters were called to account. In Siena, all the sumptuary cases which came before the court in the autumn months of 1438 concerned married women; and in 1475 the secret accusations that trickled into the office of the *Tre Segreti* assigned to sumptuary matters were also directed primarily against wives.[104] The later registers of Venice and Padua, cities whose laws show more varied sumptuary interests, record more contraventions by men, both at table and in their clothing. When the three censors of Padua heard in March 1554 that weddings in the city had been encouraging a sartorial splendour in contravention of the sumptuary laws, they visited the sites of the parties and ceremonies and prepared a list of the offenders: thirty-three men and thirteen women, only three of whom were unmarried.[105] The two extant

[100] Bistort, *Il Magistrato alle Pompe*, p. 108.
[101] *Ibid.*, pp. 111–12: Venice, 1535.
[102] Zanelli, 'Di alcune leggi suntuarie', p. 214; Pistoia, 1558.
[103] Bonardi, *Il lusso di altri tempi*, pp. 186–92.
[104] Casanova, 'La donna senese', pp. 46–50, 86–9.
[105] Bonardi, *Il lusso di altri tempi*, pp. 270–5.

Venetian registers, which begin in the last quarter of the
seventeenth century, record a variety of sumptuary offences. One is
devoted entirely to prostitutes; almost all the women in the other
are married.[106]

Although most cities appointed special prosecutors and encouraged private accusation by awarding the accuser both secrecy and a
portion of the fine, enforcement seems always to have been less
important than the invention of the law itself. They expressed in it,
or tried to, their fears for their society. On 8 May 1512, the
Venetian sumptuary official Vetor Morexini rose to speak against
Venetian women who 'formerly would dance only with a scarf, and
today will dance only with masks: they go into the fields to dance,
they dance the *balla dil capello*'.[107] He held their attention, and they
voted against the dancers; for they all knew that his motion
expressed more: a society led away by unknown women who
danced the 'balla dil capello', a French dance in which the women
picked their partners.

Women were an object of fear, their power sufficient to ruin
cities. Yet there was a gulf between most of the urban legislation
and the ecclesiastical ranting of contemporary Isaiahs who sought
to 'smite with a scab the crown of the head of the daughters of Zion'
because they 'are haughty, and walk with stretched forth necks and
wanton eyes, walking and mincing as they go, and making a tinkling
with their feet'.[108] For it was issued by men who were fully
implicated in female folly. They lived off the condemned dowries,
they paid for the forbidden dresses, whose splendour reflected their
status, and they generally appeared in court and paid the fines
demanded for contravention of the law by their women. In talking
about women, their dress and deportment, men were talking about
themselves and about their often conflicting roles as fathers and
husbands. But they did not just talk, they acted.

We must distinguish between *enforcement*, which failed, and *legislating*, which achieved objects of its own. The doge Andrea Gritti,
on the way to the ceremonies marking his coronation in 1523,
was being ostentatious in sending home a female relative to change
out of her outlawed dress of cloth of gold; just as the earlier wedding
festivities of a Corner and Loredan in the city in 1512 when 'the

---

[106] Bistort, *Il Magistrato alle Pompe*, pp. 302–9.
[107] Sanudo, *Diarii*, xiv, col. 200; Bistort, *Il Magistrato alle Pompe*, pp. 222–4.
[108] Is. iii. 16–17.

women [were] obedient to the ordinance [because] they feared the *provedadori* would condemn them', are remembered for that concern.[109] Where prosecutions were undertaken, appeal and influence often let the guilty escape. And, of course, one could simply take the fines as a kind of luxury tax, an experiment which had been tried as early as 1299 in Florence and which finds a place in the Genoese and Sienese legislation of the fifteenth century – *pagar le pompe*, as the Venetians said.[110] The process of legislating had better success. The endless codes attest to it. So does the sense of development within them of, for example, the relations between fathers and daughters, husbands and wives.

It is striking in a society whose single most important transfer of personal assets had arguably become a woman's dowry (which even in marriage she continued to own) that so much legislation was designed to keep women from wearing their wealth. This infuriated women rich in their own right, as Nicolosa Sanuti's oration shows. Some communes came to allow women to display their dotal worth, 'since all should not be equal to all', as the Genoese put it when they established jewellery limits based on the value of the dowry a woman took into her marriage.[111] But the wealth which determined what a woman might wear was always paternal wealth – what she had received as her father's daughter. When Siena toyed with this system, in 1424, it limited the gifts husbands might give to their wives at marriage and established the limit as a percentage of the dowry.[112] This system stressed patrilineal distinctions at a time when rising dowries were exaggerating them. If hungry husbands were the villains of sumptuary laws which set limits on dowries, the wealth they gained did not keep the wives who brought them from being distinguished, ever more clearly, as their fathers' daughters.

By the sixteenth century many cities had stopped legislating about women as primarily daughters or wives; for hierarchical considerations had risen to supplant lineal ones. The early laws of most Italian cities made some hierarchical distinctions, but they pertained more frequently to men than to women, and hierarchy

[109] Sanudo, xix, col. 443; cols. 161–2.
[110] Davidsohn, *Geschichte von Florenz*, IV, iii, p. 67; Mazzi, 'Alcune leggi suntuarie senesi', p. 143; A.S.G., San Giorgio, Institutiones Cabellarum, carte 170 (anno 1402); Newett, 'Sumptuary Laws of Venice', p. 259.
[111] Belgrano, *Della vita privata*, pp. 395–404.
[112] Casanova, 'La donna senese', pp. 79–80.

was used more as a means of excusing the powerful than of regulating the whole.[113] In its fully hierarchical sumptuary plan, the Bolognese law of 1474 was, however, almost a response to Nicolosa Sanuti's demands. Colour alone would have placed a woman: gold for the wives and daughters of knights, sleeves of gold for those of notaries, bankers and similar grandees, crimson for those of important artisans, but only crimson sleeves for the women whose husbands and fathers belonged to the humbler trades. Although a husband's gifts to his wife were still tied to her dowry, the limit established varied according to his rank: doctors and gentlemen might spend up to two-thirds the value of the dowry; others, no more than one-half. And women, when they married, left behind the rank of their fathers to assume a place in the hierarchy beside their husbands.[114] Given the visible consequences of such a move, daughters must have been increasingly reluctant to marry down. Rich women or the wives of rich husbands might, within the bounds of the law, still dress more splendidly or more eccentrically than their peers; but it was largely rank that distinguished them – rank which for most of their fashionable lives was in the gift of their husbands. In April 1476, Messer Lorenzo di messer Antonio de' Lanti of Siena was called before the office of the *Tre Segreti* because his wife had worn silk velvet. He tried to explain that he was a keen observer of the laws; that the gown had cost less than one of more ordinary material; and that anyway his father had been knighted by the king of Cyprus in Milan.[115] The officials would have none of it. In addition to the doubtful nature of his title, his tax assessment was not high enough to allow him entrance into the highest ranks of Sienese society. He paid the fine; and unless he intended to keep paying, his wife had to give up her velvet dress.

Hierarchical solutions created new forms of distinction, which can be most fully delineated in the seventeenth and eighteenth centuries when Italian legislation began more to resemble those

---

113 Bologna's law of 1289 let knights and doctors of law go to their graves in cloth of scarlet. Siena's of 1343 also permitted their wives to do the same; but only the men of those professions might wear cloth of gold in their lifetime. Fratri, *La vita privata in Bologna*, pp. 236–7; Casanova, 'La donna senese', pp. 52–72. The law of Pistoia of 1332, which seems to be modelled on the Florentine law of 1330, lets the wives of knights, judges and doctors wear more gold and silver and precious fur than the wives of other citizens were allowed. Ciampi, *Statuti suntuarii*, p. xi.

114 Fratri, *La vita privata in Bologna*, pp. 245–8.

115 Archivio di Stato, Siena, Tre Segretti sulle vesti, n. 1, f. 2, quoted by Casanova, 'La donna senese', p. 38, n. 4.

codes issued by northern monarchs, who wanted to keep the economy up and upstarts down. Yet the legislation may have had its roots in the same social needs. Renaissance legislators tried to create order at those points in social organization where structure was ambivalent, particularly where social ideology was in conflict with many social practices. Their society had an ideology of orders but was in practice governed by money, which could alter position and rank. Clothes were a visible sign of this conflict: a better tax position would probably have let Messer Lorenzo's wife clothe herself in cloth of gold. Their society had a patrilineal ideology but was governed in everyday life by a confusion of cognatic, patrilineal and conjugal arrangements. This had the effect of splintering women's social identity, while giving them, as status-bearers of their fathers' lineage and their husbands', a position of increasing dominance within the household. High dowries and accompanying marital gifts were a sign of this, diminishing fathers and the economic strength of the patrimony, and at the same time diminishing the power of husbands in the home. These structural inconsistencies, for which there was no real cure, created social tensions which the legislation sought to remedy and which the *process* of legislating may have eased. They became clearly visible in Italian cities in the thirteenth century, as men who rose through money became politically significant and assumed political power and as urban governments, freed from aristocratic control, began in a concerted way to attack lineal bonds and organization. It is not a coincidence that this was when the sumptuary legislation began.

Italian sumptuary legislation was, among other things, an approach to easing tensions caused by structural problems of a local social nature. Though it resembled the legislation of the northern monarchies, and even more closely that of German and Swiss cities, it was far less hierarchical than the one and far more anti-feminist than both. But Europe did in a sense form a sumptuary whole, expressing its frustration over social problems it could not fully solve through legislative control over their outward signs. These signs can be controlled by formal, often religious means in societies where orders attain the rigidity of caste, and they are generally allowed as more legitimate expressions of identity in a society ordered by class. In Renaissance Italy, a society that dreamed of orders while facing the daily consequences of class fluidity, they had to be controlled by legislation.

5. The Blood Feud in Early Modern Scotland*

JENNY WORMALD

In March 1587, a month after the execution of Mary Queen of Scots, there was a meeting between ambassadors from England and Scotland. According to the account of the well informed contemporary Scots lawyer David Moysie, the English assured the Scots, in charmingly homely language, that Elizabeth was 'verie sorie for taking Queine Mareis lyfe', and asked what satisfaction could be offered to James VI. The Scots' reply must have sounded very odd to English ears. They stated that it was not up to James to tell them. Rather, it was the 'custome of Scotland' that the committers of a murder should make offers of compensation to the kin and friends of the victim, who would then discuss and resolve upon them. The kin and friends of a king, of course, extended far beyond his own countrymen. Mary was descended from the 'moist [most] royal bloude in Europe', and English offers of compensation would therefore be considered by monarchs abroad as well as by interested parties at home.[1] The Scots were not seriously suggesting some kind of sixteenth-century European summit on the subject of Mary's execution; this exchange, if it took place, was part of the diplomatic manoeuvring indulged in by James and Elizabeth, neither of whom wanted Scottish, far less European, reprisals. They were, however, entirely accurate in describing as the 'custome of Scotland' the practice whereby a murderer offered compensation to the kin and friends of the man he had killed. So deeply embedded was the principle of compensation in the fabric of Scottish justice

---

* I would like to thank Professor G. W. S. Barrow, Dr M. T. Clanchy, Mr C. P. Wormald, and especially Professor A. A. M. Duncan, for their help in the preparation of this chapter, originally published in *Past and Present*, no. 87 (May 1980), pp. 54–97. It appears here in a slightly shortened version, and the footnotes have been curtailed; for fuller discussion of the sources and of James I's important legislation, see the original text, pp. 57–60 and 80–1.

[1] David Moysie, *Memoirs of the Affairs of Scotland* (Bannatyne Club, Edinburgh, 1830), pp. 60–1.

that it could as well be invoked, if for diplomatic reasons, for a king as for the lowest of the gentry; for anyone, in fact, who had the means to compensate, and who had kin and friends to support him.

The sixteenth-century English ambassadors may well have been as baffled as the thirteenth-century English clerk who wrote in bewilderment: 'Find out what the law of *galanas* is.'[2] No doubt they regarded this 'custome of Scotland' only as further evidence of the backwardness of the Scots. Four centuries later, however, Moysie's account no longer looks like a description of a Scottish anachronism. The remarkable pioneering work of Bertha Surtees Phillpotts offers an impressive range of evidence which shows that the blood feud, or some form of it, survived in many parts of northern Europe well into the medieval period, and in some cases beyond.[3] Within the British Isles, it was eradicated 'with marvellous suddenness'[4] in England by the thirteenth century, but England was the exception; it continued in Ireland, and it lingered on even in post-Conquest Wales until the early sixteenth century.[5] Moreover the feud is now seen in a new light, the light cast on it by Max Gluckman and other social anthropologists able to describe it as a living reality.[6] Gluckman's concept of the 'Peace in the Feud' has been revolutionary. Condemnation has been stilled, if not entirely silenced. Feud can no longer be regarded as a matter of rival groups slogging it out to the death of themselves and their descendants, until time, exhaustion or a more powerful authority brought it to an

[2] Cited in R. R. Davies, 'The Survival of the Bloodfeud in Medieval Wales', *History*, liv (1969), p. 338; *galanas*, as Davies explains, meant both the blood feud and money compensation in settlement of feud.

[3] Bertha Surtees Phillpotts, *Kindred and Clan in the Middle Ages and After* (Cambridge, 1913).

[4] F. Pollock and F. W. Maitland, *The History of English Law before the Time of Edward I*, ed. S. F. C. Milsom, 2 vols. (Cambridge, 1968), ii, p. 458.

[5] Davies, 'Survival of the Bloodfeud in Medieval Wales'; F. W. Maitland, 'The Laws of Wales – The Kindred and the Blood-Feud', in his *Collected Papers*, 3 vols. (Cambridge, 1911), i, pp. 202–29; T. Jones Pierce, 'The Laws of Wales – The Kindred and the Blood-Feud', *Birmingham Univ. Hist. Jl.*, iii (1951–2), pp. 119–37.

[6] M. Gluckman, *Custom and Conflict in Africa* (Oxford, 1956); M. Gluckman, *Politics, Law and Ritual in Tribal Society* (Oxford, 1971). I have also found especially helpful Lucy Mair, *Primitive Government* (Harmondsworth, 1970); J. Middleton and D. Tait (eds.), *Tribes without Rulers* (London, 1970 edn); P. Bohannan (ed.), *Law and Warfare* (New York, 1967); P. Bohannan and J. Middleton (eds.), *Kinship and Social Organization* (New York, 1968); I. M. Lewis (ed.), *History and Social Anthropology* (A.S.A. Monographs, vii, London, 1968).

end; and historians turn to the anthropologists in their search for a fuller understanding of the complex forces, the loyalties and hostilities within feuding groups, which bring peace as well as war.

Yet greater awareness that feud is a complex business has not resolved all problems of interpretation. In particular the idea persists that public and private order, represented by government and kindred respectively, conflict because they are essentially incompatible. One of the great writers on the feud in the pre-Gluckman era, Julius Goebel, spoke of feud continuing 'incompatible though it may be with the ends of the rudimentary state'.[7] R. R. Davies, summarizing current thinking about feud, says 'it is now . . . much more clearly realized that feud as an organized and recognized institution is largely a phenomenon of the stateless society, where lordship is weak and underdeveloped . . . preservation of law and order is in large part based on the strength of the ties and obligations of kinship'.[8] And where society is not 'stateless', even Gluckman describes how 'underneath the patent framework of government control . . . I found feud and the settlement of feud at work',[9] almost suggesting no possible interaction between the two. But the demarcation between state or government on the one side and kindred and blood feud on the other may be too rigid.[10] Just as the feud itself is a complex subject, so the question of the relationship between public and private order is also complex. There are infinite variations in the attitude and impact of governments on the blood feud. It is already well known, for example, that lords began to claim a share of compensation originally due only to the kin, for their part in bringing about settlement of feud; such settlement could be reached in the courts as well as by private arbitration.[11] It may also be the case that the

[7] Julius Goebel, *Felony and Misdemeanour* (New York, 1937), p. 21; see also, for example, H. Loyn, 'Kinship in Anglo-Saxon England', in P. Clemoes *et al.* (eds.), *Anglo-Saxon England* iii (Cambridge, 1974), pp. 197–209.

[8] Davies, 'Survival of the Bloodfeud in Medieval Wales', p. 341.

[9] Gluckman, *Custom and Conflict in Africa*, p. 4.

[10] The notable exception to this theme is the seminal article by J. M. Wallace-Hadrill, 'The Bloodfeud of the Franks', in his *The Long-Haired Kings and Other Studies in Frankish History* (London, 1962), pp. 121–47; see also J. M. Wallace-Hadrill, *Early Germanic Kingship in England and on the Continent* (Oxford, 1971), esp. ch. 2.

[11] For example, Davies, 'Survival of the Bloodfeud in Medieval Wales', pp. 344ff.; K. Nicholls, *Gaelic and Gaelicised Ireland in the Middle Ages* (Gill History of Ireland, iv, Dublin, 1972), pp. 53–7; Goebel, *Felony and Misdemeanour*, pp. 25–44.

justice of the feud could survive and be acceptable to a government without the necessary survival of large kindreds and strong kin-solidarity. There are three, not two, factors to be considered – government, kindred and blood feud – and all of them are variables.

Two extreme examples provide a starting-point. One is modern Albania, where there exists a set of rules about the blood feud, of a complexity which would do justice to an Edward I, but which are not devised to restrict bloodshed. The Albanian blood feud is not about order and stability; it is about honour. Intervention by government or church has not succeeded in replacing the passion for vengeance with honour by the less heroic but infinitely more peaceful process of emendation. The blood remains in the feud; and the situation can become so intolerable that it is not surprising to find other societies in which kin-groups themselves seek alternatives, the classic example being the Nuer, a society with agnatic clans of aristocrats, but without chiefs, without government institutions.[12] The other extreme is medieval England, where before the Norman Conquest public authority had already taken over at least part of the responsibilities of the kin, and where within two centuries after it the blood feud itself had been replaced by a concept of crime enshrined in a uniquely comprehensive system of royal justice. No government impact in Albania; almost total government impact in England. These are clear enough; but these are the exceptions.

Between them there is a large and fluid area in which the question of interaction between public and private justice is at its most problematic. One part of that area, Scotland, has not so far been studied in this context. Traditionally it is the country where kings were weak and kindreds strong, and feuds raged endlessly and

---

[12] I. Whitaker, 'Tribal Structure and National Politics in Albania, 1910–1950', in Lewis (ed.), *History and Social Anthropology*, pp. 253–93; M. Hasluck, *The Unwritten Law in Albania* (Cambridge, 1954), pp. 219–60. As Maitland recognized, 'Neither manslaughter nor what we call murder was, strictly speaking, a crime at all. It was a legal justification for a blood feud': Maitland, 'Laws of Wales – The Kindred and the Blood-Feud', p. 217. The idea that emendation was dishonourable is seen in the rejection quoted by Goebel, *Felony and Misdemeanour*, p. 22 note: 'I will not carry my dead son in my pouch.' Both these aspects of the historical blood feud are fundamental to the Albanian feud. Impressive though the concept of honour is, it created a situation in which apparently many people remained cowering in their houses, fearing vengeance because of feud between their ancestors as yet unappeased – a description I owe to Professor Peter Stein. The different solution found by the Nuer is the subject of Gluckman's revolutionary study: Gluckman, *Custom and Conflict in Africa*, ch. 1, 'The Peace in the Feud'.

bloodily. In fact it is a society which has left remarkably rich and exceptional evidence both about the feud itself and about the relationship between royal and private justice.[13] This evidence shows what happens when the justice of the feud was accepted by the government. It enables us to consider a society in which people knew all about the feud and compensation, but would have been utterly lost had they been asked to produce a Radcliffe-Brown table of their kin-groups. It may therefore suggest lines of inquiry for other societies also.

Evidence for the survival and development of the blood feud before 1400 comes from the highly problematic 'Auld Lawes', a miscellaneous collection of twelfth- to fourteenth-century law, with one tract, *Leges inter Brettos et Scottos* – a tariff of compensation payments – going back possibly to the tenth century.[14] This is not sufficient to permit the kind of question so familiar to Irish and Welsh historians about the authenticity of their early laws and the degree to which they reflect or obscure social reality.[15] But the Auld Lawes do show two things: the geographical extent of the blood feud and the attitude of the crown at a time when royal control was becoming stronger. The blood feud continued to survive throughout Scotland, not just in the Gaelic west. The forces which modified and ultimately eradicated it in the lowlands will be discussed later in this article. But because it is the differences rather than the

---

[13] I use the phrase 'private justice' here to refer to the justice associated with the feud: personal arbitration and settlement by kin and lord outside the courts. It does not here denote the courts and jurisdictions of the nobility and gentry.

[14] A detailed list of manuscripts is in *Acts of the Parliaments of Scotland*, ed. T. Thomson and C. Innes, 12 vols. (Edinburgh, 1814–75; hereafter *A.P.S.*), i, pp. 175–210, and texts are printed here. The 'Lawes' include the so-called Assizes of David I and William the Lion, and *Regiam maiestatem* and *Quoniam attachiamenta*; another version of these last two is in *Regiam maiestatem*, ed. T. M. Cooper (Stair Soc., xi, Edinburgh, 1947).

[15] Maitland, 'Laws of Wales – The Kindred and the Blood-Feud'; Pierce, 'Laws of Wales – The Kindred and the Blood-Feud'; the articles in *Welsh Hist. Rev.*, special number on 'The Welsh Laws' (1963); see also R. R. Davies, 'The Twilight of Welsh Law, 1284–1536', *History*, li (1966), pp. 143–64, and Goronwy Edwards, 'The Historical Study of the Welsh Lawbooks', *Trans. Roy. Hist. Soc.*, 5th ser., xii (1962), pp. 141–55. D. A. Binchy, 'The Linguistic and Historical Value of the Irish Law Tracts', *Proc. Brit. Acad.*, xxix (1943), pp. 195–228; this paper and reprints of papers by D. Jenkins and others on Irish and Welsh law, together with a translation of R. Thurneysen, 'Celtic Law', are collected in D. Jenkins (ed.), *Celtic Law Papers* (Études présentées à la Commission internationale pour l'histoire des assemblées d'états, Brussels, 1973).

similarities between the highlands and lowlands which tend to be emphasized, it is worth stressing here that, as far as we know, there was no basic distinction in attitudes to crime and justice between the two societies; rather, despite linguistic differences, there was a unity of approach which is a valuable reminder that interaction between them was a feature of the period up to the late sixteenth century, and that we should not simply look for division and enmity. This is readily illustrated by the continuing operation of the law of Clan Macduff, kin-based law in Fife, first described in any detail by a local chronicler, the early fifteenth-century prior of Lochleven, Andrew of Wyntoun, and still in use in the mid-sixteenth century.[16] More generally, there is the evidence of language. In *Leges inter Brettos et Scottos* there is a group of words of Irish, and in one case Welsh, origin: *cro, kelchyn, enach, galnes* (Welsh, *galanas*). All refer to compensation or honour-price, although the distinctions between them are not all entirely clear.[17] They appear in sections of *Regiam maiestatem* other than the *Leges*; as D. S. Thomson says, 'it appears that some of the traditional Celtic legal terminology was considered relevant in a fourteenth-century law treatise compiled in lowland Scotland', a point which is further supported by the late use of *cro*, in the form *croy*, in legislation of 1432.[18] But by the sixteenth century these words were relics of the past. In 1597 John Skene of Curriehill, lawyer and editor of the Auld Lawes, produced a fascinating dictionary of legal terms, *De verborum significatione*.[19] All these words appear in this work, but their precise meaning eluded Skene. He attempted, for example, to define *enach* as

---

[16] *The Original Chronicle of Andrew of Wyntoun*, ed. F. J. Amours, 6 vols. (Scot. Text Soc., Edinburgh, 1903–14), vi, ll. 2273ff. A case of the law being successfully invoked in 1548 is described by Balfour: *The Practicks of Sir James Balfour of Pittendreich*, ed. P. G. B. McNeill, 2 vols. (Stair Soc., Edinburgh, 1962–3) (hereafter Balfour, *Practicks*).

[17] For these and other words discussed here, see *A Dictionary of the Older Scottish Tongue, from the Twelfth Century to the End of the Seventeenth*, ed. W. A. Craigie and A. J. Aitken (Chicago and London, 1931–). Gaelic words are discussed in J. Cameron, 'Celtic Law', in *The Sources and Literature of Scots Law* (Stair Soc., i, Edinburgh, 1936), pp. 348–50; D. S. Thomson, 'Gaelic Learned Orders and Literati in Medieval Scotland', *Scot. Studies*, xii (1968), pp. 57–78. The clearest account of the distinctions is in A. A. M. Duncan, *Scotland: The Making of the Kingdom* (Edinburgh, 1975), p. 107; see also F. Seebohm, *Tribal Custom in Anglo-Saxon Law* (London, 1911), pp. 309–14.

[18] Thomson, 'Gaelic Learned Orders and Literati in Medieval Scotland', p. 57; the act of 1432 is in *A.P.S.*, ii, p. 21, c. 5.

[19] John Skene of Curriehill, *The Lawes and Actes of Parliament . . .* [including] *. . . De verborum significatione . . .* (Edinburgh, 1597, S.T.C. 21877).

compensation for a fault, citing rather misleadingly *Regiam*'s provision for compensation to a serf whose wife had been ravished by his lord;[20] and the lowland lawyer had to ask the highland earl of Argyll what *Gailchen* meant.

Two other Gaelic legal terms did survive into the sixteenth century and later: *culreach* (Irish, *cúlráith*), a surety for repledging; and *colpindach*, a calf, used always in the context of compensation payment or penalty. And as the Gaelic words for compensation fell into disuse, a new group of words took their place. Two were certainly of English derivation. *Assyth* (Middle English, *assithe*) is known by the late fourteenth century; in the later form of 'assythment', which first appears in an act of 1425, it became the standard word for compensation, used by Skene to explain the older words, but too familiar to merit an entry itself. The second and slightly less frequently used term was *kinbut*, from the Anglo-Saxon *cynebot*, a rare word found only in two early eleventh-century texts; one of these is, significantly, the only self-professed record of Northumbrian law, that is, law in northern England and southern Scotland.[21] But whereas *cynebot* seems to have been the penalty paid to public authority for the murder of a king, late medieval Scottish *kinbut* always referred to compensation to the kin. Skene said, logically enough, that 'ane man-bote is assithment for the slauchter of ane man, kin-bote for the slauchter of ane kins-man'. In fact by his time *kinbut* was used indiscriminately, but *manebot* had once appeared much earlier, in 1249 when border law and custom had been codified in the Latin *Leges marchiarum*.[22] The third of the new terms is *slanis*, a word used in fifteenth- and sixteenth-century Scotland always to describe the letter ('lettres of slanis' or 'letter of slains') issued by the kin of the victim of crime, stating that full and acceptable assythment had

---

[20] *Regiam maiestatem*, p. 114.
[21] Nordleoda Laga, 1, in *Gesetze der Angelsachsen*, ed. F. Liebermann, 3 vols. (Halle, 1903–16), i, pp. 458–9; *English Historical Documents, c. 500–1042*, ed. Dorothy Whitelock (English Historical Documents, i, 2nd edn, London, 1980), no. 51(b), pp. 469–70. I am indebted to Mr C. P. Wormald for this reference and for the reference to Anglo-Saxon laws in note 31.
[22] Skene, *De verborum significatione*, s.v. 'Bote'. The *Leges Marchiarum* are printed in *A.P.S.*, i, pp. 415–16; see G. Neilson, 'The March Laws', in *Stair Society Miscellany*, i (Stair Soc., xxvi, Edinburgh, 1971), p. 21; G. W. S. Barrow, *The Kingdom of the Scots* (London, 1973), pp. 158–60, which argues for the antiquity of these laws; Duncan, *Scotland: The Making of the Kingdom*, pp. 537–8.

been made by the criminal and his associates. *Slanis* has hitherto been thought to derive from the Anglo-Saxon *slean*, to slay. But a more probable origin is the early Irish *slán*, *sláinte* and its variants, signifying health, safety, wholeness; spiritual salvation; and legally, freedom from liability; this obviously fits much more exactly the idea of the letter of slains than does the verb 'to kill'.[23] We do not know how old these words are in Scottish usage; we know only when they began to be documented. *Kinbut* is first recorded as late as 1478, because one Robert Cargill of Livingston refused to pay the compensation – 'kynebut' – agreed between himself and Walter Blair, and Blair raised an action before the lords of the council.[24] *Slanis* is known entirely because of its association with the letter to which it gave a name. These things reflect the growing use of the written record, the growth of lay literacy, in late medieval Scotland. But the words themselves are clearly older. Even in terms of the documentary evidence, they were already coming into use by the time the first group of words finally disappeared in the lowlands; this, along with the early use of *manebot*, and the continuing use of *culreach* and *colpindach*, indicates the extent of chronological overlap. Moreover from the eleventh to the sixteenth centuries there is evidence of the same contacts and influences. The earliest record of the Scottish blood feud, *Leges inter Brettos et Scottos*, shows contact with Ireland, Wales and Northumbria;[25] at the other end of the period, Celtic and northern English influence can still be seen in the terminology of the blood feud. In general, therefore, it is clear that there was continuity between the early and the late medieval blood feud, and continuity with both a Gaelic and an Anglo-Saxon past.

This continuity is an important consideration in the context of the

---

[23] This derivation of *slanis* was suggested to me by Professor G. W. S. Barrow. I am most grateful to Mr Donald Meek, Department of Celtic, University of Edinburgh, and Mr A. J. Aitken, editor of the *Dictionary of the Older Scottish Tongue*, who have confirmed Professor Barrow's idea, crucial to the argument advanced here. See *Contributions to a Dictionary of the Irish Language*, ed. M. E. Byrne and M. Joynt (Dublin, 1953), s.v. *sláinte, slán, slánachus*; Nicholls, *Gaelic and Gaelicised Ireland in the Middle Ages*, pp. 51–2, 187.

[24] *The Acts of the Lords of Council in Civil Causes, 1478–1495*, ed. T. Thomson (Edinburgh, 1839), p. 9.

[25] Linguistic evidence and the name of the laws show contact with Ireland and Wales. Norse and Northumbrian influence is suggested by Seebohm, *Tribal Custom in Anglo-Saxon Law*, pp. 306–7, 315, and also by H. M. Chadwick, *Studies on Anglo-Saxon Institutions* (Cambridge, 1905), pp. 25, 77, 97 note, 104.

second point raised by the Auld Lawes, the attitude of the crown. We do not know what this was before the twelfth century. It is tempting to think that it was perhaps similar to that of the early seventh-century King Aethelberht, who 'is not consciously limiting the free play of feud for those many occasions when it is still the best solution; nor has he any moral objection to it. Rather he supplements the procedure where it fails, and perhaps makes something out of it for himself'; but that may ascribe too positive a role to early Scottish kings.[26] Only lack of objection is actually indicated, by the fact that the earliest, French, version of the *Leges inter Brettos et Scottos* gives the *cro* of a king;[27] and there is no hint at all of conflict between emerging public and private order. The problem of the crown's attitude becomes more acute with the coming of the Normans; for in the twelfth and thirteenth centuries royal justice became insistently pervasive, while on kin-justice there is little but silence, both at the time and therefore also among legal historians of the period. I am wholly indebted to G. W. S. Barrow for offering the convincing reason for this silence: that the Normans, who came to Scotland not as conquerors but as settlers, were kinless men; and it was the king who was responsible for the men without kin. Hence royal justice had a new and particular importance; and it was royal justice which was recorded.[28] A similar explanation can be offered for the apparent decline of kinship, which in the same period seemed to give way to 'feudal' lordship; again, it was lordship – lordship of land – which was recorded, with help from and advantage to the lawyers.[29] But because the Normans did not come as conquerors, they never became the wholly dominant ruling élite that they did in England. Instead, as in Ireland and Wales, they were assimilated into local society and established their own kindreds, with such success that many of the great

---

[26] Wallace-Hadrill, *Early Germanic Kingship in England and on the Continent*, p. 43. Only from the twelfth century, however, is it possible to substantiate the parallel. There are dangers in drawing earlier parallels from a position of lack of Scottish evidence; but see the discussion of pre-twelfth-century kings in Wales by Wendy Davies, 'Land and Power in Early Medieval Wales', *Past and Present*, no. 81 (Nov. 1978), pp. 3–23.   [27] *A.P.S.*, i, p. 663.

[28] On the development of royal justice, see Duncan, *Scotland: The Making of the Kingdom*; Barrow, *Kingdom of the Scots*; and also *Regesta regum Scottorum*, i, *The Acts of Malcolm IV*, ed. G. W. S. Barrow (Edinburgh, 1960), and ii, *The Acts of William I*, ed. G. W. S. Barrow and W. W. Scott (Edinburgh, 1971).

[29] Duncan, *Scotland: The Making of the Kingdom*, pp. 407–9, is a succinct and masterly discussion of legal form and social reality.

'Scottish' family names of the late middle ages are in fact those of the Anglo-French settlers. As they did this, they adopted the existing methods of justice, while at the same time introducing into native society a greater degree of royal involvement than it had hitherto known.

Inherent in this situation was the possibility of conflict between king and kin. In fact the attitude of the post-Norman kings does seem to have been that of King Aethelberht. Penalty to the crown was now clearly added to compensation for the kin. 'The king ordains (*Statuit dominus rex*)' were the opening words added to the Latin version of *Leges inter Brettos et Scottos* included in *Regiam maiestatem*; that version gives the penalty due to the king if a man was slain within the king's peace, a provision extended in *Assise regis David* to cover payment to the king and assythment to the kin.[30] Even more positive underwriting of the justice of the feud is seen in one of the laws in *Assise regis Willelmi*, dealing with a specific case of potential conflict: what happened if the kin of a man who died 'by law of iron or water' took vengeance on the informer who had brought him to law. The Scottish answer, in this case unlike that of the Anglo-Saxons, was to acknowledge the principles of the feud; the king would grant them his peace, provided the informer's kin gave their assent. Moreover it stated something which was to become a recurrent theme of late medieval and early modern legislation: if the king should grant his peace without the knowledge of the kin of the man who was slain, that kin still had the right to take vengeance.[31] It is impossible to explain this in terms of royal weakness or backwardness. Twelfth- and thirteenth-century Scottish kings consistently pursued an aggressive and expansionist policy, building up their control of their kingdon with conspicuous success. Yet here the crown took a lead in reducing an area of tension. In the wisdom of their ability to compromise and adapt may lie part of the reason for their success.

---

[30] *A.P.S.*, i, p. 663. The provision in *Assise regis David* is in *ibid.*, p. 320, c. 14. This is first recorded in the early fourteenth-century Ayr MS.; Duncan has pointed out to me, however, that the penalties, in cows, are more characteristic of the thirteenth, or the twelfth, century.

[31] *A.P.S.*, i, p. 375, c. 15. The rights of the lord were also recognized and protected: *ibid.*, p. 320, c. 14; *Regiam maiestatem*, pp. 166–7, quoted in Balfour, *Practicks*, ii, p. 552. On Anglo-Saxon law, Laws of Wihtred (695), 26.1; Laws of Ine (688–94), 17, 28: *Gesetze der Angelsachsen*, ed. Liebermann, pp. 14, 96–7, 100–1; *English Historical Documents*, ed. Whitelock, no. 31, p. 398, and no. 32, pp. 401–2.

Acknowledgement of the rights of the kin was accompanied by a willingness to 'supplement the procedure' and offer palliatives for the irritants which could hold up the settlement of feud. Both *Assise regis David* and *Quoniam attachiamenta* provided a solution to the problem of the injured man who claimed too much compensation: the man, for example, who insisted that he had been robbed of more than he actually owned, or who demanded a greater sum for the murder of a kinsman than was owed by law. In these cases, loyal and trustworthy men of the court should be brought in to estimate the amount of compensation due. Indeed, in the first case, the thief was directed not to answer the charge while an assize inquired into the wealth of his victim; if that had been exaggerated, the thief was acquitted.[32] How old these procedures were, cannot be known. But their existence in post-twelfth-century Scotland shows the crown using, and improving on, an ancient method of dealing with theft and murder.

A crucial effect of this was that the law came to look beyond the 'value of the blood spilt', the single-minded intention to end feud with status as the sole criterion. It is scarcely believable that distinctions between types of crime and motive, recognition of the varying needs of the victim or his kin and the varying abilities of the criminal to make reparation, were not well known long before the thirteenth century.[33] But only then is there evidence that they began to become effective in law. Royal writs of the thirteenth and fourteenth centuries, for example, offered protection to the man who had killed in self-defence; directed the sheriff to hold an inquest to determine whether or not a homicide was justifiable; commanded the kin and friends of a pauper to contribute towards any fine imposed on him for murder.[34] And a provision in *Regiam maiestatem* carefully distinguished between the amount of compensation owed when a horseman in a village rode down and killed

---

[32] *A.P.S.*, i, p. 375, c. 15; *Regiam maiestatem*, p. 364, c. 69. An earlier example of the king's recognition of compensation, in the assize of 1197, is suggested by the translation of 'vindictam' as compensation by Duncan, *Scotland: The Making of the Kingdom*, p. 201.

[33] An argument put forward with devastating effect in D. Daube, *Aspects of Roman Law* (Edinburgh, 1969), chs. 2–3; see esp. pp. 163–75.

[34] *Register of Brieves, 1286–1386*, ed. T. M. Cooper (Stair Soc., x, Edinburgh, 1946), pp. 50, 58, 51. In an important article, R. Black, 'A Historical Survey of Delictual Liability in Scotland for Personal Injuries and Death', *Comparative and Internat. Law Jl. of Southern Africa*, viii (1975), p. 53, argues that the 'fine' imposed on the pauper was compensation payment rather than criminal penalty.

a pedestrian, and when he killed one by backing his horse into him; compensation for the first, being the rider's responsibility, was far greater than for the second, when the pedestrian should have been more careful.[35]

Thus by about 1400 the features of the blood feud as it existed in the fifteenth and sixteenth centuries are already detectable. The king had long been involved; not surprisingly he had demanded his share in the current method of justice. In addition the obligation of the crown to provide justice for those without kin had relaxed the earlier rigidity which had existed at least in theory. And the courts were beginning to be brought into what, as far as is known, had previously been a private matter. The interaction of public and private order can therefore be seen in the Auld Lawes, sparse though that evidence is. Even although the developing royal justice of the twelfth and thirteenth centuries owed much to English example, it had not undermined, far less challenged, the principle of compensation to those wronged which lay at the heart of the justice of the feud. In the fifteenth and sixteenth centuries royal justice continued to expand, to such an extent that by the end of the sixteenth century the formal structure of the Scottish legal system had undergone as much transformation as it had in the twelfth and thirteenth centuries. Yet throughout this period the justice for which the kin had originally been wholly responsible was still available. Private agreements between lords and men show how kin and lord made it available;[36] government and legal records demonstrate that it was also part of the justice offered by crown and courts. It is this remarkable combination of public and private record which gives the Scottish blood feud of the fifteenth and sixteenth centuries its particular importance and fascination.

Discussion of it must inevitably start with the role of the kindred, for general references to the kin abound in the documentary evidence of feud and settlement. The late sixteenth-century lawyer James Balfour of Pittendreich stressed the point that it was the kin, never the individual, who must accuse and pursue the criminal.

---

[35] *Regiam maiestatem*, pp. 269–70; *cro* and *galnes* are the words used for compensation.

[36] There is a remarkable collection of over eight hundred surviving private agreements, the subject of my thesis, Jennifer M. Brown, 'Bonds of Manrent in Scotland before 1603' (Univ. of Glasgow Ph.D. thesis, 1974), and discussed briefly in my article 'The Exercise of Power', in Jennifer M. Brown (ed.), *Scottish Society in the Fifteenth Century* (London, 1977), pp. 54–8.

Letters of slains had to be given by the 'four branches of kin', two on the father's side, two on the mother's. The initial impression is that the Scottish kin-group was still an immensely large unit, whose part in private justice was still of fundamental importance.

It is clear that men did retain a strong sense of kinship and of the obligations it imposed. In practice the Scottish kin-group remained a powerful force in social and political life.[37] One reason for this was that it was agnatic, and therefore more likely to survive, because problems of conflicting loyalties are less in agnatic than in cognatic kindreds.[38] The maternal kin was not ignored in the settlement of feud. But it was a distinct social unit. Marriage brought two kindreds into juxtaposition; it did not impose mutual obligations of kinship on the husband and the male relatives of the wife. The distinction is already indicated in *Leges inter Brettos et Scottos*.[39] In the later middle ages, when the surname had come into common use, the wife did not take her husband's name, and this strongly suggests that she, and certainly her kin, were not truly assimilated into the kin of her husband. The relationship between her husband and her brothers is illustrated in a letter from Adam Bothwell, bishop of Orkney, to his brother-in-law, Archibald Napier of Merchiston, in which Bothwell referred to Napier's house – his kinsmen – and to his friends, among whom the bishop numbered himself.[40] Thus it was relatives on the father's side who recognized

[37] This is discussed in, among others, G. Donaldson, *Scotland: James V–James VII* (Edinburgh, 1965), pp. 12–16; Brown, 'Exercise of Power', pp. 57–65; J. W. M. Bannerman, 'The Lordship of the Isles', in Brown (ed.), *Scottish Society in the Fifteenth Century*, pp. 212ff.

[38] Brown, 'Exercise of Power', pp. 58–60, where the point is discussed more fully. The famous debate between Karl Leyser and D. A. Bullough in *Past and Present* makes clear the complexities of the terms 'agnatic' and 'cognatic': K. Leyser, 'The German Aristocracy from the Ninth to the Early Twelfth Century: A Historical and Cultural Sketch', *Past and Present*, no. 41 (Dec. 1968), pp. 25–53; D. A. Bullough, 'Early Medieval Social Groupings: The Terminology of Kinship', *Past and Present*, no. 45 (Nov. 1969), pp. 3–18; K. Leyser, 'Maternal Kin in Early Medieval Germany. A Reply', *Past and Present*, no. 49 (Nov. 1970), pp. 126–34; here, and in 'Exercise of Power', I use the terms in their simplest meaning of kinship through one line (in practice, the father's) and kinship through both father and mother.

[39] The section on *kelchyn* says that if a wife is slain, her husband (if she is free) or her lord (if unfree) shall have the *kelchyn*, and her kin (*parentes*) the *cro* and *galnes*: *Regiam maiestatem*, pp. 227–8, where *parentes* is wrongly translated as 'friends'. Cf. Seebohm, *Tribal Custom in Anglo-Saxon Law*, pp. 317–18, 466, 498.

[40] M. Napier, *Memoirs of John Napier of Merchiston* (Edinburgh, 1834), p. 111. 'Friend' originally denoted 'kinsman', and was still occasionally used thus in sixteenth-century Scotland, especially where the relationship between distant

kinship. And the strength of the agnatic group was reinforced by another factor, that its unity came not only from ties of blood but also from geographical cohesion. This is always a relevant consideration in determining kin-groups; in a country with Scotland's geography it is not surprising to find a strong commitment to the local unit or community which it was not easy to break down. No attempt was made to do so in this period; Scottish kings, far from trying to create a centralized state, made good use of the local unit as a means of extending royal control into the localities.[41]

In general terms the Scottish kin-group becomes relatively easy to identify, not only for the historian, but also, it seems, for people at the time, because of the use of the surname. This became the test of kinship, the words 'name' or 'surname' becoming synonymous with kindred. Even so, problems of size and extent of kin-solidarity remain. Size cannot be established with any certainty; at no time was it enunciated as a principle that kinship should be extended only to third cousins, for example. Only occasionally does one come across lists of names of kinsmen. Forty-one lairds of the surname of Murray, along with the unnamed remainder of their kin, all recognizing a common obligation in the language of the Three Musketeers, 'that anis [one's] cause shall be alle, and alle shall be ane', are an impressive enough group; so are the 227 names contained in two lists of Hamilton kinsmen.[42] But these numbers may be unusually large. Indeed the solidarity of the politically immensely important Hamilton kindred seems to have been worthy of note among contemporaries. The sixteenth-century *Diurnal of Remarkable Occurrents in Scotland* has a lot of information about the confused politics of the second half of the century and the people involved. Normally it gives long lists of individual names. But it consistently refers simply to 'the haill [whole] Hamiltonis'.[43]

It is not mere question-begging to suggest that concentration on

---

kinsmen was hard to pinpoint; for example, Robert Lindsay of Pitscottie, *Historie and Cronicles of Scotland*, ed. A. J. G. Mackay, 3 vols. (Scot. Text Soc., Edinburgh, 1899–1911), ii, p. 82. But normally it meant people who would act as kinsmen.

[41] Brown, 'Exercise of Power', pp. 52–3, 64–5.

[42] Scot. R.O., Dalguise Muniments, GD 38/1/73a and 38/1/85a; *Registrum honoris de Morton*, 2 vols. (Bannatyne Club, Edinburgh, 1853), i, pp. 65–6.

[43] *A Diurnal of Remarkable Occurrents in Scotland, 1513–1575* (Maitland Club, Edinburgh, 1833), p. 151: 'the haill Hamiltonis . . . come to Linlithgow' is a typical reference.

the problem of the size of the kindred and scope of kin-solidarity may anyway be misplaced. Certainly it can go to absurd lengths. In 1750 William Blackstone published his *Essay on Collateral Consanguinity* for the benefit of All Souls College, for which the preference for founder's kin in the election of fellows was by then an embarrassment. It can hardly have reassured the college when Blackstone's table of geometrical progression showed that, barring accidents, the number of founder's kin in the twentieth generation would be 274,887,906,944.[44] My impression is that fifteenth- and sixteenth-century Scotsmen were not obsessed by problems of identification of remote kinsmen. Obligation to an unknown relative might be grudgingly admitted. In 1590 John Grant of Freuchy declared himself justly incensed by the murder of one Alan Grant and another Grant whose Christian name he apparently did not know, for it is not recorded; his interest had to be expressed because, as he said, they were of his kin or 'at the leist being ane of his surname'.[45] But generally it is hard to find evidence of extensive kin-recognition or kin-solidarity. Men needed other men to speak for them, give them support, and they were not only to be found within the kin, least of all the remote kin. Moreover late medieval Scotsmen knew very well that even close kinship did not necessarily ensure amity, and might even be the cause of particular hostility. No doubt their predecessors were also aware of this, as much aware as the members of the early medieval German aristocracy;[46] any reference to kindred at any time may be shorthand for what is actually both a smaller and a more disparate group.

Kin-solidarity was, however, probably becoming weaker by the fifteenth and sixteenth centuries, partly because there were more alternatives available, and partly because there were increased stresses on the bond of kinship. In the late sixteenth century the great lawyer Thomas Craig of Riccarton, a man with a genius for telling his countrymen unpalatable truths, pointed out that, 'so far from acting as a protection against discord, community of blood often intensifies the bitterness of family quarrels, and the most violent hatred of which human nature is capable occurs between

---

[44] Cited by J. D. Freeman, 'On the Concept of the Kindred', in Bohannan and Middleton (eds.), *Kinship and Social Organization*, pp. 257–8.

[45] W. Fraser, *The Chiefs of Grant*, 3 vols. (Edinburgh, 1883), iii, pp. 177–8.

[46] As argued in Leyser, 'German Aristocracy from the Ninth to the Early Twelfth Century'.

brothers and sometimes even between father and son'.[47] In practice there are few known cases of extreme hostility between father and son such as led to the violent action of Alexander Ogilvy of that ilk, who in 1545 disinherited his heir in favour of the third son of the earl of Huntly, who took the name of Ogilvy.[48] But Craig was writing at a time when the strains imposed by primogeniture had been reinforced by the increasing practice of entailing lands. In addition the Reformation had at least reduced, if not wholly closed the doors to, the chance of a lucrative career for younger sons in the church; and with the disappearance of the old church went the crumbling of the traditional alliance with France, that haven for the Scots soldier of fortune abroad, leaving a gap which may not have been wholly filled until the outbreak of the Thirty Years War. The effect of these problems can be seen in the appearance, in sixteenth-century Edinburgh, of younger sons of lairds who trained in the law and, by the end of the sixteenth century, had not only broken the clerical dominance as professional lawyers and administrators, but were beginning to found their own legal dynasties.[49] It was in this transference of close kinship ties into the new world of the professional lay lawyer that there lay the as yet unrecognized seeds of the decline of the blood feud itself. But already obvious were the factors which speeded up the decline of traditional obligations of kinship, at least in the lowland areas of Scotland.

The vastly comprehensive terms, therefore, in which a murderer was forgiven by, for example, 'all & syndry our barnis [children], kyne, frendis, anerdance [allies] and branchis of kin' reflect theory, not practice.[50] In both private and public records, references to the whole kin appeared only at the point of settlement. The people who actually brought about the settlement were a much smaller group, those closest to the victim of crime: father, sons, brothers, sometimes wife, acting in private cases with the head of the kin or the lord. Even the 'four branches of kin' whose consent was

---

[47] Thomas Craig of Riccarton, *Ius feudale* (Edinburgh, 1732; first published London, 1655), trans. by J. A. Clyde, 2 vols. (Edinburgh, 1934), 2.11.13.

[48] *Registrum magni sigilli regum Scotorum*, ed. J. M. Thomson *et al.*, 11 vols. (Edinburgh, 1882–1914), iii, no. 3157.

[49] G. Donaldson, 'The Legal Profession in Scottish Society in the Sixteenth and Seventeenth Centuries', *Juridical Rev.*, new ser., xxi (1976), pp. 1–19, is a fascinating analysis of this subject. See also G. Brunton and D. Haig, *The Senators of the College of Justice* (Edinburgh, 1832).

[50] Scot. R.O., Register House Charters, no. 596.

necessary to a letter of slains were not all obliged to send along representatives. Balfour, having stated the principle, went on to say that three, or fewer, would be sufficient. Thus the perfectly valid letter of slains given at the settlement of feud between Neil Montgomery of Langshaw and Robert, Lord Boyd, of Kilmarnock was issued by Neil himself and two members of his paternal kin; the maternal kin was represented only by Archibald, earl of Argyll.[51] Moreover, while the kindred of the victim were always mentioned in letters of slains, the kindred of the murderer were not. In Scotland, as in other such societies, the kin on whom the burden of compensation fell, quite naturally resented it; and there was even less kin-solidarity with the murderer than with the victim.[52]

Myth and reality went hand in hand in the settlement of feud. Formally it was the kin who acted; in practice it was the 'kin frendis and parttakaris', and sometimes only the 'frendis and parttakaris'.[53] Yet reference to the whole kindred was not simply vague sentiment about a half-remembered or imagined past. It had a practical purpose. When feud came to an end, it was important to include as many people as possible, even unknown people; Grant of Freuchy had, after all, suddenly been involved in the murder of unknown kinsmen. The motive was similar to that which prompted many of the thirteen competitors to claim the Scottish crown in 1292: no chance, however remote, should be allowed to go by default. Even more important was the strength of the ideal of kinship. The support given to friends and neighbours, be they kin or not, was understood entirely in terms of the obligations of kinship. This enabled reverence for the idea of being a member of a large kin-group, descended from a great ancestor whose mighty deeds inspired pride and poetry, to exist in harmony with the realistic recognition that the people most likely to give help were those most nearly related, and those neighbours with whom support was a

[51] Balfour, *Practicks*, ii, pp. 517–18; Scot. R.O., Boyd of Kilmarnock Papers, GD 8/170.

[52] A theme much discussed by Philpotts, *Kindred and Clan in the Middle Ages and After*; see, for example, her chapters on Iceland and Norway. See also Nicholls, *Gaelic and Gaelicised Ireland in the Middle Ages*, pp. 56–7.

[53] Cf. Davies, 'Survival of the Bloodfeud in Medieval Wales', p. 355 and note, describing an indenture of 1523 which referred to the 'part takers' of the victim's kin 'as will hav ther part of the mendis'. In Scotland, 'Parttakaris' were those who took a man's part; I have not come across anything like the Welsh indenture, which clearly shows that they also took part of the compensation payment, but this use of the word is suggestive, and it is not unlikely that they did.

matter of mutual advantage. The 'whole kindred' was something of a myth. But it had the appeal of invoking an ancient concept, and that gave it its own reality.

It was because of the strength of the ideal that the language of kinship was taken over into the language of lordship. Scottish society offers little support for the view that powerful lordship is exercised at the expense of kinship. Even during the period of Norman feudalization it is probable that kinship was not so much weakened as unrecorded. In the later middle ages and early modern period there is no doubt that they were complementary, each strengthening the other. The records of lordship were no longer primarily concerned with land grants, but with the personal relationship between the lord and his friends and dependants which, in this increasingly document-conscious and literate age, was now described through the written word. Men made bonds of friendship, maintenance and manrent to assure one another of protection and service, the obligations as implicit in lordship as in kinship. They made these bonds precisely because they were not kinsmen, and so put into writing the obligations which, for the kin, were fundamental and unwritten. They referred repeatedly to the 'kindness' (kinship) which would exist between them; and they included such phrases as the promise that a man would act towards his lord 'in affectione and obediens as he war [were] my fader naturell and I his sone naturell', because his lord 'has grantyt gret kyndenes to me and rescavyt [received] me til his familiarite as his awin sone'.[54]

Thus lords acted *in loco parentis*. Their bonds of friendship show a strong awareness of their responsibility, not to keep their men free from the consequences of their crimes, but to involve themselves personally in, and provide a solution to, disputes between their followers. That was both their right and their duty. In their bonds they regularly promised to act together to deal with the disputes of their followers; as a sanction against any who refused to accept their authority, they agreed to withhold their protection from such a man, who would be, as one contract succinctly put it, 'schakin off'.[55] Colin, earl of Argyll, for example, in his bonds with William, earl of Glencairn, in 1576 and John, earl of Mar, in 1578, made the provision that if any slaughter or dispute should occur between any

[54] Scot. R.O., Curle Collection, GD 111/iv/3.
[55] Montrose Muniments, Auchmar House, Drymen, 1, 44.

of their kin or dependents, it should not threaten their friendship, but should be amended by them with the advice of their friends. In the second of these contracts it was further agreed that if 'wariance [variance]' should happen between the earls themselves – as God forbid – they would submit their differences to their 'wyss [wise] freindis'.[56] Other agreements added in details, sometimes naming particular people who would be called in when disputes arose, and more generally suggesting that at least four arbiters were thought necessary.[57]

These agreements show the survival of the private settlement as a customary and practical method of dealing with crime or civil dispute. It did not conflict with public justice. Alexander Ogilvy of that ilk and Walter Ogilvy of Baddinspink could quite naturally agree to settle their dispute over land 'by siche [sight] of frendis or lawe as they think expedient', while William, Lord Graham, and John, Lord Oliphant, said that should they fail to settle the actions of any of their men, the plaintiff could take the case to court.[58] There is no evidence here of a sinister desire to keep cases away from the government and its justice. What is evident is the much more prosaic consideration of using whatever method would be effective. This was what mattered; people wanted, then as now, straightforwardness, speed – and a victory in their case.

Certainly the private settlement could have the advantage of speed, in contrast to the frustration caused by the endless delays to which action before the central courts could be subject. It could also have the advantage of effectiveness in an age when the intense localism of society meant that a man who lost an action might be more readily persuaded to accept the dictates of the local lord than the judgement of a court remote in Edinburgh. Complaint to the government in 1545 did nothing for Walter Ogilvy of Dunlugus in his attempt to gain his rightful possession of the lands of Sandlaw in Banffshire, held by another laird, Thomas Baird, who was less powerful than Ogilvy but who still managed to sit tight. After a year Dunlugus turned to the head of his kin, Ogilvy of that ilk, and to the

---

[56] Argyll MSS., Inverary Castle, vol. 4/136 and 4/162.

[57] For example, Scot. R.O., Drummond Castle Muniments, GD 160, box 3, bundle IV; Hamilton Muniments, Lennoxlove, box 102.

[58] *Illustrations of the Topography and Antiquities of the Shires of Aberdeen and Banff*, ed. J. Robertson and G. Grub, 5 vols. (Spalding Club, Aberdeen, 1843–69), ii, pp. 102–3; J. Anderson, *The Oliphants in Scotland* (Edinburgh, 1879), pp. 47–8.

most powerful local magnate, George, earl of Huntly; and they brought about a settlement within a month.[59] Dunlugus now had the big battalions on his side in his dispute with a family who had been thorns in the flesh of the Ogilvies long before 1545. But justice was done and seen to be done. Dunlugus gained his lands; but the Bairds were given sweeteners, the most substantial being the cancellation of their debt of one thousand merks to Dunlugus.[60] The head of the kin and the local lord were, therefore, not simply backing their man, but doing justice, and doing it in such a way that there would be hope of reasonable relations between the disputing parties in the future. Peace after the feud depended on acceptance of a settlement by both sides. Harsh treatment of the loser, left to nurse his resentment against the neighbour who had won, reduced the chance of that. This element in Huntly's and Ogilvy's judgement was therefore as important as their legally correct decision that the lands of Sandlaw belonged to Ogilvy of Dunlugus.

If private justice worked well in disputes over land, it worked equally well in criminal cases, for the same reason: it took the tension out of a local situation. In 1554 a Forfarshire laird, George Drummond of Leidcreif, was murdered by the lairds of Drumlochy, Ardblair and Gormok.[61] The government took some action, in response to an appeal from the widow, children, kin and friends of the murdered man. The sheriff of Perth was directed to take sureties that the murderers and their accomplices would underly the law; and two of these accomplices were tried and executed.[62] But a more effective figure, David, Lord Drummond, became involved when the principal murderers approached him with offers of assythment. The first offer, made jointly by the three lairds, was by no means bad; it included one thousand merks, masses for the soul of the dead man and four pilgrimages. This compares very favourably with, for example, the assythment by the Elphinstones to the kin of William Calder in 1553, which 'after the modificacioun and consideracioun of freindis' amounted to only three pilgrimages

[59] Scot. R.O., Abercromby of Forglen Muniments, GD 185, box 2, bundle 11.
[60] *Ibid.* Other concessions included the restoration of lands leased to the Bairds: *ibid.*, bundle 10.
[61] Scot. R.O., Abercairny Muniments, GD 24/1/824 (a volume of original papers relating to this case); this reference covers the following account, except where otherwise stated.
[62] R. Pitcairn (ed.), *Criminal Trials in Scotland from 1488 to 1624*, 3 vols. (Edinburgh, 1833), i, pt. 1, pp. 367, 374.

and ten merks.[63] But Lord Drummond rejected it with furious contempt. He cared nothing for masses and pilgrimages; and a thousand merks was insultingly paltry for 'sa heych [high] crewell and abomenabill slaychteris and mwtillacionis' of a kinsman who had, he asserted, done nothing to offend his murderers. There is no further record of two of the lairds, Ardblair and Gormok. We know only about the settlement with the third, William Chalmer of Drumlochy. Chalmer was unable to offer any money at all. He had none to give, as he explained to Lord Drummond, because he had been ruined by lawsuits. No doubt he exaggerated, even if sixteenth-century lawyers' fees were high; but his plea of poverty disposes of the idea that settlements of this kind were only for people too powerful for the law to touch. Chalmer could, however, offer two things: first, his bond of manrent, promising allegiance and service to Drummond for life; and secondly, that his son and cousin should marry the daughter and sister of his victim, without dowry.

These offers Drummond accepted. They exactly fulfil two basic conditions of the settlement of feud. The first restored order; it ensured peace between the murderer and the kin of his victim, for he would now serve the head of that kin. The second did even more. It was fundamental to the system of compensation that when crime was committed, what mattered was not punishment as retribution or deterrent, but reparation in a form which would as far as possible restore the *status quo* which the crime had upset. In this case Chalmer had deprived his victim's daughter and sister of their natural protector, the head of their family. It was now his responsibility to redress that loss by making provision for them without any material advantage to himself. However bizarre it may seem that crime could be dealt with by marrying the son of a murderer to the daughter of the man he had murdered, Chalmer was exactly meeting the demands of the principle of assythment.[64]

These settlements, and others like them, depended less on the

---

[63] *Illustrations of the Topography and Antiquities of the Shires of Aberdeen and Banff*, ed. Robertson and Grub, iii, pp. 466–7.

[64] This may well have been done by a much earlier and much more famous figure. Shakespeare, seeking to compliment a Scottish king by writing *Macbeth*, might, as well as introducing witches (for James VI's interest in witchcraft had lessened considerably), have introduced the blood feud; for it is possible, as Barrow has suggested to me, that Macbeth was involved in the killing of Lady Macbeth's first husband, Gillecomgain, mormaer of Moray, and therefore that this marriage was, in part, in settlement of feud.

existence of a large kin-group acting as a unit than on the power of the individual head of kin or local laird. Certainly his power to impose settlement derived from his position as the man who commanded a large following. But it derived also from the extent to which he was a personality who could command respect. Not all men willingly followed the dictates of their lords; and lordship in the hands of a weak man was weak lordship. Such a man was Archibald, fourth earl of Argyll (1529–58), whose position brought him into national and local affairs, but who dithered so ineffectively in both that John Knox's conventionally worded record of his death, that he was called by God 'from the miseries of this life', has a peculiar appropriateness.[65] Much of his misery arose from his failure to control even his dependants, one of whom, John Lamont of Inveryne, was able to resist the earl's attempts to settle two land disputes by being simply bloody-minded. In the first case, Lamont and his opponent appointed arbiters, in the accustomed manner; and Lamont accepted their decision on the assythment he should make for the murder of his opponent's son. But neither they nor the earl could persuade him to accept a judgement awarding the disputed lands to his opponent; all they could do was to advise the opponent to take his case to court, and ineffectually suggest that Lamont should be 'contentit . . . bot ony grwnching [without any grouching] or rancour of mind'. In the second case Lamont, summoned before the earl in the sheriff court of Argyll, turned up with a royal letter directing Argyll not to hear the case, on the grounds of his feud with Lamont – a feud which, as Argyll correctly said, was invented.[66] It was not normally wise for their dependants to defy the earls of Argyll. This earl could be defied with impunity; his lordship produced stalemate, not settlement.

These cases are a reminder that settlement after murder could be more easily achieved, because it was to the advantage of both parties, than resolution of land dispute, which involved gain to one and loss to the other. Not every feud was as readily settled as the dispute over Sandlaw. The successful settlement depended on two

[65] John Knox, *History of the Reformation in Scotland*, ed. W. C. Dickinson, 2 vols. (Edinburgh, 1949), i, p. 138.
[66] The first case is in Argyll MSS., Inverary Castle, vol. 5/44; *An Inventory of Lamont Papers, 1231–1897*, ed. N. Lamont of Knockdaw (Scot. Rec. Soc., liv, Edinburgh, 1914), pp. 34, 36; the second is in Argyll MSS., vol. 5/78. Both are discussed in detail in Brown, 'Bonds of Manrent in Scotland before 1603', pp. 260–9.

things: first, allies, be they lord or kin, powerful enough to act for the wronged party; and secondly, an agreement which, if it was a criminal matter, removed from the murderer the fear of reprisals, and if civil, gave the loser some measure of compensation. It was a delicate business persuading local families who were rivals or enemies to live at peace. The desire to do so, which produced the element of compromise in the successful settlement, lay also behind the last act of this kind of justice, the publicity which was deliberately encouraged when settlement was reached. Justice should be seen to be done not only by the parties involved, but also by the people in the locality of the dispute, for that too offered some guarantee that peace would be kept. The Baird–Ogilvy dispute was finally resolved in the public ceremony of the handing over of documents relating to Sandlaw and to the debt cancelled by Ogilvy, in the parish church of Banff, six weeks after the judgement; during that six weeks Dunlugus and one of his servants were active in announcing the date of the ceremony.[67] After a case of murder, public reconciliation could be even more spectacular. The murder of Neil Montgomery of Langshaw by Robert, Lord Boyd, in 1547 was eventually settled by the sons of both in 1561. Their contract, made at Glasgow on 10 February, included the promise that Montgomery would formally forgive Boyd at Irvine, the scene of the crime, on 23 February. There, at the market cross or church, Boyd and his associates would

> humbly for God's cause implore and seek the said remit and forgiveness for the said offence . . . in plain audience of the people, and there upon their knees . . . ask God forgiveness . . . and subsequently the said Neil . . . and shall offer to the said Neil a naked sword by the point, in token of their repentance from the bottom of their hearts.

This being done, and, more prosaically, eighteen hundred merks assythment having been paid, Neil gave Boyd his letter of slains. Two years later the head of Neil's kin, Hugh, earl of Eglinton, made a contract of friendship with Boyd which referred, with sweeping disregard for past events, to the love which had existed between their predecessors.[68] The element of humiliation which Baird and Boyd had to suffer, and the human pleasure felt by Ogilvy and

[67] Scot. R.O., GD 185, box 2, bundles 11, 18.
[68] Scot. R.O., GD 8/167 (the contract), GD 8/170 (letter of slains), GD 8/177 (contract of friendship).

Montgomery, were certainly part of the publicity, but only part. Once immediate emotions were submerged or satisfied, what remained was the fact of the publicity, and the pressure which that put on the parties now reconciled.

Peace after the feud: what was achieved, or at least desired, was the situation succinctly described in a letter of slains given by the kin of John of Caldwell to the Cunninghams, that there would be friendship between them 'lyke as the slachtyr of the said John of Caldwell had nevir bein committit'.[69] The means of achieving it were very old, and still very effective. But it is not enough to discuss the fifteenth- and sixteenth-century feud in these terms. The question arises why it continued to exist at all in this period of notable development of 'central' justice. At the beginning of the fifteenth century Scotland had a network of local courts: regality, sheriff, baronial, burgh and so on. But there was no central court as such; the king's justice was sought in parliament and council. In 1426 a new and separate court was established, the Session. Initially it was peripatetic; the intention was that it should meet two or three times a year in major Scottish burghs, using a different group of local magnates, clerics and burgesses at each sitting or 'session'.[70] Only in the late fifteenth century did it begin to sit regularly in Edinburgh. In so far as a distinction can be drawn between criminal and civil law, it was the supreme civil court. Criminal justice was still a matter of going out into the localities, 'driving' the justice ayres. By the end of the sixteenth century the picture was dramatically different. The Session had been erected into the College of Justice with a president and fourteen salaried 'ordinary' lords of Session, with varying numbers of 'extraordinary' lords added. This was a distinct advance on the fifteenth-century practice of using trained churchmen and amateur landowners who were expected to bear their own expenses as part of the work which naturally went with their high position.[71] There was now a central criminal court.[72] Edinburgh had become indisputably the capital,

---

[69] Scot. R.O., Register House Charters, no. 596.
[70] *A.P.S.*, ii, p. 11, c. 19; A. A. M. Duncan, 'The Central Courts before 1532', in *Introduction to Scottish Legal History* (Stair Soc., xx, Edinburgh, 1958), pp. 329–39; J. J. Robertson, 'The Development of the Law', in Brown (ed.), *Scottish Society in the Fifteenth Century*, pp. 143, 146–7, 152.
[71] *A.P.S.*, ii, p. 48, c. 4.
[72] W. C. Dickinson, 'The High Court of Justiciary', in *Introduction to Scottish Legal History*, pp. 410–11.

for the law as for government; most notably it was the home of the lay legal profession, where lawyers could do well – that is, make money – as advocates.[73] So it is against this background of growing centralization, organization and professionalism that the place of the older system of the justice of the feud has to be considered.

The first consideration is the role of the crown. Kings in Scotland are normally assumed to have taken the initiative, in the teeth of opposition from powerful vested interests, in offering justice – their justice, better and more impartial – to their subjects; the corollary is that even heritable jurisdictions and certainly private kin-based justice were detrimental to that policy. But the evidence can be interpreted very differently. Certainly kings were expected to provide justice. Very often, however, it was forced out of them, rather than offered by them, to an extent which makes it debatable whether it was indeed the crown which was responsible, wholly or even mainly, for the increasing centralization of justice. In the fifteenth century kings rarely tried to attract men to their courts. What they did was to panic at the threat of increased business and try to push it back to the localities; hence, for example, there was legislation insisting that men went back to their local courts in the first instance, and used royal justice only for appeal.[74] James III was savagely criticized by his parliaments for showing no interest in justice other than the profitable sale of remissions (pardons).[75] His failure is well known. Less well known, but very convincing, is the argument that James I, the king with a high reputation for determination to impose law and order on his kingdom, in fact founded the new court, the Session, in order to free his council from the burden of judicial work so that it could concentrate on cases concerning lands to which the crown might have a claim.[76] A century later, in 1532, the Session was erected into the College of Justice. This date is regarded by lawyers as a great turning-point, the end of the 'Dark Age' of Scottish legal history. Historians are

---

[73] Donaldson, 'Legal Profession in Scottish Society', pp. 12–17, and Appendix.

[74] For example, *A.P.S.*, ii, pp. 9, 94, 107, 111, 177–8; the last of these, an act passed in October 1487, was repealed in January 1488, but that was exceptional; R. G. Nicholson, *Scotland: The Later Middle Ages* (Edinburgh, 1974), pp. 311, 429; Duncan, *Scotland: The Making of the Kingdom*, pp. 332–4.

[75] *A.P.S.*, ii, pp. 104, 118, 139, 165, 170, 176.

[76] A. A. M. Duncan, *James I, 1424–1437* (Univ. of Glasgow, Scot. Hist. Dept., Occasional Papers, i, Glasgow, 1976). There is no evidence that, for the rest of his reign, James made any attempt to ensure that his new court functioned.

more cynical, because the establishment of the college was little more than an excuse, used by James V as a device to extort money from the church; for it was heavy clerical taxation, allowed by a compliant papacy fearful of Henry VIII's pressure on his nephew the Scottish king, which provided the finance, ostensibly for the college, but actually for the king's coffers – so much so that after James's death in 1542 the judges threatened strike action.[77]

Kings of late medieval and early modern Scotland were not lofty and high-minded creatures thinking of ideals. They used justice for their own ends and, being the most powerful people in the kingdom, did so with conspicuous, sometimes ruthless success. They were heavily involved in the hurly-burly of justice; from the mid-fifteenth century they had their own advocate, whose duty was to act for the crown in cases in which it had a personal interest. Only in the late sixteenth century did the king's advocate become in any sense a public prosecutor, and then, significantly enough, only when approached by private individuals or kindreds, or if the kin or other parties involved failed to pursue an action themselves.[78]

All this, however, only argues against the danger of seeing these kings as men with a vision of impersonal 'state' justice as we understand it today. It does not mean that they were not interested in justice. They were; all the Stewart kings, with the exception of James III, had a deservedly good reputation in their day. That reputation came from their understanding that the most effective justice was still primarily local justice, and that compromise and compensation might be a better answer to crime than a penal code. Their approach had much in common with the lord in his locality. At every level of judicial activity, the premium was put on defusing a violent situation, formally or informally. The baron courts, for example, were filled with cases of petty violence, arising from the irritations of everyday life in small rural communities, where an unco-operative neighbour allowed his cattle to stray once too often

[77] R. K. Hannay, *The College of Justice* (Edinburgh, 1933), p. 75.
[78] *The Register of the Privy Council of Scotland*, ed. J. H. Burton *et al.*, 1st ser., 14 vols. (Edinburgh, 1877–98), iii, p. 173 (1579), and *A.P.S.*, iii, pp. 144 (1579), 457 (1587), are the earliest clear examples of the king's advocate acting as a public prosecutor. In his illuminating work, I. D. Willock, *The Origins and Development of the Jury in Scotland* (Stair Soc., xxiii, Edinburgh, 1966), pp. 153–4, discusses the development of the office of king's advocate, but stresses that 'throughout the sixteenth century, prosecution was still regarded as primarily a matter of private concern'.

and became the victim of attack, or where a persistent drunkard made life intolerable. These courts were supplemented by the 'birlaw' courts, informal courts held by men whose only right to hear cases was their local reputation for good sense, and who were simply concerned with good neighbourhood; how ancient these were can be guessed at from the Scandinavian origin of their name.[79] At the other end of the scale, the effective king was still, like his predecessors, the king who supplemented the justice of kin and lord. Even James I, who spent eighteen years of his life witnessing the unique system of English justice, and who came back to Scotland with his head no doubt filled with novel ideas, very quickly adapted his approach to the realities of Scottish society and underwrote the crucial connection between remission and assythment. His legislation was re-enacted by his son, with the additional provision in 1458 that a pardoned criminal would have forty days to assythe the injured party before the remission became null.[80] And in the late sixteenth century, legislation of James VI was still insisting that remissions were valid only if due assythment had been made. By that time, vastly increased bureaucracy led to insistence on greater formality; hence there were complaints that remissions lacking proper authorization were being handed out, and a demand for written evidence in the form of a 'sufficient lettre of slanis', to be inspected by the treasurer.[81]

The emphasis on remissions, in legislation dealing with the justice of the feud, is highly informative about the crown's attitude to justice. What could be more revealing than the spectacle of a group of men known as 'lordis componitouris' (lords compositors) accompanying the justiciar on ayre and, at the beginning of the ayre, in effect putting up a notice telling those who were to be tried to give in 'thair desyres for thair componitouris' – that is, to bargain for remissions.[82] Before a single case was heard, it was known that

[79] *The Court Book of the Barony of Carnwarth, 1523–1542*, ed. W. C. Dickinson (Scot. Hist. Soc., 3rd ser., xxix, Edinburgh, 1937), amply demonstrates these irritations; the burlaw men are discussed in Appendix A, pp. cxiii–cxvi. Duncan, *Scotland: The Making of the Kingdom*, p. 106.

[80] *A.P.S.*, ii, pp. 3, 8, 9, 21 (James I); 34, 50 (James II). For examples of the forty days' rule, see *Criminal Trials in Scotland*, ed. Pitcairn, i, pt. 1, pp. 69–71.

[81] *A.P.S.*, iii, p. 298, c. 12 (1584), p. 426 (1586) p. 575, c. 67 (1592); iv, pp. 18–19, c. 16, and p. 22, c. 23 (1593). *Criminal Trials in Scotland*, ed. Pitcairn, i, pt. 1, pp. 355–6, gives a case in 1547 in which the treasurer was involved.

[82] *Accounts of the Lord High Treasurer of Scotland*, ed. T. Dickson *et al.*, 13 vols. (Edinburgh, 1877–1978), xii, pp. xxvi–xxvii; Dickinson, 'High Court of Justiciary',

the outcome for the guilty who could pay was likely to be pardon. For the king the obvious advantage was financial; payments for remissions in the justice ayre of October 1494 to April 1495, for example, brought James IV £1,225,10s.[83] A king like James III, who thought only of financial gain, was heavily criticized. The other Stewart kings were not subjected to such attack, because they accepted that profit to them was of no satisfaction to the victims of crime. Thus a bargain was struck. That the crown did not always keep its side of the bargain is clear enough from the repeated legislation. But in theory and at least sometimes in practice, assythment was acknowledged as the essential prerequisite to royal pardon.

The groping towards an acceptable balance between royal and private justice, evident in the early laws, was now resolved, with the emphasis still on the fundamental point of compensation to those wronged. Royal justice and kin-justice could work together, to the mutual advantage of both. The advantage was not only material. In two other ways the crown gained from the welding together of remission and assythment. It offered an ideal method of dealing with those whose usefulness as crown servants far outweighed their individual crimes. Cases of treason, or the occasional exceptionally outrageous act, did provoke royal reaction, and the offender was executed; but this was comparatively rare.[84] The king's greatest servants were sometimes criminals; much more important, they were also the opponents of crime. As James I's legislation indicated, and James VI's book on kingship said, men of influence in the localities were 'the armes and executers of your [the king's] laws'.[85] Moreover, by putting its authority behind the justice of the feud, the crown gained not only in its dealings with the magnates

---

p. 410. Being a 'lord componitour' was clearly a pleasant business; the expenses of those who sat for a month at Jedburgh in 1566 were high, and included payment to a lutanist and a player of the pipe and whistle: *Accounts of the Lord High Treasurer of Scotland*, ed. Dickson, xii, p. 31.

[83] *Ibid.*, i, pp. 212–15. These remissions were, of course, particularly useful to a monarchy which rarely taxed its subjects: Brown, 'Exercise of Power', pp. 38–40.

[84] For example, in 1490, when the Drummonds burned one hundred and twenty Murrays in the kirk of Monzievaird, there was no question of remission; the master of Drummond was executed. His sister subsequently became James IV's mistress, which suggests that Scottish kings could act with severity against their powerful subjects and still keep their respect and loyalty – or even more, as in this case.

[85] *The Basilikon Doron of King James VI*, ed. J. Craigie, 2 vols. (Scot. Text Soc., Edinburgh, 1944–50), i, pp. 87–8.

and lairds but, through them, strengthened its links with the localities; for it used as its officials the lords and heads of kin-groups who were already implementing private settlements. There was no conflict between public and private justice because, for the people who did the work, there was no difference. It has been convincingly argued in an English context that kings who made a strong effort to strengthen royal justice were supplementing magnate justice, not mounting a 'full frontal attack' on it.[86] This argument is applied to private jurisdictions; it is equally valid when extended to the Scottish justice of the feud. By accepting the principles of that justice, and enabling the great men of the localities to put them into effect with the blessing of the crown, as part of its justice, the monarchy only enhanced its power and prestige.

For the kin there was the advantage of some solution to the problem of parties to feud who would not settle. The government in its role of a court of appeal was of course not always successful. But men did turn to it, and sometimes were satisfied. The case of 1478, already cited, when the lords of council ordered a man's goods to be distrained for the assythment due to his opponent, is one instance.[87] The privy council intervened in a number of feuds where its help was sought. It was at their direction that many bonds of assurance were made. Their authority was invoked in a case which reflects another of the problems which could arise in the settlement of feud: where the offenders were prepared to make assythment, but the injured party could not ensure that all those on his side would accept it.[88] On another occasion they stage-managed the reconciliation of Matthew Campbell of Loudoun, sheriff of Ayr, with Gilbert, earl of Cassillis, and George Crawford of Leifnores, insisting on the publicity which was so much a feature of private settlements when they directed the parties not only to embrace one another in their presence, but also to assemble their friends and servants in Ayr, there to 'ressave utheris in hartlynes, tendirnes and freindschip . . . quhairunto the Lordis of Secrete Counsale interponit thair autorite'.[89]

[86] J. R. Lander, 'Bonds, Coercion and Fear: Henry VII and the Peerage', in J. G. Rowe and W. H. Stockdale (eds.), *Florilegium historiale: Essays Presented to Wallace K. Ferguson* (Toronto, 1971), pp. 327–67.
[87] *Acts of the Lords of Council in Civil Causes*, ed. Thomson, p. 9.
[88] *Register of the Privy Council of Scotland*, ed. Burton *et al.*, i, pp. 407–8, 422–3.
[89] *Ibid.*, pp. 261–3.

The government's acceptance and use of the justice of the feud sheds light on what was meant when in 1425 James I's parliament enunciated the famous principle of justice: 'als wele to pur as to rych but [without] fraude or favour'.[90] There was an element of propaganda about that assurance; after fifty years of weak royal and regency government, there was now a strong king speaking authoritatively through parliament, and promising justice to all. He was not, however, as has sometimes been assumed, attacking the position of the rich. What was promised was not the same kind of justice for rich and poor, but that the poor would get justice as well as the rich, who already had it in the justice of the feud. To that extent, although it was followed up by the introduction of the poor man's counsel, the act was an expression of good intention rather than reality. In the absence of any statistical information it is of course impossible to define 'pur' and 'rych' in any terms other than the most general: the distinction between those who could pay compensation, and those who could not. So basic was the principle of compensation that there is some indication that the justice which depended on it was at least on offer to more than the aristocracy and gentry, and that some of the 'pur' were given the chance to make assythment.[91] But lack of means obviously barred a considerable section of the community from the justice of the feud. The harsh reality was that the poor suffered more, benefited less, from the law; when have they not? Yet to think of this as a matter of the rich getting away with crime where the unfortunate poor did not, is to miss a crucial point about this justice. Murder by the rich was as much a crime as murder by the poor; there was no longer any concept of 'legal justification' for killing in the feud.[92] But a different way of dealing with it was accepted, because the rich criminal could do what the poor one could not, himself offer justice in tangible form to those he had wronged. This was summed up in an anonymous poem of maxims to a king, written in the mid-fifteenth century, which said that:

[90] *A.P.S.*, ii, p. 8, c. 24.
[91] *Criminal Trials in Scotland*, ed. Pitcairn, i, pt. 1, pp. 69–71, gives examples of people below the rank of laird producing remissions at the justice ayre at Jedburgh in 1510, and being given forty days to find sureties for assythment; otherwise they would be hanged. See Nicholls, *Gaelic and Gaelicised Ireland in the Middle Ages*, p. 54, for a similar Irish example.
[92] Maitland, 'Laws of Wales – The Kindred and the Blood-Feud', p. 217.

Gude justice has twa partis principale
The tane is dome and richtwis [righteous] jugement
The tothir is to mak the scathis hale [injuries whole] . . .

and the judge who failed to do this was 'dettur verraly' – truly a debtor.[93] Two parts: rightful judgement and reparation, the essential elements in good justice, whether it be the king's justice or the justice of the feud.

The attitude of the crown was a powerful factor in the survival of the blood feud. It was maintained right up until the end of the sixteenth century, when James VI was still reiterating older legislation; when he and his parliament ratified a bond of manrent in 1592 given as assythment for slaughter, because it was 'ane necessar and guid caus viz . . . for keping . . . the parties in perpetuall quietnes'; when he settled feud himself, or tried to, by feasting his magnates in Holyrood and then making them proceed up the Royal Mile each holding the hand of his enemy.[94] Yet this same king issued an act entitled 'Act anent [concerning] removeing and extinguischeing of deidlie feids [feuds]'; it was passed by a convention in 1598, and ratified by the next parliament, in 1600, to leave no doubt about its binding authority. It is a curious compilation. It begins traditionally, setting out in detail the process by which feud should be settled by friends of the parties, backed up if necessary by king and council. It then lists three kinds of feud: no slaughter on either side; slaughter on one side; slaughter on both. The first should be dealt with by the procedure described; in the third and most savage, the king should compel the parties to agree to mutual compensation, 'according to the qualitie of the offence and personis offendit'. This takes up less than a third of the act, and none of it is new. The remainder discusses at inordinate length the

---

[93] *Liber Pluscardensis*, ed. F. J. H. Skene, 2 vols. (Edinburgh, 1877–80), i, p. 398; the poem emphasizes the problem of defaulting judges and the duty of the king to punish them; 'dettur verraly' recalls the 1432 act which ordered defaulting judges to assyth the wronged kin: *A.P.S.*, ii, p. 21, c. 9. But it also stresses the uselessness of rightful judgement if the injured party is not compensated. One victim of assault has left us a very precise comment on what he wanted from his assailant, and why there was a distinction, therefore, between rich and poor. In their action for assythment against Adam Tweedy of Dravey in 1566, Robert Rammage and his brother asked for a notarial record that 'thai nevir persewit the said Adame of his lyffe, bot onlye for amendis to be maid for the cryme': *Criminal Trials in Scotland*, ed. Pitcairn, i, pt. 2, p. 475.

[94] D. H. Willson, *King James VI and I* (London, 1966 edn), p. 63.

second type of feud, and insists that in this case the aggrieved party must go to law. And it ends with the king's promise that he will grant no remissions, even if the parties to the case agree between themselves.[95] This is a dramatic departure. It does not, however, seem to have been inspired by the king. Of course James deplored feuding; he said so in memorable prose in *Basilikon Doron*. But he was not unique. It was only because many people deplored feud that there was the justice of the feud at all; and James had clearly found that justice acceptable. The emphasis in the act itself is that the estates agreed on it, and the king then promised before them all that he would cease from giving remissions. When, therefore, in 1604 the council talked about the act as 'certane articles pennit be his Majesteis awin selff' we may assume that the king's own contribution can be most clearly seen in those sections of the act in which he was still involved, still using the old methods. But the instigators of the one significant change are introduced in the part which described the change, the insistence that the second kind of feud must be dealt with only by remedy at law: the people who would provide that remedy, the professional lawyers.[96]

Obviously their resistance to private settlement did not suddenly come into existence in 1598. Yet what is mainly apparent in the fifteenth and sixteenth centuries is the extent to which their attitude to the justice of the feud was, like that of the crown, favourable. There was much in common between their justice and the justice of the feud. Scots lawyers had long been accustomed to arbitration, which was regular practice by the thirteenth century. Formal arbiters and the more informal *amicabiles compositores* were familiar figures in judicial processes.[97] That part of *Regiam*

---

[95] *A.P.S.*, iv, pp. 158–9, c. 1, and pp. 233–5, c. 31. This last provision is comparable in intent to what happened in practice in England in 1221, when a man was hanged for murder in spite of making his peace with the family of his victim – a peace ratified by marriage and sanctioned by the sheriff – and the widow was amerced for discontinuing her appeal: Pollock and Maitland, *History of English Law before the Time of Edward I*, ii, p. 485. It is of some interest that sixteenth-century Scotsmen defined 'feud' so widely, including what was clearly non-violent dispute.

[96] *Basilikon Doron of King James VI*, ed. Craigie, i, pp. 83–4; *Register of the Privy Council of Scotland*, ed. Burton et al., vi, p. 594; I am indebted to Mr Keith Brown for this reference.

[97] T. M. Cooper, 'From David I to Bruce, 1124–1329', and David Maxwell, 'Civil Procedure', in *Introduction to Scottish Legal History*, pp. 9, 11, 414, 416; T. M. Cooper, *Select Scottish Cases of the Thirteenth Century* (Edinburgh, 1944), pp.

maiestatem which was based not on Glanvill but on Roman and canon law had a lot to say about them, and what it said was repeated in Balfour's *Practicks* in the sixteenth century, and in the seventeenth, in the *Major Practicks* of Thomas Hope, lord advocate of Charles I;[98] this reflects the frequent use, in central and local courts, of arbitration, a procedure whose popularity had been further encouraged in the fifteenth century by Scottish contact with the Roman Rota.[99] It has been suggested that 'this reliance on arbitration was bound to have a detrimental effect on the elaboration of the rules of law and slow down the pace of legal development in the fourteenth century'.[100] But it had a positive effect on the justice of the feud, for resorting to the arbitration of lord, kin or friends was very much part of the private settlement; the process which was a commonplace of legal procedure had its exact counterpart in the more informal private justice.

Moreover there was considerable overlap between the two. The Auld Lawes already show the development of a more formal kind of arbitration being used in the feud, when trustworthy men of the courts were called in. Equally, lawyers in the fifteenth and sixteenth centuries were entirely aware of the strength of kinship, when they were lobbied by kinsmen and friends of a man involved in a court action, or saw them actually coming into court on his behalf. Partiality in a judge was resisted; the judge with known connections with one of the parties to a case could be, and often was, prevented from hearing it, even if he was as important a figure as Archibald, earl of Argyll, hereditary justice-general.[101] But bringing one's kin and friends into court was entirely acceptable, provided they did not amount to a young army. Men were entitled to have at least a few 'maist honest wyss substantious freindis habill to gif counsall with thair advocattis';[102] no doubt the lawyers were prepared to tolerate this, so long as the friends reinforced, and did not replace, the advocates. And the pressure put on lawyers in advance of a case

xlix–l, lii–lv; P. Stein, 'The Source of the Romano-Canonical Part of *Regiam maiestatem*', *Scot. Hist. Rev.*, xlviii (1969), pp. 107–23.

[98] *Regiam maiestatem*, bk. ii, cc. 1–10, pp. 105–11; Balfour, *Practicks*, ii, pp. 411–17; *Hope's Major Practicks*, ed. J. A. Clyde, 2 vols. (Stair Soc., iii–iv, Edinburgh, 1937–8), ii, pp. 58–63.

[99] Robertson, 'Development of the Law', pp. 145, 147, 151–2.

[100] Stein, 'Source of the Romano-Canonical Part of *Regiam maiestatem*', p. 112.

[101] *Acts of the Lords of Council in Public Affairs 1501–1554*, ed. R. K. Hannay (Edinburgh, 1932), pp. 409–10; *Criminal Trials in Scotland*, ed. Pitcairn, i, pt. 1, pp. 163–6.   [102] *A.P.S.*, ii, p. 495, c. 15.

is marvellously illustrated by the engagingly blatant letters to Patrick Waus of Barnbarroch, senator of the College of Justice. He himself, before becoming a senator in 1576, had been asked to come to court in support of a kinsman; the request came from a laird who had the responsibility for producing his kinsman in court, and who said that he would do so, but honour demanded that he went along himself and brought others, including Waus, with him. And as a senator, Waus was the recipient of magnificent appeals to do only what was right and honest – and find for the kinsman or friend of the writer of the appeal: 'do nathing . . . bot quhilkis aggreis [but which agrees] with guid conscience and honesty, and to decern the eretabill richt of the landis to pertene to the Laird of Calderwoid', as John, Lord Hamilton, wrote on behalf of a relative.[103] Today, as Lucy Mair succinctly puts it, 'it may not be wrong that people should want to help their kinsmen, but it is wrong that they should be able to'.[104] In sixteenth-century Scotland it was not thought wrong; the kin turned up to help in the courts as they did in the localities.

Practice was reinforced by theory. The late sixteenth century did not only produce professional lay lawyers, judges and advocates to whom the kin and friends of their clients were a familiar sight. It also produced a little group of highly educated academic lawyers who looked at and tried to rationalize the great jumble that was Scots law. Throughout the whole period from the reign of James I onwards, there had been interest in the Auld Lawes, reflected in the number of surviving manuscript collections and the commissions set up to codify the laws.[105] Most came to nothing. But in the late sixteenth and early seventeenth centuries much was achieved through the work of Balfour and Skene.[106] They knew all about the justice of the feud in the past; and Skene's attempt to attribute *Regiam maiestatem* and much else besides to the great twelfth-

---

[103] *Correspondence of Sir Patrick Waus of Barnbarroch*, ed. R. Vans Agnew (Edinburgh, 1882), pp. 85–6 (1576 letter), 460 (Hamilton letter); other examples of such appeals are on pp. 317, 458.

[104] Mair, *Primitive Government*, p. 237.

[105] *A.P.S.*, i, pp. 21–30; Nicholson, *Scotland: The Later Middle Ages*, pp. 309, 428–9; *A.P.S.*, ii, pp. 10, 97, and iii, pp. 40, 89, 105; *Registrum secreti sigilli regum Scotorum*, ed. M. Livingstone *et al.*, i (Edinburgh, 1908), no. 1546.

[106] McNeill, introduction to Balfour, *Practicks*, i, pp. xxvii, xxxviii–xl; Cooper, introduction to *Regiam maiestatem*, pp. 1–5; Cooper, '*Regiam maiestatem* and the Auld Lawes', pp. 71–7 (with occasional inaccuracies in dates and references); *A.P.S.*, i, p. 24.

century king David I, the Scottish Justinian for these lawyers, shows the pride they took in the antiquity of their law. Thus in the highest legal circles of sixteenth-century Edinburgh, kin and assythment were not unsavoury relics of a less civilized age, but a part of justice which had all the aura and authority which ancient law could give.

The clearest evidence of the attitude of the lawyers, and also of the way in which the courts were beginning to take over the private amateur justice of kin and lord, is in the *Practicks* of James Balfour of Pittendreich. This was an early account of the substantive law of Scotland, based on the Auld Lawes and on citation of sixteenth-century case-law, written in the last decade (1574–83) of the life of a remarkable lawyer-politician, clerk register, lord president of the court of Session and, as the great eighteenth-century historian William Robertson described him, 'the most corrupt man of his age'.[107] However corrupt he was, his *Practicks* is an impressive work. Two sections of it describe the link between public and private justice: 'Anent slaughter' and 'Of assythment for slaughter'.[108] The first begins with what sounds like a voice from the past, the invocation of the law of Clan Macduff by one Alexander Spens, murderer of John Kynninmouth, who claimed the privileges of this law on the grounds that he was of the kin of Macduff. The claim was allowed by the deputy of the steward of Fife; the date was 1548. Balfour gives us no details about the content of the law. But he does show us a local kin-based law, turning up and accepted by a late sixteenth-century lawyer.

Thereafter he spends some time on the place of the kin and the principles of compensation. In writing about the kin and their responsibility for accusation against a murderer, he is heavily dependent on *Regiam maiestatem*. But his section on assythment reflects the extent to which the courts had become involved, for all his references are to court actions. His account begins traditionally enough: assythment or *kinbut* are given 'for skaith incurrit . . . and for pacifying of . . . rancour'. He then demonstrates how far the thinking about compensation had developed, a development already outlined in the Auld Lawes and evident in the act of 1425. Balfour provides the most detailed account we have of the criteria used in the attempt to assess realistically who lost most because of crime, and who therefore deserved most compensation. The crime,

---

[107] Balfour, *Practicks*, i, pp. xi–xxxii.   [108] *Ibid.*, ii, pp. 511–18.

the committer's substance and riches, the state of the murdered man and the number and age of his children were all to be considered. Most interesting are the provisions for the children. The person who should benefit least was the heir, who would in any case have his inheritance. Unmarried daughters should have twice as much as any of the sons, a provision entirely in line with the solution reached in the Chalmer–Drummond case. And bastards, although they did not have the right to raise an action for assythment, should have half as much as the legitimate children. This suggests an impressive degree of social concern and sophisticated thought about the problem of criminal liability, so much so that it is surprising to find it stated, in the otherwise excellent modern introduction to the *Practicks*, that 'it is clear that Balfour regards the apparatus of assythment, letter of slains and remission as a mode of escaping criminal liability as much as an item of reparation'.[109] That sees a clarity in Balfour which is not objectively self-evident, and confuses what was the essential point of sixteenth-century Scottish justice with a general problem of any judicial system.

Balfour's account is reinforced by the records of the acts of the lords of council and Session. One case which came before them – cited by Balfour, and recorded in terms very close to his own – was an action for assythment raised by Michael Fraser and his sisters for the murder of their father Andrew, against George Piat, who had obtained a remission at the justice ayre of Aberdeen; the lords of council directed the sheriff of Aberdeen 'to take cognition of the state, substance and degree of the said Andrew, the number, sex and age of his children, and of the wealth, state and condition of said George', and report accordingly. In a similar action raised by the kin of the murdered Huchan Lewis, the lords themselves set a time for proof to be made to them of the estate, degree and number of Huchan's children, and the value and substance of the murderer's goods.[110]

These cases, and Balfour's account, show the link between public and private justice. But they show something more. This was a period of extraordinary richness of evidence for the flourishing of an ancient kind of justice; at the same time it was the Indian summer of the blood feud in Scotland. The crucial point in Balfour's

---

[109] *Ibid.*, i, p. xlviii.
[110] *Acta dominorum concilii et sessionis, 1532–1533*, ed. I. H. Shearer (Stair Soc., xiv, Edinburgh, 1951), pp. 94–6.

description of assythment is that it was the judge who should decide the amount. This reflects the extent to which the sixteenth century was a period of transition. The lawyers never challenged the principles of the feud. They did something much more fatal; they approved of them and took them over. Their intervention inexorably worked against private justice. Whereas royal approval gave strength to amateur justice in the localities, the approval of the lawyers began to take kin-justice out of the localities and bring it into the developing world of the professional. At one level, law and legal procedures are the creation of the lawyers. Their very existence opens up and then widens the gulf between the lawyer bringing his specialist knowledge to bear on crime and civil dispute, and the layman imposing a practical but amateur settlement in language understandable to his fellows; there is a curious feeling of security in paying for something obscure, and that appeal seems already to have existed in late sixteenth-century Scotland. As the 'tired structure' of feudalism owed much to the early medieval lawyers,[111] so the decay of private justice owed much to those of the sixteenth century. Scottish society, becoming more literate, better educated, began to turn its attention away from the amateur to the professional. The so-called 'Education Act' of 1496, which directed eldest sons of landowners to learn 'perfyte Latyne' and then study law, was an early attempt to provide the local courts with judges with a training which enabled them to do more than apply common-sense rules.[112] A century later there was a clear distinction between the school- and university-educated lairds who rose in government, administration and the law, and those who remained in the relative isolation of their estates. In the fifteenth century dissatisfied litigants had come to council or parliament to have their cases heard by amateur lay lords backed up by trained clerical lawyers; in the sixteenth they came to the supreme central court in Edinburgh, where they found professional expertise and a high degree of self-confidence, for after 1532 the court of Session was successfully taking unto itself a much wider competence than it had hitherto possessed.[113] All these developments were slowly beginning to create a milieu in which formality, the forms and procedures

---

[111] Duncan, *Scotland: The Making of the Kingdom*, p. 408.

[112] *A.P.S.*, ii, p. 238, c. 3.

[113] A. L. Murray, 'Sinclair's *Practicks*' (lecture given at the Third Conference of British and American Legal Historians, Edinburgh, 1977).

of the law, the written authenticated record, had an appeal and an authority which would in the end far outweigh the amateur justice of lord and kin.

Even at the beginning of the seventeenth century, however, the process was very far from complete. In 1603 Francis, earl of Erroll, could still receive a bond of manrent and give a letter of slains on behalf of his kin in settlement of feud.[114] Even the act against feuding was only a partial attack. The lawyers themselves were described by an English observer in 1580 as being 'but few, and those about the Court of Session at Edinburgh, for in the shires all matters are ordered after the great men's pleasures'.[115] Moreover the new and powerful appeal of these lawyers lay primarily in the field of civil justice. As had always been the case, it was civil rather than criminal matters which provided the lawyers with most of their work; actions concerning land, rather than cases of murder, drove men to the professional lawyer with his knowledge, and the central court with its enhanced authority. If anything, the effect of this was to make the formerly hazy dividing line between civil and criminal justice very much more clear.

Yet this in turn began to affect criminal justice. The very success of the civil justice available in Edinburgh is the background to the heightening of the feeling, evident in the late sixteenth century, that criminal justice must be better organized, more efficient and regular.[116] Attempts to achieve this included the idea of using lords of Session as justices; these attempts were as yet ineffective, but they were a move towards a changing future instead of the reinforcement of a continuing past. And a few men were actively questioning that past. Alexander Arbuthnott, principal of King's College, Aberdeen, and a member of one of the commissions set up to codify the laws, wrote a neat little quatrain attacking the obligation to support one's kin.[117] Thomas Craig, the great

---

[114] Erroll Charters, New Slains, Aberdeenshire, 'Bonds of Manrent', no. 45; *Miscellany of the Spalding Club*, ed. J. Stuart, 5 vols. (Spalding Club, Aberdeen, 1841–52), ii, pp. 281–2.

[115] Quoted by Donaldson, 'Legal Profession in Scottish Society', p. 13.

[116] Dickinson, 'High Court of Justiciary', pp. 410–11.

[117] Quoted on the title-page of R. W. Munro, *Kinsmen and Clansmen* (London, 1971):

> I luif [love] justice, and wald that everie man
> Had that quhilk [which] richtlie dois to him perteine,
> Yet all my kin, allya or my clan
> In richt or wrang I man [must] alwayis mantene.

contemporary of Balfour and Skene, scathingly rejected *Regiam maiestatem* as having been fraudulently passed off as Scots law;[118] the impact of this at the time was minimal, for his work remained unpublished until 1655, but his was the voice of the future, heard and repeated by the 'greatest systematic writer' of all Scots lawyers, and the man regarded as the founder of modern Scots law, James Dalrymple, Viscount Stair.[119]

It was in the century after 1600 that the transformation clearly took place, the crucial period being the mid-seventeenth century. As late as 1633 Thomas Hope, 'the son of Balfour rather than the father of Stair', produced his *Major Practicks*, which was very much cast in Balfour's mould.[120] Fifty years later Stair's *Institutions*, a work of overwhelming influence, made it clear that private kin-based justice had gone. Assythment was now entirely a matter for the courts, of Exchequer, Justiciary and Session.[121] Moreover it was limited to cases of 'casuall' or culpable homicide, as distinct from cases of murder. In terrifying language, the parliament of 1649 had declared all remissions null; those who held them were to be pursued by the justice-general and his deputies, and punished by death, the punishment dictated

> both by the Law of God and Law or practick of this kingdome By which remissions and respits Gods law is presumptuouslie Dispensed with . . . The wholl Land polluted with sin . . . and the Lord provoked in his wrath to plague the Land and to doe justice upon the Inhabitants theirof becaus of the neglect of the magistrat heerin.[122]

Less than a decade earlier the God of the Covenanters had not yet made his wrath clear, and remissions and assythments were still linked together.[123] Now, this act was followed up by another which defined the restricted number of cases classed as homicide, to enable the justices to decide who merited death and who did not.

---

[118] Craig, *Ius feudale*, 1.8.11.
[119] James Dalrymple, Viscount Stair, *The Institutions of the Law of Scotland*, ed. J. S. More, 2 vols. (Edinburgh, 1832), i, p. 17, and ii, p. 624.
[120] *Hope's Major Practicks, 1608–1633*, ed. J. A. Clyde, 2 vols. (Stair Soc., iii–iv, Edinburgh, 1937–8), p. xv.
[121] Black, 'Historical Survey of Delictual Liability in Scotland', p. 59; see also pp. 63–4.
[122] *A.P.S.*, vi, pt. 2, p. 173, c. 95.
[123] *Ibid.*, v, p. 710, parliamentary proceedings, 1641; *ibid.*, vi, pt. 1, p. 235, commission to the Exchequer, 1644.

The man convicted of homicide was liable to imprisonment, or to a fine imposed by the court, to be used for the dead man's wife, children and nearest of kin.[124] A fine imposed by the court was the logical development of the sixteenth-century practice whereby judges determined the amount of compensation; but it had fundamentally changed the nature of assythment.

The hideous imagery of the act of 1649 introduces a new element: the dominance of the extreme Covenanters in Scotland, led by Archibald, marquis of Argyll, and that most tortured spirit of the age, Archibald Johnston of Wariston, lawyer and diarist, lord of Session since 1641 and lord clerk register from 1649.[125] The parliament of 1649, wholly reflecting the views of the covenanting party, produced in its legislation something which the church had sought, with no more than partial success, since the earliest days of the Reformation: the fusion of church and state in combating and punishing law-breaking not as crime against the human, but as sin against God. Hitherto Calvinist theology, with its stress on punishment by the magistrate as God's instrument, had made little impact on the justice of the state; in 1596, for example, the general assembly of the church had thundered impressively but ineffectually against the 'flood of bloodsheds and deadlie feids [feuds] . . . adulteries, fornications, incests . . . drinking and gluttony . . . universall neglect of justice both in civill and criminall causes, as namelie, in granting of remissions and respitts for blood, adulteries and incests . . .'.[126] In 1649, almost symbolically, the church and the law came together in the figure of Wariston; the wrath of God swept away the puny consideration of the wrath of the injured kin.

The more general question of the effect of the reformed church, with its undoubtedly profound impact on Scottish society, on the justice of the feud, can be raised here only very briefly. Calvinist emphasis on discipline, imposed in Scotland by a hierarchy of church courts, from the kirk session at parish level to the general assembly at national level, did cut across the traditional social hierarchy; for it was lairds and burgesses, not the nobles, who sat on

---

[124] *Ibid.*, vi, pt. 2, pp. 173–4, c. 96.

[125] *Diary of Sir Archibald Johnston of Wariston, 1632–1660*, ed. G. M. Paul, D. Hay Fleming and J. D. Ogilvie, 3 vols. (Scot. Hist. Soc., lxi, Edinburgh, 1911–40).

[126] *The Booke of the Universall Kirk of Scotland: Acts and Proceedings of the General Assemblies of the Kirk of Scotland from the Year MDLX*, ed. T. Thomson, 3 vols. (Maitland Club, Edinburgh, 1839–45), iii, pp. 874–5. See also D. Shaw, *The General Assemblies of the Church of Scotland, 1560–1600* (Edinburgh, 1964).

the local church courts, so that the nobility was now, at least in theory, subject to discipline by their social inferiors. Moreover the staggering success of the kirk sessions in rooting out and imposing ecclesiastical punishment for moral offences – usually sexual – and the undoubted concern of the reformers for the poor, which lay behind the formal recognition of the parish as the unit for organizing poor relief, do suggest a new level of institutionalization in dealing with problems formerly the province of kin and good neighbours. Yet kin and good neighbours were by no means replaced after 1560; and those on whom the church imposed its discipline were not, on the whole, those involved in the justice of the feud – once again there was a difference between the poor and the rich. The reformed church certainly had a role in gradually creating a different milieu and changing social attitudes, which would in time affect the whole of society; but on the justice of the feud, both locally and nationally, its impact seems to have been fairly minimal, except for the brief and short-lived period in the 1640s, when influential laymen were prepared to accept the judicial demands of an extreme Calvinist ministry.[127]

That there had been a change of attitude to the justice of the feud is, however, very clear by the late seventeenth century. In 1677 the earl of Strathmore commented, rather smugly, that castellated houses 'truly are quite out of fashion, as feuds are . . . the country being generally more civilised than it was of ancient times'; the centuries of condemnation of the feud had begun.[128] Five years earlier 'the trend towards professionalism was completed' when the

---

[127] My ideas have been much influenced by J. Bossy, 'Holiness and Society', *Past and Present*, no. 75 (May 1977), pp. 119–37, and his 'Blood and Baptism: Kinship Community and Christianity in Western Europe from the Fourteenth to the Seventeenth Centuries', in D. Baker (ed.), *Sanctity and Secularity: The Church and the World* (Studies in Church History, x, Oxford, 1973), pp. 129–43; also by discussion with Professor A. A. M. Duncan, Dr I. B. Cowan and Dr J. Kirk; and by Professor G. Donaldson's unpublished paper, 'Church and Community: The Changing Environment', which he kindly allowed me to read.

[128] Quoted by Donaldson, *Scotland: James V–VII*, p. 396. Further evidence of the changed attitude is found in David Hume, *Commentaries on the Law of Scotland respecting Crimes*, 2nd edn, 2 vols. (Edinburgh, 1819), i, pp. 284–5, which shows the confusion which already existed when he describes it as a 'point of controversy' whether assythment was damages or 'the remains of an old and barbarous usage, before the full establishment of public justice, when the criminal redeemed his blood, and pacified the resentment of the kindred, by the payment of a stated composition'. There was no idea of peace in the feud as far as this eighteenth-century lawyer and others from the late seventeenth century onwards were concerned, conscious as they were of their great system of 'public justice'.

high court of Justiciary, consisting of five lords of Session along with the lord justice-general and lord justice-clerk, was established;[129] this was, for criminal justice, what the court of Session had been for civil, in the sixteenth century. The blood feud and its justice had, in Scotland also, 'with marvellous suddenness' disappeared. The suddenness itself may be explained in the comparatively immediate terms of the effect of the Covenanters and the collapse of traditional lordship under the strains of civil war and Cromwellian rule. But this was only the tip of the iceberg. Far more crucial was the long-term impact of the lawyers, that group to whom, paradoxically, we owe so much of the extensive record of the Scottish blood feud, and also the reasons for its decline. All that remained after the mid-seventeenth century were a few actions for assythment coming before the courts until the late eighteenth century, and a final remarkable action raised in 1970, which sent the Scottish law lords into a flurry of inaccurate historical debate, and which ensured the final removal of this anachronism from the statute book. The action itself was of course unsuccessful; belatedly, and yet appropriately enough, the lawyers had a very definite last word.[130]

In his article 'The Bloodfeud of the Franks', J. M. Wallace-Hadrill writes: 'to the legal historian feud dies a slow inevitable death, yielding to the superior equity of royal justice; chaos and bloodshed give place to good order because they must. But it is possible to see the matter otherwise.'[131] In sixteenth-century Scotland crown, lawyers and landowners did see the matter otherwise. Their society was one in which the blood feud showed a remarkable ability to survive. It did so because a kind of justice originally associated, or apparently associated, wholly with the kin became integrated into the much more complex justice offered by kings, lords and lawyers. The evidence which this society has left us makes it quite clear that kings on the one hand were not necessary opponents, and extensive kindreds on the other not necessary prerequisites, of the blood feud. Kinship and its obligations were of fundamental importance. The remote kinsman was not. Men sought some kind of safeguard for possessions, livelihood, life, the

---

[129] Donaldson, *Scotland: James V–VII*, pp. 223–4; Willcock, *Origins and Development of the Jury in Scotland*, p. 45; Dickinson, 'High Court of Justiciary', pp. 411–12.
[130] Black, 'Historical Survey of Delictual Liability in Scotland', pp. 65–70.
[131] Wallace-Hadrill, 'Bloodfeud of the Franks', p. 146.

basic need met in societies such as modern Britain – with varying degrees of success – by 'state' justice, police force and insurance company. In early modern Scotland it was met, also with varying degrees of success, in part by royal justice and in part by the support of close kinsmen and of local friends and allies who were prepared to act as the kin were expected to do. The continuing localism of this society was far more relevant to the survival of the blood feud than massive kin-solidarity, for it meant that impersonal justice – though not impartial justice – was virtually inconceivable. Because of the essential smallness of environment, any Aberdeenshire assize, for example, was almost inevitably composed of dependants of the earls of Huntly and Erroll; jurors were thought of as witnesses who could tell one's side of the story, not as impersonal listeners to legal argument;[132] Huntly as sheriff was always the earl of Huntly, never the dehumanized robed representative of the justice that is blind. Justice was always seen in terms of personal intervention, personal support; and on that the justice of the feud depended.

Kings maintained its principles, because they offered the chance of order in the localities. Lawyers adopted them and made legal procedures out of them. But the lawyers, the professional élite, were both products of their society, and men peculiarly well placed to leave their imprint on that society. Their influence, not that of the crown, was decisive; the final decline of the blood feud came in the century after James VI's departure from Scotland in 1603, when Scottish monarchy was absentee monarchy, and effective control had passed to a privy council dominated by the new lay lawyer-administrators. The strength of their impact is seen in the speed with which they created a new milieu in the lowlands, in which men thought with pride of their modern civilized society and looked back with increasing horror to the barbarities of the past, forgetting or only half-remembering that there was any link between the compensation which was the basis of the justice of kin or lord, and the compensation awarded by the courts. And not only back; with the decline of the blood feud in the lowlands went an increase of suspicion and hatred of the highlander, and men looked sideways to the highland area of their country without understanding, but with embarrassment, fear and violent hostility.[133] To

---

132 Willcock, *Origins and Development of the Jury in Scotland*, p. 154.
133 The argument put forward in the latter part of this chapter clearly does not apply equally to all Scots in all parts of the country. The impact of the Edinburgh

lowland Scotsmen of the late seventeenth century, Moysie's comment would have been an embarrassment.

Only a century earlier it had not been an embarrassment, but a matter of general acceptance. Before James VI went to England he had offered his own comment on his feuding society: 'The most part of your people', he told his son, 'will ever naturally favour justice.'[134] He was quite right; and the blood feud had survived because they, like the king himself, found in the justice of the feud one answer to the perennial problem of crime and violence.

lawyers and administrators was much smaller, indeed minimal, in the highland area – which can be roughly defined as the area north and west of the Great Glen, rather than simply the area north of the Forth. The traditional values of that society were not significantly undermined until the late eighteenth century, and that is another subject altogether; but certainly the role of the government was to be crucial, as it had not been on the lowland blood feud two centuries earlier.

[134] *Basilikon Doron of King James VI*, ed. Craigie, i, p. 63.

6. *A Golden Age of Litigation: Castile, 1500–1700**

RICHARD L. KAGAN

In view of the supposed litigiousness of western society, it is odd that studies of lawsuits and litigants in European history should be so few. Rarely have historians examined who made use of the courts, for what purposes, and under what conditions. Further-more, the extent and character of litigation in past centuries, and, more importantly, its relationship to economic, social and political conditions remain practically unknown.

Whether this essay, restricted to a brief examination of Castilian litigation between 1500 and 1700 contributes anything whatsoever to these broader topics is best left for others to judge. My aim is simply to explore in this south-western corner of Europe what might be described as a 'legal revolution' – an age in which the formal adjudication of disputes was sharply and dramatically on the rise. I also intend to explore, albeit in a very tentative and speculative way, some of the reasons why this legal revolution, and the litigious spirit which accompanied it, gradually ran out of steam.

I

Castile was not the first European state to experience what I have called a legal revolution. The litigiousness of the medieval church prefigured that of secular society and by the late fourteenth century civil litigation was already commonplace in the city states and republics of northern Italy, the *bailliage* courts of France, and the central courts of London. But in the course of the late fifteenth and sixteenth centuries litigation, as the growing backlog of cases in most European courts would appear to suggest, assumed record proportions. In England, one recent study has demonstrated, even

---

* Parts of this chapter are reprinted from Richard L. Kagan, *Lawsuits and Litigants in Castile, 1500–1700*, by kind permission of the University of North Carolina Press. Copyright 1981.

a rapidly increasing supply of lawyers was unable to keep up with the growing demand for legal services.[1] Meanwhile, in France, Henry II in 1554 was obliged to create an entire network of new tribunals – the presidial courts – in order to keep up with demand. Admittedly, the French crown had its own reasons for creating these courts; it welcomed the opportunity to create, and to sell, a new variety of judicial offices. But in the decree (1554) establishing the *présidiaux*, it also acknowledged that 'the practice of litigation was never as commonplace nor as widespread as it is now'. This same document refers to litigation as a 'disease', as if to suggest that the habit of seeking legal redress was endemic in French society at the time.[2]

In Spain too something of a legal revolution was under way. The sixteenth century in Castile – heart of the Spanish monarchy in the sixteenth and seventeenth centuries – was an era when Castilians flocked in record numbers to settle their differences in court. Beginning late in the fifteenth century and continuing almost uninterrupted until the second quarter of the seventeenth century, the number of lawsuits climbed sharply, especially in royal tribunals which, by the middle of the sixteenth century, could barely cope with the demand. At the *chancillería* of Valladolid, for example, the most important of the monarchy's regional high courts, incoming cases flooded each of the ten *partidos* or administrative divisions into which new cases were filed. The records of these *partidos* are incomplete, but those of that known as *villa*, reserved for cases of a middling sort, indicate that the number of lawsuits registered went from 2,584 in 1560 to 3,550 in 1594.[3] By the end of the century the *chancillería* was receiving approximately 7,000 cases annually, a figure no other Castilian tribunal could match. Admittedly, only a fraction of these lawsuits ever reached final judgement, mainly because the litigants involved managed to settle out of court. Even

---

[1] See Peter Clark, *English Provincial Society from the Reformation to the Revolution: Religion, Politics, and Society in Kent 1500–1640* (London, 1977), and the essays by C. W. Brooks and Wilfrid Prest in *Lawyers in Early Modern Europe and America*, ed. Wilfrid Prest (London, 1981). Also useful is C. W. Brooks, 'Litigants and Attorneys in the King's Bench and Common Pleas 1560–1640', in J. H. Baker (ed.), *Legal Records and the Historian* (London, 1978).

[2] *Recueil général des anciennes lois françaises*, ed. M. Isambert, xiii (Paris, 1882–3), doc. 184, 'Edit d'érection des sièges présidiaux dans toute l'étendue du royaume'.

[3] *Libros civiles, cajas* 32, 35–6, 40. For more on this tribunal, see Richard L. Kagan, *Lawsuits and Litigants in Castile, 1500–1700* (Chapel Hill, 1981).

so, each of the sixteen judges attached to this tribunal was asked to work at a feverish pace. Writing at mid-century, for example, one judge tells us that

in view of the great number of litigants and the impossibility of dispatching all of their cases before Christmas, the heads of the tribunal's four chambers decided to put off decision of the major lawsuits until after Easter and to dispatch the others with alacrity. Thus in twenty-seven days we announced final decisions in 432 cases, a number which I myself counted. The intermediate orders (writs) I could not count because they are innumerable; normally, there are three or four times more writs than final decisions.[4]

In total, the number of lawsuits reaching final judgement at the *chancillería* rose from around 530 in 1500 to around 1,400 in 1580, an increase of well over 250 per cent and one that explains why its judges were so pressed for time.[5]

Busy as it was, the *chancillería* was not unique. Increases of a similar order were recorded in most of the crown's other tribunals, including the Royal Council of Castile, the kingdom's highest court of appeal.[6] In the meantime, many municipal and seigneurial jurisdictions attracted new litigants, although records for these courts, most of which dispensed justice orally, are exceedingly sparse. Little is known about church courts during this era, but the tribunals of the Inquisition throve on hundreds of cases of slander, 'injurious words' and blasphemy despite strong competition from secular courts.[7]

So great was the increase in the number of legal actions brought to Castile's courts that contemporaries could hardly fail to take note. In 1532 the Castilian Cortes complained that 'the number of lawsuits has grown and continues to grow so rapidly that cases

---

[4] 'La vida y cosas notables de . . . don Diego de Simancas', in *Autobiografías y Memorias*, ed. M. Serrano y Sanz (Madrid, 1905), p. 155.

[5] See Kagan, *Lawsuits and Litigants*, p. 6.

[6] Statistical data are not available for this tribunal until the seventeenth century, but qualitative evidence suggests that the number of lawsuits it dispatched was steadily increasing. See, for example, 'Advertencias que hizo Felipe II al Sr. Covarrubias cuando le elegio Presidente del Consejo (1572)', Biblioteca Nacional (Madrid), MS. 11261, in which the monarch, who was concerned that the council was spending too much of its time on legal business and too little on other matters of state, instructed Covarrubias to correct this imbalance.

[7] See Bartolomé Bennassar, *L'inquisition espagnole* (Paris, 1979), a collection of essays which examines various aspects of the work of the Holy Office.

cannot be dispatched with the speed that is necessary'.[8] Subsequent inspections of royal courts uncovered a 'multitude of lawsuits', 'crowded dockets', and long, interminable backlogs of cases which allowed some lawsuits to become 'immortal'.[9] Writing in 1566, Gabriel Monterroso y Alvarado, a scribe working in the *chancillería* of Valladolid, noted that 'lawsuits and conflicts among the populace are growing daily . . . ; already, the world is so engulfed and involved in these disputes that almost nothing is decided except by the cloth of legal judgement'.[10] His contemporary, Tomás Cerdan de Tallada, a Valencian lawyer, also acknowledged that 'lawsuits were multiplying', and in a book published in 1581 he attempted to explain why.[11] Some years later the humanist writer Baltasar Alamos de Barrientos calculated that at least three-quarters of Castile's population was regularly engaged in lawsuits.[12] His estimate is probably inflated, but nevertheless suggests the degree to which educated Castilians believed that theirs was a litigious society in which everyone, rich and poor alike, was accustomed to going to court.

The reasons for this dramatic increase in the volume of cases brought to Castile's courts are still poorly understood. Some contemporaries explained this phenomenon in traditional Augustinian terms. The saint had condemned litigation as evil; it was therefore apparent to many churchmen and moralists that the rise in litigation was the result of Castile's increasing godlessness and greed. 'What was once the art of lawsuits', wrote one scribe in 1566, 'has been converted into the art of lucre.'[13] In contrast, many lawyers argued that the monarchy was at fault since it had failed to reform Castilian law according to basic principles of Roman jurisprudence. Bad and confused law, they liked to point out, served only to foster the lawsuits about which everyone complained.[14] Bad and confused law, however, could just as easily have served as a deterrent to litigation and possibly encouraged

---

[8] *Cortes de los antiguos reinos de León y Castilla*, iv (Madrid, 1882), p. 638.

[9] The records of these inspections (or *visitas*) are housed in the Archivo General de Simancas (henceforward A.G.S.): Cámara de Castilla, *legajos* 2711–39.

[10] *Practica Criminal y Civil* (Valladolid, 1566), p. 2v.

[11] *Verdadero govierno desta monarchia* (Valencia, 1581), p. 88.

[12] Hispanic Society of America (New York): MS. HC 380/80, 'Advertencias politicas sobre lo particular y publico desta monarchia', fo. 133.

[13] Monterroso y Alvarado, *Practica criminal*, p. 2v.

[14] See, for example, Cerdan de Tallada, *Verdadero gobierno*, ch. 8.

disputants to settle their differences outside a legal forum. On the other hand those lawyers who argued that 'too many laws' were an important source of lawsuits were undoubtedly correct.[15] Beginning in the reign of Ferdinand and Isabella (1474–1503), Castile was inundated with an avalanche of royal decrees, laws and pragmatics which were gradually, but relentlessly, altering the fabric of Castilian life, from the way in which the price of bread was established to the way in which parents could bestow property upon their children. The Laws of Toro (1505), for example, liberalized rules concerning the establishment of entails (*mayorazgos*), paving the way towards widespread entailment of large portions of the Castilian landscape in perpetuity. *Mayorazgos*, however, violated traditional customs and usages which allowed for equality of inheritance among all heirs. The result was thousands of disputes over the creation of entails, the property rights of disgruntled heirs, and the amount of land which could be alienated for this purpose, many of which, given the importance of these issues, were likely to wind up in court.

Changes in the amount and substance of Castilian law were therefore instrumental in determining the amount of litigation brought to the courts. Litigation, however, as many modern legal scholars would agree, has to be explained in terms of a variety of factors, legal and non-legal. In Castile's case, it is clear that demographic growth and economic expansion were also responsible for the rise in litigation. Castile's land market in the sixteenth century has not yet been adequately studied, but it is certain that population increases put land at a premium and led directly to title disputes over lands which in earlier epochs had only been put to marginal use. Economic expansion also increased the number and the value of commercial transactions, thus increasing the likelihood of disputes on a scale sufficiently large to warrant a protracted lawsuit. Growth in the economy also contributed to litigation by helping to forge Castile's traditionally regionalized economy into a more unified whole, a development which resulted in commercial and financial disputes which went far beyond the capacity of local guild courts to resolve. Traditionally, guilds in Castile required their members to arbitrate disputes, without recourse either to lawyers or to a formal court of law, but in an age in which the orbit of these

---

[15] Sancho de Moncada, a noted *arbitrista* of the early seventeenth century, was one of these lawyers. See his *Restauración política de España* (Madrid, 1976 edn), p. 118.

merchants was expanding rapidly, they turned instead to lawsuits in royal tribunals which alone had the means to settle disputes on a national or even international scale.

Also contributing to the increase in litigation was the Habsburg monarchy. Determined to eradicate private violence and feud, the Habsburgs openly encouraged use of royal courts as a means of resolving disputes, since this was a means by which they could extend their influence in judicial matters at the expense of jurisdictions outside their control. Charles V (1516–56), schooled in humanist traditions of kingship, was also personally committed to the idea of a 'rey justiciero' and this was a view of monarchy that he passed on to his son, Philip II (1556–98). Accordingly, both of these monarchs did what they could to improve the quality of the justice rendered in their name. New tribunals were erected, trained jurists appointed as judges, and the sale of royal judgeships strictly prohibited. Furthermore, both Charles and Philip attempted to keep a close watch on their judicial officials, and strict penalties were meted out to those who did anything to tarnish the justice administered in their name.[16] Gradually, therefore, the king's justice achieved a reputation for honesty and fairness that encouraged Castilians to adjudicate their disputes before a royal judge. This is not to say that the king's justice was perfect, but for many it was far better justice than that offered by local and seigneurial courts, better too than simply 'lumping it' and forgetting about one's case. By setting a high standard of justice, the Habsburg monarchs contributed directly to the litigiousness of the times.

Who were the people in the sixteenth century to make use of the courts? The single most litigious individual in this society was, as might be expected, the king. Through his *fiscales* (royal attorneys), the monarch was annually party to thousands of cases involving the defence of the royal patrimony, challenges to the jurisdiction of royal officials, attempts to defraud the royal fisc, and a variety of other cases, both civil and criminal. The aristocracy was almost equally litigious. As property owners and heirs to vast landed estates, grandees and *títulos* were caught in an endless web of disputes over dowries, entails, inheritances, property rights and seigneurial obligations which, since the mid-fifteenth century, were

[16] The records of the *residencias* and *visitas*, the judicial reviews used by the Habsburgs to keep their officials in line, are housed in the A.G.S.: Cámara de Castilla and Consejo Real.

increasingly resolved by means of lawsuits. In addition, the aristocracy in this century was dragged almost continuously into court by peasants who considered a lawsuit in a royal tribunal the only effective means of challenging the power and authority of their lords.[17] As a result most of Castile's leading houses were obliged to retain expensive retinues of lawyers to advise them on legal matters and to protect their interests in court. The legal staff of the duke of Béjar, for example, numbered at one point nearly twenty.[18] So burdensome was the expense of litigation that a number of noblemen got into serious financial trouble. Among them was the count of Rivadavia who, in 1634, partly on account of his heavy legal debts, declared bankruptcy.[19]

The aristocracy was not alone in having to pay for the costly services of advocates, attorneys, solicitors and other legal agents. Continuous litigation required guilds, confraternities, hospitals, cathedral chapters, monasteries, municipalities, and a host of other institutions to keep a number of lawyers on hand. In 1585, for example, the city of Seville had no fewer than eighty-five different lawsuits pending simultaneously in a variety of courts, and to administer these and other legal business Seville was obliged to retain the services of at least twelve lawyers.[20] As for the aristocracy, the financial burden of these lawsuits was often more than many institutions could handle. Throughout the sixteenth century petitions came regularly to the king from towns and villages asking for permission to raise special taxes to pay for their mounting legal debts.[21]

Countless ordinary citizens also made regular use of the courts. Much has been made of the litigiousness of the painter El Greco, long time resident of Toledo, but the truth is that this artist was little different from other artisans and craftsmen of the Golden Age.[22] In

---

[17] As an example, see Ildefonso Mozas Agullo y Juan Bautista Vilar, 'Un conflicto de señoríos en la España del siglo XVI: Pleito, entre la villa de Alhama de Murcia y su señor el marques de los Vélez (1548–92), *Estudis* (Valencia), no. 6 (1977), pp. 27–70.

[18] Archivo Histórico Nacional: Osuna, *legajo* 249, secc. 1, fo. 1. In 1640 the duke had at least twenty-nine different lawsuits pending, fourteen in the *chancillería* of Valladolid, fifteen in the Royal Council of Castile.

[19] Archivo Histórico y Provincial de Valladolid: Protocolos, *legajo* 2019, fo. 403.

[20] Archivo Municipal de Sevilla: Secc. III, *tomo* 12, fos. 1–48.

[21] Many of these petitions can be found in the Archivo Histórico Nacional: Consejos Suprimidos, *legajos* 4043–53, 51362–65; and *libro* 1419.

[22] For more on the lawsuits of El Greco, see J. Gállego, *El Pintor de artesano a artista* (Granada, 1976).

the world of Castilian business, lawsuits were neither extraordinary nor unusual occurrences but commonly accepted means of determining ownership, establishing the value of goods sold and services rendered, and collecting debts. Creditors, for example, found lawsuits a useful means of harassing their debtors whereas the latter regularly employed lawsuits to put off their creditors and delay payment as long as they could. In this respect lawsuits were not dysfunctional expressions of a community unable to resolve its disputes, but an indication of how sophisticated Castilian business, even at the local level, had become. It is not surprising, therefore, to discover that in the royal *chancillería* of Valladolid 'nine out of ten litigants who come to this royal tribunal are tanners, dyers, innkeepers, and other tradesmen'.[23]

Were the mass of Castilians, the vast majority of whom were illiterate peasants and workers often lacking the funds to bring cases to court, as litigious as Alamos de Barrientos would have us believe? In theory the poor were entitled to free legal services, and many, according to available records, took advantage of this service to bring their cases to the attention of important royal courts. Case registers at the *chancillería* of Granada, for example, indicate that approximately 10 per cent of the lawsuits filed at this appellate court were labelled '*de pobres*' (of the poor),[24] and at the *chancillería* of Valladolid paupers initiated between two hundred and three hundred cases each year.[25] These included Marita, a slave, who in 1551 sued Antonio Alonso, resident of Alba de Tormes, 'for her liberty'; Juan de Hermosa, a poor peasant from Medina del Campo who sued a local shopkeeper 'over money'; and a woman from Traspiñedo whose suit against the governing council of that village in 1580 demanded that 'they send someone out of the town to go find her husband', absent for several years.

But such examples tell us relatively little about the ways in which ordinary Castilians made use of the courts. Presumably most of their cases were filed in local courts and of these only a fraction would ever come to the attention of an appellate tribunal such as the *chancillería*. Thus in order to reconstruct the uses of litigation

---

[23] A.G.S.: Cámara de Castilla, *Legajo* 2719, Visita to the *chancillería* of Valladolid (1589).

[24] Archivo de la Real Chancillería de Granada: Libros de repartimientos for the years 1594, 1600, nos. 547–8.

[25] Archivo de la Real Chancillería de Valladolid (henceforward A.R.C.V.): Libros Civiles, *caja* 32.

among ordinary Castilians it would be necessary to have at our disposal the records of courts of first instance. Unfortunately, the records of these tribunals – if they ever existed – have been lost with the exception of those of the *fiel del juzgado*, a judge with jurisdiction over the Montes, a poor, mountainous region just south of the city of Toledo.[26] Ordinarily, the *fiel*, or his lieutenant, heard cases on appeal from village magistrates, but his tribunal, especially in civil matters, also served as a court of first instance. Its records provide a good approximation of what litigation on the local level may have been like.

Having examined several hundreds of the cases which came to the *fiel* in the course of the sixteenth and seventeenth centuries, I have concluded that the inhabitants of the Montes generally employed the lawsuit as part of a larger strategy designed to force a settlement in what were ordinarily elaborate and protracted disputes. Thus in 1577 Juan Calderon, a resident of Navahermosa, took his illegitimate brother Alonso to court. Their father, Bartolomé Calderon, had recently died, and Alonso, the illegitimate son, had appropriated for himself some of the property belonging to the estate. Juan, citing laws which prohibited 'natural sons' from inheriting property, went to court in order to force Alonso to relinquish the property in question. But Alonso was determined to make it a fight. He claimed that the property in question only represented what 'my father owed me for the many years of service that I gave him'. And he added that Juan deserved nothing because 'he did not do any work around the house but spent all his time learning how to read, write and count'. Notwithstanding the logic of Alonso's defence, the village magistrate, in keeping with Castilian inheritance laws, found in Juan's favour; Alonso, reluctant to part with his property and perhaps thinking that a compromise might be arranged, appealed first to the *fiel* in Toledo and then, after another judgement against him, to the *chancillería* of Valladolid. Several years later the case was still pending at the *chancillería*, and Juan, who had not yet collected, complained that 'the appeal was only intended to postpone and hold up the execution of the judgement and to delay what is owed me'.[27]

The obvious intent of Alonso's appeal to the *fiel* was to force Juan

---

[26] The records of this tribunal are housed in the Archivo Municipal de Toledo (henceforward A.M.T.).

[27] A.M.T.: Pleitos civiles, Navahermosa, 1577.

either to abandon his case or agree to a compromise. Most of the other litigants who came before the *fiel* employed similar tactics, which seem to have been a rather effective means of resolving disputes. The vast majority of cases which came to Castile's courts never reached a final decision in court. At the *chancillería* of Valladolid – the only tribunal for which this kind of information is available – unfinished lawsuits outnumbered those which obtained a final judgement by a ratio of 15:1, a difference so large as to suggest that the parties involved were willing to compromise in order to bring the lawsuit to a halt. It would probably be right to assume that litigants in the *fiel*'s court were similarly inclined.

What did the inhabitants of Montes litigate about? Most of the cases which came before the *fiel* involved simple demands concerning breach of contract, violation of property rights, failure to pay certain debts; in other words, the kind of cases that one might expect to find in a small local court. Less important numerically were those involving family matters such as curatorships, tutorships, dowries and inheritance. Many of these involved women, particularly widows seeking to protect their property, dowries and estates. At least one-fifth of the cases heard by the *fiel* involved widows, typically one who was seeking to protect her dowry from her dead husband's creditors. Luisa de Aguilera, for example, began this kind of suit after her husband, Bernal Hernández, died in 1582 with debts amounting to over 11,000 maravedís (mrs).[28] This was not a lot of money but at the request of his creditors Hernández's property had been seized by a local magistrate. Luisa protested, and in a lawsuit filed in the *fiel*'s court, asked him to separate the goods belonging to her dowry from her husband's estate. The *fiel* so ordered and in similar cases involving widows he generally did the same. Ostensibly, the *fiel* appeared as a champion of widow's rights, but he was only acting in accordance with laws which stipulated that dowries, on the husband's death, were to be returned to the widow intact. In any event the recurrence of such cases suggests that widows in this male-dominated society, together with other women, looked regularly to the courts for aid and support.

With the exception of widows, it is difficult to identify all the litigants who came to the *fiel*'s court. It nevertheless appears that

[28] A.M.T.: Pleitos civiles, Ventas, 1583.

the most populous class in the Montes, the landless dayworkers (*jornaleros*) who constituted around 65 per cent of the region's inhabitants, rarely initiated lawsuits except as debtors seeking to halt a court-ordered seizure of their property. Appearing much more frequently were the region's *labradores*, the peasant prop- rietors who represented about 10 to 15 per cent of the local population. Their suits were supplemented by that of the region's small middle class – a mixed group of artisans, shopkeepers, innkeepers and itinerant merchants. The recurrence of such individuals in the *fiel*'s court can be easily explained. In the first place, as property owners, they had inheritances and investments to protect. Secondly, as small moneylenders and buyers and sellers of land, houses, livestock and other goods, they were certain to become involved in a variety of contractual and other disputes, many of which were destined to wind up in court. Finally, most of these artisans, *labradores* and merchants were literate. Presumably, they also knew about law, legal process and lawyers, and this special knowledge is perhaps the best explanation why this particular type cropped up with such regularity in the *fiel*'s court.[29]

But were the peasants and the other inhabitants of the Montes litigious, that is, eager to bring disputes and conflicts to court on a regular, recurring basis? Some, like Pedro Albarran, a rag dealer from Ventas, who was involved in at least three lawsuits in as many years, might be classified as such.[30] In contrast, most of the region's litigants resembled what one legal scholar has labelled 'one- shotters', or individuals who litigate intermittently.[31] Litigiousness, however, should not be thought of strictly in quantitative terms. Litigiousness is also knowing how to exploit courts and legal procedures for one's own advantage, how to wrap up a determined adversary in legal red tape, how to force a settlement out of court, and how to help one's lawyers plan a successful case. Litigants in the Montes used lawyers, but many cases, particularly those in the villages, were initiated without expert legal help. It appears, therefore, that the peasants of the Montes knew what litigation was like. These were no ignorant countrymen, duped and befuddled by

---

[29] For more about this region, see Michael R. Weisser, *Peasants of the Montes* (Chicago, 1977).
[30] A.M.T.: Pleitos civiles, Ventas, 1583–5.
[31] Marc Galanter, 'Why the Haves Come Out Ahead: Speculations on the Limits of Legal Change', *Law and Society Review*, ix (1974), pp. 95–160.

the complexity of legal process, but shrewd individuals well acquainted with the use of the courts. One scholar has recently described the complex and often confusing procedures of Castile's courts in the sixteenth century as resembling the Cretan labyrinth.[32] The image is apt, but this was a labyrinth through which, despite its complexity, most Castilians could easily find their way.

II

It may be surprising that Castile, a somewhat underdeveloped, largely pastoral country in which no more than 25 per cent of the male population was literate, could support a litigious society; but its litigiousness was part of a legal regime typical of much of early modern Europe, which was open and relatively unstructured, and granted to individuals considerable freedom in the way legal disputes were to be resolved.[33] It was as if Castilians of this era shopped around for justice in an open market-place. They lived in a quarrelsome, 'hair-trigger' society though they were gradually learning to sublimate their penchant for violence and channel conflict into the courts. But their reliance on lawsuits did not reflect any willingness to resolve conflicts peacefully: a lawsuit was generally considered an unwelcome, highly unsatisfactory method of obtaining justice, and most of the cases brought to the courts had the distinct marks of a fight.[34] They were passionate, frequently reckless and spontaneous, and generally conducted without reference to rules of gentlemanly conduct or fair play. In a word, litigation was untamed and, in the absence of a fixed set of courtroom procedures, subject only to a minimum of rules and restraints. The absence of checks helps to explain, for example, why taboos against fighting with members of one's own lineage were forgotten as lawsuits erupted regularly between cousins, siblings, even fathers and sons. The open, unrestrained character of litigation also helps us to understand why a litigant, in the middle of a lawsuit, could realistically ask the court to have his opponent

[32] I. A. A. Thompson, *War and Government in Habsburg Spain, 1560–1620* (London, 1976), pp. 45–8.
[33] See William J. Jones, *The Elizabethan Court of Chancery* (Oxford, 1967), p. 305.
[34] *Cortes de León y Castilla*, iv, petition 35, p. 638, and v, petition 111, p. 690. In these petitions, the Cortes complains about the disruptions and enmities which lawsuits produce and suggests that the king appoint an official arbitrator in every town whose job would be to see that lawsuits be kept to an absolute minimum.

provide him with the wherewithal to pursue his case.[35] Furthermore, litigation, owing perhaps to the lack of other kinds of suitable investment, served the interests of those seeking outlets for surplus cash: many lawsuits were purely speculative ventures, and the lack of consensus over what was permissible and right only multiplied such cases.

If litigation in the sixteenth century exhibited a distinct lack of restraint, it reflected the relative flexibility of a legal regime which was only on the verge of establishing a fixed set of rules, procedures and behavioural norms. Law in this century was still very confusing, even for supposed experts. Despite attempts at systematization, legal texts were frequently ambiguous and ill-defined, rules variable and changing. Law courts were equally unstructured, particularly local ones. Most were open, administrative forums performing tasks and services which in later centuries would be performed by a variety of non-judicial agencies, both in and out of government, and settled without recourse to adjudication. In the sixteenth century, every law court served multiple functions: commercial clearing house, family counsellor, land bureau and watchdog of public morals and behaviour.

This multiplicity was matched by a judicial market-place which, despite efforts by the monarchy to impose some sort of regulation, stubbornly refused to be regulated. Generally speaking, jurisdictional limitations were ill-defined, and even when they existed usually ignored by tribunals which actively competed with one another for business, aiming to improve their share of the judicial market and so augment their reputation. Rules governing this competition were practically unknown, and few of the kingdom's law courts hesitated to interfere in cases which legitimately belonged to another, to steal cases, or even to entice litigants away from other tribunals by offering preferential costs or by rearranging their timetable. The magistrates rarely involved themselves directly in these activities, most of which were handled by lesser judicial officers whose livelihood, like that of modern salesmen, depended upon the amount of business which they could drum up. In this

---

[35] A.R.C.V.: Reales Ejecutores, *caja* 981, August 1560, Pedro Arias de Avila v. Conde de Puñonrostro. Arias informed the *chancillería* that 'he had no money to continue the case since he was broke after selling his goods in order to pay for the lawsuit'. He asked the court to order Puñonrostro to advance him 750,000 mrs, which he needed to pay his attorneys and solicitors. The court, however, required the count to pay only one-third of that sum.

respect, courts of the sixteenth century were not passive observers of legal disputes, but interest groups, actively selling a particular brand of justice to the public.

Similarly, membership of the legal profession was open and constraints upon its members few, despite attempts by the crown to establish guidelines for 'professional' behaviour.[36] Its practitioners, taking advantage of a situation in which the demand for legal services probably outstripped the supply of available lawyers, reaped great profits without having to worry much about reputation, qualifications for practice, or ethical rules. Many in fact resembled legal adventurers, entrepreneurs who were willing – for a fee, of course – to pursue any kind of suit. One such practitioner, a certain Lic. Teruel, advocate at the royal *chancillería* of Granada, was known to 'take on unjust and desperate cases and to defend them with craftiness and cunning; he takes pride in this and, as a result, all of the deceitful litigants run after him shouting, "Teruel, take this one" '.[37]

Teruel was something of an exception, but the readiness of lawyers to take even the most trivial of cases to court is one other characteristic of a legal culture which, in contrast to that of later centuries, encouraged litigation as a means of resolving disputes. As we have seen in the case of Toledo's peasants, litigation was a device from which relatively few Castilians, even unschooled members of the peasantry, shied away. For one thing, familiarity with the law and legal process promoted it. To be educated in the sixteenth century was to be acquainted with the law, and thanks to the proliferation of legal dictionaries, handbooks and other manuals, most literate Castilians had at least some access to law and legal procedure. Many had also studied law at the university. Matriculations in the law faculties at Castile's universities during this epoch reached record heights, and at Salamanca alone, as many as 4,000 students a year matriculated in the law faculties, the majority of whom were sons of the gentry and middle classes interested in the subject primarily for reasons of education rather than career.[38] Meanwhile those who could not attend university or manage a law book learned about litigation through experience.

---

[36] See my 'Lawyers and Litigation in Castile, 1500–1750', in Wilfred Prest (ed.), *Lawyers in Early Modern Spain* (Baltimore, 1974), ch. 9.

[37] A.G.S.: Cámara de Castilla, *legajo* 2738, no folio.

[38] See my *Students and Society in Early Modern Spain* (Baltimore, 1974), ch. 9.

The law court, which was centrally placed in most villages and towns, served both as a school and a theatre, helping to teach the illiterate and semi-literate what litigation entailed. Indeed, it was principally by listening and watching that Castile's peasantry, her artisans and her women learned how best to manipulate the courts for their own advantage.

The result was a litigious population in which law courts served multiple functions and lawsuits were widely employed to satisfy a broad range of interests and aims. The courts' basic material consisted of disputes over contracts, inheritances, questions of jurisdiction and ownership, together with other issues concerning the conduct of public officials and the limits of seigneurial power. Courts, however, were also expected to rule on hazy areas of personal conduct and private behaviour. Damage suits over alleged insults, libels and other 'crimes' in which an affront to one's honour was the central issue at stake figure prominently in both lesser and higher jurisdictions. One reason for the recurrence of such actions was the monarchy's strong stand against duelling, yet it is also clear that the courts of this epoch were responsive to these 'honour' cases despite the hearsay quality of much of the evidence and the difficulties of separating fiction from fact. Little wonder then that Castilians, to borrow a phrase applied to English tribunals of this epoch, used their law courts as 'cockpits of revenge'.[39]

Of course, lawsuits involving libels, insults and related matters can be found in most other societies, and it is impossible, in view of the lack of comparative evidence, to know whether Castilians living in the sixteenth century were any more or less prone to litigation than Englishmen, Frenchmen or Italians. One thing appears certain. Litigation normally accounts for only a small fraction of the disputes and tensions to which society gives rise. In this regard, Castile was no exception. Yet, given the *laissez-faire* character of its legal regime, it is likely that the size of this fraction was, albeit by some unknown quantity, sharply increased.

III

A century later Castilians were still litigious, but the spirit of litigation, and indeed its character, had changed. In the first place,

[39] See William Willcox, 'Lawyers and Litigants in Stuart England: A County Sample', *Cornell Law Quarterly*, xxiv (1938–9), p. 541.

the king's justice had lost much of its authority and respect. The later Habsburgs, in sharp contrast to Charles V and Philip II, had little interest in the management and administration of justice. Responsibility passed into the hands of officials who were generally more interested in furthering themselves and their families than in promoting a just and efficient rule of law. In the course of the seventeenth century, therefore, standards of royal justice deteriorated, costs rose, and, in the process, the king's tribunals lost much of their previous clientele. The financial predicament of the monarchy made matters worse. Philip III (1599–1621), in order to get Castile's cities to approve a tax known as the *millones*, granted municipal courts the authority to consider cases previously decided by royal magistrates with the result that the volume of business in tribunals such as the *chancillería* of Valladolid fell off sharply. As early as 1635 scribes attached to this tribunal wrote to Philip IV complaining that 'we have nothing to do';[40] by the end of the century the number of cases dispatched by this tribunal was only about one quarter of what it had been in the days of Philip II.[41]

In consequence royal justice gradually became remote justice, difficult and expensive to obtain, while what was purveyed by municipal courts was subject to the whims of the narrow circle of patrician familes who governed most of Castile's cities and towns. Tied to the interests of a narrow socio-economic élite, these local courts commanded little in the way of authority and respect and therefore served as a deterrent to litigation, persuading the populace to resolve their disputes by other means. The state of the Castilian economy in the seventeenth century was such that less money was available for litigation, even among the nobility. In short there were fewer persons in a position to invest in lawsuits whose costs, owing to runaway corruption, had risen sharply. The flood of so-called 'minor' lawsuits which had choked royal tribunals in the sixteenth century receded, leaving behind a plethora of

---

[40] See the complaints of these officials in the Archivo de los Condes de Bornos, *libro* 110, letters of 15, 16 February 1635.

[41] Nor was the *chancillería* of Valladolid the only tribunal to suffer. The number of lawsuits completed at the *chancillería* of Granada declined by approximately 50 per cent in the course of the century (cf. Archivo de la Real Chancillería de Granada, *libros* 326–84, *de ejecutores*). The volume of legal business brought to the Royal Council of Castile expanded dramatically in the first part of the century, but by 1640 litigation at this tribunal registered a decline similar to that of the provincial courts, thus ruling out the possibility that administrative shuffling was the sole cause of the *chancillería*'s decline.

under-utilized courts whose magistrates and other officials were underemployed. This was certainly true, for example, in the Montes, whose population in the sixteenth century had demonstrated a remarkable skill in its ability to make use of the courts. Admittedly, this region by the late seventeenth century was probably more impoverished than most, but whether it was poverty, the cost of a lawsuit, or a growing suspicion of the efficacy and honesty of institutionalized justice, after 1660 the peasants of this region, judging from the records of the *fiel del juzgado*, rarely ventured into a civil court.

Accompanying this loss of legal business, and in some respects a cause of it, was a change in the character of litigation itself. Litigation in the sixteenth century had been unrestrained, the legal regime empirical, but by the end of the seventeenth century both were what can only be described as professional. By this I mean that litigation had lost much of its passion and spontaneity and instead had become rather cool and calculated in tone; it was less of a speculative or even a vindictive venture than a legal stratagem launched after considerable forethought and preparation and then only in certain, specified disputes. To be sure the change did not proceed evenly, and may in fact have been limited to the higher tribunals which, by the end of the century, dealt only with cases of major importance and worth. Presumably, in small village courts, older ways persisted, but in the cities, and above all in Madrid, a lawsuit was no longer a free-for-all but a carefully controlled contest conducted according to a fixed set of rules.

Although difficult to document, one cause of this change was economic; the high cost of litigating in major tribunals ruled out lawsuits of a frivolous, speculative and purely spiteful nature. Another was the gradual crystallization of procedural law and the development of a fixed body of rules which governed litigation in all parts of the kingdom. Credit for this development must go to the authors of practical legal handbooks such as Juan de Hevia Bolaños, whose *Curia Philipica* set a standard for all courts to follow. This enormously successful work, which dealt with a wide variety of procedural questions, effectively served as Castile's legal bible until well into the nineteenth century.[42]

Another cause was the emergence of a royal judiciary united in its

---

[42] The book was first published in Lima, 1603, and in Spain at Valladolid in 1605. Subsequent editions number at least twenty-three.

attitudes towards law and legal procedure. Royal magistrates in the sixteenth century were a relatively diverse group, but those who served in the king's tribunals in the seventeenth century were increasingly homogeneous in social background, education, career, style of life and experience. Unfortunately, little is known about what these judges thought, but as members of a legal caste, with close ties to the aristocracy, they appeared as defenders of order, property, and especially the institutions, that is the *Colegios Mayores*, to which they were attached.[43] They also tried to impose order on law and litigation, to do away with 'captious delays' together with the 'men who impede justice and its execution either by means of their pleas . . . or by other evil roads which disturb the peace and good government', and finally to create a world in which their privileges and those of the aristocracy would be guaranteed.[44]

Even more than the judges, it was the lawyers who were chiefly responsible for changes in the character of litigation brought to the courts. Advocates by the end of the century showed numerous signs of professional behaviour, especially in Madrid where the important legal work of the kingdom was increasingly concentrated. Their quest for gentility and recognition by the king had led to the organization of colleges, new rules of ethical conduct and behaviour, and even regulations barring practitioners of base and ignoble birth.[45] Attorneys had similar pretensions, and their efforts to achieve higher standards were instrumental in the demise of that symbol of legal entrepreneurship, the solicitor, who was institutionalized by Philip IV and turned into a docile officer of the court.[46] At first these changes were limited to Madrid, but by the eighteenth

---

[43] J. Fayard's otherwise admirable work, *Les membres du conseil de Castile à l'époque moderne (1621-1746)* (Geneva, 1979), says relatively little about the ideas and politics of the judges who served on this council. More helpful is Jean-Marc Pelorson, *Les letrados: juristes castillians sous Philippe III* (Poitiers, 1980).

[44] Juan Alonso Bustamente, *Discurso sobre gobierno eclesiástico* (Granada, 1624), p. 1v.

[45] See Kagan, 'Lawyers and Litigation in Castile, 1500–1750'.

[46] Spanish solicitors (or *solicitadores*) were legal agents who had established legal practices independent of the judges' (and the monarchy's) scrutiny and control. The established attorneys (or *procuradores*) complained bitterly about these legal 'upstarts', and a determined effort on their part to rid themselves of this unwelcome competition helps to explain why Philip IV in 1632 banned *solicitadores* from practising in the crown's tribunals. They were replaced by a limited number of '*agentes de negocios*' who were initially required to buy their offices for 450 ducats apiece.

century they had spread to other parts of the kingdom as well. The establishment of provincial '*colegios*' for both advocates and attorneys in this century suggests that the seeds of a closely knit profession had been planted on a national scale.

It might be going too far to suggest that these efforts on the part of Castile's advocates to organize themselves, establish new standards of recruitment and discipline, and improve their social standing and prestige were akin to modern processes of 'professionalization', but whatever we call it, it is certain that the advocates helped to reshape the nature of litigation in Castile. In the sixteenth century advocates, especially those who worked for the great nobles and municipal corporations, served their clients more as loyal servants than as independent legal experts solicited for counsel and advice. A century later, in Madrid at least, the opposite was true. Melchor Cabrera Núñez de Guzmán even suggested that advocates should not automatically accept a client's case, but rather act as 'first judge' and decide whether litigation was desirable or necessary.[47] Of course, the so-called 'hedge' lawyers who worked on the basis of contingency fees and who deliberately cheated their clients by needlessly fomenting litigation or writing superfluous briefs still abounded. But in larger cities, and especially in Madrid, established advocates, seeking to create an image of themselves as responsible practitioners worthy of promotion to the royal bench, probably acted as a brake upon litigation, reminding clients of the unnecessary costs and delays a lawsuit would incur. Cabrera Núñez, spokesman for the advocates who belonged to the important *colegio de abogados* of Madrid, instructed advocates to work independently on a salaried basis, and to reject any case in which they had a personal stake. These practitioners were also those responsible for developing new modes of arbitration and other devices designed to ensure their importance to the legal process yet also designed to keep their clients out of court.

Unfortunately, little is known about Castilian methods of arbitration. The law itself had allowed for '*escrituras de compromiso*' since the middle ages, but information about these agreements is scattered and incomplete. Apparently, the procedures involved were relatively simple. The disputants, many of whom were already locked in litigation, designated two or more

---

[47] *Idea de un abogado perfecto* (Madrid, 1683), ch. 14.

advocates to serve as arbitrators. The advocates were then given a set period of time (frequently twenty days) in which to work out an equitable solution of the dispute in question. In the case of Maria Guillamas, who had several lawsuits pending with her son, the advocates, one representing either party, were given the power 'to look over the lawsuits and competing claims' and then, 'either orally or in writing' and 'either keeping or not keeping to the judicial form', to arrange for a compromise settlement. Once the decision was reached, the parties further agreed to pay a stiff indemnity should either 'continue with any of the lawsuits pending or threaten new ones'.[48]

It is impossible to keep track of these settlements or even to estimate how many there were. Examples garnered from notarial archives in Madrid and Valladolid suggest that relatively humble persons as well as nobles entered into them. Naturally, an element of risk was involved; enforcement of the compromise was difficult; in many cases it provoked a new lawsuit. There is little doubt, however, that this procedure provided an alternative to litigation and for this reason it was probably promoted by the advocates themselves, particularly in the seventeenth century when court costs were steadily on the rise. By acting as arbitrators, advocates could earn as much as by going to court; they also benefited since the money they earned from arbitration was not subject to any limitation whereas that earned from litigation was.[49] Advocates, therefore, had every reason to eschew lawsuits since they could offer their clients an alternative yet still legalistic method of terminating disputes.

What I am suggesting is that the legal profession itself was instrumental in subjecting the *laissez-faire* legal culture typical of the early Habsburg era to new professional constraints. They established new ground rules concerning litigation, use of the courts, and even limits on the jurisdiction of individual magistrates and courts, regulations which in the course of the eighteenth century would gradually be written into law. In a sense, they provided order where there had only been chaos, but they did so

---

[48] Archivo Histórico y Provincial de Valladolid: Protocolos, *libro* 2019, fo. 171.
[49] Royal laws stipulated that advocates were to receive fees worth no more than 1/20 of the value of a case, with a maximum ceiling set at 30,000 mrs. Advocates resented these restrictions and found innumerable ways to avoid them. Their receipts, however, were subject to periodic scrutiny and control.

less in the name of reason than to augment their own authority, reputation and prestige.

Thanks to the lawyers, as Castile entered the eighteenth century a new 'professionalized' judicial culture was gradually taking shape. Courts were becoming specialized institutions, limited in jurisdiction and scope; indeed, by the end of the century many of their administrative and executive duties – legacies of an earlier epoch – would have been stripped away. Litigation was also subject to new restraints, and would in fact diminish in importance as more and more of the administration of law and of justice was dispatched without recourse to a formal lawsuit. Lawyers were thus able to appropriate for themselves many of the functions previously performed by magistrates, private servants and friends. Acting, alternately, as legal experts, counsellors and arbitrators, they had constructed a new legal order which paralleled that of the courts but was independent of external supervision and governmental control. The primary aim of this order was to promote harmony and minimize disputes, but in doing so, it increased the dependence of the lay public upon lawyers while ensuring for lawyers a new importance and respect.

For centuries, lawyers throughout Europe had served as the agents of a pragmatic world in which the law would be set free from the over-riding concerns of God, church and state and allowed to develop independently along the lines established by the lawyers themselves.[50] This law, as it emerged in Spain, would be national in character, rooted in custom rather than in Rome, and justified by the history and traditions of Spain itself. Not surprisingly, it was also designed to enhance the primacy of lawyers, and in this respect the lawyers of Castile were the architects of their own lasting success. Towards this end litigation was tamed, courts curtailed, and even the monarchy persuaded that lawyers merited promotion to higher places.

What I have attempted in the latter part of this essay is to suggest some of the reasons why the litigiousness characteristic of Castile's Golden Age was gradually curtailed. Castile, however, was not the only European state to experience this transition. Studies of litigation patterns in early modern Europe are relatively few, but there is evidence to suggest that the incidence of litigation, after

[50] Cf. William S. Bouwsma, 'Lawyers and Early Modern Culture', *American Historical Review*, lxxviii (Apr. 1973), pp. 303–27.

having reached a peak in the early part of the seventeenth century, declined gradually in the course of the late seventeenth and eighteenth centuries.[51] Castile's experience with litigation might then serve as a starting-point for the systematic study of lawsuits in other parts of pre-industrial Europe.

[51] See, for example, Wilfrid Prest, 'The English Bar, 1550–1700', in Prest, *Lawyers in Early Modern Europe*, and Colin Kaiser, 'The Deflation in the Volume of Litigation at Paris in the Eighteenth Century and the Waning of the Old Judicial Order', *European Studies Review*, x (July 1980), pp. 309–36. For continuing shrinkage in the nineteenth century see V. Aubert, 'Law as a Way of Resolving Conflicts: The Case of a Small Industrialized Society', in Laura Nader (ed.), *Law in Culture and Society* (Chicago, 1969), pp. 282–303. See also José-Juan Toharia, *Cambio social y vida jurídica en España* (Madrid, 1974) and B. Schnapper, 'La litigiosité en France au XIXᵉ siècle', *Annales E.S.C.*, xxxiv (Feb.–Mar. 1979), pp. 399–419.

7. 'Such Disagreement betwyx Neighbours': Litigation and Human Relations in Early Modern England

J. A. SHARPE

It would not, perhaps, be too much of an exaggeration to say that historical writing over the last decade has promoted a new 'conventional wisdom' about the nature of human relationships in the pre-industrial English village. Earlier interpretations of this subject, which emphasized the mutual co-operation thought to be natural to the inhabitants of such settlements, have been rejected, and the tendency to idealize and romanticize the concept of 'the community' in the past exposed as fallacious.[1] Instead, an interpretation has arisen which stresses the degree of potential disharmony within the village, and the high price at which such harmony as did exist was obtained. This development can be demonstrated by reference to the works of two of the major practitioners of early modern English social history, Keith Thomas and Lawrence Stone. Mr Thomas, in his description of how suspicion of witchcraft might be focused on certain individuals, remarks on the 'tyranny of local opinion and lack of tolerance displayed towards nonconformity or social deviation' current in the sixteenth and seventeenth centuries. Communities within which such values flourished formed a 'tightly-knit, intolerant world', where social nonconformity could be easily detected, and combated by means ranging from the skimmington to indictment at the assizes.[2] This view of village life in earlier times has been taken further by Professor Stone in his history of the family and sexual

---

[1] For a recent critique of 'the myth of the community', see Alan Macfarlane, Sarah Harrison and Charles Jardin, *Reconstructing Historical Communities* (Cambridge, 1977), pp. 1–4. Macfarlane's ideas on the subject are developed further in his article 'History, Anthropology and the Study of Communities', *Social History*, no. 5 (May 1977), pp. 631–52. These ideas are themselves criticized by C. J. Calhoun, 'History, Anthropology and the Study of Communties: Some Problems in Macfarlane's Proposal', *ibid.*, iii (1978), pp. 363–73.

[2] Keith Thomas, *Religion and the Decline of Magic* (London, 1971), pp. 526–30.

relations. He comments on the 'lack of warmth and tolerance in interpersonal relations at the village level', and declares that 'the Elizabethan village was a place filled with malice and hatred, its only unifying bond being the occasional episode of mass hysteria, which temporarily bound together the majority in order to harry and persecute the local witch'.[3] Although other more limited and cautious studies have implied that this view may be somewhat pessimistic,[4] the main drift of current thinking suggests that human relationships in the pre-industrial English village were more likely to have been tense or hostile than otherwise.

Those supporting such a view might, and indeed do, derive considerable backing from the taste for litigation which was so obviously a major feature of life in the Tudor and Stuart periods. The litigiousness of the English was already well established in the Middle Ages,[5] became a notable element of aristocratic and gentry life in the sixteenth century as lawsuits became more fashionable than personal violence,[6] and was also apparently current among the lower orders.[7] Practically every court, whether civil or criminal, experienced an increase in business between the mid-sixteenth and mid-seventeenth centuries, and the degree of individual participation in legal proceedings could be remarkable. In the 1630s William Powell, a pluralist Welsh vicar, attempted to further a feud with one of his parishioners by commencing twenty-six suits against him in a six-year period, involving him in legal action in seven courts ranging from the local Consistory to the King's Bench.[8] In Wiltshire, at a slightly earlier date, disputes between three gentry and yeoman families led to litigation in the county quarter sessions, the local Consistory court, Star Chamber, Common Pleas, King's Bench and

[3] Lawrence Stone, *The Family, Sex and Marriage in England, 1500–1800* (London, 1977), p. 98.
[4] See for example, the discussion of kinship and neighbourliness in David G. Hey, *An English Rural Community: Myddle under the Tudors and Stuarts* (Leicester, 1974), pp. 209–18.
[5] As D. M. Stenton pointed out, 'the medieval Englishman was incurably litigious': *The Earliest Lincolnshire Assize Rolls*, ed. Stenton (Lincoln Record Soc. publications, xxii, 1926), p. xvii.
[6] Lawrence Stone, *The Crisis of the Aristocracy 1558–1641* (Oxford, 1965), pp. 240–2.
[7] For a perceptive study of this topic see M. J. Ingram, 'Communities and Courts: Law and Disorder in Early-seventeenth-century Wiltshire', in J. S. Cockburn (ed.), *Crime in England 1550–1800* (London, 1977).
[8] Stone, *Crisis of the Aristocracy*, p. 241.

Chancery.[9] Such cases were doubtless exceptional, but the number of contacts that the early modern Englishman had with legal process remains striking. In the Essex township of Earls Colne, it has been discovered, a thousand inhabitants experienced some two hundred such contacts, ranging from proving a will to involvement in an accusation of theft, between 1589 and 1593.[10] Even if we accept that most of these contacts were necessary, fairly trivial, and in no way malicious, there would still seem to be some justification for those contemporary commentators who numbered litigiousness in the compendium of sins to which the early modern English were addicted. The preacher of an assize sermon at Norwich in 1619, for example, felt moved to censure the current popularity of 'frivolous suites, of trifling trialls, which a Common Yeoman were Iudge fitte enough to end in his chaire at home'. Continuing his attack upon the litigious, he declared that 'upon every occasion to go to Law, is to be an Outlaw of God, whose whole Law is fulfilled in Love'.[11] Despite such exhortations, the court records of the period contain numerous examples of eager or over-eager participants in lawsuits.

The frequency and geographical spread of references to the subject indicate that launching suits on slight or malicious grounds, with an intention to further a feud, was a national problem. The articles against a Staffordshire man, subject of a complaint to the county bench in 1591, described him as

> a comen pyker of quarrels a comen haunter of Alehouses a dronkard and a comon mayntener and partaker of dyvers and manye accions and sutes that have growed . . . within the parish of Norton and Lyttle Wyrley to the great disagreement trouble and expense of moste of the neigbours there.[12]

A few years later John Barret, another man complained against to the Staffordshire magistrates, had allegedly paid an attorney £22 a year for 'suytes in lawe', which was felt to have contributed to 'the Impoveryshinge of manye poore people'.[13] In 1608 complaints were

---

[9] Ingram, 'Communities and Courts', p. 120.

[10] Macfarlane *et al.*, *Reconstructing Historical Communities*, p. 183.

[11] Samuell Garey, *A Manuall for Magistrates: Or a Lanterne for Lawyers: A Sermon Preached before Iudges and Iustices at Norwich Assizes, 1619* (London, 1623), p. 55.

[12] *Collections for a History of Staffordshire: The Staffordshire Quarter Sessions Rolls, vol. II 1590–1593*, ed. S. A. H. Burne (William Salt Archaeological Soc., 1930), p. 1.

[13] *Collections for a History of Staffordshire: The Staffordshire Quarter Sessions Rolls, vol. V 1603–1606*, ed. S. A. H. Burne (Staffordshire Record Soc., 1940), p. 212.

sent to the Somerset bench about Jeffrey Smith, clerk of West Hatch, who was alleged to have stirred up 'many frivolous actions' against his parishioners.[14] Some twenty years later in the same county John Fackrell, describing himself as a 'very poore and impotent person', reported that vexatious suits brought against him at the instigation of a local enemy were leading to 'the utter undoeing of the said John Fackrell, his wife and children'.[15] The victim of a vexatious or malicious suit could, of course, seek more direct remedies than those offered by complaint to the quarter sessions. In 1680 the northern assizes heard how William Batley, a Leeds yeoman, had reacted to being sued by a local knight. Batley had declared his intention of being revenged on his adversary by committing perjury against him in a lawsuit; according to one witness, he was consulting no less than four almanacs in the hope of finding the most propitious time for so doing.[16] These examples, which could be multiplied, obviously provide ammunition for those seeking to portray the rising litigation of the sixteenth and early seventeenth centuries as an indicator of generally hostile human relationships in the period.

One of the types of litigation most peculiar to the age, and one which is especially unfamiliar to the first-hand experience of the modern historian, was that constituted by suits for defamation. The history of the law of defamation is complex, not least in the sixteenth century when the law concerning verbal abuse was in an uncertain and evolutionary phase.[17] Up to about 1500, slander had been the concern of the ecclesiastical courts, or of local tribunals. From that date the common law courts began to interest themselves in this type of suit, and rapidly developed a wide cognizance in this area. This extension was obviously a response to a growing demand by would-be litigants over words: it seems that the inhabitants of

[14] *Quarter Sessions Records for the County of Somerset, vol. I, James I, 1607–1625*, ed. E. H. Bates (Somerset Record Soc., xxviii, 1907), p. 22.

[15] *Quarter Sessions Records for the County of Somerset, vol. II, Charles I, 1625–1639*, ed. E. H. Bates Harbin (Somerset Record Soc., xxiv, 1908), p. 63.

[16] *Depositions from the Castle of York Relating to Offences Committed in the Northern Counties in the Seventeenth Century*, ed. James Raine (Surtees Soc., xl, 1861), pp. 246–7.

[17] For two good recent discussions of the law of defamation in this period see S. F. C. Milsom, *Historical Foundations of the Common Law* (London, 1969), ch. 13, 'The Rise of the Modern Law of Torts', especially pp. 332ff.; and *The Reports of Sir John Spelman*, ii, ed. J. H. Baker (Selden Soc., xciv, 1977), 'Introduction', pp. 236–47.

Tudor and Stuart England were extremely sensitive to slights against their good name. The exact reasons for this sensitivity remain obscure, but its impact on the courts is undeniable. From the mid-sixteenth century onwards, the tribunals of both the common and ecclesiastical law experienced a rapid increase in the number of suits for defamation. This increase, and the related growth in the complexity of the law of defamation, has attracted considerable attention from legal historians; so far, however, this marked expansion of litigation over matters of honour and reputation has been of little concern to the social historian.[18] This is unfortunate, as the subject obviously offers an important perspective on certain aspects of the mentality of our Tudor and Stuart forebears; it is no accident that Professor Stone should adduce 'back-biting' and 'malicious slander' as evidence of the lack of affective relationships in the Elizabethan village.[19] A study of defamation suits, it could therefore be argued, might illuminate some important areas of social attitudes in the past.

There are a number of surviving bodies of archival materials from sixteenth- and seventeenth-century courts upon which this study might be based. The records of the ecclesiastical courts at York must be among the more voluminous and rich of these.[20] York, as the administrative centre of the northern province, was the location of a number of church courts, three of which had jurisdiction over defamation. In the number of suits dealt with, the two most

[18] Two historians who have attempted to view defamation in its social context, both of them using ecclesiastical court materials, are C. A. Haigh, 'Slander and the Church Courts in the Sixteenth Century', *Transactions of the Lancashire and Cheshire Antiquarian Soc.*, lxxvii (1975), pp. 1–13; and M. J. Ingram, 'Ecclesiastical Justice in Wiltshire, 1600–1640, with Special Reference to Cases Involving Sex and Marriage' (Univ. of Oxford D.Phil. thesis, 1976), ch. 9, 'Defamation Causes'.

[19] Stone, *Family, Sex and Marriage*, p. 98.

[20] The work of the church courts at York in the late sixteenth and early seventeenth centuries is described in R. A. Marchant, *The Church under the Law: Justice, Administration and Discipline in the Diocese of York, 1560–1640* (Cambridge, 1969). Post-Restoration developments are covered by Barry Till, 'The Ecclesiastical Courts of York 1660–1883: A Study in Decline' (unpublished typescript deposited at the Borthwick Institute of Historical Research, York, 1963). The most detailed account of the functioning of the York courts in the period with which this chapter is concerned, however, remains Carson I. A. Ritchie, *The Ecclesiastical Courts of York* (Arbroath, 1956). The records of these courts form much of the subject-matter of J. S. Purvis, *The Archives of the York Diocesan Registry* (St Anthony's Hall publications, ii, 1952).

important were the Consistory court and the Chancery court, while the Dean and Chapter court, which had a peculiar jurisdiction over a number of parishes, also heard a steady trickle of cases dealing with slander. For these courts, as for so many others in early modern England, such cases formed one of the main areas of business. Causes for defamation rose steadily from about 1560, and stayed high until the Civil Wars put a temporary stop to the activities of the church courts. When they resumed operations after the Restoration, suits for slander began to increase, and by the early eighteenth century were again a numerically important part of the courts' business.[21] Exact statistics relating to fluctuations in this type of litigation have yet to be worked out, but some impression can be gained from samples. These show that something like a third of new causes entering the Consistory court in the 1590s,[22] about a third of those entering the Chancery court in the 1630s,[23] and the overwhelming majority of those entering the Chancery at the turn of the seventeenth and eighteenth centuries,[24] were for defamation.

First appearances, therefore, would seem to confirm the impression that defamation was an important source of litigation in this period, and that the contemporary Englishman was unusually willing to protect his reputation through waging law. Moreover, the details of some of these defamation suits do much to support the view that the litigation of the period is a useful index of the supposedly permanent undercurrent of antipathy between individuals: certainly such cases as that involving two servant-girls in neighbouring houses in post-Restoration York which was eventually pursued on appeal to the Court of Delegates, do indicate a degree of interpersonal tension.[25] A closer examination of the records, however, suggests a rather more complex situation. If we turn to the Dean and Chapter court act book covering the mid-1590s, we find that between the beginning of January 1596 and the end of December 1598 twenty-seven causes for defamation

21 The extent and nature of the defamation business coming before the ecclesiastical courts at York are discussed more fully in J. A. Sharpe, *Defamation and Sexual Slander in Early Modern England: The Church Courts at York* (Borthwick papers, lviii, 1980).
22 Marchant, *Church under the Law*, table 8, p. 62.
23 *Ibid.*, table 9, p. 68.
24 Till, 'Study in Decline', p. 250.
25 Borthwick Institute of Historical Research, Consistory court cause papers, C.P. H/2758.

were initiated.[26] This fits neatly into the expected pattern, defamation forming between a third and a half of all business, and rivalled in numerical importance only by tithe disputes. However, of these twenty-seven causes, only five continued to a decision and final sentence against the defendant. This small sample of suits suggests that people were very willing to initiate litigation, but were considerably less willing to fight a suit through to its conclusion. This, of course, raises obstacles for any interpretation which portrays the rising litigiousness of the age as an indication of intrinsically sour social relationships.[27] Any student of the litigation of this period must address himself to the task of discovering what factors were in operation when suits were discontinued.

In many cases, naturally enough, proceedings were dropped when the initial anger which had prompted legal action cooled, and the plaintiff became aware of the costs and trouble that litigation invariably involved. Court fees and legal advice could be expensive, while litigants would have to meet other costs; it was customary, for example, to reimburse witnesses for any expenses or loss of earnings they might have incurred while giving evidence. Calculating the average cost of a suit is difficult, but it has been estimated that fighting a suit through to its conclusion at the York courts in the later seventeenth century would probably have entailed spending £8, a fair sum at a time when a labourer would do well to earn more than a shilling a day.[28] As might be imagined, although a short-lived anger might encourage the launching of a suit, the outlay of considerable amounts of time and money would be a daunting prospect for a poor litigant, especially if he or she lived in an up-country or coastal parish forty or fifty miles from York. Many causes, we must therefore conclude, were simply dropped once passions had cooled. There is, however, suggestive if scattered evidence that more positive factors might work towards the early termination of a suit.

This evidence consists of the numerous cases where those involved in litigation attempted to end their differences out of

---

[26] Borthwick Institute of Historical Research, D/C AB 8, fos. 51–188v.

[27] Preliminary work on the criminal archives of other countries suggests that this phenomenon was by no means limited to England: for evidence from a French jurisdiction in the period under review, see Alfred Soman, 'Deviance and Criminal Justice in Western Europe, 1300–1800: An Essay in Structure', *Criminal Justice History: An International Annual*, i (1980), p. 7.

[28] Till, 'Study in Decline', p. 157.

court, either through arbitration or other forms of settlement, or were advised to do so by their friends and neighbours. These cases were fairly common, and their nature can be conveyed easily by quotation from cause papers. Thus we find such examples as that of Peter Roger, initiator of a suit against Robert Andos, who had accused him of theft. The suit 'by consente of bothe the said p[ar]ties was compromitted to the orderinge and arbitremente of foure of there honeste neighbours who all mett in Egton churche or chapple upon all Soules Day laste paste for the ord[er]inge of the said matter'. The outcome of the arbitration was that Andos was to pay £3 to Roger, 'and so the said action ceased'.[29] When John Buttarie and Thomas Stor fell out in 1594, Thomas Postgate of Hutton Buscel, 'being brother to both ther wif[es]', attempted to reconcile them.[30] In another case, again from the 1590s, a neighbour speaking on behalf of one of the participants in a suit expressed his sorrow that law was being waged, and 'trusted the matter to be ordered and ended by frendes att home w[i]thout chardges or trouble in Lawe'.[31] About a century later, Edward Crowther, a tailor from Burnsall, made a similar effort to bring about a reconciliation when two of his female co-parishioners became involved in a defamation cause. He went to the defendant, and advised her 'to aske pardon & make submission and agreement', a suggestion which, sad to relate, was rejected.[32] This last case notwithstanding, it seems safe to conclude that a large proportion of the defamation suits initiated at the York church courts were settled out of court. It was, of course, a principle of the canon law that litigants should be given every opportunity to reach a reconciliation, and there is some evidence that the ecclesiastical authorities encouraged such practices. In 1598, for example, in the course of a lengthy suit between Margaret Spender and John Browne, the defendant asked to be allowed to litigate *in forma pauperis*, being thus liable to only minimal fees. At this the judge 'did move the said Browne to put all matters betweene Spender and him to order. Spender was verie willing so to do. Browne utterlie refused whereupon the Judge refused to admit him *in forma pauperis*'.[33]

[29] Borthwick Institute of Historical Research, C.P. G/2192.
[30] *Ibid.*, /2790.   [31] *Ibid.*, /2738.   [32] *Ibid.*, H/4359.
[33] Borthwick Institute of Historical Research, D/C AB 8, fo. 135v. It is possible that the prospect of losing fees for what must have promised to be a very lengthy suit may have encouraged the court to try to effect an early settlement rather than allowing Browne to litigate *in forma pauperis*.

As these examples suggest, arbitration, however informal, was widely accepted as an alternative to fighting a suit through to the bitter end, and was something which members of the litigants' community might be anxious to help bring about. There were obvious immediate advantages to those involved in a suit if this course of action were followed: costs and trouble would be avoided. Some of the more detailed accounts of attempts to bring about arbitration, however, indicate that there was a widespread attitude which regarded litigation as a breach of proper neighbourly relations, and which saw arbitration or less formal methods of reconciling those at law as an attractive method of healing such a breach. Such a set of values seems to have been in operation when Thomas Pullen, the vicar of Pontefract, was asked to act as an arbitrator in a suit in 1600. He recounted how he was called into the house of John Walker, one of his parishioners, where he found Thomas Hammond, a local gentleman. Hammond told him 'heare is a matter betwene your neighbour Browne and Christ[ofer] Hurst . . . I wold yow and I might make them frendes . . . yow and I will take this matter upon us & make them frendes', suggesting that he should act for Hurst, and the clergyman for Browne and his wife. Pullen agreed, 'yf the parties will give there consent[es]', and Hurst at least accepted that 'whatsoever Mr Hammonde shall doe for me I will give my consente & agree to yt'. Another witness deposed how Hurst had approached him and another man and asked them to put pressure on Browne to 'refarr the matter . . . to order'. These efforts, unfortunately, came to nothing. Nevertheless, the details of the case demonstrate a deep-seated desire to end disruptive litigation between neighbours, and 'make them frendes'.[34]

Two other cases provide even more striking evidence of this desire in action. The first occurred in the late sixteenth century, and involved two women from Snaith, Katherine Hodgekinson and Emott Belton. The curate of the neighbouring parish of Rawcliffe deposed how he, the two litigants, and 'dyvers others', met in an alehouse there. One of the company, Jane Mapples, 'beinge then and there presente said unto the said Katherine and Emott I would to God yow two were frend[es], for this is not the beste meanes neighbours one to sue an other'. Belton answered that she bore Hodgekinson 'no more evill will than the child that is newlie borne'.

[34] Borthwick Institute of Historical Research, C.P. G/3268.

At this, Hodgekinson commented sharply that if that were indeed the case, Belton would not have slandered her, but 'the said Jane Mapples still contynewynge in desiring theme to be frend[es] the said Katherine Hodgekinson said I could be contented to be frend[es] w[i]th her . . . so that my frend[es] were satisfied for the costes and charges they have bene at'. Another witness gave evidence that Hodgekinson, after drinking to Belton, told her 'that she loved no suites nor troubles and if her frend[es] were so contented and her husband recompensed, she could finde in her harte that all were lovers and frend[es]'.[35]

The second case again arose from a defamation suit between two women, Jane Hutchinson and Jane Orton. The actual incident which sparked the suit off was unremarkable enough: Hutchinson called Orton 'a rotten faced or rotten mouthed queane', to which Orton apparently responded in kind. The court papers record that after this contretemps

> the said Jane Orton and the said Jane Hutchinson by both there mutuall consent[es] referred all actions suites and controversies had or to be had betwixt theme and especially for or concerninge the word[es] before ment[i]oned to the arbitrament of frend[es] by whose mediat[i]on they . . . were made lovers and frend[es] and thereupon drunke and eate together and did then and there remitt and release the one to the other all Act[i]ons Suites and controversies whatsoever from the beginning of the world untill that time.[36]

Even if the language in the final clause is a little hyperbolic, the sentiments expressed in this case hardly support the view that the inhabitants of early modern England lived in a society ridden with hostility and a relative lack of affective feelings in human relationships.

Such cases provide remarkable insights into the way in which members of a community might attempt what was virtually a formal reconciliation between litigants, and they must modify the view which portrays interpersonal relationships in this period as characteristically hostile or malicious. Faced with co-parishioners locked in litigation, members of a village, knowing that it was 'not the beste meanes neighbours one to sue an other', would try to

---

[35] *Ibid.*, /2636.
[36] *Ibid.*, Trans. C.P. 1625/2. I am grateful to Dr W. J. Sheils for bringing this case to my attention.

'make them frendes'. At times, there is evidence that a breakdown in neighbourly relations, far from being regarded as a normal state of affairs, provoked real disquiet within a parish. In the early 1560s, for example, the township of Kirkby Overblow was seriously disrupted by a feud between two of its members. Witnesses in some of the litigation which arose from this feud declared that 'ther was such disagreement malice and hatred betwyx them as is articulate and that was notorious & openly known and dayly spoken of'. A number of attempts had been made at reconciling the parties, most notably at Easter 1562 when the rector of the parish had tried to persuade one of them, Richard Ampleforth, 'to be in charitye and to come up and Receave the hoolye com[mun]ion as other p[ar]ishioners then did'. Ampleforth's refusal to do so was just one incident in which the two men had failed to settle their differences, and it is evident from the depositions relevant to the case that parochial opinion was deeply offended by the continuing rift. Witnesses told how the parish 'did grudge and were much offended at the malice and hatred and disagreement betwix the p[ar]ties', and that the villagers were 'offended that such disagreement as is articulate should be betwyx neighbours'.[37] The conception of proper social relations that is implicit in these statements suggests that the sixteenth-century Englishman had more optimistic expectations about such matters than some modern historians have been willing to credit him with.

Moreover, as the references to arbitration in these York cause papers frequently indicate, those involved in suits were themselves often anxious to arrive at a settlement out of court, and sought arbitration as a means of so doing. This raises some important questions about the motivation which underlay the decision to initiate a defamation suit. As we have seen, comparatively few suits were fought through to the bitter end. It is conceivable that those which were might have caused further disruption, and left a bitterness which might erupt into yet more litigation, or other forms of hostility, at a later date. The widespread evidence of malicious and vexatious litigation in this period, already alluded to, reminds us that the law could be used as a weapon to further a feud, and that a decision in a lawsuit was no guarantee of future harmony between erstwhile litigants. However, as a historian of the ecclesiastical

[37] *Ibid.*, G/1066.

litigation of the Middle Ages has pointed out, 'one of the principal goals of any legal system must be to bring quarrelling people to amicable settlement'.[38] It could be argued, although perhaps a little paradoxically, that a system allowing litigants ample opportunity to settle out of court might preserve the peace more effectively than one which ensures a decision in every case. On the evidence of the York archives, we may safely conclude that the system of ecclesiastical justice in Tudor and Stuart England allowed every chance for a more or less amicable settlement to be reached between litigants. Given this, the initiation of a suit for defamation might be interpreted as the first step towards bringing neighbourly tensions to a close, as well as a symptom of such tensions as already existed.

Certain aspects of the background to and objectives of litigation over defamation must be set in the context of the ecclesiastical law dealing with the subject.[39] This had long offered a remedy against words of defamation or reproach, and dealt not only with slander proper, but also with words spoken in a spirit of malice. Indeed, the idea that defamation constituted a breach of Christian charity – or, as it might be translated into more secular terms, a breach of neighbourly ethics – lay behind much of the church law's thinking on defamation. Certainly, lay and clerical writers on defamation and related topics were not loath to dwell on the offence it offered to Christian charity and to social harmony. Hence the bishop of Gloucester, preaching against slander in 1685, after commenting that it arose from 'a great want of charity', pointed out that 'just as the Slanderer is thus highly Injurious to Those who are the Objects of his Slanders, so he is the most Pestilent Creature to the Community of which he is a member'.[40] Josiah Woodward wrote in

[38] R. H. Helmholz, 'Canonical Defamation in Medieval England', *American Journal of Legal History*, xv (1971), p. 267.

[39] A number of contemporary works on the ecclesiastical law have useful sections on defamation. Among the fuller of these are John Godolphin, *Repertorium Canonicum: Or, an Abridgement of the Ecclesiastical Laws of this Realm, Consistent with the Temporall: Wherein the Most Material Points Relating to Such Persons and Things, as Come Within the Cognizances Thereof, are Succinctly Treated* (London, 1678); *Praxis Francisci Clarke, tam jus dicentibus quam aliis omnibus qui in foro ecclesiastico versantur apprime utilis*, ed. Thomas Bladen, 2nd edn (London, 1684); and John Ayliffe, *Parergon juris canonici anglicani: Or, a Commentary, by Way of a Supplement to the Canons and Constitutions of the Church of England* (London, 1726).

[40] Edward Fowler, *The Great Wickedness and Mischievous Effects of Slandering, Represented in a Sermon Preached at St. Giles without Cripplegate, on Sunday Nov 15 1685* (London, 1685), pp. 3, 8.

1729 that 'the sin of slandering is a high breach of that Charity, which is the Life and Soul of the Christian Religion . . . if the grand Principle of Charity be wanting, all our Deeds, how specious soever, are nothing worth'.[41] Dod and Cleaver held that 'everie man is bound to have a charitable opinion, and good conceit of his neighbour, with a desire of his good name and credit',[42] while a leading commentator on the ecclesiastical law held that through defamation 'charitie between man and man is violated, and the peace of the Common-wealth is many times broken and disturbed'.[43]

The concept of Christian charity was, therefore, an important one to the writers of sermons and tracts. The York archives contain a number of references which suggest that the concept was also of some relevance to the population at large. Despite the extent of religious indifference and negligence, this was a society which was deeply permeated by at least some of the church's teachings, and it seems likely that those which were felt to be most useful to everyday life might enjoy a wide currency.[44] Hence it comes as no surprise to find witnesses in defamation causes occasionally making references to the notion of charity: in one case, for example, a witness excused herself from giving detailed evidence by claiming that she left the room where the slander was spoken because she was 'wearyd w[i]th

---

[41] Josiah Woodward, *The Baseness and Perniciousness of the Sin of Slandering and Back-biting*, 3rd edn (London, 1729), p. 10.

[42] John Dod and Robert Cleaver, *A Treatise or Exposition upon the Ten Commandments, Grounded upon the Scriptures Canonical* (London, 1603), p. 94v.

[43] Sir Thomas Ridley, *A View of the Civile and Ecclesiasticall Law: and Wherein the Practice of them is Streitned and may be Relieved within this Land*, 3rd edn (Oxford, 1662), p. 344.

[44] Popular ideas on what constituted 'Christian charity', and the connection of this concept with less overtly religious views on the proper nature of human relationships, are subjects which would repay further investigation. Certainly the idea of 'charity' as a force for social harmony enjoyed a wide currency, and is to be found in the most unexpected contexts. In 1668, for example, Hannah Blay, a prostitute described as 'very rude, and debauched, being seldom sober, except at such times as she could by no means procure drink to be drunk withal', was in prison awaiting execution for her complicity in a murder committed at Ratcliffe, near London. On the night before her execution, the Ordinary of Newgate offered her the sacrament, which she refused, 'saying she could not die in Charity with some whom she Named, judging them to be the cause of her . . . Execution': Robert Franklin, *A Murderer Punished and Pardoned: Or, a True Relation of the Wicked Life and Shameful Death of Thomas Savage, Imprisoned, Justly Condemned, and Twice Executed at Ratcliffe, for his Bloody Fact, in Killing his Fellow Servant, on Wednesday, Octob. 28, 1668*, 12th edn (London, 1669), p. 41.

hearyng such uncharytable speaches'.[45] More remarkable from the point of view of legal history are a number of cases, dating from the late seventeenth century, in which a suit was commenced at the Consistory or Chancery courts following an allegation of theft. In theory the remedy for this type of slander, in that it imputed a common law rather than an ecclesiastical offence, should have been an action at common law.[46] The papers dealing with these suits usually contain a note to the effect that the words at issue constituted a breach of Christian charity, thus providing a justification for their being dealt with by an ecclesiastical jurisdiction.[47] It is, moreover, significant that the plaintiffs in these causes apparently preferred the remedies offered against defamation by the ecclesiastical courts to those available at common law. Many inhabitants of early modern England must have felt that the formal penance and apology enforced on the defamer by the church courts were more appropriate remedies for an attack on reputation than were the pecuniary damages awarded by the common law. As one contemporary writer remarked, the satisfaction that a successful plaintiff derived from the defendant in a suit for ecclesiastical defamation was rather 'to reduce him to a Recantation, than to augment his [the plaintiff's] Costs by his own Credit's diminution'.[48]

This hypothesis lends further support to the contention that the litigants of the period were aware that they were acting within a context of some sort of community social values, and were concerned that their conduct should be, and should be seen to be, broadly in accord with those values. The type of apology made by a defamer in the course of his penance served to clear the reputation of the offended party, and might thus have formed a sounder basis for reconciliation and an end to future malice than the payment of pecuniary damages. In 1692 James Webster, a York man, was sued successfully for calling George Thwing 'Rogue and Rascall'. He was sentenced to go to the house of one of Thwing's kinsmen, and there to do penance in the presence of several local worthies. A detailed

[45] Borthwick Institute of Historical Research, C.P. G/3282.
[46] Godolphin, *Repertorium canonicum*, p. 516.
[47] E.g. Borthwick Institute of Historical Research, C.P. H/4478, where the defendant allegedly said that the plaintiff was a 'Theife & that she had stolne a Ferkin of Butter from her late Master', it was noted that the words were 'contra bonos mores et fraternam Regulam Charitatis'.
[48] Godolphin, *Repertorium canonicum*, p. 515.

description of what he had to say by way of apology survives, and runs as follows:

> I doe here acknowledge that I spoke the said Word[es] wrongfully, rashly and unadvisedly, and am hertily sorry for my passion and unadvisedness therein, and doe here declare that I had noe just cause for speakeing the said word[es], wishing you all here present to thinke no worse of him the said George Thwing by reason of my speakeing the said words[es].[49]

Such an apology might well have provided the wronged party with a satisfaction more welcome than mere financial recompense. It is also, perhaps, not entirely fanciful to suggest that it would be less likely to impede restoration of good relationships between the two parties than would an award of damages. Even when a cause was fought through to the finish, it would seem that the objective of the church courts' treatment of defamation was to ease tensions rather than give them a legal framework within which to develop freely.

This essay has concentrated upon evidence relating to one offence in one set of courts, and hence cannot claim to offer a complete reinterpretation of the social significance of litigation in early modern England. It is, however, possible to raise a number of general issues on the basis of the evidence provided by these York defamation causes about litigation, litigants and contemporary notions on the proper nature of human relations. Firstly, the idea that judicial proceedings might sometimes be initiated, not as a means of furthering a dispute, but as a first step towards a settlement, seems to have been applicable to other courts, and other offences, than those which have constituted our main concern here. Forcible disseisin, for example, is an offence which, like defamation, has caused some puzzlement to modern historians.[50] It becomes more understandable when it is realized that, to quote one authority on the agrarian history of the period, 'most intrusions were made with the intention of drawing on a suit of trespass by which title could be tried, rather than defying the law'.[51] The

[49] Borthwick Institute of Historical Research, C.P. H/4302.
[50] E.g. F. G. Emmison, *Elizabethan Life: Disorder* (Chelmsford, 1970), p. 130, follows an earlier commentator in remarking that 'it is curious and perplexing that throughout many generations people persisted in so turbulent and futile a way of asserting their claim to real estate'.
[51] Eric Kerridge, *Agrarian Problems in the Sixteenth Century and After* (Historical Problems, Studies and Documents, vi, 1969), p. 82.

historian of the court of Chancery in Elizabeth's reign has offered some general observations on this way of using litigation. He argues that many legal problems which today would be settled without going to court could, in the period under discussion, only be resolved by using a lawsuit to bring on a decision. Whereas in modern England such decisions are easily obtained without recourse to court action, he claims that

> In Tudor times this could rarely happen, and the only sanction of reliability could be found in at least beginning formal proceedings in some court of law . . . only litigation offered a glimmer of certainty to the citizen seeking to avoid more serious contention, for only the courts could give some measure of immediate and contemporary authority to what might be little more than a private agreement or composition.[52]

Given such a state of affairs, the early modern taste for litigation becomes more comprehensible and less sinister. Without doubt many suits or criminal charges were brought on slight, vexatious, or malicious grounds: conversely, it is patent that other suits were initiated for reasons which even the least litigious modern historian would find logical.

If it is accepted that many of the lawsuits of the period were launched in hopes of hastening the settlement of disputes, preferably without having to fight them through to the end, the numerous references to arbitration in the law books and court records of the period should cause little surprise. If people went to law with the honest intention of obtaining a decision in a disputed matter, or of obtaining a settlement over some differences, there is no reason why they should not have done so in the cheapest, quickest, and most amicable way possible. Similarly, if, as we have seen from the York materials, there was a genuine dismay at the spectacle of two neighbours locked in litigation, there is every reason why people within the community should encourage such a settlement. This acceptance of arbitration flourished not only among the populace of Yorkshire, but is also evident in works of

[52] W. J. Jones, *The Elizabethan Court of Chancery* (Oxford, 1967), pp. 266–7. It is probable that this practice of initiating a suit in order to facilitate a settlement out of court, and the discontinuation of litigation when such a settlement was reached, was common to most of Western Europe in the late medieval and early modern periods. Something very like it, for example, was practised in the Toledo area of Spain in the early seventeenth century: Michael R. Weisser, *Crime and Punishment in Early Modern Europe* (Hassocks, Sussex, 1979), p. 61.

legal theory and the practice of many contemporary courts. An eminent civilian, writing on the civil and ecclesiastical law, commented that 'many times, things which otherwise can have no speedy end by law, are compounded by Arbitrement',[53] an observation which is obviously in line with the main drift of our argument. Similarly, arbitration was perfectly acceptable to common lawyers. One such, author of an anonymous book on the subject published in 1694, declared that 'arbitrement is much esteemed and greatly favoured by our Common Law; the end thereof being privately to compose Differences between Parties by the Judgement of honest Men; and to prevent the great Trouble and frequent Expense of Law-Suits'.[54]

This view was widely diffused among lawyers, court officials, and the population at large; the archives of any tribunal active in the period will provide at the worst scattered references to arbitrations, compositions, or other forms of settlement out of court. It is, perhaps, in the nature of the phenomenon that no systematic study of it will ever be possible, and that we shall never be able to discover, for example, what proportion of suits were ended by arbitration or related types of settlement. For the moment, however, it would seem undeniable that both the litigating populace and the legal profession accepted, as one recent student of the church courts has put it, that 'the burgeoning weeds of litigation did not altogether hide from view the ancient aim of reconciliation'.[55] Indeed, some contemporaries were manifestly anxious not to give the weeds a chance to burgeon. Thomas Peacocke, a wealthy clothier from Coggeshall in Essex, in 1580 made Mr Justice Southcote and Sir William Cordell, Master of the Rolls, the overseers of his will. This document directed that 'if there shall arise any trouble between the executors, or between any person and them touching my will', the two worthies should 'have

[53] Ridley, *View of the Civile and Ecclesiasticall Law*, p. 105.
[54] *Arbitrium redivivum: Or, the Law of Arbitration; Collected from the Law-books Both Ancient and Modern, and Deduced to these Times. Wherein the Whole Learning of Awards and Arbitrements is Methodically Treated* (London, 1694), sig. A 3.
[55] Ralph Houlbrooke, *Church Courts and the People during the English Reformation 1520–1570* (Oxford, 1979), p. 265. For some wider comments on how the church had an important role to play in easing social tensions, see John Bossy, 'Blood and Baptism: Kinship, Community and Christianity in Western Europe from the Fourteenth to the Seventeenth Centuries', in *Sanctity and Secularity: the Church and the World* (Studies in Church History, x, 1973).

the hearing and determining of such matters, without any suit of law'.[56]

There are, of course, a number of other problems relating to what arbitration tells us about general attitudes to litigation, although detailed examination of them is impossible in a short exploratory essay of this nature. Perhaps the most urgent of them, however, is the need to develop a typology of arbitration. Legal textbooks prescribed a relatively formalized procedure for arbitration, in which disputants chose representatives to argue their case for them in a way not dissimilar from that adopted by feed lawyers in court: this model, obviously enough, is very different from the informal neighbourly pressures which seem to have been operating at a more popular level. This divergence serves to remind us that the use of the term arbitration in this chapter has been imprecise, and that its employment has been loose and descriptive. Future research on the subject will doubtless provide the materials upon which a more sensitive analysis of the phenomenon might be based.

One method of approaching this problem might be through forming an impression of the type of person chosen as arbitrator. Legal theory suggested that such persons should be 'sufficient and indifferent',[57] but evidence from other courts and other areas supports the impression provided by the York ecclesiastical records that in practice this was given a wide interpretation. The local clergyman was an obvious mediator, and should in fact have regarded it as part of his pastoral duties to end disputes. Ralph Josselin, the Essex vicar whose diary affords so many insights into the daily work of the seventeenth-century country clergyman, often noted his involvement in his parishioners' differences. After arbitrating in one dispute, he wrote that they had found 'my endeavours acceptable to them all, and above all I know 'tis an acceptable service unto god to continue peace and concord among brethren'.[58] The gentry, naturally enough, might be called upon to end disputes, or might intervene on their own initiative in the hope of so doing. Thus we find a Wiltshire gentleman of the early seventeenth century involving himself in trying to end a pew dispute, expressing his dislike of 'such unnecessary suits' in forceful

---

[56] F. G. Emmison, *Elizabethan Life: Wills of the Essex Gentry & Merchants* (Chelmsford, 1978), p. 302.   [57] *Arbitrium redivivum*, p. 18.
[58] *The diary of Ralph Josselin, 1616–1683*, ed. Alan Macfarlane (Records of Social and Economic History, new ser., iii, 1976), p. 69.

terms, and eventually effecting a reconciliation with the help of the minister of the parish and 'a chief parishioner'.[59] Members of social strata below the gentry were also often involved, and village notables drawn from the yeomanry or of even lower rank were frequent participants in arbitration.

It would seem, therefore, that the initiation of a lawsuit with the aim of achieving an extra-legal settlement, and the frequent recourse to arbitration as a means of reaching this end, were two of the distinctive characteristics of litigation in Elizabethan and Stuart England. To some extent, this would agree with the prevailing orthodoxy about differences over time in attitudes towards the law. It has been argued, at times a little crudely, that whereas the medieval period enjoyed an emphasis on law in its personal context, as a means of settling personal disputes, in modern industrial societies law is seen mainly in impersonal terms, and lawlessness as something which threatens 'the state' or 'society'.[60] It might be argued, however tentatively, that those aspects of popular attitudes towards litigation and litigants upon which we have concentrated in this essay indicate that opinions about the nature and function of the law in the period in question fall somewhere between the 'medieval' and the 'modern' poles. If this hypothesis is correct, the use of litigation as a means towards solving disputes which the law itself could not always solve, and the use of arbitration to adjust the law to local needs, might be interpreted as evidence of how the law was performing a function both for the state, and for the individual and his or her community. As has been pointed out elsewhere, arbitration, through its flexibility, and its consideration of local conditions, probably came nearer than anything else available at the time to providing what the layman thought of as 'justice'.[61] The

---

[59] Ingram, 'Communities and Courts', p. 126.

[60] This interpretation seems to provide the main theme of Weisser, *Crime and Punishment in Early Modern Europe*. The notion of such a transition is also raised in two other recent essays attempting an analysis of broad changes in the law and attitudes towards it in Europe in the early modern period: Soman, 'Deviance and Criminal Justice'; and Bruce Lenman and Geoffrey Parker, 'The State, the Community and the Criminal Law in Early Modern Europe', in V. A. C. Gatrell, Bruce Lenman and Geoffrey Parker (eds.), *Crime and the Law: The Social History of Crime in Western Europe since 1500* (London, 1980).

[61] Jones, *Elizabethan Court of Chancery*, p. 279, where it is suggested that 'the intermingling of experts and amateurs over all parts of the country and from diverse institutions makes the system of reference and arbitration one of the more significant aspects of Tudor and Stuart society'.

relationships between law and society, or between law and human needs, were very subtle in this period. Arbitration, through its necessary adjustment to the circumstances of the individual case, gave the settlement of suits between parties as much flexibility as was given to the application of the criminal law by its adjustment to meet the peculiarities of individual offenders.[62]

This conclusion forces us to return to the wider problem of assessing what the litigation of the period tells us about contemporary human relationships. As was suggested at an earlier point, the most obvious use to which the historian might put the undoubted rise in suits at law in Tudor and Stuart England is as evidence of the general affectionlessness of human relationships at that time. On the other hand, the practice of bringing suits on with the object of effecting a speedy settlement to an otherwise intractable dispute indicates that this interpretation would be over-simplified. Moreover, the widespread recourse to arbitration would seem to support the contention that contemporaries were anxious to maintain some sort of harmony in their communities, and saw a bitterly contested lawsuit as a threat to that harmony. Witnesses in causes for ecclesiastical defamation brought before the courts at York, as we have seen, thought that it was 'not the beste meanes neighbours one to sue an other', or claimed that they 'loved no suites or troubles', and were 'offended that such disagreement . . . should be betwyx neighbours'. When confronted with litigating co-parishioners, they often did their best to 'make them frendes'. Such people make a poor advertisement for a society 'filled with hatred and malice', and if their view of proper neighbourly conduct amounted to 'a tyranny of local opinion', it was a tyranny which was humane, even laudable, in many of its objectives and some of the methods by which it sought to attain those objectives. If the litigation of the period makes it impossible to portray human relations in early

---

[62] For two discussions of this flexibility of the criminal law's application in a somewhat later period than that covered by this essay, see Douglas Hay, 'Property, Authority, and the Criminal Law', in Douglas Hay, Peter Linebaugh, John G. Rule, E. P. Thompson and Cal Winslow (eds.), *Albion's Fatal Tree* (London, 1975), pp. 40–9; and J. M. Beattie, 'Crime and the Courts in Surrey, 1736–1753', in Cockburn (ed.), *Crime in England*. Less explicit sources than those used by Hay and Beattie suggest that something very like the situation they describe was already obtaining in the seventeenth century: J. A. Sharpe, 'Crime in the County of Essex 1620–1680: A Study of Offences and Offenders at the Assizes and Quarter Sessions' (Univ. of Oxford D.Phil. thesis, 1978), pp. 282–9.

modern England as a Rousseauesque idyll, the opinions expressed
in the York defamation causes make it equally difficult to interpret
the contemporary taste for lawsuits as proof of the existence of a
Hobbesian war of all against all.

8. Household Disputes and the Law in Early Modern Andalusia

JAMES CASEY

There seems to be some conflict of evidence or interpretation about the willingness of pre-industrial populations to use courts of law in order to settle disputes. On the one hand we have the very persuasive thesis that they only used them as a last resort or against outsiders to the community, preferring by and large more informal methods of regulating conflict.[1] Since these traditional, face-to-face societies were kept together by the complexity of the relationships of their members, disputes would be difficult to limit to the specific point at issue but must tend to become general, socially divisive and ultimately unresolvable by simple adjudication. The very publicity of a court case would become a factor in its own right, damaging to the authority or prestige of the plaintiff himself, inasmuch as he was tacitly acknowledging that someone had thought him weak enough to be taken advantage of in the first place.[2] In early modern Spain, still fundamentally a federation of small-scale agrarian communities, such attitudes are not hard to find. 'Litigation is war', affirmed the author of one book of conduct; while an Augustinian friar cautioned his countrymen: 'Though one can litigate about property without building up general resentment and hostility, it will be difficult.'[3] But if these considerations suggest why people might

---

[1] See, for example, T. J. A. Le Goff and D. M. G. Sutherland, 'The Revolution and the Rural Community in Eighteenth Century Britanny', *Past and Present*, no. 62 (1974), pp. 96–119; Michael Weisser, *The Peasants of the Montes* (Chicago and London, 1976), p. 111.

[2] Julian Pitt-Rivers, *The Fate of Shechem: Essays in the Anthropology of the Mediterranean* (Cambridge, 1977), p. 9; and on the reluctance of present-day rural Andalusians to use the courts, see his classic exposition in *The People of the Sierra* (Chicago, 1954), pp. 129–30 and 141–54. My page references are to the second edition of 1971.

[3] Cristóbal Suárez de Figueroa, *El Pasagero: advertencias utilísimas a la vida humana*, 1617, ed. Francisco Rodríguez Marín (Madrid, 1913), p. 340; Marcos Antonio de Camos, *Microcosmia y Govierno universal del hombre christiano* (Barcelona, 1592), i, p. 205. John Davis makes a rather similar point aptly from the

189

have approached the courts with caution in pre-industrial Europe, they do nothing to explain the readiness to litigate which other authors have charted. Richard Kagan has drawn our attention to the huge impact which the higher royal courts made on the lives of the ordinary Spanish people in the sixteenth century.[4] His analysis of the ratio of unfinished lawsuits to sentences – something like 15:1 – has parallels with phenomena elsewhere. Richard Helmholz has pointed out, for example, how ready people seem to have been to air their marital disputes in court in fourteenth-century England, only to compromise very often before the case reached its conclusion.[5]

It is particularly, perhaps, in the realm of household quarrels that one must ask whether the publicity of a court proceeding might not undermine any possible remedy hoped for. As part of a more general study of the structure of the family in southern Spain I found my attention captured by a neglected section of the episcopal archives labelled, disarmingly, '*Varia*' in the diocese of Granada and, more boldly '*Divorcio*' in the diocese of Cordoba. Though probably purged during the nineteenth and twentieth centuries when the whole nature of divorce changed and the word itself became loaded with obnoxious connotations of liberalism and secularization to an embattled Catholic church, the surviving documentation is full enough to cast a curious light on the relationship between priest, judge and family under the old regime. For the diocese of Cordoba there survive approximately 350 divorce suits from the period 1600–1800 (the estimate is my own, since no inventory exists). The coverage is geographically and chronologically so spotty that it at once raised the question: how big was the original archive? For example, almost all the surviving cases from the seventeenth century relate to the agro-town of Montilla, some 35 kilometres south of the diocesan capital. From this peasant population of 2,288 families (census of 1587), equivalent perhaps to 10,000 men, women and children, we have no fewer than thirty-three divorce suits for the first fifty years of the century.

perspective of the present-day anthropologist: 'You cannot sue an acre; a boundary dispute is not a dispute with a boundary'. See his *Land and Family in Pisticci* (London, 1973), p. 157.

[4] *Lawsuits and Litigants in Castile 1500–1700* (Chapel Hill, North Carolina, 1981); and see above ch. 6.

[5] R. H. Helmholz, *Marriage Litigation in Medieval England* (Cambridge, 1974), p. 137.

There were actually some years in which two separate families were initiating divorce proceedings. In the eighteenth century the city of Cordoba becomes visible in the documentation for the first time: sixteen cases from the city for the years 1738–46, twenty-five suits from 1774–86, an average at both periods of two suits per year for a population of about 11,000 families. In Granada the surviving documentation is even more haphazardly distributed and has to be physically unearthed from bundles of miscellaneous material. I could not actually find more than fifty-two divorce suits for the early modern period, but there may well be more awaiting the enterprising researcher who enjoys climbing ladders and untying ancient knots. Of the fifty-two trials, nearly half occurred in the four years 1796–9. If this is a representative survival (and the internal evidence of the suits themselves makes it clear that there was nothing unusual about these years) then the 14,225 families of this thriving provincial capital may have been trying to divorce at the rate of five couples a year towards the end of the *ancien régime*.

The figures may appear surprisingly high. Spain had a reputation among foreign travellers for discretion in household affairs and particularly for the withdrawal of its married women from the theatre of public affairs. One of the numerous French travellers in the seventeenth century, Madame d'Aulnoy, remarked: 'it is very rare to see quarrels between husband and wife, and even rarer that they should separate as they do in France'.[6] Yet divorce litigation may well have been as common as in northern Europe. In the city of Rouen in the 1780s (population 80,000–85,000 people) there seem to have been on average three attempts at canon law separation a year – before the dramatic secularization of the divorce law by the French Assembly in 1792 led to nearly ninety petitions a year. In the diocese of Cambrai the norm seems to have been between five and ten ecclesiastical divorce suits annually in the eighteenth century, for a diocesan population of perhaps 250,000 (the diocese of Cordoba, by comparison, had 237,355 inhabitants towards the middle of the eighteenth century, that of Granada 234,904).[7]

---

[6] Juan García Mercadal, *Viajes de Extranjeros por España y Portugal: Siglo XVII* (Madrid, 1959), p. 1074.

[7] R. Phillips, 'Demographic Aspects of Divorce in Rouen 1792–1816', *Annales de démographie historique* (1976), pp. 429–41; Alain Lottin (ed.), *La désunion du couple sous l'Ancien Régime* (Lille, 1975), pp. 16–17 and 113–14. Cf. Nancy Cott, 'Eighteenth Century Family Life Revealed in Massachusetts Divorce Records', *Journal of Social History*, no. 10 (1976), pp. 20–43. There were approximately

Though divorce in both France and Spain under the old regime was overall extremely rare, I think it may actually have been more 'popular' than it was to become in Catholic countries at a later period. In Spain, until the secularization of divorce just recently, these were difficult cases to fight, reserved for an upper bourgeoisie of money and connections: 'two to three years of paperwork, an outlay of 500,000 to 3,000,000 pesetas' (£2,700–£16,200).[8] Yet the surprising thing about Cordoban and Granadan divorce litigation is how lowly the social background of many of the plaintiffs was (see table 1). It is possible to guarantee, from the evidence of the trials

Table 1. *Social background of divorce litigants*
Of 178 divorce cases analysed for the purposes of this chapter, 142 gave information on occupation.

	Montilla & Lucena 1600–1700	Cordoba 1700–1800	Granada 1700–1800
Aristocrats	6	8	7
Professionals	2	10	5
Clerks	2	1	0
Merchants	2	2	7
Master craftsmen	6	14	18
Journeymen	1	6	5
Peasants	7	11	6
Labourers	4	8	1
Unknown	15	21	3
Total	45	81	52

themselves, that these occupational classifications (often notoriously imprecise in the old regime) correspond roughly to specific social categories. Though journeymen were frequently only youths awaiting succession to master craftsmen fathers, a good two-thirds of our litigants were, in fact, 'small men' of little property or letters.[9]

fifteen requests for divorce a year in the archbishopric of Mexico in the early nineteenth century, Silvia M. Arrom, *La Mujer Mexicana ante el Divorcio Eclesiástico 1800–57* (Mexico, 1976), p. 14. For the population of the dioceses of Granada and Cordoba, Juan Sáez Marín, *Datos sobre la Iglesia Española Contemporánea 1768–1868* (Madrid, 1975), pp. 93–4.

[8] See the inquiry in the periodical *Cambio 16*, 12 Oct. 1981, pp. 110–31.

[9] Arrom, *La Mujer Mexicana*, p. 31, also notes the considerable participation of the poor (though not of the Indians) in divorce proceedings in early nineteenth-century Mexico.

What were they litigating about?

Table 2. *Causes alleged against the defendants in divorce suits*

M: main cause
A: ancillary cause(s)

Number of suits in which the respective allegations appear

	Montilla & Lucena 1600–1700		Cordoba 1700–1800		Granada 1700–1800	
Annulments	M	A	M	A	M	A
Coercion into marriage	3	0	0	0	1	0
Impotence	2	1	4	0	2	0
Separations						
Wife-beating	28	8	34	17	17	11
Insults & general cruelty	8	1	19	3	16	2
Wasting dowry & neglect	3	12	12	18	5	16
Adultery & venereal disease	1	5	12	9	11	15
Total	45	27	81	47	52	44

The Andalusian courts seem to have stretched the letter of canon law pretty widely. Our foremost authority, the Cordoban Jesuit Tomás Sánchez, who spent most of his working life in Granada at the end of the sixteenth century, laid most of his emphasis on the technical reasons for the breakdown of a marriage – that is, the incapacity of one of the parties to consent to the original contract through the impediments of consanguinity, impotence or coercion. The possibility of separation of 'persons and property' (*a mensa et thoro*) after a valid contract mostly arose for Sánchez when one of the parties had committed adultery – no question, of course, in canon law of the double standard, unlike the royal law of Castile which had much more savage punishments for female adultery.[10]

---

[10] Tomás Sánchez, *Disputationum de Sancto Matrimonii Sacramento*, 3 vols. (Madrid, 1602–5), especially book vii on impediments and book x on divorce. This treatise became a standard authority on marriage in Catholic Europe in the early modern period. Though it was edited and included in J. P. Migne, *Theologiae Cursus Completus*, xxv (Paris, 1860), pp. 387ff., there is a tremendous need for an up-to-date edition. A classic justification of the double standard in the criminal law comes in the great medieval lawcode *Las Siete Partidas del Rey Don Alfonso el Sabio*, facsimile reprint of the 1807 official edition, 3 vols. (Madrid, 1972), 4/9/13.

He did, indeed, pay some attention to cruelty, another recognized cause of separations, but like most canon lawyers he tended to fight shy of the subject, since the degree of brutality required was uncertain.[11] The problem was that the Andalusian courts of the old regime were being asked to adjudicate cases for which they had no very clear guidelines in canon law. Though some of the suits were simple enough, involving (especially among the rough peasants of seventeenth-century Montilla) severe bodily lesions, many others drew the courts into the delicate area of incompatibility of temperament. My husband never actually beat me, confessed the wife of the postmaster of Granada, but 'his contempt for me was so great that perhaps physical ill treatment would have been preferable'; a landowner's wife from a village (Fuenteovejuna) whose pride has been immortalized in Castilian literature, objected to being treated like a maid by her husband, 'taking the bread to the oven, fetching the water from a fountain which is outside the village, going to wash the clothes a quarter of a league away and having to carry them there and back'.[12] It was not only women who stood on their dignity. Men complained bitterly that their wives called after them from the balconies of houses, waylaid their customers and blackened their characters, fetched them home to bed from a tavern or a friend's house. 'Am I a child', protested one Montilla landowner, out late playing cards, 'that you had to send after me so often?'[13] The courts, in other words, were being asked to adjudicate upon difficult questions of honour – not surprisingly, perhaps, since the Castilian criminal codes attached at least as much importance to insult as to wounding.[14]

Execution of the wife and her lover, carried out personally by the husband, or at his suit by the royal courts, remained permissible until the end of the old regime in Spain. There is an example of the latter practice in the sixteenth century in *Casos notables de la Ciudad de Córdoba*, Sociedad de Bibliófilos Españoles (Madrid, 1949), pp. 160–3. Francisco Tomás y Valiente, *El Derecho Penal de la Monarquía Absoluta (Siglos XVI–XVII–XVIII)* (Madrid, 1969), p. 395, makes the point, though, that the usual practice was probably murder in the seventeenth century, giving way to gaol for the adulterer in the eighteenth.

[11] Cf. Francisco Gómez Salazar and Vicente de la Fuente, *Tratado teórico-práctico de procedimientos eclesiásticos*, 4 vols. (Madrid, 1868), iii, p. 11.

[12] A(rchivo) D(iocesano) de G(ranada) V(aria)/68/6, Arilla v. Alfaro, 1756; A(rchivo) D(iocesano de) C(órdoba) D(ivorcio)/2/11, Ríos v Sánchez Mellado, 1741.

[13] A.D.C. D/1/43, Rosal v. Oliveros, 1687–8.

[14] *Siete Partidas*, 7/8/1–16 (homicide), 7/9/1–23 (dishonour) and 7/10/1–18 (violence). These twenty-three laws on insults were made more specific by the *Novísima*

Something similar could be said about adultery. Some of these cases clearly related more to reputation than to damage of the kind which canon law had in mind. Fighting an unsubstantiated charge of adultery, the wife of one rural doctor remarked: 'Jealousy is an indiscreet passion; it clouds a man's thinking and, unless he takes a stand against it, will enslave his mind and drive him mad.'[15] Though women were the most prominent plaintiffs in the divorce courts – all but 27 of our 178 cases – men were surprisingly willing to vent their complaints of adultery or bad treatment in the public theatre. This is a problem, since it seems to contradict the image of a society governed by honour and keen to avoid judicial publicity. I hope to show here that divorce litigation was indeed inappropriate to the needs of these small agrarian communities of Andalusia, and that we have to go beyond the record itself to understand why, in spite of everything, the courts were involved in household disputes.

People might well have thought twice before taking their problems to law. In a federation of face-to-face communities like Andalusia[16] honour was a real consideration. No village seems to have been too small to escape the jurisdiction of the divorce court; nor was any town big enough to be impersonal, for many of the parishes of Granada and Cordoba were autonomous neighbourhoods of peasants and artisans. Honour and reputation were tangible assets, ranked by contemporaries themselves as one of the bundle of factors, including wealth and birth, which determined social standing: everyone, said a peasant of Verja, had some, except perhaps the gypsies.[17] It did no good to the reputation of the peasant Juan Hernando of Ohanes to be dragged through the divorce courts: even his friends, while agreeing that he was innocent, had to admit he had shown himself 'so poor spirited by nature that it was only to be expected that this would happen with his wife'.[18] As the Castilian authors of the Golden Age were fond of

---

Recopilación de las Leyes de España mandada formar por el señor D. Carlos IV, 1805–7, facsimile reprint, Boletín Oficial del Estado, 6 vols. (Madrid, 1976), 12/25/1–10 – incorporating ten edicts of the later medieval and early modern period.

[15] A.D.C. D/6/8, Cañas v. Reyes, 1775–6.

[16] Splendid introductions to the historical landscape are Antonio López Ontiveros, *Emigración, Propiedad y Paisaje Agrario en la Campiña de Córdoba* (Barcelona, 1974), and Joaquín Bosque Maurel, *Geografía Urbana de Granada* (Zaragoza, 1962). See also Manuel Garzón Pareja, *Historia de Granada* (Granada, 1981).

[17] A.D.G. M(atrimonio)/798, Verja, Gutiérrez/Robles, 10 May 1775.

[18] A.D.G. V/68/7, Hernando v. Hernando, 1735.

repeating, a man's reputation in the market-place could be undermined by failure to control and run his household.[19] Nor were the clerical judges sympathetic to divorce litigation. For the ecclesiastical writers of early modern Spain, the pursuit of justice through the courts, licit in itself, could have adverse effects on the soul of the litigant as he was driven to either trickery or despair. Throughout the records of the trials the point is made time and again that charity is stronger than law. 'Cousin, bear these beatings patiently', the aristocratic doña Teresa de Pareja of Lucena was told by her friend, 'since it is the Lord Our God who has given you this cross.'[20] Meanwhile the Granadan and Cordoban judges made it plain to litigants that self-sacrifice outranked the pursuit of happiness in their order of priorities. Go back to your husband, the vicar-general of Granada told the fifteen-year-old bride of a carpenter who had complained of his impotence and brutality, 'and bear as best you may the upsets and quarrels which occur'; four years later the pair told the vicar-general that they had decided to drop the case 'and suffer and tolerate each other so that God may forgive each of them in his turn'.[21] It often required a good deal of simple courage on a woman's part to petition for divorce. 'Now that it has become public in this town [Lucena] that I have gone to court', lamented doña Francisca de Paula Serrano, a clerk's wife, 'my husband has persecuted me and I have had to leave town and go into hiding in a village elsewhere.' In the same town earlier in the eighteenth century, doña Victoriana de Mesa called on the local priest to witness that she could not petition openly for a divorce for fear of the violence of her husband. In the tiny, remote village of Bubíon, stuck up in the Alpujarras, the landowner's wife doña Maria Josefa de Mendoza had to go secretly to priest and notary, warning them that, if her husband found out, he would retort with 'unhelpful actions'.[22] It was indeed extremely difficult for married women, at least of the respectable classes, to leave the house in rural Andalusia to go anywhere, except to mass.

[19] For example, Pedro de Luxán, *Coloquios Matrimoniales*, 1550 (Madrid, 1943), pp. 21–4, or Juan de Pineda, *Diálogos Familiares de la Agricultura Cristiana*, 1589, Biblioteca de Autores Españoles, 5 vols. (Madrid, 1963–4), iii, p. 395, or Camos, *Microcosmia*, ii, p. 76.

[20] A.D.C. D/1/5, Pareja v. Cuenca, 1682–8.

[21] A.D.G. V/65/2, Romero v. Rivas, 1793–7.

[22] A.D.C. D/6/43, Serrano v. Casas, 1786–91; D/2/20, Mesa v. Ruiz de Carmona, 1707; A.D.G. V/65/25, Mendoza v. Enciso, 1797–8.

There was also the cost. Divorce cases had to be determined in the diocesan capital, since the archdeacons in Spain, as in the rest of Europe, had been losing their jurisdiction over marriage cases from the later middle ages, before it was finally taken away at the Council of Trent in 1563.[23] This centralization was a severe blow, when the furthest village, like Ohanes, might lie some 75 kilometres from the diocesan capital, and over some very rough territory if the diocese was Granada. Small wonder that the villagers of the Alpujarras petitioned, unsuccessfully, for a vicar-general of their own in 1565.[24] Though less expensive in some ways than the civil courts (there was no stamped paper), the court of the vicar-general or *Provisor* operated with the same basic procedures as the royal *chancillería*: that is, with written submissions deposited by attorney and attested to by special ecclesiastical notaries, and with witnesses nominated by the parties, who were interrogated on a list of questions drawn up by advocates and approved by the judge.[25] All the technicalities of appeal and filibuster familiar to the civil courts were fully in evidence in the church courts too. One Montilla litigant kept a case from getting heard in this way for over a year: on 6 September 1632 he appealed against the supposed bias of the examining judge, and then against an interim award of alimony to his wife, first to the *chancillería* and then to the bishop of Cordoba's superior, the archbishop of Toledo. Both appeals got nowhere – except to prevent the hearing of witnesses until 14 December 1633.[26] If nothing else, such tactics could have made it prohibitive for the other side to proceed.

[23] Juan Tejada y Ramiro (ed.), *Colección de Cánones y de Todos los Concilios de la Iglesia Española*, 5 vols. (Madrid, 1849–55), pp. 73–4, article lviii of the Council of Seville 1512. Cf. Helmholz, *Marriage Litigation*, pp. 143–5.

[24] Tejada, *Cánones*, v, p. 364. Since the Alpujarras were Morisco territory at the time, the reluctance of the Curia to decentralize may be understandable; afterwards they were heavily depopulated. It should be borne in mind that there were 77 villages and towns in the diocese of Cordoba, 186 much smaller units of settlement in the demographically equivalent archdiocese of Granada, Sáez Marín, *Iglesia Española*, pp. 93–4.

[25] Many of the details in Kagan, *Lawsuits and Litigants*, ch. 2, could be applied straight to the church courts. Francisco Ortiz de Salcedo, *Curia Eclesiástica* (Madrid, 1749) is a law clerk's manual, not very helpful for the general historian. John T. Noonan, Jr., *Power to Dissolve: Lawyers and Marriages in the Courts of the Roman Curia* (Cambridge, Mass., 1972) is illuminating about divorce litigation at the top, including, incidentally, one appeal from the diocese of Cordoba.

[26] A.D.C. D/1/15, Alva v. Gómez de la Gama, 1632–4.

The lowest estimate of costs which I have seen for a divorce suit was the 101 reals which a woman of Montilla spent in 1656, in official fees alone, in the first six months of her suit against a violent husband; the latter alleged that he had spent 500 reals over the same period.[27] With the average divorce suit taking seventeen months on average to prosecute to a conclusion, total fees for a case, *pro rata*, may have come to a minimum of 300 reals around the mid-seventeenth century. They do not seem to have climbed much in the eighteenth century: it was 300 reals which one woman was awarded for the cost of her divorce suit in 1774.[28] It has to be said that the figures we have for the bourgeoisie and aristocracy often go far higher then this: 4,400 reals for one merchant of Granada in 1624, 5,500 for another in 1704.[29] The difference may partly be accounted for by the greater readiness of this class to appeal to Toledo or to the Nuncio or to Rome, or it may be due to the fact that the larger sums come from testaments, which would include incidental expenses of travel and the like which do not figure in the judicial record of award costs. In any case, even 300 reals could be a heavy burden for the peasants and artisans who constituted the basic clientele of the diocesan courts. A journeyman silversmith in Cordoba in 1784, earning four reals a day, had to borrow from his master to defend his suit, paying him back at the rate of two reals a day deduction from wages – which left the poor litigant with the bare minimum to buy food.[30] Clearly, a divorce suit was a major financial undertaking, though on average it cost less than the 700 reals needed to fight a property case before the *chancillería*,[31] There were, indeed, exemptions from fees in hard cases: but they were very few. More often the solution would be for the judge to make an interim award of alimony to the weaker party (almost always the wife, but very

---

[27] A.D.C. D/1/11, Fernández v. Morales, 1656.

[28] A.D.C. D/6/1, Vela v. González, 1774–82.

[29] A(rchivo de) P(rotocolos de) G(ranada) E(scribanía de)/Luis González/1624, testament of Alvaro Muñoz, 29 Sept. 1624; E/Palacio/1703–4, fos. 352–7v, testament of don Jerónimo de Aranda Sotomayor, 13 June 1704. The higher figures seem closer to those cited in Arrom, *La Mujer Mexicana*, pp. 25–31, where a full trial seems to have cost 100 pesos (1,500 reals) in the early nineteenth century.

[30] A.D.C. D/6/8, Luque v. Castro, 1784–5.

[31] Information from the notarial archives of Granada and Cordoba. Cf. Earl J. Hamilton, *American Treasure and the Price Revolution in Spain 1500–1650* (Cambridge, Mass., 1934), p. 402. On fees before the *chancillería*, Kagan, *Lawsuits and Litigants*, p. 39.

occasionally the man). Divorce suits could, indeed, only be fought as family affairs, with the backing of kinsmen, friends and patrons. Of our 178 cases, 117 give clear indications of a woman taking refuge outside the home – in 88 cases with her parents, sibling or cousin. A doctor's wife in the village of Iznajar acknowledged that her funds came from a loan from her brother, the local parish priest.[32]

The decision taken, the cost calculated, one had to reckon with the chances of proof, which depended on getting the greatest number of witnesses together to swear to the truth of one's case. Where the number was equal the defendant would be absolved, though some litigants tried to claim that their depositions were better, and there was some doubt in their minds (though none in that of the judges) whether women and the poor should rank equally with solid male citizens.[33] The theory was that witnesses gave their testimony impartially, as in Iznajar in 1775 when the judge quizzed seven-year-old Isabel de Blancas about a wife-beating case. 'His Worship asked her what she understood by having made the sign of the cross and having taken the oath, and she replied that it was to tell the truth and anyone who does not commits a sin.'[34] Though the courts sometimes objected to the use of kin in divorce proceedings, except in cases where impotence was at issue, there was no agreement that the testimony of relatives was to be rejected out of hand. In the tiny community of Ohanes, the mayor thought that second cousins might be tempted to lie, but more distant cousins hardly at all; a peasant woman was categoric that 'she would not do so for any relative of hers, breaking her oath'.[35]

Most people were naturally more cautious about incurring the enmity of the other side. 'I cannot forbear telling you', wrote a friar to the man for whom he had testified in the *chancillería*, 'that don Francisco Guerra came to see me in the convent and mentioned the

[32] A.D.C. D/6/8, Cañas v. Reyes, 1775–6. And cf. D/1/1, Aguilar v. Gómez Bernal, 1611–12 for the award of interim alimony to a struggling lawyer against his propertied wife.

[33] A.D.C. D/1/45, Cruz v. Ramírez de Simon, 1659, for objections to women and the poor, objections on which the court failed to act. Though concerned with civil and criminal jurisprudence, Juan de Hevia Bolaños, *Curia Filipica*, 1602 first edition (Paris, 1853), is fundamental to the understanding of court procedure generally in Castile of the old regime. I am very grateful to Richard Kagan for drawing this work to my attention. See particularly pp. 90–4 on testimony.

[34] A.D.C. D/6/8, Cañas v. Reyes, 1775–6.

[35] A.D.C. V/68/7, Hernando v. Hernando, 1735.

lawsuit he was fighting against you. He told me how upset he was at the testimony I had given, and I know he told my family the same. I didn't know what to say, for since he is my friend I am sorry he thinks I am trying to harm him.'[36] Don Francisco's irritation was natural enough since testimony was nearly always an effect of personal obligations to the litigant. Though they may look innocent neighbours, we soon find out from the challenges (*tachas*) presented against them that an intricate network of godparenthood, affinity, employment or close friendship bound them to their principal.[37] Even if these connections were spotted by the other side, there was really very little the judge could do about it. In one divorce suit before the *chancillería*, a merchant's wife was condemned to costs for false pleading on adultery and beatings, and her male witnesses were warned with a spell 'in the garrisons in Africa' and the female with the home for fallen women if they were caught giving false testimony again.[38] But in the absence of any generalized system of cross-examination of witnesses, such cases were rare. Finally, there was little reliable medical evidence to be had, though the canon law had largely abandoned the concept of *maleficium* in cases concerned with impotence, and took doctors' advice in these matters and where venereal disease was involved.[39]

Since the law was such a blunt instrument why did not people settle their domestic disputes outside it? The men in particular were indeed keen to keep things quiet. Summoned for wife-beating in 1718, Cordoban notary Diego Sánchez declared: 'I thought it better to say nothing in my own defence than to have the rantings of someone so close to me ring about the courts.'[40] Even in adultery cases discretion often seemed the better part of valour. When a peasant of Montefrío found his hired hand in bed with his wife, he spared them both when the culprit fell to his knees, 'begging me not to kill him, for he was in mortal sin'; the case only surfaced later, when the guilty pair 'made the offence worse by talking about it'.[41] In the 1670s, when the dramas of honour vengeance were playing to packed houses, a pastry-cook of Granada only took his wife and her

[36] A(rchivo de la) R(eal) C(hancillería de) G(ranada) 512/2365/5, Guerra v. Soria, 1718.
[37] A.D.G. V/65/15, Cortes v. Sánchez, 1796.
[38] A.D.G. V/65/23, Varela v. Riancho, 1798–1800.
[39] Gómez Salazar, *Tratado*, iii, pp. 12–13.
[40] A.D.C. D/2/23, Fuentes v. Sánchez, 1718–23.
[41] A.D.G. V/65/9, Arco v. Nieto, 1795.

lover to court after neighbours made fun of his plight.[42] Particularly among the lower classes, unhappy partners might quietly pack their bags and leave. As one illiterate old woman who sold wine put it in her testament, her second husband 'didn't bring any of his wages home and I had to keep him, and he ill-treated me so that after four or five months of marriage we quarrelled so much that he left my house and has not come back since'.[43] Many other examples could be given from those unique personal records, the deathbed confessions (for that is what the will was in the old regime) of the Andalusian poor, which give us an idea of the 'dark figure' of real divorces.[44] Very occasionally we get the formal, notarial agreement of a middle-class couple to separate amicably: a Granadan notary and his wife calmly noted in 1631 that 'their temperaments are not in harmony, which has caused much quarrelling and unhappiness, and if something is not done about it they are both heading for an early grave'.[45] True, this sort of agreement was illegal: a married couple living apart of their own accord, in the eyes of the Andalusian church, were giving scandal. Bishops would periodically order their vicars to take action *ex officio* against such couples, and some of our divorce cases are simply the response of the separated parties to investigation of this kind.

Yet there were physical and social difficulties in the way of such private arrangements. The pattern of settlement left no room for the isolated farmstead. Nor was there much in the way of privacy in a land where thin adobe walls were commonplace.[46] The linen-

[42] A.P.G. E/Melchor Manuel Venegas/1676–8, fo. 1231v; E/Venegas/1681–2, fos. 272–3.

[43] A.P.G. E/Jacinto de Piña Ladrón/1787–92, fos 406–9v, testament of María de Moya, 29 Jan. 1789.

[44] For example, A.P.G. E/Luis de Morales/1622, fos. 241–4v, testament of Pedro de Arellano, peasant, 2 Apr. 1622, or E/Gonzalo Hernández Segado/1620, testament of María de Leyva, 9 Apr. 1620. To date, something like 18 of the 1,500 testaments I have looked at so far from Granada and Cordoba testify to this kind of separation.

[45] A.P.G. E/Francisco López Tenorio/1620–32, fos. 1008–9v, Salazar/Herrera agreement of 11 Aug. 1631. Already in 1480 the synod of Toledo had condemned the practice of mutual separation before judge or notary, cf. Bartolomé Bennassar (ed.), *L'inquisition espagnole XVᵉ–XIXᵉ siècle* (Paris, 1979), p. 314. But it was in the nineteenth century that the practice seems really to have worried the church, cf. Gómez Salazar, *Tratado*, iii, p. 9.

[46] French travellers constantly commented on the scarcity and poor quality of building materials in Spain, e.g. Bartolomé Joly (1603–4) or Antoine de Brunel (1665), in García Mercadal, *Viajes de Extranjeros*, pp. 120, 124 and 407. The Genoese merchant, Lantery, refers to the old style of making party walls in Cadiz

weaver's wife Maria Delgado 'was in such pain that the neighbours could not get to sleep' – which made her venereal disease a public not a private matter.[47] The frequency of lodgings, even for the middle classes, in a region where building materials were scarce and expensive, further diminished the intimacy of family life. The doctor of Iznajar's bedroom was only separated by a curtain from his landlady's living room.[48] The kitchen quarters of the principal families were open to ex-servants, to their families and friends. The affairs of the aristocratic Aceijas family of Puente Genil were thus common gossip in this little market town, one of the purveyors of information being the illiterate sister-in-law of a muleteer, whose aunt was married to the local schoolmaster for whom don Juan de Aceijas had stood as best man at his wedding – a remote connection, but good enough to give her regular visiting rights.[49] One of the witnesses to the divorce suit of doña Ana Teresa de Pedregosa against her husband don Jerónimo de Ortega had been a servant in the household,

> and having left about three months, I went back about a month ago for old time's sake (*con el cariño de aver estado en ella*) to see everybody, and asking Sebastiana, who sells wine in the house, how the whole family was, she told me that they were all well except mistress Ana de Pedregosa because master Jerónimo, her husband, had given her a whacking.[50]

At a lower social level, the tradition that work was carried on inside the household was so highly developed that any rigorous separation of 'private' and 'public' domains would be meaningless. The pack-saddle maker, Feliz Martín, brought workmen into his home even on Sunday mornings, where they were prime witnesses to his ill-treatment of his wife; the wife of the lawyer don Juan Rubio de Villegas waylaid the attorneys and clients who came to consult him, 'ruining my business'.[51]

'just of mud', though the practice was evidently dying out in the seventeenth century, cf. *Memorias de Raimundo de Lantery, mercader de Indias en Cádiz 1673–1700* (Cadiz, 1949), pp. 318–19.

[47] A.D.G. V/65/18, Delgado v. Martín, 1797.
[48] A.D.C. D/6/7, Cañas v. Reyes, 1775–6.
[49] A.R.C.G. 3/1004/7, Aceijas v. Aceijas, 1668–9; and cf. similar cases of the 'visiting rights' of clients and ex-servants in 3/1687/2 (Ecija, 1644) or 3/427/4 (Jerez, 1694).
[50] A.D.G. V/68/2, Pedregosa v. Ortega, 1699.
[51] A.D.G. V/65/21, Piñar v. Martín, 1795; V/68/19, Rubio de Villegas v. Romero, 1762.

Above all, marriage was not the conjunction of two individuals but an alliance of two families – and if there were no children the wife's property passed back to her kin and not to her husband.[52] Though the nuclear family household was the norm, there was much coming and going between kin. Indeed the very concept of a separate household is rather misleading. In the village of Dalías, at the foot of the Alpujarras, where the diocese of Granada gives way to Almería, the house of one of the notables adjoined that of his brother-in-law, 'so that they have access to each other from inside, while having separate front doors to the street'; a Granadan carpenter lived for a time beside his parents, whose idea was similarly to open a door in the wall separating the two houses.[53] The separation of houses did not necessarily reduce relations with one's kin. The daughter of a landowner in Montilla continued, after her marriage, to send her bread to be baked in her father's oven, while 'the linen from my father's house and that from our own were washed together in a stream belonging to my father, and then taken to our place for drying, since we had more room and more sun'.[54] Altogether 36 of our 178 divorcing couples had experienced an extended household for all or part of their married life, and a further 43 had close relations with their kin.

These were for women solid attachments cutting across their loyalty to their husband, and also to their children. Though at least 61 of the 178 women had children or were pregnant by the marriage and another 13 had stepchildren, custody of the offspring was never an issue for them. One aristocratic mother took her two daughters with her in her flight to her brother, sent two children to kinsmen, and left her two boys to wander the streets, nominally under the care of their brutal father, until they were taken in by neighbours.[55]

---

[52] A classic denunciation of the formality, coldness and suspicion which this arrangement bred in Castilian households, from the perspective of the new liberal bourgeoisie of the nineteenth century, comes in Segismundo Moret y Prendesgast y Don Luis Silvela, *La Familia Foral y La Familia Castellana* (Madrid, 1863), pp. 118–19.

[53] A.D.G. V/68/4, Peralta v. Arcos, 1762; V/65/2, Romero v. Rivas, 1793–7. The examples could be multiplied.

[54] A.D.C. D/1/23, Fernández v. Alderete, 1606–10.

[55] A.D.C. D/2/7, Ulloa v. Lobo, 1742–6. The courts granted her the separation. Migne, *Theologiae*, p. 481, noted that under old canon law the children went automatically to the mother for the first three years, and then to the father; but in his day, in the mid-nineteenth century, the secular courts were beginning to adopt the practice of awarding custody to the innocent party. Gómez Salazar, *Tratado*,

The law relating to dowry, the shortness of expectation of life, the value system, all combined to undermine the privacy and autonomy of the nuclear family. Household disputes could rarely be private quarrels between a man and a woman, since women especially were so dependent on their families of origin. One coachmaker's wife refused to follow her husband from Granada to his new business in Andújar, because 'his aim was just to deprive me of the protection of my family'; the wife of a hood-maker insisted that her husband come back from Vélez Malaga to Granada 'so that my father and kin could keep an eye on him'.[56]

The ramifications of kinship and household, which might bring matters into court, might also of course help to keep them out. The first moral authority for intervention in household disputes unquestionably lay with the kin. 'All the neighbours are terribly sorry for the poor wife', declared a Granadan weaver in one divorce suit of 1793, 'and have got together to tell . . . her grandfather that, if he does not act, they will'; while in Puente Genil around 1668, when the neighbours witnessed the too frequent visits of an aristocrat to the wife of a muleteer, they went first to tell the woman's *comadre* (co-godparent).[57] The rule seems to have been for affines to cede first rights of disciplining the guilty partner to the latter's own kin. Thus in Dalías a landowner's wife got her brother-in-law to 'scold' her husband for his ill-treatment of her, and in Murtas another landowner's wife resorted first to his kin – 'people of respect' – before trying to divorce her husband for adultery.[58] Within the household landlords, servants or employees might serve the same function. Given the importance of rented accommodation in Andalusia, a landlord's ire was a terrible thing. In Santa Fe in 1793 a peasant woman, who was separated from her husband, was refused the renewal of her lease when it was found that she was entertaining men; while in Iznajar the doctor was given

---

iii, pp. 16–17, notes that the church courts had lost the power of awarding custody in Spain too by this time. In general, I have the impression that the notion of the sanctity of the family and the good of children was only really developed by the church in the course of the nineteenth century, cf. Noonan, *Power to Dissolve*, pp. 158–283.

56 A.D.G. V/65/12, Martínez v. Sánchez, 1796; V/68/5 Díaz v. Martín de Castilla, 1758.

57 A.D.G. V/65/2, Rivas v. Romero, 1793–7; A.R.C.G. 3/1004/7, Aceijas v. Aceijas, 1668–9.

58 A.D.G. V/68/4, Peralta v. Arcos, 1762; V/65/3, López Jiménez v. Maldonado, 1793.

notice to leave by his landlady when she saw him hit his wife.[59] Servants in Andalusia had a complex relation with their employers, and were quite capable of criticizing them to their faces. In Montilla a landowner was lectured by his seventy-two-year-old housekeeper about going round arm in arm with his young wife, 'for it looked bad if anyone came in from outside'. The journeyman barber Gonzalo Molina had only been in his master's shop four months when he started scolding the latter's wife about her fights with her husband. In the little town of Hinojosa an illiterate foreman was asked by the wife of the rich peasant for whom he worked, 'to tell her husband, when they're out with the herds, to give up gambling, stay home more often, and not be so quarrelsome'; the advice might have looked impertinent since the foreman was only thirty years old, but the master only laughed it off with a shrug.[60] Usually, no doubt, the roles were reversed, and it was patrons who assumed rights of lecturing and arranging disputes. When the parish priest of Valsequillo found out about the adultery of the wife of his sharecropper, Felipe Morales, he tried to mediate, 'for charity's sake'.[61] Readers of Pitt-Rivers will wonder about the *vito*, the Andalusian equivalent of the charivari – also to be seen in the famous Hoefnagel drawing of sixteenth-century Seville, with a willing cuckold being flogged along the road on an ass.[62] But, as Pitt-Rivers points out, such demonstrations were illegal and possible only away from built-up areas – and what dispersed settlement there is in Andalusia rarely predates the nineteenth century. The anti-charivari laws date in Spain from 1765–87: 'anyone who has any particular grievance to air must go before the courts', they ran (though a law of 1564 had already prohibited lewd ballads in the streets, and, indeed, any charivari must already have run foul of the provisions against dishonouring contained in the great medieval lawcode, the Siete Partidas).[63] References to public satire of individuals are actually rather scanty in the Andalusian

[59] A.D.G. V/65/5, Molina v. Jiménez, 1794; A.D.C. D/6/8, Cañas v. Reyes, 1775–6.
[60] A.D.C. D/1/43, Rosal v. Oliveros, 1687–8; A.D.G. V/65/4, Cuero v. Moreno, 1794–5; A.D.C. D/2/2, López de Marmoleja v. Morales, 1739.
[61] A.D.C. D/6/34, Morales v. Sánchez, 1783–4.
[62] Pitt-Rivers, *People of the Sierra*, ch. xi. The Hoefnagel drawing can be seen, for example, in Antonio Domínguez Ortiz (ed.), *Historia de Andalucía*, iv, *La Andalucía del Renacimiento* (Madrid/Barcelona, 1980), p. 92. For the context, cf. the account of Bartolomé Joly in 1603–4, in García Mercadal, *Viajes de Extranjeros*, p. 118. [63] *Novísima recopilación* 12/25/6–10.

documentation of the old regime. One gets them typically in the episcopal archives, as an argument for dispensing with banns in the case of the remarriage of a widow or widower. In more serious cases of moral disapproval, the charivari was almost certainly regarded as inappropriate. The one example of its use which I have come across comes from the village of Fortuna in 1787, where the peasants went through town in a cart, singing rude songs about their local judge and his mistress, the wife of a rich peasant. But this was a calculated act of rebellion in a situation where judicial remedies were, *a priori*, out of the question.[64]

Nor, finally, did simple vendetta provide effective competition for the courts, though warring couples and their families stood to lose little by passing from words to acts. In Montilla in 1675 there was a classic confrontation between the peasant Acisclos el Rubio and his wife's brother, Pedro García de Baena. Acisclos pursued his estranged wife back to her parents' home, where, after some heated verbal exchange, Pedro 'asked his brother-in-law to step out into the street, whereupon Acisclos pulled a dagger and stabbed him in the right shoulder . . . and when his mother intervened to save her son, she received a stab in the hand'.[65] For one of the fathers of social science in nineteenth-century Spain, Pascual Madoz, Andalusia was the classic home of self-help, its people 'more akin to Orientals than to their European brothers . . . with a passion for the shotgun and the jacknife, a quarrelsome, disputatious race'. Even the modern, merchant city of Cadiz seemed terribly unsafe to the Genoese trader Raimundo de Lantery in the 1680s; 'tempers were brittle here, and it was the done thing to take life in those days'.[66] Possibly; but this is not what one would deduce from the transcripts of criminal trials stuffed into the wads of divorce papers. In 68 out of our 178 lawsuits the royal judges had intervened at some time to check violence. The impression they give is that, though violence certainly flared up in the course of matrimonial disputes, and indeed constituted the biggest single cause of divorce proceedings, it was quickly enough contained by the judicial process. The notion

[64] A.R.C.G. 321/4391/39, López Ríos v. Palazón and Torralbo, 1787–8. In general, the section *Expedientes Matrimoniales* of the diocesan archives of Granada and Cordoba, provide veiled references to the charivari.

[65] A.D.C. D/1/42, El Rubio v. García de Baena, 1675–7.

[66] Pascual Madoz, *Diccionario Geográfico-estadístico-histórico de España y sus Posesiones de Ultramar*, viii (Madrid, 1847), p. 471; *Memorias de Raimundo de Lantery*, p. 160.

of Andalusian, and Castilian, honour has perhaps been taken too much from contemporary drama, where only blood can erase the stain of a wife's infidelity.[67] A better guide to Andalusian morals would seem to be books of conduct of the period, whose message is quite the opposite of the theatre's. Echoing a commonly found opinion, the early seventeenth-century moralist Suárez de Figueroa noted that 'the greatest and finest victory to which a man can aspire in this world is that over himself'.[68] Honour came from good breeding, which taught a man the respect due to others.[69] Its essence was prudence, the curbing of instinct and passion by the use of reason, which constituted the very basis of civilized relationships as early modern Spain understood them. It was not an ethical system which indulged the hot-blooded man. As the future Vice-Chancellor of the Crown of Aragon and later Regent for Charles II, don Cristóbal Crespí, put it in a letter of advice to his younger brother, 'to retort to an insult is right and proper, but let it come in its due season . . . Only the foolish man feels no resentment, but it is the job of the wise man to wait his moment.'[70] This sort of scheming could accommodate itself better with lawcourts than with reckless violence. Inability to master anger is frequently cited in the divorce records as a telling indictment of the other side: 'a man who cannot control himself', 'a proud, rigid man', 'a quarrelsome fellow who shouts at everybody'.[71] Taking matters into one's own hands was not in conformity with the dominant ethos nor did it bring a man much advantage. It was also dangerous. The law of 1390 forbade general defence leagues or associations; that of 1480 outlawed the duel, and was stiffened in 1716 and 1757 by the death penalty.[72] The right to avenge oneself for a wife's adultery was hedged about with restrictions – that it be *in flagrante delicto*, that the lover be not of superior social status, that the wife be killed as well as the lover, and (after 1505) that one

[67] C. A. Jones, 'Honor in Spanish Golden Age Drama: Its Relation to Real Life and Morals', *Bulletin of Hispanic Studies*, xxxv (1958), pp. 199–210.
[68] *El Pasagero*, p. 300.
[69] Pineda, *Diálogos*, iii, pp. 324–5, insisting that there was no dishonour in pages of good family learning to serve on their knees.
[70] Printed in Eugenio de Ochoa (ed.), *Epistolario Español: Colección de Cartas de Españoles Ilustres, Antiguos y Modernos*, Biblioteca de Autores Españoles, 2 vols. (Madrid, 1856–70), ii, pp. 63–5.
[71] A.D.C. D/1/9, D/1/6, D/1/40 are only the most telling cases.
[72] *Novísima Recopilación* 12/12/1 and 12/20/1–2.

abandon any claim to the wife's dowry.[73] That classic of Castilian literature, Alarcón's *Three Cornered Hat*, which is such an excellent guide to social mores in Andalusia at the end of the old regime, turns on the theme of a miller's response to the supposed adultery of his wife with the local judge (*corregidor*). 'I can't use you', he says to his shotgun. 'Everybody would pity them afterwards . . . and I would be hanged. After all, he is a corregidor.'[74] By the eighteenth century, and as I would argue long before, honour vengeance was generally regarded as inappropriate.

Law was then supreme in Andalusia, though it worked in its own way. The organization of local justice was so highly developed in these close communities, with their formally elected *regidores* and *alcaldes* and appointed *corregidores* or *alcaldes mayores*, that trouble had a way of getting to court very quickly. The *alcaldes* acted as both policemen and judges, patrolling their towns on foot, throughout the old regime. In the village of Dalías, at the foot of the Alpujarras, one July evening in 1762, 'don Melchor de Aranda, *alcalde* of this village, going to ring the bell for curfew before setting out on his rounds at eleven o'clock, as is his wont, met the notary at the church door, who told him that he had noticed quarrelling in don Ramón de Arcos' house . . . They agreed to pay him a call to warn him to be quiet.'[75] The formality of the record for such a simple, village intervention reminds us of the legalism of the political regime in even the smallest Andalusian communities, which in this case brought a domestic dispute straight into court. The mingling of police, judicial and administrative powers in the hands of the *alcalde*, and the failure to distinguish private and public domains, turned the judge into a 'little father' of his community. As in communities studied by anthropologists, law was general rather than specific; it filled the gaps in individual and domestic relations.[76]

---

[73] *Siete Partidas* 7/17/13; *Novísima Recopilación* 12/28/5.

[74] Pedro Antonio de Alarcón, *El Sombrero de Tres Picos*, 1874 (Madrid, 1979), p. 122. Pope Alexander VII had already condemned in 1665 the killing of a wife or lover in this way, cf. Tomás y Valiente, *El Derecho Penal*, p. 71. By the eighteenth century honour vengeance seems to have been regarded by Spanish writers as no longer a problem, cf. Antonio Domínguez Ortiz, *Hechos y Figuras del Siglo XVIII Español* (Madrid, 1973), p. 242.

[75] A.D.G. V/68/4, Peralta v. Arcos, 1762. A good example of the formality of village political life in Andalusia can be had from the notarial records of elections to office of alcaldes and municipal officials – e.g. elections in Saleres, where there were just nineteen heads of household, A.P.G. E/Bernardo Messía/1651–4, fos. 117–18.

[76] John Beattie, *Other Cultures* (London, 1964), p. 156.

The great legal writer Castillo de Bobadilla, frequently reprinted throughout this period and himself a *corregidor*, makes the point eloquently, leaving considerable discretion in the hands of the judge to use a *corrección* (a scolding) rather than *coerción*, or to use secret trials to avoid scandal in the case of adulterous women.[77] Similar sentiments are to be found in the advice to a new *alcalde mayor* in Cordoba from a friend: he was to 'warn' rather than punish, be a good policeman rather than a good judge, to go on the beat and stifle every spark before it became a conflagration.[78] In their capacity as policemen the courts acted first and investigated afterwards, drawing up an indictment and gaoling a man once a statement of grievance was lodged with the judge, supported by two hearsay witnesses, before the individual had said a word in his own defence. From the pardons granted by victim to accused we gather that indictments were frequently incorrect.[79] This wide-ranging authority was systematized in the vagrancy law of 1745, parallel to French legislation of 1639 and 1763, which extended the definition of a vagrant to include disobedient children, neglectful husbands and bad workmen.[80] The edict was used in Andalusia to conscript for the army, without trial, on the order of the *alcalde*, adulterers and wife-beaters.

In theory the criminal courts, then, should have worked

---

[77] *Política para corregidores y señores de vassallos*, 2 vols. (Madrid, 1597), p. 692. Other writers of the period who advocated a flexible hand for the judge in handling criminal cases include Pineda, *Diálogos*, i, pp. 366–7, and Camos, *Microcosmia*, i, p. 154.

[78] In Ochoa, *Epistolario Español*, ii, pp. 529–31.

[79] A(rchivo de) P(rotocolos de) C(órdoba) E(scribanía)/Juan Díaz de Galarza/1639–42, fos. 56–7v, fos. 115v and 125v are three separate instances of pardon where there was no proof of guilt. In something like 39 out of 150 pardons of this kind which I have seen from seventeenth-century Granada and Cordoba the uncertainty of the charge seems to have been a principal factor in the release. Hevia Bolaños, *Curia Filipica*, p. 218, provides the classic justification for seizing a man on suspicion alone.

[80] Rosa María Pérez Estévez, *El Problema de los Vagos en la España del Siglo XVIII* (Madrid, 1976), pp. 61–2. For France, see Georges Snyders, *La pédagogie en France aux XVIIe et XVIIIe siècles* (Paris, 1965), p. 256. It is interesting to note that even the liberal reformers of early nineteenth-century Spain saw fit to maintain the essence of the vagrancy code, while exempting married men from its provisions. See Francisco de Paula Miguel Sánchez, *Dirección Teórico-Práctica de Alcaldes Constitucionales* (Granada, 1821), pp. 173–6. I am grateful to my colleague David Barrass for drawing this work to my attention. The aim of these vagrancy laws was simply to provide 'quick justice' on delinquents judged to be such by rumour: once rounded up, a man was presumed guilty unless he could establish his innocence.

admirably to solve most household disputes. But their informality was in many ways a real drawback. The transcripts of trials are full of the 'scoldings' given by the *alcaldes* to bad husbands, a variant of the English system of binding over to keep the peace. They were ordered to stay away from drink 'on pain of *presidio*' (hard labour, often in the garrisons of Africa, usually for six years), or not to molest a wife 'on pain of 500 ducats fine'.[81] But, in the latter case, a renewed act of violence led only to a further warning (partly because the man was mad and in the care of his father); while in Lucena, a certain don Josef Lobo was warned in 1742 not to beat his wife on pain of six years' hard labour yet, on his re-indictment on the same charge in 1744, released again after a month.[82] As we learn from the indispensable Madoz, criminal cases in early nineteenth-century Spain were less likely to end with a full conviction than with a warning or a pecuniary indemnity.[83] It would seem that the Andalusian courts recognized a very low threshold for intervention, but having intervened, aimed more to hold the peace between the parties than to enforce a normative code of civilized behaviour. Madame d'Aulnoy had made the point already: it was easier than in France to have a person thrown in gaol, more difficult to have him sentenced.[84] To talk of criminal or divorce courts, therefore, is perhaps misleading. It may give the impression of an institution operating according to impersonal rules, whereas everything seems to have depended on an intimate connection between the judge as a man and the persons who sought his intervention.

This attitude was suitable enough to litigants whose aim was more often to harass the opposition than to get a judgement. Something like 76 of our 178 divorce suits came on the rebound from the *alcaldes*, usually after the wife had exhausted the possibilities of keeping her husband in gaol or in Africa. But the divorce suit also provided a man with a very good means of retaliating against a wife who prosecuted him in the criminal courts. The homes for fallen

---

[81] A.D.G. V/65/15, Cortes v. Sánchez, 1796; A.D.C. D/2/24, Vargas v. Martínez de Rivera, 1732. On binding over in England, J. A. Sharpe, 'Enforcing the Law in the Seventeenth Century Village', in V. A. C. Gatrell, Bruce Lenman and Geoffrey Parker (eds.), *Crime and the Law: The Social History of Crime in Western Europe since 1500* (London, 1980), pp. 115–17.

[82] A.D.C. D/2/7, Ulloa v. Lobo, 1742.

[83] *Diccionario*, pp. 471–3.

[84] García Mercadal, *Viajes de Extranjeros*, pp. 1064–5. Rather similar points were made by Joly and Brunel, *ibid.*, pp. 118 and 443.

women, set up all over Spain from the later sixteenth century, were not just for prostitutes but also a deposit for women 'under suspicion' of adultery in divorce litigation.[85] To be placed in the Granadan house, Santa María de Egipciacas, was equivalent to a sentence of civil death. In 1794, the *alcalde mayor* of Granada, handing over to the *Provisor* a charge of assault lodged by a barber's wife against her husband, since the husband had sued for divorce on grounds of adultery, said that he thought the charge of adultery was frivolous and that she should not be deposited in Egipciacas, for it would be 'very damaging to her reputation' – which was precisely, one may surmise, what the barber had in mind.[86] In the hamlet of Posadilla, near Fuenteovejuna, divorce was only granted to a peasant couple on condition that the adulterous wife 'be taken to the home for fallen women in [Cordoba], there to undergo whatever rigorous penance may be assigned her'.[87] The courts were in general unwilling to prosecute adultery *ex officio*. Though the Council of Trent had ordered such investigations by bishops, the Provincial Council of Granada rejected the ruling in 1565, basing itself on the royal law of Castile which forbade such inquiries except at the suit of the husband, 'so as to avoid the far greater trouble which can follow the publicity of an adultery suit'.[88] The general caution of Andalusian judges, ecclesiastical and royal, when it came to enforcing normative standards, their absence of an 'axe to grind', and the fundamental *ex parte* tradition of moral and criminal justice, made the courts a useful, and above all retractable tool to use to belabour the opposition. Andalusians had a basic respect, not so much for the law, as for the person of the judge as a powerful intermediary in their disputes. In the Cordoban town of Baena (population 2,000 families in 1750), we find the *corregidor* chatting with the local priests after mass in the sacristy about the family quarrels of their parishioners. His attempt to use his influence led to a charge that he was meddling with ecclesiastical jurisdiction in one particular case. His justification is a classic example of the difficulty of separating litigation and mediation in Andalusia of the old

---

[85] The best overall survey is Josefina Muriel, *Los Recogimientos de Mujeres: Respuesta a una Problemática Social Novohispana* (Mexico, 1974).

[86] A.D.G. V/65/4, Moreno v. Cuero, 1794–5.

[87] A.D.G. D/6/34, Morales v. Sánchez, 1783. She was released, with her illegitimate child, three months later, into the custody of her father.

[88] Tejada, *Cánones*, v, pp. 397–400.

regime. He had ordered this pair of separated peasants together again, he said,

> not as a judge, but as a good father and friend, trying to get them to live in peace through Christian counsel and comfort. It was never his intention to bring a suit which properly pertains to the church before himself as a judge, but merely to invoke the authority and respect which he as a person commands in the community.[89]

Mediation in the old world was frequently cast in the mould of law, and vice versa, the court simply serving to publicize and authenticate claims and counter-claims in an oral culture lacking alternative forms of record.

A high proportion of the proceedings, before both the *chancillería* of Granada in civil suits and the church courts in marriage litigation, were not lawsuits in our sense at all. In a society lacking modern concepts of contract and absolute property rights, the court served as a forum through which one would broadcast to the community one's rights, by means of the device known as the 'declaration of witnesses' (*información de testigos*). Don Antonio Alcalá-Galiano, whose memoirs are such a mine of information on aristocratic family life in Cadiz at the end of the old regime, used this tactic when ordered by the governor of the town to go back to his estranged wife. He had no intention of doing so, and no intention of fighting a court case before the governor, whom he regarded as a personal enemy of his house. So he went to see the *Provisor*, a friend of one of his uncles. 'I reminded the *Provisor* of this friendship, and told him that I was consulting him as a gentleman might any person of standing, and not only because he might one day be my judge.' And the *Provisor*, 'speaking not as a judge but as a friend', advised the use of the 'declaration of witnesses' before his tribunal as a warning shot to the governor that, if necessary, don Antonio would sue formally for divorce if the latter insisted on his injunction.[90] It worked.

Judicial paternalism shaded off into patronage and clientage, and naturally enough the nobility often took a hand. Surprisingly, in view of his importance as mediator in other Catholic peasant

[89] A.D.C. D/6/26, Argudo v. Barranco, 1782.
[90] *Memorias de Don Antonio Alcalá-Galiano, publicadas por su hijo*, 2 vols. (Madrid, 1886), i, pp. 389–90. The incident dates from about 1813.

societies we do not hear much about the parish priest.[91] There were I think two reasons for this. First, even after Trent the parochial structure, by comparison with the religious orders, was relatively weak. The lawyer's wife doña Manuela del Castillo confided her husband's impotence first 'secretly to persons of learning' which almost certainly meant friars; then she told her parents, who told the parish priest.[92] The priest of Angustias in Granada lectured the postmaster in 1756 about his ill-treatment of his wife:

> I told don Diego that his conscience was not at ease, in my opinion, and that if he did not believe me he should consult persons of learning . . . I gave him a piece of advice when he came to make his annual confession this year, hoping that he would make a good confession and go back to his wife . . . That has not happened, I don't know why.[93]

Even among the lower classes a dissolute young husband of Cordoba simply walked out when his wife invited the parish priest in to give him a lecture.[94] Andalusia was not really like those other parts of Catholic Europe, like Ireland and Brittany, where dispersed habitat and the lack of formal institutions of local government made the church a prime focus of sociability. Further, as in the case of the secular court, pastoral relations moved rather easily into the orbit of law. The equivalent of the archdeacon and the *Provisor*'s local representative was the *vicario*, often a trained lawyer and sometimes also a commissioner of the Holy Office.[95] He had summary jurisdiction in marriage cases, could hear allegations of ill-treatment or adultery, and place a woman under safeguard before remitting the papers to the *Provisor*. He would also serve at a later stage to take the depositions of local witnesses by delegation from the diocesan judge. In general, the parish priest worked by

---

[91] Charles Tilly, *The Vendée* (London, 1964), p. 101; Yves Castan, *Honnêteté et relations sociales en Languedoc 1715–80* (Paris, 1974), pp. 468–9 – but their influence in Languedoc seems rather muted and shared with a range of other intermediaries. See also Nicole Castan, *Justice et répression en Languedoc à l'époque des Lumières* (Paris, 1981), pp. 40–1; and below, pp. 234 ff.

[92] A.D.G. V/68/3, Castillo v. Alvarado, 1772–8.

[93] A.D.G. V/68/6, Arilla v. Alfaro, 1756.

[94] A.D.C. D/6/33, Piedrola v. Gómez de Figueroa, 1783.

[95] We desperately need a study of the Spanish church at diocesan and parochial level. Inevitably the Inquisition has tended to capture the limelight; but the whole system of moral control reposed on the *vicarios*, not on the Inquisitors. All my information comes from the records of their activity contained in the diocesan archives of Granada and Cordoba.

persuasion, then handed over to the *vicario* when he felt that more rigour was required. Thus in Hinojosa in 1743 the priest called a field-hand by the name of Mollera and his wife to find out why he had beaten her and she had walked out on him. Mollera complained that it was because his wife was seeing too much of an old friend of his, Juan Romero. At this stage the *vicario* was called in, ordered Romero to stay away from the Molleras' house and street, and warned Mollera's wife to go back to her husband on pain of excommunication. The wife now appealed to the *vicario* formally for a divorce on the grounds of cruelty, while Mollera got the *corregidor* to exile Romero from town for eight months ('and sixteen months more if my lady the most excellent duchess of Béjar thinks appropriate') for 'offending the honour and chastity of a marriage'.[96] The incident illustrates how the poor found themselves involved in litigation willy-nilly in the small-scale communities in the old regime, and the ambivalent role of the church, at once counsellor and judge. It also illustrates the weakness of ecclesiastical censures: time and again the priest and the *vicario* handed over pertinacious moral delinquents to the *alcalde*, not to the Inquisition. Priests would be a prime source of information for the *alcaldes* when it came to picking 'vagrants' for the inclusion in the troop levies demanded by the government.[97]

Given the informality of the judicial system and the overlapping responsibility of *alcalde* and *vicario*, it is no surprise that few divorce cases were actually finished. (See Table 3.) Adjudication, one can see, did play some part in the work of the court, though a sentence of divorce appears to have carried few terrors for the Andalusian once the dispute itself had become public. Its importance was chiefly financial. The desire for alimony encouraged one sacristan's wife in Granada to 'divorce' her husband after they had already separated amicably.[98] The frequency of interim awards probably means that after nine months of litigation many women had achieved the security of an alimony payment. No doubt divorce could bring financial hardship; but the extended family in Andalusia made the break-up of the nuclear household no very traumatic experience. My daughter Angela, commented the wealthy municipal councillor don Jerónimo de Aranda Soto-

---

[96] A.D.C. D/2/9, Mollera v. Gómez, 1743–4. Béjar was feudal lord.
[97] For example, A.D.G. V/65/5, Jiménez v. Molina, 1794.
    A.D.G. V/65/28, Gutiérrez v. Vidal, 1799.

Table 3. *Ratio of sentences to lawsuits initiated in the divorce courts* (numbers of cases terminating in the way specified under each heading)

	Granted	Refused	Interim Award of Separation and Alimony[99]	Reconciled	Dropped
Annulments					
Coercion	4				
Impotence	1	1	1	2	3
Separations					
Wife-beating	13	1	20	7	38
Ill-treatment	3	1	9	8	22
Neglect	1	2	4	3	10
Adultery & venereal disease	2	1	3	5	13
Total	24	6	37	25	86
Duration of trials from first to last recorded act (in months)	18	28	9	12	2

mayor, has been looking after us since the annulment of her marriage, and he went on to make her his favoured heir, over his son, 'for the great love I have always borne her'.[100] Lower down the social scale patronage provided a buffer against misfortune: a divorced day-labourer's wife supplemented her needlework with alms from a kindly ex-employer.[101] The civil courts did not, as in France, interfere with the financial consequences of divorce.

Over half the cases were compromised or dropped within a year. 'My wife has got all the people I most respect in this city', groaned one Granadan tailor, 'to get me to give up this case, and I cannot very well say no, since I have my trade, position and friends to think of.'[102] Mediation was assisted by the strength of the idea of Christian

[98] This refers to a custody, specifying a 'safe place' where the woman was to be kept, on an allowance from her husband, pending a judgement.
[100] A.P.G. E/Juan Bautista de Palacio/1703–4, fos. 352–7v, testament of 13 June 1704.
[101] A.D.C. D/2/31, Jurado v. Lozano, 1730.
[102] A.D.G. V/65/13, Fernández García v. Valenzuela, 1796.

forgiveness. A master baker of Granada had his adulterous wife put away in a home and excluded from care of their child; on his deathbed he pardoned her, and two years later she successfully claimed his whole estate from the *alcalde* when the infant died.[103] Several other examples could be given of the willingness of Andalusian husbands, even in the seventeenth century, to swallow dishonour and pardon faithless wives.[104] The real dishonour in early modern Andalusia was not to demonstrate, what Andalusians valued above all other qualities, prudence. Publicity about their wives did not prevent Granadan artisans carrying on very successful businesses. Nor did the courtroom publicize dishonour, because publicity had usually been there long before in these gossip-prone neighbourhoods. Rather going to court was a public vindication of honour since it applied reason to the control of anger and sexuality. Like the Delphic Oracle the law confirmed what one wanted to hear: one thinks of don Antonio Alcalá-Galiano, aristocrat of Cadiz, or Pelagio de los Reyes, day-labourer of Cordoba, setting down solemnly in writing before a judge the circumstances of the adultery of their respective wives, 'so that, having seen the record and after thinking about it, one may file the appropriate suits'.[105] Law was a cleansing ritual.

Rather than view the cases we have been studying as 'divorce suits' we should I think look on them as instances of judicial arbitration in a world which lacked those attributes of modern law, specificity and formality. This old world did not pass away suddenly, but clearly it was undermined by changes detectable in the later eighteenth century and fully visible in the nineteenth. Part of this development was the growing privacy of family and household in Andalusia. The casual, interim injunctions which we get in the old regime – an order from the *alcalde del barrio* to a carpenter's family in Granada to close the party wall between their house and that of their daughter-in-law, an 'instruction' from the *Provisor* to a father not to visit his daughter because his son-in-law did not like it – testify to a ready use of law in domains where more informal arbitration would be used at the present day.[106] The

[103] A.P.G. E/Jacinto de Piña Ladrón/1787–92, fos. 445–9v, testament of Diego Barba, 1 July 1789; fos. 763–6v, claim of Antonio Castañares, 5 July 1791.
[104] A.P.G. E/Esteban Ramos Gavilán/1700–1, fos. 216–6v, 23 Oct. 1700.
[105] A.D.C. D/6/17, Reyes v. Porcuña, 1778.
[106] A.D.G. V/65/2, Romero v. Rivas, 1793–7; V/68/17, Nicolás v. Yspero, 1762.

gradual withdrawal of the courts from interference in these matters was presaged in two instructions for secular judges issued by Charles III in 1769 and 1788: 'They will not intervene, unless asked, in domestic quarrels between parents and children, husband and wife, masters and servants . . . so as not to disturb the privacy (*el interior*) of the household.'[107] The decline of the formal dowry contract around the same time and the resort to arbitration rather than law in disputes over family property are further landmarks along the same road.[108] Richard Kagan's explanation of the decline of civil litigation at an earlier period may well apply to the church courts too: the growing professionalization of jurisprudence made it unsuitable as a workaday tool of conflict.[109] One of our best guides to the changes which liberals were trying to introduce in this domain in the early nineteenth century is the work of the Granadan lawyer Francisco Sánchez. He defined the power of the new 'constitutional' *alcaldes* as threefold: administrative, judicial and conciliatory.[110] Though there is much in his book that would be familiar to any student of Castillo de Bobadilla, what is new is surely the concept that law and mediation, adjudication and arbitration, are fundamentally different things, and that the latter should always precede the former. This disentangling may be held to signal the passing of the old regime in Spanish jurisprudence.

[107] *Novísima Recopilación* 12/32/10.

[108] Though this is a subject which remains to be explored and which I am currently investigating, I would refer the interested reader to article 1349 of the Civil Code of 1889, which I take to be (at the prompting of Moret, *Familia Foral*, pp. 110–11) an attempt to increase the husband's right to negotiate with dowry land on condition he reimburse the wife with its *equivalent*. Cf. Joaquín Costa, *Derecho Consuetudinario y Economía Popular de España*, 2nd edn, 2 vols. (Barcelona, 1885), ii, pp. 177–9, for a description of the informal dowry lists and arbitrations thereon among the peasants of La Mancha, a complete contrast to the very formal, notarial contracts which characterized this class in the seventeenth and eighteenth centuries.

[109] Kagan, *Lawsuits and Litigants*, pp. 241ff.; see above, pp. 162 ff.

[110] *Dirección de Alcaldes*, p. 189, referring to article 282 of the new liberal Constitution of 1820 which ordered the *alcaldes* always to try conciliation first, 'con el objeto de terminar las discordias de los españoles antes que lleguen a hacerse contenciosas'.

9. The Arbitration of Disputes under the 'Ancien Régime'

NICOLE CASTAN
translated by the Editor

The following is an extract from Mme Castan's book *Justice et répression en Languedoc à l'époque des Lumières* (Flammarion, Collection 'Science', Paris, 1980). The editor and the Past and Present Society are extremely grateful to Mme Castan and her publishers for permission to publish a translation here. See also Mme Castan's *Les criminels de Languedoc: les exigences d'ordre et les voies du ressentiment dans une société pré-révolutionnaire*, with a preface by Pierre Chaunu (Association des Publications de l'Université de Toulouse II, 1980).

PREFACE: THE INTERMITTENCES OF THE LAW

Tensions and conflicts are facts of civilization, and when exasperated create harm and suffering which may be deeply felt. It is the business of the political authority to decide what is permitted and forbidden, to categorize the multiplicity of illegal acts; but it is for the individual or collective victim to demand justice, satisfaction and punishment. The sources of tension, its changing occasions, the forms of penalty are therefore concealed elements of the social dynamics we need to understand. But to grasp the process in its reality, we need to add to the analysis of formal proceedings that of the settlements which are offered to those offended, and relied upon for the maintenance of prevailing rules of conduct. By investigating their terms we can appreciate the range of sensitivities and of methods of countering aggression; in the ways they reveal submission or resistance to the underlying social realities, we can grasp the subtle interaction of forces at issue and of objectives pursued.

A high proportion of the innumerable conflicts of everyday life will never be settled by official proceedings or enter into the judicial system; many offences are tolerated by judicial intention or inertia or disappear through general incompetence. This variable quantity

219

is the subject of no systematic record and extremely difficult to estimate, though it appears often enough in subsequent proceedings called for by the exasperation of an unsettled dispute. Others, in equally variable quantity, get nearer to the light through records of unofficial mediation which may survive. In this case the two parties, offender and victim, more anxious for a rapid solution than for exemplary punishment, have deliberately chosen to settle by private arrangement. Thus many solutions may be preferable to legal proceedings; yet these, however restricted their field of action, have the inestimable advantage of bringing to light matters which would be likely otherwise to remain in the dark. In turning to the law, the parties change their tactics: instead of negotiation and arbitration, the tone is that of fighting for rights which one intends to uphold to the last iota; the apparatus of the state takes over the task of resolving the conflict, and the exterior authority of the judge will dominate the course of proceedings as they evolve within the norms of the law. The rites of judicial combat are not to be regarded as simply a representation of an external state of affairs, since there is no way of measuring the distance between absolute litigiousness and judicial proceedings; what they do is to define a threshold of irritation beyond which the victim, ignoring all the consequent difficulties, will decide to pick up the challenge and seek this extreme remedy. What this threshold is, is not easy to determine, and does not depend exclusively on the nature or scandalousness of the aggression: it must be sought also by a deep analysis of the power relations which act to withdraw the affair from the private domain and the control of the parties, and to hand it over to the public domain organized by the state.

There are then three possible types of behaviour, easily distinguished in theory – inaction, compromise and judicial proceedings. In practice attitudes are often less clear-cut and may shift by hesitations and withdrawals from one to the other and back again. It remains true that formal proceedings, unhappily and to an indeterminable degree less numerous than actual disputes, offer the only source capable of exhaustive study by quantitative methods.

A study of this kind requires evidently to be placed in a particular historical and geographical context; the present context is the extensive area of judicial responsibility of the Parlement of Toulouse, the largest in France after that of Paris. During the second half of the eighteenth century the population of Languedoc

Area of Jurisdiction of the Parlement of Toulouse
Sénéchaussées: 1. Gascony. 2. Guienne.
3. Upper Languedoc. 4. Lower Languedoc.

was going to law with increasing regularity. It was not alone in this. Put generally, the reasons for this expansion seem to lie in the simultaneous and reciprocal action of changes occurring in society and in the repressive policy of the state. The monarchy, persistently attempting to rationalize its administration and its justice, was seeking to gain a stronger purchase on the action of individuals. There is some question whether this effort, beginning in the 1750s, was genuinely effective, but it had the result of deliberately expanding the volume of judicial activity. The piling up of judicial proceedings, which were expanding by geometrical progression, entailed a greater willingness in the population to go to law. Further, in these last years of the *ancien régime*, the population confronted this intensification of judicial demands in a demographic and economic climate favourable to conflicts and frustrations; social divisions were widening, pushing the poorest into marginality while the rich got richer through economic progress; disputes and assaults multiplied, promoting insecurity and driving the possessing classes to demand a peremptory intervention of the law in defence of their property. At the same time the power to pardon, which until then had wiped out a large number of cases, was becoming increasingly restricted. In short, a new legalism, a disturbed population, arbitration on the decline, all combined to put a growing burden on the judicial machine, which it might or might not be capable of bearing.

Hitherto outside or only partly inside judicial action, a number of situations and criminal actions were tending from 1750 to enter into it, but they left outside a vast and ill-defined space of private initiative and public inefficacy. Naturally, the principal evidence for this area is provided by the judicial documents themselves: a plaintiff, a witness or any other participant in the process may well relate, apropos for example of a dispute about common lands, the extra-judicial negotiations whose failure has inspired the suit. One may find interesting information in private letters, in which notables carefully expounded the details of their negotiations; and also from the comments which the public prosecutors wrote in the margins of criminal cases, to bring the inadequacies of the law to the attention of the *procureur-général* of the Parlement and of the *Garde des Sceaux*.

These uncertainties are evidently not the sole prerogative of the *ancien régime*. Nevertheless, at this point the shifting balance between resort to the law and failure to resort to it does reflect the passage from an ancient to a modern conception of the law itself. This is visible, in the first place, in the emotions surrounding it. There was certainly still plenty of life in the old conception of judicial power which, even in the most serious cases, tended to regard its intervention as an unwelcome intrusion analogous to taxation. But at the same time one sees in the increasingly clamorous appeal to public force and public justice another conception of the state and of justice, another system of domination, of clientage and solidarity. Those who do not invoke it bear witness to their own mistrust and to its fallibilities.

The first thing to be remembered about the various kinds of assault is that the law distinguished two levels, the ordinary or *petit criminel* and the extraordinary or *grand criminel*. The first included offences satisfaction for which only concerned individuals, the second crimes and misdeeds threatening public order; public and private attitudes differed markedly between the two cases. After this, there is a problem about information. Not that there is a lack of it, on the contrary: contemporary writings, account books and private letters are full of stories, reflections, advice given or received. 'Get my case finished', ordered Mme Goeffrin. 'They want money? I've got plenty, give them it. What better use can I put my money to than buying some peace?' And the rich were not the only people to approach the choice between lawsuit and mediation with a penchant for peace and economy: in the eighteenth century, one required only a modest property to run the risk of being caught in the judicial machine and to seek to escape it through compromise.

It may seem paradoxical to look for evidence of this elsewhere than in private archives or the registers of notaries, which sometimes contain its results. Besides, the judicial archives may seem biased since they were more likely to record settlements unsuccessfully planned than those achieved. But a closer look will justify the use of a source which on the face of it excluded equitable judgements from its competence: the most modest case of insult, of pregnancy or even of theft will show how intimately, in the eighteenth century, resort and non-resort to law were intermingled. If the case continued for any length of time, it would have encompassed a whole series of manoeuvres and ploys waving alternately, in the cause of subtle blackmail or prudent reservation, the stick of justice and the carrot of accommodation. If an agreement was come to, it did not necessarily stick since it lacked the force of a tribunal legally entitled to pass sentence. So it is not surprising to find a large number of such episodes in the criminal records: one might even venture the outlines of a quantitative analysis. It may be of limited interest to explain that, of 4,092 criminal cases brought on appeal before the Parlement of Toulouse between 1779 and 1790, 7 per cent mentioned either a previous settlement or one in progress: what matters is to distinguish, by means of these 306 sets of negotiations, model situations and model settlements evolving in accordance with social and mental instincts.[1]

I. THE AMBIGUITY OF MEDIATION

In a traditional society like that of Languedoc under the *ancien régime*, where the law in any case intervened rather intermittently, the inclination to compromise was reflected by the collective wisdom of every level of society. 'Better keep your money than go to law,' was the saying, not only in the Vivarais; in the Gers, 'Always mistrust the law'; and everywhere, 'A bad agreement is better than a good lawsuit.'

In the first place a duty, deeply re-instilled since the Counter-Reformation by the pastoral activities of the clergy, rested upon all Christians to seek peace and to love their neighbour. Certainly it was principally the business of the *curé* to settle quarrels, but it was up to all the faithful to co-operate. Not to do so would entail the evil opinion of all, not simply that of the church. It is worth noting that 'law-monger' was one of the most frequent insults in Languedoc, and one of the accusations most often brought by defendants against witnesses in court, since it implied that they were incapable of rational or equitable behaviour. On the other side, the peasant woman who denied having wanted to make a legitimate complaint against her father-in-law, and affirmed that she had even begged him 'on Easter eve to end the quarrel so that he could make his

[1] See J. Charbonnier, *Sociologie juridique* (Paris, 1972); Y. Castan, *Honnêteté et relations sociales en Languedoc, 1715–1780* (Paris, 1974); P. Deyon, *Le temps des prisons* (Université de Lille III, 1975); M. Foucault, *Surveiller et punir: naissance de la prison* (Paris, 1975); J. Bastier, *La féodalité au siècle des Lumières dans la région de Toulouse, 1730–1790* (Paris, 1975).

Easter duties', was seeking to place both the moral and the penal responsibility of the lawsuit on the old man who had refused conciliation. This principal concern for Christian peace was nevertheless less frequently expressed than simple mistrust or fear of the law as a strange and unknown world. People preferred settlements which enabled them to keep to a territory in which consequences could be foreseen, and to put themselves in the hands of acceptable mediators who were abreast of all the relevant facts.

The law was a terrifying machine and might trap both rich and poor, though in different ways. The labourer, victim of an offence or a crime, could not expect anything better than a compromise. How could he possibly pay the costs of an action, unless he had behind him a third party to whom he was prepared to lend his name? He was left with the way of conciliation, and so much the better for him if, in this unequal combat, he enjoyed the secure protection of his master or landowner. Wage-earners, as a rule, were unable to go to law, though if they were the aggressors it would deal with them harshly. Smitten with panic, they offered all kinds of accommodation, restitution or compensation at the merest hint of a charge.

The person of property, whether the guilty or the injured party, seems infinitely better placed: favoured by his level of culture, his orderly and respectable language, his knowledge of law, relations and protections in the legal profession, even his leisure, since law required as much time as money. Yet his wealth itself made him vulnerable: he had to weigh the chances of a victory which alone could reimburse him for his costs, assuming that the loser had the wherewithal to pay. Meanwhile he had to pay counsel and meet all kinds of expenses; on the multiplying occasions presented by the judicial process, his goods might be seized, put under judicial leases or managed as sequestered property, and this sometimes for years on end.[2] If the original damage was modest, he might as well have followed the advice of the innkeeper of Aubenas for whom 'putting up with it would cost him less than getting justice'. The probable difference between the amount of the damage and the law's

---

[2] The seizure of property by the law might be requested by plaintiffs in order to secure their rights. It put the property in question, or more usually its fruits, into the hands of the law. It entailed costs of inventory and management, and the settlement of accounts at the end of a suit provoked numerous difficulties and arguments.

unpredictable dangers calmed many a would-be litigant: an artisan's wife, insulted by her sister-in-law, might well proclaim in the middle of a street in Montpellier that she was 'ready to swallow her portion of vineyard in lawsuits', but she hesitated all the same, fearful of losing in them a good deal more than her vineyard.

Apart from peace of mind and protection for one's property, compromise might offer valuable advantages. People tolerated, even at the highest level, astonishing verbal violence and directly offensive gestures, on condition, when tempers had cooled, of 'making reparation and living together amicably thereafter'. Many people were attached to such nobilities of attitude: compromise also ensured secrecy, that is to say the negotiable safeguard of his honour, to the person who had put himself in the wrong.

Non-resort to justice was thus a convenient attitude, which became a duty when preserving the family honour was in question: people in every walk of life affirmed that 'you do not go to law with a member of the family'. The position was decently expounded by M. de Sadoul, counsellor at the *cour des aides* in Montauban, to a young cleric who had solicited his intervention in a matter of inheritance: 'He could not approve the taking of steps which would cast grave reflections on the honour and sensibility of his elder brother.' Somewhat the same spirit of solidarity governed the refusal to take to court a member of the same community: assuming that the assault had not been excessively repugnant in character, or committed by a stranger, people found distasteful the idea of introducing an exterior power into a domain considered, like the familial, as private.

Altogether, beneath these more or less explicit motivations, there was concealed a profound desire to reduce to the minimum outbreaks of illegality, to play down as far as possible a situation which, if prolonged, would destroy the balance indispensable in a community. By means of a compromise, resting on principles considered just or at least acceptable, people hoped to resolder the breach in the social contract: duly sealed by a meal eaten together, its repair restored friendship and reknitted the broken bonds. In this way the two parties and their descendants avoided the long and painful quarrels, the almost obligatory vengeances which a legal battle provoked by the dramas which it added to the affair and by the rancour and humiliation which it frequently left in the defeated party. 'Burn all the papers immediately', M. de Varroquier, the governor of Saint-Affrique, told his agent at the close of a settlement laboriously arrived at, so anxious was he that no trace of the conflict should remain.

In fact the law did not, at least in theory, allow its machinery to be so easily halted. It stipulated that in a criminal case the compromise was valid for the parties but did not impose silence on the state; and it is precisely in observing criminals struck with incredulity by the idea that a case was not over and done with when they had paid their compensation, that we can understand the gap between the legislation of the seventeenth and even more of the eighteenth century, which codified and punished with ever greater precision, and an archaic mentality still deeply attached to the right of private regulation.

2. THE STRENGTH OF MEDIATION

Although a large part of these private arrangements, those concluded and carried out without documentation, must be invisible to us, it is possible from the 306 cases discovered between 1779 and 1790 to construct a classification of offences which distinguishes between town and country and between the *petit* and the *grand criminel*.

The priorities of country and townspeople were evidently not the same. For the first, the most important were settlements concerning conflicts about property (29 per cent, as against only 6 per cent in the towns), which turned for the most part on questions of use and abuse and therefore implied a mutual responsibility of both parties;

Subject of disputes amicably settled

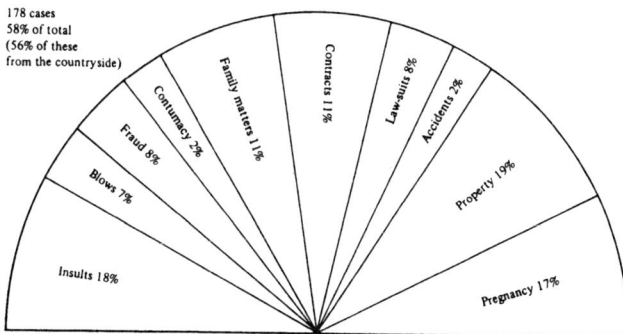

178 cases
58% of total
(56% of these from the countryside)

Contumacy 2%
Fraud 8%
Blows 7%
Insults 18%
Family matters 11%
Contracts 11%
Lawsuits 8%
Accidents 2%
Property 19%
Pregnancy 17%

Figure 1. *Petit criminel.*

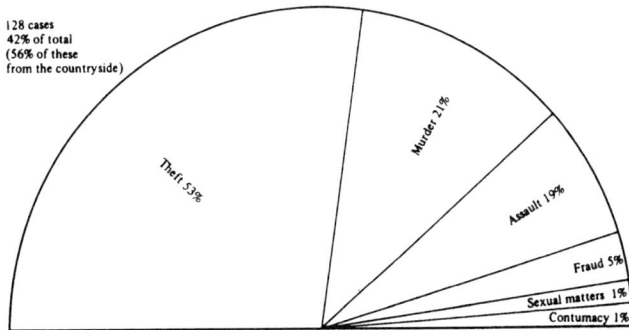

128 cases
42% of total
(56% of these
from the countryside)

Theft 53%

Murder 21%

Assault 19%

Fraud 5%

Sexual matters 1%

Contumacy 1%

Figure 2. *Grand criminel.*

they need to be seen in the context of a system of relationship and authority proper to the rural scene. Here property was above all an instrument of labour, and one undergoing change at the close of the eighteenth century: as such it provoked increasing conflicts and contraventions because of the imprecision and uncertainty of individual and collective rights; on the other hand the urgency of getting on with the job imposed a need for rapid settlements presided over by known and recognized arbitrators. Illegal pasturage was the classic case. It was relatively easy to sort out in so far as the guilty party was likely to claim that it was an accident; it was particularly difficult to charge him with acting maliciously since the normal arrangement was that the animals were watched over by the youngest member of the family or the feeblest of the servants. Everyone claimed that the animals had got out by mistake. As always, what embittered the argument and made it necessary to keep a firm grip on the discussion was the suspicion on the victim's part that he was being challenged and flouted in his own territory; the feeling had to be taken account of in the settlement, which was also a warning for the future.

In the chronicles of rural arbitration insults and blows are less prominent than they are in towns. Verbal abuse was not a characteristic of peasants, who were not much given to repartee and mistrusted words, like signatures, which obliged or compromised them. As for blows, their modest place in the *petit criminel* was partly an accidental effect of the likelihood that the brutal gestures of country people, always armed with an iron-shod stick or a knife, might produce mortal consequences, followed by desperate efforts to conceal them. Nevertheless, insults and blows represented nearly a fifth of the cases settled. People were very willing to offer reparation for unintentional excesses, committed by women who were thought not to be responsible for their actions, or under sudden impulse; a settlement might even take the place of a duel, still regarded in some circles as the method of settling conflicts of honour. So said a noble of the Vivarais whose challenge had been refused by the offender, another former officer, seeing in a settlement the best way of procuring a public reparation corresponding to the gravity of the offence.

The friendly arrangements which concluded cases of illegitimate pregnancy form a high proportion of all cases (11 per cent), when one thinks of the illegitimacy rate in the countryside which varied between 0.5 and 1 per cent of all births.[3] It was an absolute necessity for the girl and her family to preserve her honour. Everything depended, however, on the social distance between the seducer and his victim. If their social position was roughly comparable, as for the serving-girl absorbed into the family, the compromise was based on a fairly prompt resignation to an obligatory marriage or, if this was impossible, on the less exacting sense of honour of those who had to bow to economic necessity.

As soon as one rose in the social scale, even to the level of the householder and more especially to that of the rural bourgeoisie or the well established nobility, difficulties multiplied. The woman had an urgent desire for marriage, the only thing which could wipe out her sin and restore her honour; to persuade the man's family to accept her, her own had to offer compensations and benefits which would need to be argued about. The man at this level had a variety of means of, and reasons for, shirking his responsibilities if marriage did not seem to him appropriate; he might, however, accompany his refusal to marry with an offer of compensation. In short, agreement was achieved by a financially established balance and if it failed there was a lawsuit. In 1783, in the region of Toulouse, an orphan girl of a good bourgeois family with pretensions to nobility was being brought up by her uncle on a country estate where there was a shortage of distractions. An officer, lieutenant in the *régiment d'Aquitaine*, arrived at a neighbouring estate on six months' leave. Neighbourly relations occurred, and the girl turned out to be

[3] See J.-L. Flandrin, *Les amours paysannes* (Paris, 1975).

pregnant. As soon as this was known the young man, before hurriedly rejoining his unit in Champagne, handed the affair over to three ambassadors (one police lieutenant, one knight of Saint Louis, one businessman) – 'You ought to be able to fix it between you.' That, they objected, depended on what the witnesses deposed. 'For heaven's sake!', said the lieutenant. 'When I fucked the girl I didn't call any witnesses.' He rejected any suggestion of marriage, while accepting responsibility for the child. The negotiation was getting nowhere when the threat of legal sequestration of the estate forced the young man to return and adopt a more conciliatory posture. An offender of lesser status let himself be persuaded into marriage on condition that the father-in-law retired from business.

A handy way for a seducer to refuse marriage while keeping negotiations going was to say that he could not marry against the wishes of his parents since they would disinherit him, though he would offer compensation and take responsibility for the child. At this point in the argument a whole gamut of ploys might be resorted to with a view to undermining the opposition; the threat to go to law, summonses of witnesses, threats of seizure on one side, the spreading of tales which reflected on the girl's honour on the other. Everything could still be settled by the offer of substantial damages proportionate to the victim's status.

Things were very different in towns: conflicts and settlements in the field of the *petit criminel* took on another kind of significance, in the first place by their frequency. Pregnancies represented a quarter of the total, and dominated mediation in towns as those concerning damage to property did in the countryside. This was certainly due in part to a degree of sexual freedom consequent on migration into another way of life, as with servants who found places in towns. In that case the objectives and difficulties of settlement were the same as in the country: the desire, often futile, for marriage and negotiation on the sum to be paid. In these discussions one gets the impression of some shift of traditional ambitions and values. A royal judge, for example, from a family of haggling Gascons who had got him a dispensation to hold his office at the age of twenty-four, was happy enough to have as his mistress the daughter of M. de Romécourt, *seigneur* of Saint-Orens and ex-mayor of Mauvezin, but refused to marry her when she became pregnant. He grounded his refusal on his own youth and the loose character of a girl sick of family control and 'prepared to do anything to get away from home'; but the truth was different, as emerged when the young man's family threatened to disinherit him if he married her, considering 'the excessively small fortune of the young lady by comparison with his office and property'. Mme de Romécourt, at her wits end, did all she could to find an honourable solution: 'This is such a sensitive matter that we must scrape up every penny and make use of people important enough to get our point accepted.' All to no avail, in spite of a last effort by the Romécourts who clubbed together to raise a dowry of 4,000 livres.

Towns were changing more rapidly, witness an amazing verbal crudity towards anyone whatsoever, without any respect for rank: eloquence flourished, offending modesty and decency to a degree which would not later be the case. Insults and blows amounted, at 32 per cent, to a percentage of negotiations similar to that of conflicts about property matters in the countryside. It is true that in towns property was not so generally an instrument of labour, that its boundaries and its uses were more exactly defined, and that numerous conflicts were quarrels over the garden wall which rapidly degenerated into insults and threatening behaviour. But the matter in dispute was often trivial, an occasion for the manifestation of ill-temper and vapours rather than an affair of fundamental interests. Such was the case with the innumerable neighbourhood quarrels which women enjoyed having with each other, like one virtuous old woman, a priest's housekeeper, outraged at the visible social advancement of an attractive girl with a generous friend. Vitriolic letters, scandalous songs or jokes in the worst possible taste failed to stand in the way of a settlement. To enjoy yourself, like the *curé* of La Plume (Lot-et-Garonne) and his housekeeper Marie Barbe, by persuading a nine-year-old girl, the daughter of a *receveur des domaines du roi*, to wade through the outlet sewer from the hospital latrines, thirty feet long, for a sou, was an offence which might have had serious consequences had not some bourgeois hastened to settle it. The same was true of incidents in the street where the townsman, prompt to slap a face or even to draw a sword, was prepared on reflection to offer compensation and 36 livres damages in the morning.

In collective disputes which concerned groups or members of groups, what was at issue was no longer the honour and interest of the individual and his family, but the order of the community. The need to settle them was that much stronger that the play of solidarities divided the community and put its social equilibrium in danger. In that case a genuine diplomatic service was put in operation to re-establish peace and make possible a return to normal relations. I choose the example of an act of ritual violence, the *paillade*, current in Languedoc and more especially in lower Languedoc. It resembled the charivari, but its purpose was to punish not remarriage but the undue subordination of the man in a household. It was directed as much against the humiliated husband as against the trouser-wearing wife. Hence occasions for it were numerous, from a wife's adultery to imperious gestures on her part. To go and drag one's husband from among his companions in the inn was enough to set off the *paillade*; likewise the display of any attitude contrary to the mores which maintained women in apparent subordination. By his feebleness the man had betrayed the estate of masculinity, and his dishonour reflected on all males; his companions were obliged to redress the matter and to force the couple to keep to their traditional roles. This social performance was a fearsome method of collective constraint, provided that it was not allowed to get out of hand, and was played according to a very strict set of rules in which arbitration had a determined place. At Caveirac, in 1781, a pathetic householder was deceived by his wife: the matter was public knowledge and so properly taken in hand by the young, more exactly by the unmarried young. Obscene songs, chanted in chorus by all the children of the town, were the first shot, denouncing 'the cuckold whose horns laid end to end would reach from here to Nîmes'. Then came the rowdy derisive masquerade performed before the assembled population; before which how-ever, as the rites prudently required, the leading maskers had secured some 'people of consideration' as patrons of the *paillade*, just in case.

Disputes among kin, on the other hand, were not either in the rural or the urban milieu massively represented in unofficial settlements. This is surprising in a society which regularly made use of the marriage contract and the will in favour of the eldest son, arrangements which might seem designed to multiply quarrels and dissensions. The effect was very evident in formal lawsuits, especially in towns where it was intensified by the presence of a thicker stratum of the wealthy and by more marked changes in the way of life. One might have expected to find more trace of it among the settlements, though no doubt many such conflicts were settled by internal agreement and left no trace outside the family papers. Only family monographs could discover them. Those that do emerge, mainly matters of inheritance and especially legal portions, were there as a result of disputes dramatic enough to have been brought to public attention; most of them therefore came into the category of the *grand criminel* due to the degree of violence involved, which sometimes went as far as murder.[4]

The proportion of 42 per cent for cases entering into the *grand criminel* gives a misleading impression, since in most cases these concerned actual crimes in the present sense of the word. Nevertheless nearly half the equitable settlements concern such crimes: 58 per cent of them thefts, 34 per cent grievous bodily harm including 19 per cent murder. Here one can see most clearly the persistence of a traditional frame of mind. But here also the action of the state was most clearly felt in the second half of the eighteenth century, seeking to insinuate itself into existing mechanisms of self-regulation and to substitute law for privately accepted norms in the field of social relations. Here is one example. It occurred at Noé, in the environs of Toulouse, in 1785, where a peasant sharecropper killed a bourgeois landowner with so few precautions that the entire community was immediately *au courant*. To the inhabitants of the village who overwhelmed him with good advice, he replied: 'They can't do anything to me, nobody saw it,' meaning that he was sure that nobody would inform on him. 'Everyone whispers that Méras (the share-cropper) committed the murder, but that he was driven to it and that nobody is to say anything about it'; he had been 'brought to a terrible state of despair' by a pitiless landowner who refused him the corn he needed to live so as to make up for what he had lent him on account of the shortage the previous year.

Yet as soon as murder had been committed, this attitude became more difficult to maintain. For a settlement to be reached, it was essential that the crime should have been honourably motivated. The revenge of honour or reaction to particularly iniquitous

---

[4] This was the case of a merchant of Figeac who had been robbed by his brother; one night in February 1788 he threatened to kill him. Since his younger brothers had only managed to secure their legal portion by violence, he had decided to follow their example. He kept in his heart, he said 'resentment for the humiliated life which he had led in the family home, where he had been allowed nothing but the servants' black bread'.

treatment were more easily justified than mere viciousness. In general, people were prepared to excuse all unpremeditated violence committed in a state of excitement, fury or drink. Everyone recognized in such incidents his own impulse to brutality: slashes or shots exchanged at the end of a wedding breakfast or the parish feast were too spontaneous, too much part of the ritual of the occasion not to be interpreted as mere accidents which might be transformed into tragedies by the hazards of medicine.

What fundamental conclusions can one draw from these regional contrasts of town and country, *petit* and *grand criminel*? Perhaps above all the underadministration of the countryside by comparison with the towns, where a more abstract and more generalized authority was growing up. Peasants, face to face with the realities of the land and its exploitation, needed to resolve their problems as quickly as possible and without exterior interventions: the interventions of the law, foreign to them in particular by its language, were no less feared than others. Towns gave less ground for criticism on this score. Overadministered by comparison with the countryside, they possessed their own judicial authority, present on the spot, provided with officers and policemen. Here the law was in possession of effective instruments which it was commanded to make use of by a state preoccupied with the reign of order; nobody minded a great deal if Texan mores obtained in one or two remote districts, but they would not be tolerated at Toulouse or Nîmes. Hence the attitude of the subjects of the law had been formed by the close proximity of judges whose language and practices had become familiar. Even in modest towns like Frontignan there were magistrates' courts with summary procedure, well adapted to the fluidity of urban relations: such were the *bureaux de police* or the *petit consistoire* at Toulouse, whose sittings, presided over by a member of the city council, dealt every morning with a whole range of minor urban delinquency. Here immediate decisions which cost little and often took the form of a warning or light penalty calmed tensions, so that these courts played the same role as arbitration in the countryside.

3. THE INTERMEDIARIES

Short of a written and signed agreement of the parties to put their dispute to the decision of some person or persons, the intervention

Table 1. *Persons arbitrating, in town and country*

	Town	Country	Total
Clergy	15 = 29%	33 = 33%	48 = 32%
Nobility	6 = 12%	27 = 27%	33 = 22%
Bourgeois notables	11 = 21%	9 = 9%	20 = 13%
Lawyers	12 = 23%	26 = 26%	38 = 25%
Judges	5 = 10%	3 = 3%	8 = 5%
Tradesmen	3 = 6%	2 = 2%	5 = 3%
Total	52 = 34% of overall total	100 = 66% of overall total	152

of an arbitrator was in no way necessary: compromise would succeed if both parties accepted responsibility, the offender for the offence and the victim for the limitation of his claims. Word or signature given was sufficient to make a friendly agreement, and this was no doubt the procedure adopted in a mass of trivial cases which were not worth the attention of 'persons of consideration'. We have little chance of finding out about this sort of offence, except by a chance reference in a story or a letter. People reported incidentally that they had 'fixed it up', or that someone 'had decided to settle'. But if the business got complicated, if people's sensitivity made negotiation difficult, and it was felt that the best chance of avoiding a breakdown was to bring somebody else into the discussion; then an agreement and its execution might be guaranteed by remitting it to the objective authority of a third party, and written documentation or verbal testimony may be available.

Procedure of this kind evidently implied a hierarchical society at least some of whose higher levels possessed the esteem and authority sufficient for the conciliation of disputes. There had also to be a sense of honour which would absolutely oblige people to keep their word by reference to a set of rules which everyone accepted. The requirement of correct and responsible behaviour made precisely the difference between arbitration imposed and arbitration freely solicited. Just as every man was not capable of putting in motion the law, so all were not in a position freely to invite external intervention: everything depended on relations of power and control which those concerned were often unwilling to make clear.

Table 2. *Persons arbitrating, by sénéchaussées*

	Gascony (26 = 17%)		Guyenne (37 = 24%)		Upper Languedoc (35 = 23%)		Lower Languedoc (54 = 36%)	
	Town	Country	Town	Country	Town	Country	Town	Country
Clergy	2	9	3	11	2	7	8	6
Nobility, *seigneurs*	–	5	1	4	4	6	1	12
Bourgeois notables	1	2	2	3	2	2	6	2
Lawyers	1	4	2	9	4	6	5	7
Judges	–	–	1	–	–	1	4	2
Tradesmen	1	1	–	1	1	–	1	–
Total	5	21	9	28	13	22	25	29
(% of total for *sénéchaussée*)	19%	81%	24%	76%	37%	63%	46%	54%

It is evident in the first place that the category of persons whom law and custom treated as not responsible for their actions would find a verdict imposed upon it without argument: the mental defective, or the *fils de famille* under parental authority and so judged incapable of entering freely into a settlement. The same was true of all those who, for lack of goods and of honour, failed to measure up to the standard of economic responsibility and social esteem required to obtain the guarantee of 'persons of consideration'; these people would dictate to them the terms of a settlement in language as firm as would an exterior judge. Unless one had crossed a certain threshold of respectability and independence one was in no position to have recourse on one's own initiative to this private tribunal and possibly to choose its members.

These were not however chosen at random: notabilities of various kinds, they had to represent the indispensable networks of sociability and authority. They were therefore the skilled maintenance workers of a social equilibrium constructed on a basis of custom more or less in keeping with the law; their function was especially vital in a region like Languedoc, a distant province less firmly controlled by the royal administration than the ancient royal domain close to Paris. Underadministration, in this linguistic and cultural context, demanded the intervention of such local intermediaries, bilingual, deeply or superficially touched by French culture and the only people capable of re-establishing concord through conciliation.

The choosing of them was not an arbitrary matter but an effect of the logic of the situation in question. According to the range of local activities and peculiarities, they might emerge from the family, the parish, the *seigneurie*, the community or the craft guild, though there were also constant elements to be noted throughout the whole of Languedoc. Of the 306 negotiations already mentioned, the arbitrators were detailed in 152 cases.

Arbitration in towns

Towns make you free, it was said in the Middle Ages, and because of that they constructed their own hierarchy, which was continually adapted in accordance with demographic and economic renewal as well as with the mobility and the social intermixture of their inhabitants. Traditional authorities, and notably the *seigneurs*, who were still recognized in the countryside of the eighteenth century, were unable to transplant themselves as such into the urban environment. Distant from its base on the land, dissociated from public authority and judicial authority in particular, the dominant class was a more or less recent arrival and therefore more unstable, more heterogeneous and something of a *parvenu*, without a solid installation in the normal chain of hierarchical relations. In towns, nobody received the same unconditional recognition as the aristocratic inheritor of a long lineage. As new methods of getting rich proliferated, the growing power of money put in the shade the ancient glamour of birth; it stimulated competition among the meritocracy and hopes of social advancement, so elaborating a social and cultural hierarchy more shifting and less elementary than that of the village.

Hence there emerged possibilities of arbitration not in vertical but in horizontal relationships: mediators were judged on their competence and technical qualifications, the more so that the increasing rationalization and complexity of economic and social relations made it necessary to have recourse to specialized talents. These influential people, deeply imbued with the ethics of equality and individualism emanating from the Enlightenment, naturally questioned and transformed the norms which had hitherto governed the process of private arbitration. Rather than to a consensus founded on respect for traditional hierarchies, they appealed to the weight of a public opinion which, in towns large and small, possessed a collective authority sufficient to promote the work of conciliation. From this point it is clear that the authority of the mediator became limited and insecure, challenged and even made obsolete by an ever more penetrative state machine. The urban community, incapable henceforth of providing the support of a vertical hierarchy of orders, to some extent made up for this weakness by a cultivation of horizontal solidarities.

Not that the traditional mediators had disappeared at the close of the eighteenth century: they were in decline simply because the distinction of orders had become a factor of segregation in face of the challenge of money, and hence the authority of the first two orders had no longer the same force. Nevertheless the clergy was still in towns the principal object of requests for arbitration, presiding over 29 per cent of negotiations, as against 33 per cent in the countryside. For the town clergy had the prestige of birth, wealth, education and diversity of function which distinguished it from the rural parish priests. Take the case, normal for a rural capital, of Toulouse. Here the clergy occupied such a large number of offices and had such considerable resources that it was in a position to act as mediator at all levels of the population. Around the archbishop the high ecclesiastical technocracy consisted of nine vicar-generals and a secretariat; the cathedral chapter of Saint Etienne included six archdeacons, twenty-four canons, two hebdomadaries, twenty-four prebendaries and twenty-six choir priests. In short, there were at least a hundred ecclesiastics attached to the archiepiscopal see and the cathedral, all of them from the more polished ranks of society between the middle bourgeoisie and the *noblesse de robe*, and possessed of a solid education. There were forty dignitaries in the chapter of Saint Sernin; the *curés* of the ten city parishes, all with at least one vicar, two in the densely populated quarters and four at Saint Etienne; the priests of the four seminaries and six colleges, of the private chapels such as those of confraternities, and of the hospitals. This multiplicity of functions, supported at the individual level by the practice of the direction of conscience, put a variety of private negotiations in the way of the clergy.[5]

Opposition to their intervention was usually motivated by their well established reputation for greed, a conviction, it must be said, held by no less greedy families. Their presence at the bedside of the sick and dying exposed them to accusations of diverting inheritances and, by way of confession, of interfering excessively in family affairs. The *curé* of La Plume 'profits from the last moments of the dying to bring accusations against the family and make off with their papers' (in this case recognizances for debt); his defence was that 'she [the dead woman] was so poor, due to her continual illnesses, that he has been obliged to give her assistance every year, and that the poor box of the town provided her with clothes', but this seemed so implausible that an appeal was made against him to the vicar-general of the diocese.

All the same, as soon as a matter arose which concerned personal or family honour, such as illegitimate pregnancy or theft, anything in short which called for considerable discretion and would only be spread abroad by going to law, people turned by preference to a member of the clergy, carefully selecting whoever inspired them

[5] See J. Sentou, *Fortunes et groupes sociaux à Toulouse sous la Révolution* (Toulouse, 1969).

with the greatest confidence (the director of conscience, for example). At Caylus, some young bakers entrusted the archpriest with the delicate mission of persuading their mother not to remarry. Such examples could be multiplied, though they were occasional rather than universal.

Arbitration by members of the nobility was in a distinctly more marked decline, representing no more than 12 per cent of cases, as against 27 per cent in the countryside. This loss of influence by the nobility is the more surprising since there had never been so many nobles in the town populations, due both to social advancement and to the transfer of quarters from country to town by a considerable part of the seigneurial class. The migration, though mainly towards the larger towns – Toulouse, Montauban, Béziers or Nîmes – had some effect on them all: like many nobles of the region, Charles de Maffré, *seigneur* of Lastens, settled at Lavaur; Pierre Paul de Pagèze, marquis of Saint-Lieux, did the same, by contrast with his father who expressed the wish to die on his own land and kept the use of the family *château* after the distribution of his property.

Henceforth the prestige of the nobility could no longer be based on the exercise of public authority, especially of judicial authority, by the *seigneur* on his lands. Very few of them were in a position to exercise this authority in towns, and these were extremely powerful people who did not reside there. Monsieur, the king's brother, bought from Jean du Barry for 900,000 livres in 1775 the *seigneurie* of Lisle-Jourdain, and that of Grenade from the Prince de Conti, but appeared in neither place, any more than he did at Pézenas where he was also *seigneur*. On the other hand the social influence of this group remained considerable in any urban community, and especially in the smaller towns where the noble families kept their roots and enjoyed a prestige disputed by no one: at Castelnaudary the family of Hébrail, at Limoux the marquis of Hautpoul, as much in demand as the archbishop of Narbonne or the lawyer Barère de Vieuzac. But the foundations of this social influence were changing: henceforth it was founded as much on wealth as on respect, for urban property and wealth create much more distinctly capitalist relations. Further, the ancient nobility, like the new, was penetrated by contemporary ideas, whether through the 'amazing *penchant* for slumming' noted by Proust or through the appeal of social liberation. The power of money, denounced by the marquis d'Argenson ('this wind of prodigality blowing from every corner of

France'), brought together in a mongrel aristocracy a whole variety of nobles ranging from the ancient nobility to extremely rich bourgeois 'living nobly'. All of them participated, as much by their wealth as by their birth, in the social life of a rich and leisured class, and the mediating power of the nobility properly speaking became enfeebled.

Thus restricted, it was principally exercised at two levels, first in the hierarchical relation with traditional dependants like household servants, with whom the nobleman maintained a relation of patronage often originating on his country estate: at Le Puy, the count of Saint-Haon remained the natural protector of his servant Simon, born on his estate at Le Velay, and it was part of his duty to settle a matter of theft committed by him on a certain Mme de Bec-de-Lièvre. Second, and to an increasing degree, this power of arbitration was exercised within the nobleman's own circle, as horizontal solidarities prevailed over vertical ones: in the Mont-désir case the circumstances were dazzling. The salon which governed behaviour among the polite society of Montauban was that of the marquise de Tauriac, frequented by the canons of the cathedral, the nobility of the town and the members of the *cour des aides*. Here the affair was much and passionately discussed after the circulation throughout the town of a libel designating known persons by transparent names. The great game of society was to identify them. 'There was a great deal of laughter at table', said the marquise's butler, 'at the absurdity of the names.' The marquise summoned to her salon a sort of arbitration committee, one of whom, a priest, obstructed any kind of accommodation by continual wisecracking.[6]

In this oligarchy, complex and different in every town, the notabilities among the bourgeoisie occupied an increasing place in mediation on account of their number, their economic power, their numerous activities and their administrative role: 21 per cent of the total, twice as much as the nobility. Among them the lawyers, solicitors, notaries, advocates, practitioners of every type, expert in plumbing the depths of an increasingly fluid and abstract set of urban relationships, were the indispensable element. The expert in feudal law dealt with boundary problems; the notary was the

---

[6] The pamphlet was entitled *Le testament de Lord Temcourt*. The priest's brother was given the name Martial, his sister Miss Suz (*sic*), Madame de Grialou Milady Grasselsalou, etc.

normal mediator in any case which had to be concluded by a formal document, stipulating everyone's rights in a divided family or the compensation in money required for an assault. The advocate, on the other hand, would be preferred by parties strongly inclined to go to law in any case: they hesitated, clarified their rights, constructed hypothetical arguments, but might on reflection hand all the papers over to him to avoid an uncertain lawsuit and opt for a settlement where the defence prepared by the advocate would serve as a means of exercising pressure.

Respected notables and lawyers dominated negotiation in towns: not surprisingly, few craftsmen figured in it; doctors appeared only on occasion – it was still too early for them to challenge the clergy for a role justified neither by their social condition nor by the state of their science.[7] There would have been more resort to arbitration by businessmen if this function had not been performed by organs supervised by the tribunal of the Bourse, whose judgements were esteemed so highly that many towns in Languedoc requested the establishment of such institutions during the eighteenth century.

As for judges and administrators, counsellors in the sovereign courts, criminal judges, royal procurators, *subdélégués* or mayors, their position was ambiguous. As in the case of the *parlementaires* of Toulouse, they were much in demand to influence the course of a suit, and just as much avoided as potential mediators. To request arbitration from them was conceived as half-way to going to law. They were resorted to only partly as 'persons of consideration', mainly because owing to their office they possessed an authority and power calculated to instil honesty in witnesses and ensure the execution of an agreement. When they appeared, like the *subdélégué* in the Varroquier case, it is quite clear that they had been called in to bring the business to a conclusion. Theirs was very much the double role played in this society by any functionary, whether *curé*, *seigneur* or administrator: private arbitration, public judgement. On the whole the urban sector, a theatre of multiple frictions and variegated tensions, was being drained more and more of its internal autonomy for lack of adequate authority in a divided ruling class, to the benefit of an external power more vigorous and better equipped.

---

[7] Doctors were nevertheless called to play a moderating role in cases of witchcraft or poisoning, where accusations made on the spur of the moment were dismissed by the general opinion of judges and doctors.

The rural intercessor

In this respect the countryside was distinctly backward and amenable to traditional hierarchies: at least in part and on the surface, for the rural world was not immutable. Its structures too were being shaken by change gradually penetrating it in depth: something was happening in the countryside from the 1740s, just as it was in the towns. Nevertheless it remained much more distinctly under the control of unofficial jurisdictions. Everywhere, informal 'tribunals' continued to ensure the settlement of conflicts; they were composed of well known personages, at the same time mediators and protectors, drawn from the historically dominant *cadres*, above all the *seigneurs* and the church. People turned to them quite naturally, and every community knew perfectly well who was the mediator suitable to a particular case; there was in general no need to invite the intervention of external authorities.

In Languedoc it is not possible to contrast as starkly as usual an urban world governed by royal authority with a rural world under seigneurial control. Apart from the fact that he had, as elsewhere, to take account of the power of the church, the *seigneur*, in a region of written law, was obliged to deal with an ancient tradition of communal autonomy: in matters of mediation the communities of Languedoc were under the triple authority of the *seigneur*, the *curé* and the municipality, and their equilibrium depended on the successful interaction of this trinity.[8] Traditionally the *seigneur* had the greatest power, and if he collaborated with the *curé* and the *consuls* of the municipality he did so as a dominant partner. His wealth in land, the political and judicial power which he exercised, the honour to which he was entitled ensured him the role of primary mediator; in cases of difficulty his jurisdiction continued to give him a notable power of persuasion. Hence the 27 per cent of negotiations which he supervised.

As a rule, if he was diligent and responsible in his life and actions, the *seigneur* was still the person to whom people brought cases to be settled, with a spontaneity which reflected his rights of patronage, operative both in the exercise of internal arbitration and in the protection of members of the community in their relations with the outside world. Isolated by their oral culture and their language,

---

[8] See G. Frêche, *Toulouse et la région Midi-Pyrénées au siècle des Lumières* (Paris, 1975).

they could only communicate with it through intermediaries, preferably powerful ones. So the *seigneur* as such was eminently suited to intervene in their name with outsiders, though to preside effectively over the regulation of internal conflicts he needed to be on the spot and to cultivate personal relations with the population. An example taken from the Lauragais demonstrates the persistence of such relations: the *seigneurie* in question was that of Calmont (*sénéchaussée* of Castelnaudary), in the possession of the family of Saint-Marcel de Paulo until the Revolution. A vagrant woman from the Ariège gave birth to a child in a barn in March 1786. After baptizing it, she later maintained, she smothered the baby and threw it down a well; she attempted neither to conceal the fact nor to deny it. The peasants, not knowing what to do, took her spontaneously but rather brutally, despite her protests, to the *château* ('let me go, you'll get me killed, let me go and do penance, God will forgive me.'). The countess, unlike the peasants, took a charitable view: one can see in the depositions of the witnesses the deep trust of peasants attached by long tradition to a family which had managed to maintain its authority.

But such cases were bound to become rarer as the nobility deserted the countryside,[9] leaving a vacuum to be filled by bourgeois, peasants and lawyers at a time when rural communities were in any case in the throes of demographic growth and fundamental economic change. The behaviour of the seigneurial class was such that it did nothing to mitigate the consequent tensions, but either observed them without doing anything about them or made them worse by its own demands. In either case, the *seigneur* came increasingly to underestimate the genuine character of personal bonds entailing reciprocal obligations, to attend exclusively to his dues and his rights. As the history of the *seigneurie* tended to make of him a stranger or an enemy, he was in no position to continue exercising the role of the essential mediator. Little respected, baited by a body of young people whose behaviour he had no way of influencing, he found himself reduced in public judgement to the status of a mere mortal, no longer an arbitrator but a cause of dispute: the tempo and geography of this evolution was to be fixed with some exactitude by the riots of 1789. And even if he kept his authority and prestige inside the rural community, he

[9] The discussion of this subject in the original version of the text is omitted here (ed.).

would no longer be conceived as arbitrator of more than one segment of matters in dispute: what people were anxious for now was the use of his social power and his network of connections with the outside world. Who would take his place?

The parish clergy, *curés* and vicars? In essence, yes: they exerted in the villages an influence comparable to that of the clergy in the town environment. Especially since the social equilibrium of the countryside was suffering from the loss of its terminal categories, the nobility and even the bourgeoisie at the top and the poorest at the bottom. Though the loss of the latter did not in this context matter very much, the place left free by the 'élites' would be the object of prolonged struggles for the domination of communities, in which the *curé* would not fail to be a fairly frequent victor. First, because he was the sole priest available: the unique resource which he offered depended on his complete knowledge of a milieu which he entered because of his function and judged according to his experience. This became very obvious in 1790 when *curés* were excluded from certain tasks, especially that of the distribution of charity, by the new municipalities: as the *curé* of Mauguio (Hérault) complained, 'the shame-faced poor get no assistance because they have no confidence and are embarrassed to expose their needs'.

Further, the *curé* was constantly resident: exceptions were few and always caused a great deal of trouble. Absenteeism mainly occurred on the outskirts of towns, especially where these were of some size and had a bilateral relationship with the countryside, sucking its lay and even clerical *cadres* but also colonizing it through the acquisition of property. The environs of Montpellier were dominated by large estates in the hands of head servants whose masters lived in the town 'except at harvest time', and fairly thick with 'rural parishes which have never required the residence of the *curé*'. The acts of diocesan visitations also reveal some absences near Toulouse: the *curé* of Le Falga preferred to live at Saint Félix de Caraman, a town of 1,000 or so inhabitants where he had the company of three teachers, a doctor, three surgeons and some Sisters of Mercy.

The effects of assiduous residence were frequently intensified by a long incumbency: at Azereix, three priests took up the whole of the eighteenth century with respectively 29, 22 and 31 years: at Murviel, the prior had been there for 34 years, and although this was unusual it was normal to find *curés* who had lived in the same village for fifteen or twenty years. They were also recruited, if not from within the diocese, at least from within the region, with a preponderance from neighbouring dioceses. And even if there were variations between regions producing a surplus of priests (the mountain regions of Auvergne, Rouergue, Dauphiné or the Pyrenees) and those with a deficit (like the plains of lower Languedoc), it remained true that the *curé* shared a civilization and a language with his flock, in spite of differences of dialect and pronunciation. He was somewhat more segregated from his flock by his social origins, normally bourgeois or even noble, and by an education not always very advanced, but certainly better than in earlier periods and characterized by the trilingualism (Latin, French, *langue d'oc*) which in Languedoc was the mark of the educated classes.

They had the advantages, furthermore, of a financial security which placed them above most country people, as one may deduce from the frequency of theft in presbyteries and from their practice of making loans: the *curé* of Castelbajac, according to the calculations of J.-F. Soulet, lent 475 hectolitres of corn and 4,000 livres in money between 1740 and 1774.[10] The priest was also an administrator much used by the crown since the sixteenth century, for lack of local officials, in the tasks of government: apart from his well known duties as registrar, he was a censor of morals and above all a channel of information for an unlettered population ignorant of French and of the mode of expression of the state. He informed, explained, expounded, acted as interpreter between the state and the peasant who often enough had no other means of understanding what was going on in the world outside. Turgot wanted to institutionalize the function by turning the *curé* into an official instrument for the transformation of the countryside. One may take a good example from the Vivarais in 1783. The king sent a commission from the Parlement of Toulouse whose duty was to ensure the supersession by royal justice of local judges and legal practitioners: *curés* were instructed, during their announcements at mass, to inform the faithful of the fact and of its importance:

> Assist the *consuls* of your village, who may be illiterate, in the
> promulgation of the royal Letters-Patent, and of the Letter
> intended to inform the oppressed how they can make their

10 See J.-F. Soulet, 'A propos de l'endettement rural au XVIIIe siècle dans les communautés du Piédmont pyrénéen', *Annales du Midi* (Jan.–Mar. 1973).

grievances known. What better mark of your concern for your parishioners can you give on this occasion, than to make known to them the opportunities created for them, in his secret counsels, by a King who prefers the title of Father of his subjects to that of their Master?

This was all very well, but it is clear, in these years which marked the beginning of a great transformation, that the *curé*, while still for many the arbitrator who made up for the weaknesses of the law and of seigneurial authority, would nevertheless become himself an arm of the law in so far as his efforts failed to secure peace by private means. He would become its servant to the degree by which he made use of it as a kind of secular arm, denouncing to various authorities the violence he was unable to control.

In fact, with 33 per cent of rural arbitration, the clergy was distinctly in the lead, though shortly to be overtaken by the bourgeoisie and lawyers together, particularly by the latter with their greater expertise. Yet there seems little sign that the function was unpopular. True, the servant of the *curé* of Maignan justified in 1781 a theft against his master by affirming 'that he would never have scruples about stealing from *seigneurs* or *curés*', but this was uncommon before the troubles of 1789. Hostility was mainly directed against the regular clergy, insufficient in number and insistent on their rights, of the great abbeys of Saint Chély of Aubrac or of Saint Sardos in Gascony, while the *curés* were the subject only of modest complaint about conduct 'unworthy of a priest'. It is obvious enough that the *curé* Fautrier of Fitou, who went about armed and escorted, 'when he takes the Sacrament to the sick, like a Roman senator, with his two servants, also armed, beside him', was no more competent to act as an arbitrator than a law-mongering minor landlord. But there were kindly *curés* as well: everything depended on the individual and on the internal balance of the community.

In short, in spite of certain limitations, the *curé* was the best man to settle disputes which required discretion. Family matters and especially cases of pregnancy were taken to him, above all by humble people who found it easier to rely on the authority of the *curé* than on the technical competence of the notary, whom the bourgeoisie preferred. A case of withcraft, or more exactly of defamation, shows by its complications the ambivalent role of the *curé* in arbitration, and the limits of an authority which was not undisputed. Not for nothing was the village concerned, near Boulogne in Gascony, situated close to the centres of the witch-hunts of the preceding century. A peasant woman was accused by general consent of 'killing the cattle and doing harm to people'. She terrified everyone by her boldness and physical strength: 'She would not be so busy', they said, 'if she did not possess a mandrake root.' The problem fell into the competence of the cunning man, a surgeon who kept an inn in a neighbouring village and had a role rather like that of the *official* of the diocese: he was consulted and asked to exorcize the witch and break her spell, which he did for a fee of 6 livres for the advice and the protective objects to be put in farm buildings (double the fee of a doctor from the town). Then he ordered the witch's entire family to be shut up, which caused confusion in the village. At this point a small group of artisans decided to resort to the *curé*, not to settle the case, which was not thought to be within his competence, but to ask his permission 'to fetch in some learned person from outside' in order to decide whether magic had taken place or not. The *curé* sensibly did his best to explain to them the idiocy of what they were doing, but without avail: in the end they had to resort to outside authority. It should be said that, though in this particular type of case the intervention of the *curé* was benevolent but marginal, his arbitration would be needed as soon as those concerned felt the need to receive absolution for their evil behaviour, whereupon penance would take the place of legal repression. This transference required the *curé* to possess a firm moral authority which he must not hesitate to support, if necessary, by religious sanctions as forcible as exclusion from the sacraments.

In saying that the priest was the favourite arbitrator of this organic society (though also an indispensable one for lack of anything better), is one affirming that in the exercise of his pacifying role he could rely on the unanimity or at least a broad consensus of the population? Not exactly, for in the internal balance of rural society new divisions were appearing and alliances being created and collapsing behind shifting fronts on which the domination of communities was being fought for. At the heart of these events, a man of authority and often also a man of the Enlightenment, the priest could not withdraw from a conflict where *seigneurs*, businessmen, lawyers, rich proprieters and municipal officials were each involved either with him or against him. According to the situation the *curé* might be allied or opposed to the *seigneur*, the municipal authority representing the local oligarchy, or the population. In either case, and whether or not he was supported by a local party or an exterior power, it is very clear that he found the desertion of the countryside by the 'élites' a welcome rather than a deplorable process, since it left him without a social rival except a middle class comparable and competitive with his own. At Saumon (Lodève), the *curé* 'claims to be more important than the *seigneur*, and leads the people, who are poor and ignorant, by the nose'; at Chusclan (Montpellier) the *seigneur*, counsellor at the *cour des aides* of Montpellier, came back for the summer of 1786 to find himself insulted by his peasants 'because the *curé* who runs this community with an iron hand has no wish to have a resident *seigneur* to reckon with'.

What was emerging was a type of *curé* very different from the model propagated by the Counter-Reformation of the seventeenth century. More and more involved in the cares of the world, he concerned himself with economic and social matters as an administrator anxious to recover his whole portion of the tithe, to ensure his control of public assistance, of teaching and of the distribution of charity, in short over an increasing sector of the population. These ambitions encouraged some of them, principally in Gascony and lower Languedoc, to behave more like temple officials than devoted pastors. On the one hand they refused to do anything which was not strictly within the definition of divine service, and in particular, as was objected against the *curé* of Auzan, anything for which they did not receive a fee; they also stolidly resisted all requests from communities who were continually wanting the appointment of vicars 'to restrain and educate the young'. On the other, they vigorously exacted all their rights, and sought to establish new ones like the extension of the tithe to new crops or the upkeep of the presbytery. These selfish preoccupations made them doubly distasteful to their parishes in that they were no longer capable of a pacifying role and were indeed themselves a major cause of conflict.[11]

Equally serious, though motivated by a high spirituality, was their insistence on expurgating traditional Catholicism of all kinds of elements which they judged maleficent and heathen:

[11] See B. Plongeron, *La vie quotidienne du clergé français au XVIIIe siècle* (Paris, 1974).

processions, prayers for the cattle, blessings of the crops, pilgrimages, bell-ringing, in short on evacuating so far as possible the festal element from popular religion. Since a large number of *curés*, in concert with the upper classes, had the firm intention of suppressing a large part of the social rituals so fundamental to the sociability of the Midi (parish or calendar feasts, dancing, inns), it will be no surprise to find them raising the standard of the new bourgeois morality, preaching the values of work and order, of everything contrary to leisure, spontaneity and festivity. Nor will it be surprising to find, in dioceses where Jansenist priests had been in charge of the training of generations of seminarists, conflicts arising from a 'Reformation' so similar in its effects to those of enlightened or Anglo-Saxon philosophy.

The chief beneficiaries of the weakening of seigneurial and clerical power were the 'Messieurs'. All bourgeois in different degrees, they dominated the rural population by their property, their wealth and their culture. Taken together, with 38 per cent of the total, they certainly represented a lesser proportion of rural mediation than they did in the towns (54 per cent); they were nevertheless, even in the countryside, the first resort.[12] They form however a rather loose category within which there are important distinctions to be emphasized: its members, and not all of them, enjoyed respect for the antiquity of their wealth and residence, their education, their property and their office. Three types may be distinguished according to their function – bourgeois properly speaking, lawyers, and judges and administrators; but among the first only families of 'old and respected' bourgeoisie possessed a prestige which equated them more or less with long-established landed families. They played an essential role in certain kinds of negotiation, such as those which a father of good family had to undertake to 'arrange' the future of a compromised daughter. A bourgeois of Saint Orens (Gers), acting as confidential envoy and friend of both parties, carried a succession of proposals from one to the other, dined at the *château* and calmed susceptibilities; he prevented the crises occurring which arose from premature contact and only brought the parties together once an agreement in principle had been ratified by everyone. Among the respectable classes, such notabilities were then entrusted with unofficial

---

[12] See A. Soboul, *Les campagnes montpelliéraines à la fin de l'Ancien Régime: propriétés et cultures d'après les compoix* (Paris, 1958).

missions which enabled the guilty party or his victim to avoid losing face or making excessive concessions during the negotiation.

As 'persons of consideration', they also sorted out the most serious assaults committed by the poor, but in this case they carried the same authority as would the *seigneur* if he were resident or the *curé* if he inspired confidence. At Durfort, where as was often the case in the region people steered clear of the *curé*, a day-labourer who had murdered a householder put the matter into the hands of a respected bourgeois; a silk worker of Le Velay, involved in an unpleasant case of theft, went off to find a 'Monsieur' with a present of a bag of silk flock. It was almost exclusively the ancient bourgeoisie which took on this arbitral role: a neo-bourgeoisie in increasing quantity was setting itself up beside it, but the peasants refused to give it the same respect. Profiting from a favourable economic climate and equally favourable legislation they were getting rich as farmers of seigneurial domains, with feudal rights and tithes: they intensified economic distinctions within communities and did a great deal to upset their equilibrium. Considered as *parvenus* in an age when such people were despised, they became segregated from their dependants, controlling them but rarely acting as mediators for them. Occasionally they presided over the settlement of disputes between neighbours about boundaries, but even here people often preferred to resort to the services of a surveyor or feudal lawyer. Feared, and rightly so, they were more often found in lawsuits than in arbitrations.

It may well seem surprising that, as the figures show (26 per cent out of 38 per cent) most of the arbitration done by the bourgeoisie was in the hands of those who one way or another were engaged in the chicanes of the law. In Languedoc they were called *hommes d'affaires*, a vague term which covered notaries, solicitors, advocates and other practitioners; it would have made more sense to call them *hommes du droit*, since in this world of illiterates they possessed an undisputed monopoly of the knowledge and practice of the law. During the last years of the *ancien régime*, the *seigneur* of Laudun, comte Dormier, did not reside there, and the public prosecutor was practically illiterate: 'It's a disaster for the whole village that we have no intelligent people here, neither *seigneur* nor judge nor judge's deputy.' That left the *sieur* Dutour, notary and first *consul*, who kept the population under his thumb because he was the only person who could inform people about their rights, and he was a 'bad lot'. All the same he was the person whose skill was needed for any matter which required exact knowledge of the law: disputed letters of exchange or bills of debt, rejected tradesmen's accounts, fraudulent bankruptcies, conflicts of inheritance or property. Add to that, to get an exact notion of the man, that he was apt to collect in his hands several activities which markedly increased his grip on the inhabitants: notary, agent or *fermier-général* of the *seigneurie* where he also held the court, town clerk, first *consul*, tax-collector. Given a little skill in the exercise of these various functions, such a man could make himself not arbiter but actual master, in a position to impose settlements designed to intensify his dominion over the community. Furthermore, in these difficult years, he could use the resources at his disposal to get numerous small proprietors into his debt, with the consequent threat of seizure of their property. Thus, to give a single example, at the death in 1787 of the solicitor François Rigaud, adviser to the d'Antraygues family, his family papers deposited privately with the count in his *château* of Labastide (Villeneuve-de-Berg) revealed that he possessed recognizances for debt amounting to 20,427 livres signed by people from the entire region. People said that such men were becoming a formidable power. A perversion of the mediating function turned the pacifier into a disturber of the peace: in this way veritable mafias of lawyers got under their control whole areas of Guyenne or of the eastern flank of the Massif Central, to the point of provoking rebellion.[13]

So it is clear that, at the end of the eighteenth century, the arbitral machinery deriving from the *seigneurie*, the church or the land was falling to pieces. Its disintegration went on at different rates in different places, but was clearly accelerating in the second half of the century, as may be seen from the accompanying increase in legal business. More given to change, the towns no longer saw in it anything more than a marginal activity, a private matter dealing only with trivial or confidential affairs. It survived more tenaciously in the countryside, at least in appearance, for it too was insidiously affected. Who was responsible? One thinks first of the monarchy, which in the course of centuries had set up, with persistence though varying success, a public justice charged with the duty of gripping all its subjects in the net of universal laws and tribunals. The mediators

[13] See N. Castan, 'Caractéristiques criminelles des hautes régions du Languedoc oriental', 44ème Congrès de la Fédération Historique du Languedoc mediterranéen et du Rousillon, 1972.

themselves clearly bore some responsibility also. Whether their position was due to tradition or of recent emergence, they destroyed or proved unable to establish the kind of personal relations which bound them to communities in a reciprocity of powers and duties. What too frequently and too implacably took the place of mediation were unilateral demands of an economic or socio-cultural order, resented by the population as arbitrary since they were devoid of any compensatory element. Be that as it may, nostalgia for the tribunal of mediation, feared no doubt but also familiar, remained considerable. It was to express itself in the grievances submitted to the States-General, which looked rather for an improvement of arbitral methods than for an abstract, universal and distant law.

4. CONVENTIONS OF AGREEMENT

There was an essential difference between a compromise and the judgement which concluded a case at law. The judge's sentence summed up all the elements of the judicial process and expressed both the will to punish or absolve and the evaluation of the penalty. In a mediated settlement the parties were not simply present as people demanding their rights: by admitting their responsibility they sought a compromise which took account of the point of view of all parties. It took the form of an agreement between them, a private contract subject to the general principles governing contracts, requiring, that is to say, mutual consent and the legal capacity of the parties to agree. There was also, of course, an obligation to respect law and morality. This apart, they possessed absolute freedom to stipulate the details of compensation, with the proviso that in case the agreement was not executed they might be required to prove that it existed.

Hence they had an interest in giving a binding agreement an objective form, in providing sanctions for non-observance and keeping open the possibility of a final resort to law. One might have thought that people so anxious to avoid both the publicity and the complications of the law would have preferred agreements formalized in the simplest way, by mutual consent and a firm purpose of carrying out one's obligations. It is true that the most primitive type, a pure verbal agreement, did exist: one finds them here and there reported as having been carried out. This type was rather like the handshake which symbolized a purchase in the market. It remained current in milieux where anonymity did not exist and there was no question of evading one's word once given: the unwritten law no more required the composition of a written document in this case than it has done in respect of the obligation of honour entailed by gambling debts in other times and places. Everyone was perfectly aware of the consequence of backsliding, an alarming state of moral quarantine extremely damaging to reputation and credit.

It is also true, and especially in Languedoc, that many agreements were entered upon a written document and counter-signed by the witnesses. If these in addition were the mediators who placed upon the act the guarantee of their power (the *seigneur*), their moral authority (the *curé*) or their social standing (a notable), the value of the document was that much greater. One notices however, along with the decline of the influence of such persons, an increasing substitution of the notarial act for the simple sealed document. To the detriment of traditional authorities, notaries were mediating in an increasing number of disputes, their skills being particularly in request for cases with financial or judicial complications: it appealed to the sense of economy to employ them both as technical advisers and as mediators. A householder, intending to rescue his son-in-law from the debtors' prison, was well advised to turn up, accompanied by a notary, at the inn where the prisoner and his creditor were staying the night: the notary calmed the dispute, drew up the bill for 200 livres which the father-in-law promised to pay, negotiated the details of payment and gave himself as guarantor. A retraction made and signed in his presence was by general consent equivalent to the withdrawal of a charge in court. Everyone in short was convinced that by going before the notary, as a public officer, they were giving a more binding force to their undertakings. The act was also used as a last resort before going to law, a form of pressure much used where the parties lacked confidence in each other's word. One finds this frequently used as a threat by pregnant serving-girls about to give birth: 'She will bring a complaint at law, if the seducer does not undertake his obligation to the child before a notary.' This was more a form of blackmail than of 'arrangement', and the man was left to weigh the financial pros and cons of lawsuit or agreement.

The *vinage* or joint drink was not properly speaking an item in the agreement, but a ritual gesture which symbolized reconciliation. It concluded the negotiations which frequently took place among the lower classes at an inn or over dinner, and consecrated in renewed conviviality the setting aside of the dispute and the restoration of peace. It was so embedded in usage that it was rarely mentioned unless something memorable happened during it. It would rate a mention if it degenerated into a pitched battle, bringing all negotiation to an end; it could also be raked up as proof of the ill-faith of a party misguided enough to breach all good usage and bring the matter to law again, in which case it provided the other party with an alibi for refusing to take any notice.

By investigating the substance of agreements it is possible to measure, here and there, another aspect of the diffusion of generalized law and of its externally forged image of justice and punishment. The distance which separated the locally applied norm from the general rule of the state was a sign of survivals and refusals, as well as of lines of force and relations of power well understood by the parties but rarely mentioned. The general rule which governed mediation was the restoration of material or moral order according to modulations which reflected certain aspects of economic and social reality. The reparation of honour applied, as at law, to any insult, libel or breach of a person's moral integrity, whether or not accompanied by physical violence, in an order reflecting the gravity of the offence and possibly even more than at law the social status of the victim: it is obvious that the honour of a poor girl was worth less than that of a girl of quality.[14] Precise dispositions related to particular classes of offence. For any attack on a person's reputation, the reparation had to be made in public, like the offence: on the model of the judicial ceremony which required the accused to make his declaration before the clerk of the court or in the courtroom and in the presence of witnesses, agreements obliged the offender to undergo a ritual equally public and humiliating, withdrawal before a notary or carefully chosen witnesses. The accompanying request for pardon was a different matter, since it consisted of a supplication to the offended party to renounce his right of punishment and limit himself to a request for damages, in

[14] Public insults between peasants were 'arranged' for six to ten livres, while among members of the bourgeoisie a figure of some hundreds of livres was not exceptional. In cases of illegitimate pregnancy, the sum varied with the status of the victim: 4,000 livres for example for a daughter of the bourgeoisie and a few *écus* for a country serving-girl. The circumstances of the seduction and the degree of anxiety to keep the matter secret were also important considerations.

the hope that by this means the conflict might be appeased. There were legal difficulties if the matter was scandalous or there had been an infringement of public order: none the less in 1791 the newly appointed arbitrators still accepted the retraction of an eighteen-year-old day-labourer outraged at what he considered the scandalous rate at which wages had been fixed: 'Anyone who pays 10 sous for a day's work will be hanged; the labourers, owners and agents will have their heads cut off.' The gesture by which the offender withdrew his remark was the same, but the task of arbitrator had changed hands; it was no longer the business of the *seigneur* or the *curé*, but of the new municipal officers whose vocation to peace-making was fundamentally the same as theirs.

Reparations of a material kind, and more especially the negotiations which led to them, shed much light on the manipulation of money and its various substitutes. Since the fundamental principle was to extinguish the offence and all its consequences, including moral ones, the best thing was to produce an overall evaluation of the damages to be paid to the victim. Negotiations therefore generally turned on a round figure, 6 livres for an insult, 36 for a theft, but a hundred louis for a lampoon. Once the figure was fixed the means of payment had to be stipulated. The sum agreed upon was very often only a valuation of the offence and did not entail immediate payment; there had therefore to be clauses dealing with delays and equivalences; as in all pre-industrial societies the handling of money was minimized at every level. So the general custom at this point was to sign a bill, which would be accepted as long as the signer inspired confidence or had a guarantor; which was where forms of solidarity and protection revealed their strength. The best example of this which I have found is the purse put together by some soldiers and their officers to save the skin of one of their comrades who had committed an accidental murder. People who were settled, especially if they were well off, had an obvious advantage at this point. If he had no ready money, a householder could easily promise to sell some wood, or a rich peasant offer an advance of 850 livres on account of 3,000; but what guarantee could the servant caught with his hand in the till give of his promise to pay a bill of 20 livres, since he had no property and no guarantor? Often enough, persistent inability to pay was what finally brought the matter into court.

In this unfortunate situation, labourers had nothing to offer but

their labour, and might propose, in return for a piece of cloth
stolen, 'to come and work' for the victim 'until they have made up
the price', an offer accepted for lack of anything better; at law, their
prospects would be even bleaker. Bills, obligations, promises of
service or labour were current throughout a Languedoc more used
to exchanges in kind than in money. A curious dialogue shows
clearly the down-to-earth character of negotiations describing in
the minutest detail a compensation intended to disarm the
adversary and prevent him complaining to the public prosecutor. In
1788 a daughter of a peasant in Quercy was seriously wounded by a
workman who specialized in nocturnal theft. Her father, mistrustful
of the law, wanted a settlement and went to sound out the offender.
'Why did you do that?' 'I'm really awfully sorry: look, I've got a
shroud, it's absolutely new, you can have it. Hire a servant in place
of your daughter, I'll pay her wages. You can get bread at the
baker's on my account, and come here for a chicken to make a
stew.' Stranger still was the offer made to his victim by a
day-labourer from the environs of Béziers to go off and steal an
identical quantity of grapes from the vineyard where he was
working.

To get nearer to the truth one would need to be able to analyse
the strength of the bonds of dependence and clientage and
consequently of the reciprocal services which constitute one of the
most obscure of the various substitutes for money. All the same,
one cannot write the history of arbitration by an account of the
means of paying compensation; this history lies much more clearly
in changes in the arbitrating parties and in the objects of
negotiation. From now on, by negotiation people hoped above all
to bring pressure on their opponent, to penetrate his lines of
resistance, and were happy to break it off if the agreement was not
thought satisfactory. In the past the parties had sought to conclude
the matter at any cost, since they had no alternative solution. The
efforts of mediators were turning into skirmishes of light horse.

CONCLUSION: MEDIATION IN TRANSFORMATION AND DECAY

What is one to say at the close of a difficult investigation in an area
where many things are not said? One would have liked to get to
know it better, to have been able to penetrate more deeply the
images or dreams of justice which occasionally emerge from the

contents of an agreement. Still, it is something to have been able to offer a statistical sketch of the way it functioned in the period before the Revolution, since a period of crisis may reveal concealed structures and conflicting values. To outline different forms of arbitration, within the institutions of the *ancien régime* at its close, is to measure the progress of the monarchical state in the area of law.

The shifting pattern of arbitration during the eighteenth century expressed changing conceptions of law and power, as it did changes in the internal balance of a society. This was certainly no innovation: over the centuries the structure of royal legislation built upon the foundations of the apparatus of the state had been rising to overshadow the equitable justice founded upon unspoken law. The rules applied there, which were neither fixed custom nor pure deductions from the general law, made arbitration a living thing and gave it a special attraction. They are certainly as interesting as those of formal jurisprudence.

The eighteenth century confirmed a tendency which had begun in the seventeenth, the passage from a private to a public order; the mediatory process reflected it. Widely resorted to, it was the index of an uncompleted state. The plurality of juridical fields and particularist cultures demonstrates how far the notion of a general law was from having triumphed before the Revolution. True, in the exercise of judicial power the state asserted and put increasingly into practice the principle of a public order infringed by crime. But the will to repression was obstructed by the obstacles of an ill-equipped administration, anxious where possible to leave matters to private regulation, and of an atavistic mistrust of all exterior interventions. Groups and communities, concerned above all to maintain their own cohesion, did their utmost to smother discords by reconstituting as quickly as possible the web of normal relations. Hence the longevity of the idea that crime was the exclusive affair of the local community. Meanwhile, however, administrators were slowly converting the idea of a common law into reality, and erecting the judge as arbiter of disputes and defender of public order. The more the state extended its action, the more mediation decayed.

Besides the ambitions of the state, we have also to consider the novel requirements of a population confronted by fundamental change. Equitable justice was the effect of an intensely hierarchical society. It rested as much on clientage and fidelity as on the basic human solidarities, which were intensified in a closed economy by collective constraints on work and life. The intercessors, whose position was in principle that of a dominating class, could therefore depend upon a consensus which recognized them as legitimate: without this legitimacy there was no authority, and negotiation ended in the hazards of conflict. Once the economy was opened up such social relations were shaken. The rise of a capitalism which undermined human relations, the progress of agrarian individualism and the removal of 'élites' to the towns increased social mobility and dislocated communities. The traditional hierarchies were weakened in their mediatory role; it became increasingly urgent to resort to external intervention.

Insidiously, and especially in towns where things changed more quickly, there emerged a state of mind adapted to a more flexible environment. Authority became more concentrated, monopolized by the agents of the crown and confronted by groups of looser structure and less intense sociability. In face of the rise of an egalitarian spirit disinclined to admit the legitimacy of traditional hierarchies, the ancient mediators, whether present or absent, would tend to be superseded. The *seigneur* was no longer a public figure: entirely concerned with his private interests, he saw justice as meaning the respect of his rights and a strict economy of his expenses. The church, by the demand for a new kind of religious practice on the part of its *curés* and vicars, upset its familiar relation with the people. But they did not leave an empty seat: one way and another the representatives of a rapidly rising middle class were keen to take their place, and to succeed to the domination of communities. In the wake of these modifications and substitutions, mediation was more and more felt to be an expression rather of particular interests than of values held in common; at the same time people continued to insist that it was in principle to be preferred. The new authorities were not united; the intervention of royal agents had the disadvantages of depersonalizing judicial authority and of attaching it to the administration of the state. There was of course something to be said for that: the new regime had the merit of avoiding the arbitrariness inherent in situations of social hegemony, and many people felt more secure with an abstract and uniform law. But this was not the only question: one needs also to know whether the state was actually capable of exercising the function claimed. In any event, the profound wish of most people remained to put their conflicts into the hands of a judge recognized as arbitrator and conciliator. It looks as if the later eighteenth century was a phase of uncertainty and confusion between a system of autonomous social regulation in a state of collapse and a system of state regulation under construction.

SOURCES

The judicial archives of the Parlement of Toulouse, deposited at the Archives départementales de la Haute-Garonne, constitute the essential source of this work. It contains the registers of *arrêts criminels* and of prisoners, and also the bundles of civil and criminal proceedings of the seventeenth and eighteenth centuries. I have investigated some 10,000 criminal cases from the eighteenth century. I have also used the extremely important series of *Plaintes et Placets* addressed by individuals or communities to the military authorities charged with maintaining domestic and public order. It is deposited at the Archives départementales de l'Hérault at Montpellier.

10. Conjugal Settlements: Resort to Clandestine and Common Law Marriage in England and Wales, 1650–1850

JOHN R. GILLIS

Marriage has been, and will always be, an occasion of conflicts between individuals, families and communities. In 1268 a brawl between a wedding party and the men of Byram, Yorkshire, left a man dead and many injured.[1] The cause of the fray cannot be determined, but it probably involved tensions between villages, perhaps between kin-groups. Conflict was endemic in later periods as well, but by the seventeenth century disputes had lost their collective character and become more personal. They were more likely to result in witchcraft accusations than in bloody battles; and the fissures were usually between parents and children, within families, or between different strata of the community, notably between impoverished individuals and the village 'élites'.[2]

The church's success in establishing the legitimacy of its marriage ceremonies depended to a very large degree on its ability to moderate disputes such as these. From the twelfth century onwards it had successfully insinuated itself into the courtship and marriage process by offering its porch as a place of notarization for the arrangements previously made by the parties themselves. In time the rites were moved inside and the ritual kiss of peace added, but it was the publicity of the occasion, expressed in the profane as well as the sacred ritual, which created what people regarded as proper marriage. The medieval church courts also owed a considerable part of their appeal to the relatively quick and efficient adjudication of disputes arising from pre-marital contracts and the notarization

[1] George C. Homans, *English Villagers of the Thirteenth Century* (New York, 1975), p. 175.
[2] The nature of these tensions is discussed in my forthcoming book, *For Better, For Worse: A Political and Social History of British Marriage, 1600 to the Present*.

of separation agreements of married couples.[3] On the parish level, clergy acted as go-betweens, matchmakers and peacekeepers, thereby making themselves an indispensable part of the conjugal process. Before the Reformation the business of arranging a marriage contract, normally involving negotiation between families, was likely to be mediated by a priest, whose function was to negotiate between kin-groups at the time of betrothal. The Catholic clergy were also involved in disputes between parents and children, but it was not until the seventeenth century that disputes within rather than between families became the mediators' chief concern. Arranged marriage was becoming less common, especially among the middling and lower ranks, but disputes between parents and children were apparently increasing. To secure their ends young people were resorting to private betrothals which, when made in a proper manner *per verba de praesenti* before witnesses, constituted an indissoluble vow according to canon law and. therefore a legitimation of their choice should parents or others become obstructive. The presence of a clergyman at such betrothals virtually guaranteed that the church courts would uphold them. Thus, while the church dutifully exhorted 'yung folke to absteyn from privy contracts, and not to marry without the consent of such of their parents and fryends as have authority over them', the local clergy often took a more sympathetic position, one more in line with the priest's traditional role as facilitator of marriages.[4]

It seems to have become the practice of persons intending to wed to go through the formalities of a 'privy contract' even though they intended to appear in church soon after. If there was no objection to their union, then the betrothal remained just a preliminary private act without legal significance. If, however, the relationship was challenged by a third party – parents, guardians, other suitors, or, as far as the poor were concerned, the parish authorities – then the couple would claim their contract represented a public binding act equivalent to valid marriage. Church courts were generally willing

---

[3] R. H. Helmholz, *Marriage Litigation in Medieval England* (Cambridge, 1974), chs. 1 and 2.

[4] On the reconciliatory role of the priesthood, see John Bossy, 'Blood and Baptism: Kinship, Community, and Christianity in Western Europe from the Fourteenth to the Seventeenth Centuries', in D. Baker (ed.), *Sanctity and Secularity: The Church and the World* (Oxford, 1973), pp. 131ff. Also J. S. Burn, *History of the Parish Registers in England*, 2nd edn (London, 1862), p. 143.

to support this claim if presented with evidence of properly witnessed vows.[5]

On the Continent, parental anxiety encouraged the reform of the marriage law by the Council of Trent, which closed off all options besides that of church marriage. In England there were also pressures to tighten ecclesiastical discipline, but popular distrust of the church's ability to serve the purposes of patriarchal authority led to a questioning of the supremacy of the church in all matters matrimonial. Interventions by church courts in matters of family and community concern met increasing resistance in the late sixteenth and early seventeenth centuries. As economic conditions worsened and the issue of marriage became more critical, elders on both the local and national levels came to view the role of the church as unwarranted interference with the godly prerogatives of patriarchy. The objection to private betrothal was extended to the church's own rites, with the result that during the Civil War not only the church's power of adjudication but its monopoly of legitimation was abolished. During the years 1653–7 the formalities of marriage were transferred from the clergy to the civil magistrates, who, as fathers and masters, could be expected to uphold patriarchal authority more effectively. Civil marriage vested unprecedented power in parental consent and, by demoting betrothal to a purely private act, placed all those under the age of majority at the mercy of parents, guardians and, in the case of the poor, their masters. Sects like the Quakers imposed a marriage discipline so severe that, despite the efforts of members to mediate conflicts, it became a major reason for the loss of members.[6]

Civil marriage did not survive the Interregnum, but the problem of mediating marriage disputes remained unresolved. Rebellious children of dissenters could turn to the established church to solemnize their marriage choices, but for the ordinary parishioner facing a patriarchal obstruction the options narrowed. The restored

[5] Ralph Houlbrooke, *Church Courts and the People during the English Reformation, 1520–1570* (Oxford, 1979), pp. 57–66; M. J. Ingram, 'Ecclesiastical Justice in Wiltshire, 1600–1660' (Univ. of Oxford D.Phil thesis, 1976), especially chs. 3 and 4.

[6] On the period of the Civil War, see Keith Wrightson, 'The Nadir of English Illegitimacy in the Seventeenth Century', in P. Laslett, K. Oosterveen and R. M. Smith (eds.), *Bastardy and Comparative History* (London, 1980), pp. 184–6. Also Keith Thomas, 'Age and Authority in Early Modern England', *Proceedings of the British Academy*, lxii (1976), p. 227.

church courts had lost much of their efficacy in matrimonial matters and therefore resort to private betrothal as a means of legitimating marriage was now less attractive. As an alternative, many turned either to marriage by licence, a costly means of avoiding publicity and thus patriarchal intervention, or to so-called 'clandestine marriage', an irregular ceremony which, while frowned on by both civil and religious authorities, was nevertheless valid in the same way as betrothal under canon law. By resorting to a clergyman or layman who was willing to perform a marriage service without the usual publicity of banns or regardless of the usual restrictions on time and place, couples were able to circumvent both parental and parish authority. As the popularity of the 'privy contract' declined, clandestine marriage rose to take over its functions, reaching its peak of popularity in the period 1660 to 1753.[7]

I

Clandestine marriages were performed by all manner of persons, including Catholic priests, dissenting ministers, laymen and, most common of all, renegade clergy of the Church of England itself. Catholics and dissenters found it relatively easy in the seventeenth and early eighteenth centuries to make their own marriages.[8] Equally bothersome were the laymen like the Bristol barber, John Boroston, and the Berkshire dairyman, Gabriel Ross, many of whom used public houses as their place of solemnization.[9] In the parish of Llanyckil, Wales, the parson found himself competing with Evan Cadwalader, who ran his marriage business from the nearby market town of Bala. The parson was also losing marriages to the minister of a nearby parish, James Langford, who offered to wed without requirement of banns or licence, a practice that was

[7] Ingram, 'Ecclesiastical Justice in Wiltshire', pp. 127–8.
[8] Patrick McGrath, 'Notes on the History of Marriage Licences', *Gloucestershire Marriage Allegations, 1637–1680* (Publications of the Bristol and Gloucestershire Archaeological Society, ii, 1954), pp. xxi–xxx; *The Parish Registers and Parochial Documents of the Archdeaconry of Winchester*, ed. W. A. Fearon and J. F. William (London, 1909), pp. 9–10; D. J. Steel, *National Index of Parish Registers*, 3 vols. (London, 1968), ii, pp. 550–2; on Catholic marriages, *ibid.*, iii, pp. 857–72; and J. C. Aveling, 'Marriage of Catholic Recusants', *Journal of Ecclesiastical History*, xiv (1963), pp. 857–64; J. Anthony Williams, *Catholic Recusancy in Wiltshire, 1660–1791* (Newport, 1968), pp. 66, 92; John Bossy, *The English Catholic Community, 1570–1850* (London, 1975), pp. 136–40.
[9] Steel, *National Index of Parish Registers*, i, p. 314.

illicit but nevertheless indulged in by hundreds of other Anglican clergy in every part of Britain.[10] They presided over so-called 'lawless churches', located not only in towns but remote rural areas. Parsons like Nottinghamshire's Amos Sweetaple and the Gloucestershire parson John Kelham dispensed marriage to hundreds of couples who violated the spirit of the canon law by wedding outside their home parishes.[11] The church hierarchy managed to put down a few of these, but others sprang up to meet the apparently insatiable demand. When London's lawless churches were finally suppressed in the 1690s, clandestine marriage simply shifted to the precincts of the Fleet Prison, where an estimated 150,000 to 300,000 unions took place over the next fifty years.[12] At Derbyshire's Dale Abbey Chapel the curate there conducted weddings at a shilling per couple until the 1750s; and similar facilities existed in every part of urban and rural Britain.[13]

In all, these irregular marriages may have accounted for at least a fifth and perhaps as much as a third of all unions in the first half of the eighteenth century.[14] The ubiquity of Friar Lawrences and the willingness of church courts to uphold all manner of vows, especially those made before a parson, meant that all piecemeal attempts at suppression were frustrated. The participants might be disciplined, but their unions were indissoluble.[15] For many, avoidance of public marriage by banns was merely a matter of convenience. Sailors on short leave, who did not have the time to

---

[10] 'A Report on the Deanry of Penllyn and Edeirnion by Rev. John Wynne, 1730', *The Merioneth Miscellany*, no. 3 (1955), p. 8.

[11] J. D. Chambers, *The Vale of Trent, 1670–1800* (Economic History Review Supplement iii), p. 50; E. A. Wrigley, 'Clandestine Marriage in Tetbury in the Late Seventeenth Century', *Local Population Studies*, no. 10 (Spring 1973), pp. 15–21; John H. Pruett, *Clergy under the Later Stuarts: The Leicestershire Experience* (Chicago, 1978), pp. 20, 74–5, 131–41; J. C. Cox, *The Parish Registers of England* (London, 1910), pp. 95–6; G. R. Quaife, *Wanton Wenches and Wayward Wives: Peasants and Illicit Sex in Early Seventeenth Century England* (London, 1979), pp. 96–7.

[12] Steel, *National Index of Parish Registers*, i, p. 299; Roger Lee Brown, 'Clandestine Marriages in London, especially within the Fleet Prison, and the Effect in Hardwicke's Act, 1753' (University of London M.A. thesis, 1972), p. 4.

[13] *Marriage Allegations in the Diocese of Gloucester, 1681–1700* (Publications of the Bristol and Gloucestershire Archaeological Society, ix, 1960), p. xi.

[14] *The Parish Registers and Parochial Documents of the Archdeaconry of Winchester*, pp. 9–10; Pruett, *Clergy under the Later Stuarts*, pp. 131–41; Steel, *National Index of Parish Registers*, i, p. 299.

[15] F. Pollock and F. W. Maitland, *The History of English Law*, 2 vols. (Cambridge, 1911), ii, p. 372; Steel, *National Index of Parish Registers*, i, p. 315.

have their names read out on three consecutive Sundays, were frequent clients of the Fleet and other lawless churches.[16] Cost was sometimes a consideration, although clandestine marriage was not always cheaper than licence or banns.[17] People had been objecting to marriage fees for centuries, but it was not overt anti-clericalism which was behind the resort to clandestine rites, which were normally carried out either by a clergyman or someone pretending to clerical office.[18] Many sought to avoid the publicity of a parish wedding because they could not afford the celebrations that were expected of all newly-weds by their friends and neighbours.[19] Even though couples who 'stole away' diminished their costs, they usually sought a place that could provide some minimal form of celebration. The 'marriage houses' of the Fleet not only provided the parson, but offered facilities for the traditional feasting and bedding that invariably went with a wedding.[20]

Poverty by itself was not the principal factor in the rise of clandestine marriage. The desire for privacy had social rather than material origins. Widows and widowers marrying too soon after the death of a spouse or against the wishes of their families; couples disparate in age, social status, or religion; bigamists and bankrupts – all these had reasons to seek privacy.[21] Fortune hunters and persons of fraudulent intent valued secrecy, as did persons with living spouses wanting to marry again.[22] But there was a difference

[16] J. S. Burn, *The Fleet Registers* (London, 1831), p. 100.

[17] The costs of places like the Fleet marriage houses were not necessarily less than regular marriage by banns, but certainly below the cost of a licence. But the price of marriage, however small, remained an issue well into the nineteenth century. See Edward Coke, *Religious Rites made Free to the Poor* (London, n.d.), Fulham Papers 101, Lambeth Palace Archives.

[18] For a late example, see *The Unknown Mayhew*, ed. Eileen Yeo and E. P. Thompson (New York, 1972), p. 120.

[19] This was also a reason for buying privacy through licence. Vivien Elliott, 'Marriage Licences and the Local Historian', *The Local Historian*, no. 6 (May 1973), pp. 287–8; R. B. Outhwaite, 'Age of Marriage in England from the Late Seventeenth to the Late Nineteenth Centuries', *Transactions of the Royal Historical Society*, 5th ser., xxiii (1973), p. 64.

[20] Both the Fleet and Gretna Green provided facilities for feasting and bedding. In London the clergy were often employees of the marriage houses, but in some places they seem to have owned their own inns, thus taking full profit from the marriage trade. John Latimer, *The Annals of Bristol*, 2 vols. (Bristol, 1893), i, pp. 158–9.

[21] Outhwaite, 'Age of Marriage in England', pp. 64–7.

[22] Burn, *Fleet Registers*, pp. 49, 53–4, 61; W. T. McIntire, 'Gretna Green Marriages', *The Geneaologists' Magazine*, ix, no. 3 (Sept. 1940), p. 82; Brown, 'Clandestine Marriages in London', pp. 167–9.

between the privacy sought by those who had something to hide from the law and the discretion of persons who, while they might wish to keep their actions secret for the moment, also felt a powerful desire to legitimate their vows. It was they and not the wanton bigamists or the vile seducers who constituted the greater part of the Fleet's huge clientele. If the records of the Fleet are a reliable guide to the patterns of clandestine marriage throughout England and Wales, it would seem that most of those who opted for irregular marriages were neither wholly impoverished nor rootless, but persons of middling rank and just below, claiming a right conceded by canon law but not always honoured by a clergy increasingly subservient to the demands of property and patriarchy. Most who turned to the Fleet and similar places appear to have been using clandestine marriage as a means of getting their way in situations where parental or other opposition had arisen. The vicar of Almondbury, Yorkshire, reported in 1743:

> I am prepared to name three several couples, all now living in this very Town, who (when I refused to Proceed in ye Publication of Bans, because ye Fathers of ye several Girls (women I canot call them) applied themselves to me, alledging a Lawful Impediment, *vis* nonage & Want of Consent) all went away, in Contempt of their parents & were married by ye neighboring surrogates.[23]

Grudging the loss of fees and under pressure from parents to stop clandestine practices, many clergy made the same complaint to their superiors. However, elopement was a highly effective counter to parental authority. Often it resulted in some kind of reconciliation, parents ultimately accepting the union and the children returning to marry a second time in their local church. Like the seventeenth-century Somerset couple who 'got themselves into Dorsetshire and procured themselves to be married there', many were using nearby lawless churches to legitimate not only their own relations but the children, often already conceived, who resulted from those relations.[24]

---

[23] *Archbishop Herring's Visitation Returns 1743*, 4 vols. (Yorkshire Archaeological Society Record Series, lxx), i, p. 18.

[24] Quaife, *Wanton Wenches*, p. 96. Many 'stole away' marriages are recorded in the private notes of a Yorkshire nonconformist minister from the 1680s and 1690s. *The Reverend Oliver Heywood, 1630–1702: His Autobiography, Diaries, Anecdotes and Event Books*, ed. J. Horsfall Turner, 4 vols. (Brighouse, 1881), ii, pp. 130–6; and J. Horsfall Turner, *Haworth, Past and Present* (Brighouse, 1879), pp. 49–50. For instances of successful elopements using clandestine marriage, see Lawrence

A clandestine union was equally effective against objections to marriage raised by parish officials.[25] It could also be a means of protection against church and civil penalties for pre-marital sexual relations. In Llancykil parish in the 1730s the ceremonies performed by Evan Cadwalader, the layman, and Reverend James Langford, his ordained competitor, seem to have been used to legitimize sexual unions which were then later solemnized in the parish church nearer (or sometimes after) the arrival of the child:

The country people, it's to be imagin'd, are first marry'd by either this layman or else by Langord [Langford] and, to screen themselves from publick reproach, and the parson who marries [them] from punishment, they some time after apply to the parish minister. When the females want but a very few months, and sometimes but a few weeks, of lyeing in, their banns are in due and solemn form published, and, paying the parson and the clerk their respective fees, all are married without being ask'd any more questions than what the church form contains.[26]

Disreputable and subversive as such practices may be made to appear, a strong case can be made for the opposite interpretation. The clandestine marriage is best understood as a substitute for the private contract or betrothal, previously upheld by the church courts, which legitimated sexual relations and provided for any children resulting thereof. In some places children born out of wedlock were apparently still being legitimated by joining their parents 'under the care cloth' at the wedding ceremony. One such rite was performed in Somerset in the nineteenth century.[27]

Among those best served by clandestine marriage and related rites of legitimation were young persons whose marriage was opposed by parents. The conflict of generations has a very long history, but there is reason to think that tensions were increasing during the early eighteenth century, particularly in those areas of mixed agriculture and domestic industry where the family had reconstituted itself as a productive unit. Sex and age relations had

Stone, *The Family, Sex and Marriage in England 1500–1800* (London, 1977), pp. 289, 294.
[25] On the growing restrictions on marriage, see Thomas, 'Age and Authority', p. 227. The parish prevention of beggar weddings is noted in *Notes and Queries*, 8th ser., vii (1895), p. 46; *Byegones*, 2nd ser., iii (1893), p. 106.
[26] 'A Report on the Deanry of Penllyn', p. 8.
[27] This practice is discussed by Homans, *English Villagers*, p. 172; nineteenth-century example provided by Ruth Tongue, *Somerset Folklore* (London, 1965), p. 82.

become simultaneously more equal and more problematic.[28] Parents depended more on the labour of their children, particularly daughters, who tended to stay at or near home longer than in those places where only agricultural employment was available. Relations between husbands and wives were characterized by a similar interdependence; and marriage, now more likely to take the form of partnership in pursuit of a common occupation, was more a matter of individual choice than parental dictation.[29] The traditional forms of courtship had given way to new, more individualized forms of behaviour. Tensions were acute at a time when the parental need to control was increasing, while actual patriarchal power was diminishing.

These central contradictions were faithfully reproduced in the courtship and betrothal practices of those parts of England and Wales where the family economy predominated. It was there that courtship, often taking the form of night visiting, tended to be most clandestine. Where women had to be courted under the father's or master's roof, a degree of discretion was necessary. Confrontation was avoided by suitors arriving late, just as or just after the elders retired to bed. The secretive behaviour of the young and the complicity of the old 'not to know' helped avoid what both feared most, namely public rupture. It permitted time for negotiation and, if necessary, the arbitration of third parties. In Montgomeryshire the process, which lasted well into the nineteenth century, was described as follows:

> Unmarried couples rarely appeared together in public and parents' first intimation of their offspring's choice of partner

[28] This is developed in Gillis, *For Better, For Worse*. On the general problem, see Hans Medick, 'The Proto-industrial Family Economy: The Structural Functions of Household and Family during the Transition from Peasant Society to Industrial Capitalism', *Social History*, i, no. 3 (Oct. 1976), pp. 291–315; David Levine, *Family Formation in the Age of Nascent Capitalism* (New York, 1977).

[29] On the effect on women, see Ivy Pinchbeck, *Women Workers and the Industrial Revolution, 1750–1850* (London, 1930), pp. 19–21, 114–81, 246–8, 273–80. Useful local studies include Joan Thirsk, 'Industries and the Countryside', in F. J. Fisher (ed.), *Essays in Economic and Social History of Tudor and Stuart England* (Cambridge, 1961), pp. 70–88; Alan Everitt, 'Farm Labourers', *The Agrarian History of England and Wales*, iv (Cambridge, 1967), ch. 7; David Hey, *The Rural Metalworkers of the Sheffield Region* (Leicester, 1972); Marie Rowlands, 'Industry and Social Change in Staffordshire, 1660–1760', *Transactions of the Lichfield and South Staffordshire Archaeological and Historical Society*, ix (1967), pp. 39–58; G. H. Tupling, *The Economic History of Rossendale* (Aberdeen, 1927), pp. 79ff., 163–89.

frequently came from a third person, generally a relative, and thus gave them the opportunity to approve silently or vehemently oppose it.[30]

If the mediation of third parties failed and parents forbade the marriage a determined couple would go ahead with private betrothal, exchanging words and tokens, and perhaps begin sexual relations, this being both morally legitimate and, as a way of compelling parental reconsideration, quite effective. A pregnant woman could expect a change of heart on the part not only of her parents but of the parish, for the latter was particularly eager to facilitate marriages in cases where a bastard child might otherwise become a burden to the ratepayers.[31] If this failed, then elopement and clandestine marriage were the last resort.

Many parishes tried to prevent 'beggar weddings' by putting pressure on the local parson not to solemnize these.[32] But if the parish clergyman would not take their side, couples could always find an obliging cleric in a nearby parish who could afford to ignore the bride's obvious condition because the new husband's settlement was elsewhere. Apparently a high percentage of clandestine marriages involved pregnant women.[33] In 1724 Mary Moore, who was about to bear her child, was told by Mrs Hodgkinson, who kept a marriage house called the Hand and Pen in Fleet Lane, that 'for a half-a-guinea it [the marriage] might be entered backwards [antedated] in the book and would skreen her from the anger of her friends'.[34] As the parish officers were also harassing Mary Moore, clandestine marriage was doubly valuable to her.

---

[30] A. Baily Williams, 'Courtship and Marriage in Late Nineteenth Century Montgomeryshire', *Montgomeryshire Collections*, li, p. 1 (1950), pp. 117–26. On clandestine courtship and bundling, see J. Ceredig Davies, *Folklore of West and Mid-Wales* (Aberystwyth, 1911), pp. 2–4; R. B. Walker, 'Religious Changes in Cheshire, 1750–1850', *Journal of Ecclesiastical History*, xvii (1966), p. 83; Frank Ormerod, *Lancashire Life and Character* (Manchester and London, 1895), pp. 117ff.; Trefor Owen, 'West Glamorgan Customs', *Folk Life*, iii (1965), p. 27; Enid Porter, *Cambridgeshire Customs and Folklore* (London, 1969), pp. 4–5.

[31] U. R. Q. Henriques, 'Bastardy and the New Poor Law', *Past and Present*, no. 37 (July 1967), pp. 106ff.

[32] Clergy could refuse to co-operate in forced marriages. Quaife, *Wanton Wenches*, p. 116.

[33] *Ibid.*, pp. 96–7; Burn, *History*, pp. 153ff.; Burn, *Fleet Registers*, pp. 52ff.; Brown, 'Clandestine Marriages in London', p. 153.

[34] Burn, *Fleet Registers*, p. 38.

II

Together private betrothal and clandestine marriage permitted a latitude which by the mid-eighteenth century had become intolerable to the upholders of the patriarchal order. Their frustration led to the passage of the Hardwicke Marriage Act of 1753, which closed both loopholes and required parental consent for all those marrying under the age of majority. Legal marriage was confined to wedding in a properly consecrated church after the calling of banns or purchase of licence. Only Jews and Quakers were exempted from this radical remedy, a law that departed so abruptly from tradition that Blackstone declared it an 'innovation upon our antient [*sic*] laws and constitution'. Any parson caught conducting an irregular marriage was subjected to fourteen years' transportation.[35] 'A punishment little inferior to ye gallows and inflicted generally on ye most profligate and abandoned part of mankind', one clergyman confided to his register.[36] But neither he nor many of his colleagues dared disobedience.

Many clergy rejoiced to see their parishioners return to their altars and their incomes rise accordingly. London returns for 1760 show a sharp rise in both banns and licences, with the latter increasing at the greater rate. The clerk of St Botolph's Aldgate, explained that 'the Fleet no doubt took off many Marriages from ours and every other Church hereabouts'.[37] Resort to licence increased in the next eighty years and accounted for as much as a third of all recorded marriages until banns regained popularity in the late nineteenth century.[38] Licence attracted a very wide clientele, including many working people. Particularly in Wales, parts of the Midlands and the North of England, the publicity of banns was avoided wherever possible.[39] Those living close to the Scottish border resorted in growing numbers after 1753 to places like Gretna Green, Coldstream and Lamberton Toll, where a cadre of marital entrepreneurs carried on a lucrative business in supplying, in addition to quick Scots marriages, accommodation for celebration and consummation in the same way as the Fleet parsons

---

[35] *Ibid.*, pp. 18–19.
[36] Quoted in Cox, *Parish Registers of England*, p. 92.
[37] Fulham Papers 438, Lambeth Palace Archives.
[38] Outhwaite, 'Age of Marriage in England', pp. 62–3.
[39] *Ibid.*, pp. 64–8.

and other lawless clergy had previously done.[40] Until residence requirements were imposed in the 1850s, border weddings were immensely popular among young miners and agricultural workers.[41]

People in large cities had their own ingenious ways of maintaining the clandestine character of their weddings. In Exeter, country people were able to come to town on three consecutive Saturday nights and, by sleeping in lodgings, establish their residence there.[42] People had been using London for this purpose for centuries, wedding there and then returning to their native parishes. For those already resident in the town or too scrupulous to live together, there was the alternative of claiming, as a right, marriage in the 'Mother Church' of a large urban parish. Reverend Rushton, who in the 1850s presided over a huge Manchester parish, conceded that 'the parishioners have the general common law right of resorting to the Mother Church, and it is therefore impossible for me to know whether they are the parties they represent themselves to be'.[43]

These means of circumventing patriarchal authority depended to a large degree on the acquiescence of clergy. As long as they served in a mediating rather than judgemental capacity, people would bring their marriage business to the church because they valued the notarizing and legitimating functions it provided. For the unwed mother access to a register was a way of avoiding prosecution and removal from the parish. Clergy like Reverend David Jones of the north Wales district of Ceiriog appear to have been willing to enter children as legitimate as long as they were assured that some kind of marriage, even an illicit one, had taken place prior to the birth.[44]

[40] McIntire, 'Gretna Green Marriages', pp. 77–83; F. A. Milne, 'Border Marriages', *Folk-Lore*, xxxxviii (1901), pp. 452–3; 'Claverhouse', *Irregular Border Marriages* (London and Edinburgh, 1934), *passim*.

[41] Hastings M. Neville, *A Corner in the North* (Newcastle, 1909), p. 108.

[42] Report of the vicar of Barnes, Essex, 1803, Fulham Papers 101, Lambeth Palace Archives; for Exeter, see M. Cook, *The Diocese of Exeter in 1821: Bishop Carey's Replies before Visitation* (Devon and Cornwall Record Society, 1960), pp. 49, 84. In London the practice was still common in the early twentieth century. See Visitations of 1905 for St Edmund's, Lombard Street, London Guildhall Library, MS 17885, box i.

[43] *Report of the Select Committee of the House of Lords Appointed to Inquire into the Deficiency of Means of Spiritual Instruction and Places of Divine Worship in the Metropolis*, Parliamentary Papers (1857–8), ix, p. 450. Also the London Visitation of 1905, St John's, Hampstead, London Guildhall Library MS. 17895, box ii.

[44] Many children were baptized in parishes other than their own perhaps as a way of legitimating them. E. A. Wrigley, 'A Note on the Life-time Mobility of Married

Ironically, it was the Hardwicke Act, ensuring the established church a monopoly over the notarization of marriage, which, together with changes in the position of the clergy itself, finally ruptured this long standing complicity between parsons and people. As the clergy abandoned their traditional role as notary to the people's marriage business, becoming instead the constables of morality, large parts of the population were forced to turn to the court of public opinion to arbitrate their claims, thus preferring as jury people more like themselves, as the only ones from whom they could expect a fair verdict on their actions. The emergence of a new and distinctly plebeian common law practice in the decades after 1753 reflected changing class alignments, within which the clergy, now firmly identified with patrician interests, could no longer serve as arbitrators.[45] From the 1750s through the mid-nineteenth century, a sizeable part of the English and Welsh labouring classes turned away from the church to create for themselves unique rites of notarization and legitimation that were a functional substitute for the private betrothal and clandestine marriage now denied them by law. In time, these alternative ceremonies took on a life of their own and came to constitute a distinctive tradition of common law marriage and divorce, which lasted in many places well into the Victorian period.

III

Secular plebeian forms of marriage left no public record and rarely surface in memoir or biography. The educated classes, and particularly the clergy, were almost entirely ignorant of their existence. Typical was the nonconformist minister, a friend of the Welsh folklorist Gwenith Gwyn, who worked for decades among the people of south Wales before his 'great discovery' at the time of the First World War that many of the most respected members of the community were 'living tally', as common law marriage was

Women in a Parish Population in the Later Eighteenth Century', *Local Population Studies*, no. 18 (Spring 1977), p. 26; Quaife, *Wanton Wenches*, pp. 105ff.; L. Bradley, 'Common Law Marriage: A Possible Case of Under Registration', *Local Population Studies*, no. 11 (Autumn 1973), p. 43; Brown, 'Clandestine Marriages in London', pp. 131, 153; Elliott, 'Marriage Licences', p. 287.

[45] On the changing relations of clergy and people, see Eric Evans, 'Some Reasons for the Growth of Rural Anti-clericalism, 1750–1830', *Past and Present*, no. 66 (Feb. 1975), pp. 84–109; M. R. Austin, 'The Church of England in the County of Derbyshire, 1772–1832' (Univ. of London Ph.D. thesis, 1969).

then called. He was enlightened by a member of his own chapel, a man who had definite views on the subject of church and marriage:

> You have married a lot in your time . . . but I'm thinking whether couples are as happy as Tom and Mary Jones who have never been married. It strikes me that ceremony and flowers and rice and parson do not make marriage, but something else. What that is I do not know. I am no scholar.[46]

That same evening the minister visited Mrs Jones, who seemed embarrassed when he appeared at her door. When it became apparent that his purpose was a friendly one, she relaxed sufficiently to reveal the cause of her initial apprehension:

> What will the neighbours think of you Sir, calling on the likes of us? Tom and I have never been properly married Sir. We are living tally, Sir, but we are very happy. I does my duty to him and he – well there is not a better man on earth than my Tom.[47]

The encounter reveals the gulf between church and people that had developed since the late eighteenth century. Gwenith Gwyn discovered the remarkable extent of common law marriage while looking through the christening register of the Ceiriog Valley parish of Llansantffraid. He was initially puzzled by entries for the period 1768–1805, which seemed to indicate that some kind of irregular marriage had been practised there on a very considerable scale. Sixty per cent of all births were attributed to conjugal arrangements which, while not immediately solemnized in church, were nevertheless entered by the vicar, the Reverend David Jones, as distinct from those few in which no father was declared. On further investigation, Gwyn found that the unions notarized by this remarkable register were known as 'besom weddings', a public, secular rite that provided both self-marriage and self-divorce to the participants. A seventy-three-year-old woman was able to provide him with considerable detail about its practice in the early nineteenth century:

> It was a real marriage in the estimation of the public, and I should think that women thought much of it. It was the women that spoke about it when I was young. Only when speaking about very, very old people would men refer to it. The besom wedding was a wedding after this manner: A birch besom (broom) was placed aslant in the open doorway of a house, with the head of the

[46] Gwenith Gwyn MS., Welsh Folk Museum MS. 2593/24.
[47] *Ibid.*

besom on the doorstone, and the top of the handle on the doorpost. Then the young man jumped over it first into the house, and afterward the young woman in the same way. The jumping was not recognized a marriage if either of the two touched the besom in jumping or, by accident, removed it from its place. It was necessary to jump in the presence of witnesses too. I should think this form of marriage was very common in this part of the country at one time, but I never saw one.[48]

Other of Gwyn's informants were able to describe how brides kept their maiden names, their property and their rights to the children, who were regarded as equal to other children with respect to rights of maintenance and inheritance. If a couple were barren or proved incompatible within a year of their besom wedding, divorce was possible, with the couple jumping backwards over the broom in the presence of witnesses.[49] Whether Reverend David Jones was ever present we cannot know, but it must be assumed that he was privy to the practice, since he was willing to make his register notary to the claims of couples married over the broom.

When Gwenith Gwyn published his findings in 1928 he did so in *Folk-Lore*, a convenient storage for materials touching on issues that his generation still regarded as highly sensitive. Besom marriage and related common law practices remain even today in the safe keeping of categories like 'custom', 'folk life' and 'survival', nicely distanced from the present, but also exempted from historical inquiry into their extent and function. It seems time, therefore, to return them to their historical context, not only because of their apparent ubiquity during the late eighteenth and early nineteenth centuries, but also because without them the history of authorized marriage is incomprehensible. For much of that period alternative forms of marriage and divorce presented a powerful challenge to the law of church and state. Henry Mayhew described common law arrangements as almost universal among elements of the mid-nineteenth-century London street trading community. The practice appears to have been particularly appealing to London's more inbred occupations – dust collectors, chimney-sweeps, as well as costermongers – in which women worked alongside men, and children with their parents. Miners, navvies and a large part of the

---

[48] Gwenith Gwyn (William Rhys Jones), 'A Besom Wedding in the Ceiriog Valley', *Folk-Lore*, xxxix (1928), pp. 153–4.
[49] *Ibid.*, p. 156.

maritime community also resorted to it, but, as Gwyn discovered, it was equally prevalent in many rural areas, especially regions where small farms and domestic industry predominated.[50] Not all common law practice was as ritualized as the besom marriage. The vows made by Mayhew's costers were more private in character. Public witness seems to have been of less importance in cities, but even there exchange of tokens, usually a ring, was considered necessary to legitimate a marriage agreement. The return of the ring, symbolizing the termination of the contract, functioned, together with the better known rites of 'wife sale', as the equivalent of jumping backwards over the besom.[51]

The degree of ritualization appears to have been proportional to the felt sense of community. Those who lived in large cities had less reason to notarize their relations. It was the inhabitants of villages and small towns who were most creative in providing for themselves rites appropriate to their needs and conditions. Religious dissent, which offered pitifully little resistance to the Hardwicke Act, provided little comfort to those who wished to make their marriages in their own way. The Owenites provided a secular marriage ceremony which incorporated many of the features of existing common law rites, but this was not accessible to the plebeian population at large.[52] Lacking an organized alternative, it is not surprising that common law marriages took a bewildering variety of forms. They were most elaborate in those pastoral and woodland places where a mixed economy of small farming and cottage industry or mining had developed. In the arable regions of the south and east, common law practice was confined to the few forest, heath, or fenland communities untouched by the general develop-

[50] Henry Mayhew, *London Labour and the London Poor*, 4 vols. (London, 1861), i, pp. 20, 42–45; ii, pp. 177, 370; Steel, *National Index of Parish Registers*, i, pp. 62–3.

[51] Terry Coleman, *The Railway Navvies* (London, 1965), pp. 22, 32, 181–96; W. Rye, *Glossary of Words Used in East Anglia* (n.p., 1905), pp. 26, 105; S. O. Addy, *Household Tales* (London, 1895), p. 122; 'Claverhouse', pp. 14–29; J. S. Coleman, *Celtic Wooings and Weddings* (Douglas, Isle of Man, 1959), *passim*; T. Gwynn Jones, *Welsh Folk-Lore and Folk-Custom* (London, 1930), pp. 184–6; Elias Owen, *Some Old Stone Crosses of the Vale of Clywd* (London, 1886), p. 63; *Notes and Queries*, 6th ser. iii (1881), pp. 126, 258; Samuel P. Menefee, *Wives for Sale* (New York, 1981), ch. 2.

[52] On Protestant dissent, see Steel, *National Index of Parish Registers*, ii, pp. 550–2; on Catholics, *ibid.*, iii, pp. 863–7. On Owenite marriage, see Eileen Yeo, 'Robert Owen and Radical Culture', in S. Pollard (ed.), *Robert Owen* (London, 1971), pp. 101–3.

ment of large-scale capitalist agriculture taking place there.[53] Smithing villages in the Midlands, mining and navvy camps in Cheshire and south Wales, weaving settlements in the valleys of Lancashire and Cumberland, and out-of-the-way fen and moorland hamlets were places where jumping the broom and parallel rites were most common. In some places, like Woking, Surrey, these built on an earlier tradition of radical religious dissent, though resistance to episcopal authority was now detached from all organized religion and now more likely to be allied with militant secularism.[54] This remained the case well into the nineteenth century when the practices, like the communities that nurtured them, succumbed to a combination of repressive and assimilative forces.

Common law marriage and divorce were not therefore strictly urban practices of uncertain historical origin, sustained by the uprooted and adopted by those orphaned from any feeling of attachment, familial or communal. Historians have left the impression that the clientele consisted of the poorest and most alienated, when, in reality, its practitioners, whether London costers or Welsh quarry workers, had very strong feelings of social obligation. For centuries there had been those who, in the manner of the vagabond, had defied all convention by establishing informal unions, whose only symbolism was a shared bed and bowl. But this practice, given expression by the likes of Abiezer Coppe during the Civil War period, was not the progenitor of the eighteenth-century version of common law marriage, which laid so much stress on orderly process, public notarization, and the mutual rights of the participants.[55] While libertine activity no doubt continued at other social levels, the practitioners of the new common law rites were not strangers to family, community, or even, in all cases, to religion.

---

[53] Gwyn, 'A Besom Wedding', pp. 160–3; on practices in other parts of Britain: *Notes and Queries*, 7th ser., x (1890), pp. 229, 297; Olive Anderson, 'The Incidence of Civil Marriage in Victorian England and Wales', *Past and Present*, no. 69 (Nov. 1975), pp. 68–9, 73–8.

[54] Woking provides an excellent case of a dispersed heath community where social and religious nonconformity were intertwined. A. C. Bickley, 'Some Notes on a Custom in Woking, Surrey', *The Home Counties Magazine*, iv (1902), pp. 25–9.

[55] Christopher Hill, *The World Turned Upside Down: Radical Ideas during the English Revolution* (Harmondsworth, 1976), ch. 16. For the view that common law practice is the result of social disintegration, see Jeffry Kaplow, 'Concubinage and the Working Class in Early Nineteenth Century Paris', in E. Hinrichs *et al.*, *Vom Ancien Régime zur Französiche Revolution* (Göttingen, 1978), pp. 364–7.

Living tally did not necessarily signify marginal or outcast status. In many places it cut across lines of religious denomination. Whether a couple remained with church or chapel, or had the respect of their neighbours, depended on whether, as with Mr and Mrs Jones, they had managed to legitimize their union by reputation if not by law. Common law rites, together with popular practices grafted on to church ceremony, were essential to that process, serving to notarize arrangements which, for a variety of reasons, could no longer be served by the rites of the church and state.

IV

There is no way that the actual extent of common law marriage can be measured; and the object of this chapter is the exploration of historical context and function rather than statistical analysis. The broad geographical distribution of rites similar to the besom wedding suggests that these were by no means the product only of the secular city or the industrial revolution in its urban phase. What appeared to Victorians as something produced by the factory and the slum had, in fact, a much longer history. 'Before there was a church, before there was a priest, jumping the broom was the custom,' was the way one rural Welshman explained the origins.[56] His construction of the common law tradition is only partially correct however. Besom marriages may pre-date Christianity in Wales and elsewhere, but the task at hand is the explanation of the renaissance of the practice in the eighteenth century, when it and other common law rites took on that distinctly plebeian and uniquely secular form which marked a break with both private betrothal and clandestine marriage, and thus with the church itself.

A closer look at the clientele in terms of age, gender and previous marital status suggests that the renaissance of common law practice can be explained by the social and sexual tensions of the late eighteenth and early nineteenth centuries. There were good reasons why, as Gwyn's informant put it, 'the women thought much of' common law rites such as the besom wedding. Before 1753 church and local courts had often upheld marriage agreements that provided for the autonomy of married women in matters of

---

[56] Recording of Tom Morgan, Dyfed, in the collections of the Welsh Folk Museum.

property and trade.[57] With the Hardwicke Act only one status of married women, *femme covert*, was recognized. As Blackstone put it: 'by marriage, the husband and wife are one person in law; that is, the very being or legal existence of the woman is suspended during marriage'.[58] For those who for any reason wished to maintain separate legal identity, resort to common law marriage was one way of establishing a contract that would stand up in civil court (until 1843) or, what was often more important, in the court of public opinion.[59]

Besom practice maintained the woman's right to her name, property and children. Such provisions are found in other common law practices and the Irish in some large towns found vows before a Catholic priest, while having no legal standing, useful in other ways as well:

These marriages satisfy the conscience of the wife and while the parish requires no relief, their invalidity is unknown or are unattended to. But as soon as the man becomes chargeable and the parish proceeds to remove him and his family, he shows that he is not legally married, and his children claim settlement on the parishes in which they were born.[60]

In some cases, couples ignored marriage and simply drew up an agreement, such as that between Emily Hickson and William Capras, which came to light in a Birmingham court in 1853:

It is hereby mutually agreed upon, by and between said William Charles Capras and Emily Hickson, that they the said shall live and reside together during the remainder of their lives, and that they shall mutually exert themselves by work and labour, and by following all their business pursuits, to the best of their abilities, skill, and understanding, and by advising and assisting each other, for their mutual benefit and advantage, and also to provide for themselves and each other the best supports and comforts of life which their means and income can afford.[61]

[57] Katherine O'Donovan, 'The Male Appendage – Legal Definitions of Women' in Sandra Burman (ed.), *Fit Work for Women* (London, 1979), p. 131.
[58] William Blackstone, *Commentaries on the Laws of England*, 4 vols. (Oxford, 1778), i, p. 442.
[59] Gerhard O. W. Mueller, 'Inquiry into the State of a Divorceless Society: Domestic Relations and Morals in England, 1660–1837', *University of Pittsburgh Law Review*, xviii (1956–7), pp. 545–78.
[60] *Report of His Majesty's Commissioners for Inquiry into the Poor Laws*, Parliamentary Papers (1834), p. 99.
[61] *Notes and Queries*, 1st ser., vii (1853), p. 603.

This agreement was drawn up by a lawyer, but for those who could not afford a written document there were other ways of notarizing intent; and it was not uncommon for couples to use the church ceremony itself for this purpose. It was believed that if a woman married only in her smock she could legally keep her financial obligations separate from those of her husband. The parish register of Marsham, Yorkshire, provides both the rationale and description of a so-called 'smock marriage' that took place there in June 1723:

> The woman to prevent a creditor coming on her newly wedded husband for debts contracted by her former husband had nothing to cover her nakedness during the solemnizing of the wedding but her shift.[62]

At Whitehaven in 1766 the ceremony was the same, but the financial embarrassment was the husband's, 'upon which account the girl was advised to do this, that he might be entitled to no other marriage portion than her smock'.[63] Smock weddings were frequent until the 1840s, especially in the north, where clergy appear to have been more willing to participate in them. Even those who disapproved could understand the logic behind the rite:

> I suppose that the original notion arose from some ingenious rustic special-pleader's interpretation of the character of certain portions of our conveyance-like marriage service.[64]

The feature of popular church rites that best served the female desire for a firm contractual basis to marriage was the ritual of the dow purse and the ring. The ring and coins were placed on the service book at the point in the ceremony when the groom speaks the words 'with all my worldly goods I thee endow'. By the eighteenth century the propertied classes had forsaken this practice, stigmatizing it as archaic superstition and substituting for it the marriage settlement drawn up in lawyers' chambers.[65] But humbler folk insisted on it, and were outraged when clergymen mistook the coins placed on the service book as a generous fee. Women were particularly sensitive to these lapses because both the coins and the ring symbolized their right to maintenance:

---

[62] *Ibid.*, 13th ser. i (1927), p. 169.
[63] *Ibid.*, 7th ser., i (1886), pp. 70–1; also *Monthly Chronicle of North Country Lore and Legend* (1887), p. 186.
[64] *Notes and Queries*, 3rd ser., vi (1852), p. 561.
[65] John C. Jaeffreson, *Brides and Bridals*, 2 vols. (London, 1872), i, p. 187.

Oh, sir, you should have put the siller [silver] into the bride's hand; the money's given to you that you might do so.[66]

Especially in the north and west of England and in Wales local clergy were still playing the major mediating role expected of them by the people. They entered into the service more actively than the liturgy required, blessing the ring and sanctioning a plebeian form of dowry. When in the late nineteenth century they began to withdraw these services, it was the women who saw their interests threatened. They transferred the meaning previously attached to the ring to the marriage certificate, which now became their marriage contract. At South Molton a man deserted his wife and stole her marriage paper, which he intended to give to another woman so she could claim his Chepstow parish settlement. The abandoned wife promptly acquired a duplicate, which she sent to the Chepstow overseers with the warning that 'my right is to his Parish and no other woman can have a right to it during my life time'.[67] Still, the ring retained much of its traditional meaning. Giving and accepting rings remained the most frequent act of common law marriage in the nineteenth century. Breakage, loss, or return of the ring was regarded as equally significant, the latter being the woman's form of self-divorce in both Shropshire and Wales, a counterpart to the better known and generally male-initiated divorce by wife sale.[68]

For women who wished to keep a separate legal identity, common law rites were extremely attractive. Conventional wedding endangered a woman's access to trade, and Mary Vinson, a London chimney-sweep with her own business, was well aware of this when she placed this announcement in the newspaper in 1787:

Many in the same Business have reported I am married again, which is totally false and without Foundation, it being calculated to mislead my Customers.[69]

For the same reasons a widow with a jointure which would lapse if

[66] James Vaux, *Church Folk Lore*, 2nd edn (London, 1902), p. 101.
[67] Ivor Winters, *Chepstow Parish Records* (Chepstow, 1955), p. 57.
[68] *Cupid's Pupils: From Courtship to Honeymoon: Being the Recollections of a Parish Clerk* (London, 1899), pp. 253ff. The importance of the ring is evident in the bigamy cases tried in the London Central Criminal Court during the nineteenth century, where exchange of rings was a common form of second marriage among persons who were separated but could not afford a legal divorce. Also Charlotte S. Burne (ed.), *Shropshire Folklore: A Sheaf of Gleanings* (London, 1883–6), p. 295; *Byegones*, ii (Oct. 1874), p. 128.
[69] Quoted in Pinchbeck, *Women Workers*, p. 285.

she remarried sought the secrecy of a Fleet wedding earlier in the century.[70] Servants, apprentices, soldiers and others who were bound to celibacy needed a way of putting their relations on a permanent footing without exposing their positions to risk. The same was true of farmers' sons who would not have a place of their own until their fathers' deaths, yet wanted to legitimate their lovers and any possible offspring. This may well have been a major reason for the popularity of besom marriage in Wales, where many waited years before having a home of their own.[71] Through the besom rite both they and the woman they intended to marry retained the respect of the community and a popular right to parish support.[72] And both sexes benefited from the kind of conditional contract that allowed men to pick up and move on without damage to the reputation or material condition of the women involved. Just as the urban Irish used this device, miners and other highly mobile workers resorted to the 'little weddings' described by Lewis Morris as very popular in Wales in the 1760s:

> Some Couples (especially among the miners) either having no friends, or seeing this kind of public marriage too troublesome and Impracticable, procure a man to wed them Privately which will not cost above two or 3 mugs of ale. Sometimes half a dozen Couple[s] will agree at a merry meeting, and are thus wedded and bedded together. This they call *Priodas vach* [i.e. the Little Wedding] and is frequently made use of among miners and others to make sure of a woman . . . The little wedding doth not bind them so Effectually, but that after a months trial they may part by Consent, when the Miner leaves his Mistress, and removes to a Minework in some distant Country, and the Girl is not worse look'd upon among the miners than if she had been an unspotted virgin, so Prevalent & Arbitrary is custom.[73]

The little wedding appears to have licensed intercourse for the purpose of testing fertility, while at the same time providing protection to the woman. There was a general understanding that

[70] Burn, *Fleet Registers*, p. 63.
[71] This was true of late nineteenth-century Wales. See D. Jenkins, *Agricultural Community in South-West Wales* (Cardiff, 1971), pp. 142, 155. Also Jennie Kitteringham, 'Country Work Girls in Nineteenth Century England', in R. Samuel (ed.), *Village Life and Labour* (London, 1975), p. 130.
[72] Burn, *Fleet Registers*, pp. 38, 54; Brown, 'Clandestine Marriages', pp. 172–3.
[73] Dafydd Ifan, 'Lewis Morris ac Afrerion Prioidi ygn Ngheredigion', *Ceredigion*, viii, no. 2 (1972), p. 201.

such a relationship could be terminated, but only on the consent of both parties. Self-divorce required witness, which explains the elaborate ritual of the wife sale. Leading the wife to market in a halter, 'auctioning' her to the highest bidder, and then notarizing the transaction by a bill of sale served the same purpose as jumping the broom backwards or returning the ring. When John Osborne and his wife Mary parted by wife sale in 1815, they made the conditions of their divorce quite explicit:

[John Osborne] does agree to part with my wife, Mary Osborne and child, to William Serjeant, for the sum of one pound, consideration of giving up all claim whatever.[74]

In the seventeenth century radical dissenters were known to authorize divorce, although they seem to have abandoned the practice by 1700.[75] For a time divorce was among the services offered by the Fleet and other lawless churches. Susannah Hewitt, an Enfield widow, married Abraham Wells, a butcher, there in 1729. Seven years later she returned to the Fleet parson who had wed them, complaining that 'her husband had beat and abused her in a barbarous manner, and she had much rather be esteemed his W—— [Whore] that she might have proper recourse against him'.[76] Others sought divorce by the same simple means of erasing the register, but they were not always so successful. The Fleet parsons were careful not to be too obliging, for they took their role as notaries and mediators quite seriously.[77] So too did the secular arbitrators of marriage in the later eighteenth and early nineteenth centuries. Self-divorce did not automatically have the support of the community; and the powerful sanction of rough music was often used to restore conjugal rights and force quarrelling couples to live in peace with one another.[78]

---

[74] Steel, *National Index of Parish Registers*, i, p. 325; many examples provided by Menefee, *Wives for Sale, passim.*

[75] Mueller, 'A Divorceless Society', pp. 547–50; Steel, *National Index of Parish Registers*, i, p. 322; Chilton L. Powell, *English Domestic Relations, 1487–1653* (New York, 1917), pp. 66, 80; Roger Thompson, *Women in Stuart England and America* (London and Boston, 1974), chs. 6 and 8.

[76] Burn, *Fleet Register*, p. 53.

[77] Brown, 'Clandestine Marriages', pp. 154–5; Steel, *National Index of Parish Registers*, i, pp. 327–8.

[78] On the variety of purposes served by rough music, see Edward P. Thompson, ' "Rough Music:" Le Charivari Anglais', *Annales: Économies, Sociétés, Civilisations*, xxvii, pt. 2 (Mar.–Apr. 1972), pp. 285–315.

V

From the 1750s onwards two standards of legitimacy, and two conceptions of marriage, were at war with one another. Lewis Morris observed that in Wales 'the late Act of Parliament [Hardwicke's Act] is looked upon as a Cruel and wicked restraint upon the liberties of the Mine Country'.[79] By providing for civil and dissenting marriage by reform of the law in 1837, and legislating civil divorce two decades after that, church and state ultimately moved to end open defiance of the law. But these changes did not alter the substance of marital relations. Parental consent continued to be required of those under age; wives were still *femme covert*. Civil divorce remained beyond the material means of working people until well into the twentieth century and, while they did eventually respond to the offer of civil marriage, the acceptance of this alternative did not wean them from their common law tradition as immediately as the reformers intended. Initially civil weddings by registrar were associated with the hated poor law administration and were therefore unacceptable to most working people. Equally important, the abbreviated civil ceremony lacked the tangible, contractual elements that had been part of both the common law rites and the popular amendments (the dow purse, etc.) to the church's own ceremonies. London poor law guardians were willing to pay George Stiffell to marry Ellen Barrett in the 1840s, but he balked at the idea of marriage without a ring. 'I said at the office that it would not do without the ring, and they said I could put that [the expense] into my pocket.' His best man, a silk-weaver named Thomas Green, was no less perturbed by the omission: 'Never saw such a marriage in my life . . . There was no ring put on.'[80] Ellen Barrett's reaction was probably even more emphatic, though we have no record of her feelings. For those who took the business of marriage seriously, the three-minute ceremony was not enough. 'Is that all . . . Am I married?' were characteristic responses to the civil marriage service.[81]

Olive Anderson has shown that civil marriage eventually made inroads into common law practice, even where that tradition was most entrenched.[82] The Registrar became by the 1870s the resort of

[79] Ifan, 'Lewis Morris', p. 201.
[80] Testimony in a bigamy case, 1850. Old Bailey Sessions Papers, 14 June 1850.
[81] *Cupid's Pupils*, p. 381.   [82] Anderson, 'Civil Marriage', pp. 86–7.

pregnant brides and other persons who, for reasons both economic and social, did not wish to have a full-scale public wedding. The fact that register weddings came to be called 'broomstick marriages' suggests that they came to serve the purposes which first clandestine and then common law marriages had earlier.[83] And it is significant that it was in those regions where common law rites had previously flourished that civil marriage became most popular in the course of the later nineteenth century.

In addition to changes in the law there were other reasons why common law rites were declining by 1900. Access to the anonymity of the towns and the decline of the kind of close-knit community that required public validation of private life were both factors that led to the recession of the more elaborate practices. Families were ceasing to be units of production. The intergenerational relations were altered; and so too were the conditions of marriage itself. As children's labour declined in importance, parents were more willing to accept early marriage. In the early twentieth century age of marriage fell dramatically, and the role of the family in the courtship and nuptial process was significantly altered.[84]

The decline of common law marriage also reflected the changing position of women. The Married Women's Property Acts of the 1870s and 1880s, together with laws securing the mother's right to her children, probably encouraged women to look more favourably on conventional church marriage. Although legal divorce was still beyond their means, it was possible by 1900 for working-class wives to gain separation orders from the police court and thus protect themselves against brutal husbands. In some places magistrates had begun to act like a kind of family court, providing a setting for arbitration and reconciliation that had been unavailable through church and state since the eighteenth century.[85] But the late nineteenth and early twentieth centuries also saw a decline in many

[83] On linguistic evidence, see J. Harvey Bloom, *Folk-Lore, Old Customs and Superstitions in Shakespeare's Land* (London, 1929), p. 10; Gwynn Jones, *Welsh Folk-Lore*, p. 185; Owen, *Some Old Stone Crosses*, p. 63. On the function of register office weddings, see Ormerod, *Lancashire Life*, pp. 124–5; A. N. Cooper, *Round the Home of a Yorkshire Parson* (London, n.d.), p. 201; C. Stella Davies, *North Country Bred* (London, 1963), p. 153.

[84] Diana Leonard Barker, 'A Proper Wedding', in Marie Corbin (ed.), *The Couple* (Harmondsworth, 1978), pp. 56–77; also Diana Leonard Barker, *Sex and Generation: A Study of Courtship and Weddings* (London, 1980).

[85] *Report of the Royal Commission on Divorce and Matrimonial Causes*, Parliamentary Papers (1912–13), xviii, pp. 90–100.

areas of married women's employment, and a growing economic dependence of wives on husbands.[86] Working women who testified about divorce in 1911 were all too aware of their continued powerlessness. One recounted how, after failing to get protection against her husband from the civil authorities, she finally resorted to the device of showing her marriage certificate to her neighbours, then publicly removing her ring, thus qualifying herself as what was popularly called a 'grass widow', a woman with the popularly acknowledged right to live apart from her husband while retaining her reputation as a respectable person. She hoped fervently for the passage of a progressive divorce law: 'I cordially long to regain that freedom which will relieve me from the necessity of passing myself off as a widow.'[87]

Gwenith Gwyn may be forgiven for thinking that by the First World War common law marriage and divorce had all but disappeared. They had undoubtedly diminished, but there were those who, like his elderly informant, either looked back nostalgically to the older plebeian traditions or, like the grass widow, resurrected them when faced with intolerable marital situations. In the long term, divorce and marriage reform erased the memory of the popular rites and the plebeian culture of which they were an expression. But these same reforms were not nearly so successful in removing the inequalities of sex, age and class which had given rise to the common law alternatives in the first place. If common law marriages constitute less than 3 per cent of contemporary conjugal arrangements, this may be due to the fact that greater access to divorce makes it so much easier to terminate a legal marriage.[88] But changing partners does not resolve the fundamental contradictions inherent in modern marriage. It is just another way of dealing with them, a further development in the long and very complicated history of marital disputes and settlements.

[86] O'Donovan, 'The Male Appendage', p. 136.
[87] A 'grass widow' could be either a wife living alone or an unwed mother. *Cupid's Pupils*, p. 59; example of self-divorce from *Working Women and Divorce: An Account of Evidence Given on Behalf of the Women's Cooperative Guild before the Royal Commission on Divorce* (London, 1911), p. 63.
[88] Of women living with men surveyed in the 1970s, only 3 per cent were found to be cohabiting. Most of these arrangements were short term, and of the women involved only 2 per cent thought of themselves as being in a real marriage. It seems that despite the increase in pre-marital intercourse and numbers of couples 'living together' before marriage, the older common law tradition has virtually disappeared. Karen Dunnell, *Family Formation 1976* (London, 1979), pp. 7–8.

11. *Postscript*

JOHN BOSSY

My qualifications for offering some general historical reflections on the contents of this volume are modest. What I had in mind when proposing the topic for a conference was the idea of a social history which would be a history of actual people; a feeling that the record of law and especially of litigation was a good place to find out something about them; some experience in the history of the social institutions of Christianity considered as peace-making rituals, and a wish to pursue the subject of arbitration and peace-making as an important matter in itself; and an interest in the theory of marriage represented in *Romeo and Juliet*. It has been an agreeable experience to discover that these preoccupations are shared by people with expertise as various as that of the ten contributors. Bearing in mind Simon Roberts' recommendations to avoid treating one's typology as if it were an evolutionary scheme, and supposing that one method of settling disputes is inherently more attractive than another, I shall try to summarize what I have learned from them.

I do not think it will be violating Roberts' principles to say that three extremely powerful images have governed the resolution of disputes in the West since the disintegration of Roman authority: the image of feud; the image of charity; and the image of the law (or the state). The first requires that offences be retaliated; extends the obligation for offence and retaliation to others than the individuals offending and offended, and especially to kinsmen; and creates a social universe distinguished for any member into his friends and his enemies. It is represented here by the sixth-century feud of Sichar and Chramnesind, which inspired the intervention of Gregory of Tours; and by Jenny Wormald's account, particularly valuable for the amount of written evidence she is able to use, of a European population where the image of feud dominated the settlement of offences until the seventeenth century, that of Scotland. Her account bears comparison with Wallace-Hadrill's of feud among the Franks, and with Otto Brunner's of the institution in late medieval Germany; in the second case there are strong resemblances in both argument and chronology.[1] It has been, I suppose, a fading image. At the time when it was being finally abandoned in Scotland, Casey sees it as not much more than a topos of the theatre in Spain; in the eighteenth-century Languedoc of Nicole Castan it was subdued to a marginal practice of the duel, and to a general sense of honour which was always negotiable, though it required something more than monetary satisfaction. Whether it has been at any time so exclusively aristocratic an image as is often suggested seems a matter for discussion. We should be careful of underestimating its force at any level of the population and at any period in the history of the West. It has been a silent presence behind the workings of law and love, and where neither law nor love prevail will no doubt continue to govern the relations of individuals, communities and states.

The image of charity requires that offences be not retaliated, which is not to say that it requires them to be ignored; that conflicts should be amicably settled; that an obligation of love extends to enemies as well as to friends; and that certain outward signs of amity should be generally observed. It seems quite likely that it responds to something in human character as deeply rooted as the image of feud, though it has been widely held to be contrary to nature. In practice, in European experience it has been generally associated with Christianity, and indeed for most people at most times has been what Christianity was thought to be chiefly about. It has been generally felt compatible with the objective existence of a social world divided into friends and enemies; and it may well be true that it and Christianity lose a good deal of their force where this is no longer the case.

First among our contributions to this theme must be Michael Clanchy's exposition of the text that love must conquer law, the classic form of a contrast which is probably the principal theme of the history of European legal systems considered as social

---

[1] J. M. Wallace-Hadrill, 'The Blood-Feud of the Franks', in *The Long-Haired Kings* (London, 1962); perhaps I should say that I have no quarrel with the definition of feud given here (p. 122), nor with the view expressed that arrangements for composition are part of a system of feud, not a different system. Otto Brunner, *Land und Herrschaft: Grundfragen der territorialen Verfassungsgeschicte Österreichs im Mittelalter*, 4th edn (Vienna/Wiesbaden, 1959), pp. 1–110.

institutions. We can bear in mind that in a feudal regime love may be compulsory, and do justice to Wycliffe's comment that the settlement of disputes by love rather than law may favour the strong at the expense of the weak. This is also to some degree the message of Nicole Castan from eighteenth-century Languedoc. But if all lovedays had been of this nature we could hardly account for the strength of the image of charity through the centuries, for its governing to the degree which it did the behaviour of the seventeenth-century Yorkshire villagers described by J. A. Sharpe, or those of Wiltshire recorded elsewhere by Martin Ingram.[2] Although the prudential factors in favour of arbitration have been emphasized by Nicole Castan, it must surely mean something that the question of motive has arisen in almost exactly the same form for almost all the contributors, including herself. On the spur of the moment all kinds of feelings were no doubt involved; but whenever people's submission to arbitration was seen in perspective, not only by the learned but by themselves, it was seen as an act of Christianity. The rituals of reconciliation or *amicitia*, performed in the church or churchyard, in the alehouse or elsewhere, were modelled on (or possibly models for, I doubt if it makes much difference) the rituals of penance and communion: in the case of penance they were practically indistinguishable. The Scottish term for the formal indemnity granted to one who has made compensation seems to be a form of *salus*, and evokes the *salus* and *incolumitas* which the Christian was invited to pray for, for himself and all his, in the mass. Love is not only better than law, it is the way to salvation, especially if it involves some surrender of right.

That the intervention of charity did not in principle require the intervention of the church narrowly defined may be illustrated from the communities investigated by Sharpe and Casey; before them, it would perhaps be the principal lesson of the history of fraternal institutions in the Middle Ages and after. In a variety of circumstances priesthood has certainly been an obstacle to it. But reconciliation on earth, as between earth and heaven, normally requires a mediator, and there has been a general conviction that it

[2] M. J. Ingram, 'Communities and Courts: Law and Disorder in Early Seventeenth-century Wiltshire', in J. S. Cockburn (ed.), *Crime in England, 1500–1800* (London, 1977), pp. 110–34, esp. pp. 125ff. For a non-compulsory loveday in the late sixteenth century, see *Depositions and Other Ecclesiastical Proceedings from the Courts of Durham* (Surtees Soc., xxi, 1845), pp. 87ff., a reference for which I am indebted to Miranda Chaytor.

has been the business of the church to supply the function. Gregory of Tours reflected the view that the intervention of the church was particularly called for where simple negotiation might favour the stronger party. In the phase of Christianity with which we begin, as in other cultures mentioned by Simon Roberts, the mediating power seems to have operated through a strong and physical sense of the holy, both personal and local: analysed elsewhere by Peter Brown and others, it is represented here by Edward James' account of the early history of sanctuary.[3] The relation of local and personal sanctity to the reconciliation of disputes is a theme which might be pursued at least as far as the sixteenth century: what the story of Gregory of Tours seems to be pointing to is the attribution of the function to the institutional sanctity, first of bishops and later, perhaps particularly after the time of Pope Innocent III, of the parish clergy. By the close of the Middle Ages, except for the still considerable areas where the parochial institution was a shadow, and barring personal and other quarrels, the officiating parish priest was the appropriate agent of charitable settlement. His mediation or participation seems to have been the most usual case, the nobleman and the notary being important competitors or allies. Both before and after the Reformation the duty was impressed upon him both from above and from below,[4] though there were probably elements in the Reformation, such as the abolition of sacramental penance, which may have made it more difficult or more distasteful to perform. To some extent from the sixteenth century, and certainly in the nineteenth, the parish clergy were apt to be told that they had better things to do than to compose the quarrels of their parishioners; it is difficult to know if they were victims, in the end, of changes in the conception of their role, or in the economic system, or of a kind of functional obsolescence.

The image of the law affirms that most offences are not in the first

[3] Peter Brown, 'The Rise and Function of the Holy Man in Late Antiquity', Journal of Roman Studies, lxi (1971), pp. 80–101; H. Mayr-Hartung, 'Functions of a Twelfth-century Recluse', History, lx (1975), pp. 340ff.

[4] Three examples: Gabriel le Bras, Institutions ecclésiastiques de la Chrétienté médiévale, ii (A. Fliche, V. Martin et al. (eds.), Histoire de l'Eglise, xii, pt. 2) (Paris, 1964), p. 407 (synodal statutes of Tournai, 1306); Alessandro Pastore, Nella Valtellina nel tardo Cinquecento (Milan, 1975), p. 55 (agreement between people and priest of a (Catholic) village in the Valtelline); Alfred Soman, 'Deviance and Criminal Justice in Western Europe, 1300–1800: An Essay in Structure', Criminal Justice History, i (1980), pp. 18ff. (reformed consistories of Meyrueis and Coutras, sixteenth to seventeenth centuries).

place offences against other persons, but against the state or the law itself, to which exclusively falls the obligation of retaliating them. In most cases this has entailed the construction by the secular authority of a more or less comprehensive code of permitted and forbidden behaviour; it always involves the erection of a system of courts where offenders against these rules can be tried and convicted, and the more or less compulsory offer of facilities for adjudication where the state is not primarily a party. It has the effect of creating a class of legal officers and practitioners whose experience in the formal presentation and resolution of disputes makes them competitors with older agents of pacification. Derived, as Michael Clanchy presents it in his model of the Emperor Frederick II, from Rome and the Old Testament, it made its way through Christendom in an apparently inexorable process recently charted by Bruce Lenman and Geoffrey Parker and illustrated here by Richard Kagan's Castile.[5] The inpouring of the people's disputes into the tribunals of the crown of Castile from the close of the fifteenth century seems to have constituted a golden moment in the image of the law; the same thing was happening in France and Tuscany,[6] perhaps also in England. Quite how the image of the law, or the state or the crown, had managed to acquire a sanctity, a moral force of this order seems rather a problem, but it was clearly in some sense here to stay. In so far as one may take the view that its principal object was to get rid of the simpler forms of feud, it seems to have been broadly achieved, as in seventeenth-century Scotland; on the whole, and rather contrary to Clanchy's notion of the twelfth century, it does not look as if it created more disputes than it resolved. But everyone seems agreed that it did not supersede the practice of composition or arbitration, and that one of the reasons for welcoming it was that it provided a fairly efficient incentive for private settlement. Those who thought that the beginning of law was the end of love would have been consoled by this, as by the flight from the Castilian courts from the late seventeenth century: whether they would have been gratified by the passage of the arbitral faculty into the hands of the advocate is less clear, though

---

[5] Bruce Lenman and Geoffrey Parker, 'The State, the Community and the Criminal Law in Early Modern Europe', in V. A. C. Gattrell, B. Lenman and G. Parker (eds.), *Crime and the Law: The Social History of Crime in Western Europe since 1500* (London, 1980), pp. 11–48.

[6] Samuel Berner, 'Florentine Society in the Late Sixteenth and Early Seventeenth Centuries', *Studies in the Renaissance*, xviii (1971), pp. 227–35.

they had accommodated themselves to the notary in the past.

Kagan's demonstration of the retreat of royal jurisdiction in eighteenth-century Spain is another reminder not to take types of conflict settlement for phases in a historical process, or to see the crowned image of law as a fatal denouement. Even Nicole Castan, who seems most nearly, among our contributors, a believer in the inevitable supersession of arbitral by adjudicative processes, in the decay of mediation with the decay of traditional hierarchies, leaves us with something of a question about what happened in France after 1800. Neither in France nor in Spain, it appears, did the rise of the liberal state entail the disappearance of arbitration, and a layman's acquaintance with British experience in divorce and industrial relations might suggest the same for ourselves. There is some suggestion that the image of the law is rather a myth. If so, I suspect that we should take the fact, as for the image of feud and the image of charity, as evidence of the importance of myths.

Three of the contributors have written about the history of marriage, as a substantial topic in the history both of disputes and of their settlement. For a marriage, as Clanchy says, is a loveday; the rites of reconciliation and the rites of marriage are the same, and both are social victories, as well as social armistices. Diane Hughes, who has already written on the history of dowry,[7] has here chosen a peculiarly rule-bound area of law, the sumptuary *ordini* of medieval and renaissance Italian cities. Behind the arguments about sleeves and cleavages we find legislators grappling with the mores of matrimonial alliance practised among their patrician families, endeavouring to subject the social machine to the demands of the whole. The display of fashion by brides and wives, product of dowry and bride-gift, demonstrated the potency residing in the union of lineages, the triumph of negotiation over conflict, the power of the ring. Here the image of law is at symbolic odds, not directly with the image of feud, but with the image of reconciliation; the personal relations of wives and husbands, though not a negligible matter, recede behind the mechanisms of alliance. Among Casey's Andalusian couples, we naturally see more of them, though misalliance is as much a public matter as alliance. The union of individuals does not supersede the prior bond of consanguinity,

---

[7] Diane Owen Hughes, 'From Brideprice to Dowry in Mediterranean Europe', *Journal of Family History* (Sept. 1978), pp. 262–96.

though even in these unsuccessful cases affinity means a good deal. Her consanguinity is a refuge for the unhappy wife, and the process of divorce will bring into play the contrary loyalties of two sets of kinsmen and turn alliance to discord, leaving the judge to disentangle the facts and seek to promote reconciliation before affinity is finally dissolved. Yet as privacy creeps up on even these ill-insulated households, the tensions of conjugal society seem to loom larger, superseding arguments about dowry, murder at the marriage feast and the influence of the aiguillette as the principal hazard in the constitution of alliance by marriage.

There is no sign in Andalusia that access to judicial separation was restricted to the upper classes, or that married life among peasants and artisans was more brutal or male-dominated than among anyone else. Others, including Nicole Castan, have held the contrary.[8] John Gillis implies a third view, which seems popular among English-speaking historians, that 'plebeian' marriage was more likely to nurture successful human relations than a patrician marriage over-concerned with property, and his account of the clandestine and common law tradition of English and Welsh marriage is an eloquent testimony to this. I wonder myself whether affectionate conjugal relations are not compatible with almost any regime of law, custom, economy or demography, and whether marital dispute or spouse-murder were more common among couples married in church. But there is clearly a good deal of force in his picture of a clergy failing to appreciate what was intended by the bride who placed coins on the Bible that the priest might convey them to her groom, and in general to live up to its historic role as maker of alliance and guardian of its most potent symbol, the ring. This at least was not a case of functional obsolescence.

In the course of the conference I took the liberty of recommending to the participants a certain *naïveté* about words like love and friendship as an aid to understanding in the history of human relations. I expect this will seem dangerous advice to many, but think it worth repeating. It is after all what I imagine they, in their own relations, would be likely to recommend to themselves.

---

[8] Nicole Castan, 'Puissance conjugale et violence maritale', *Pénélope*, no. 6 (Paris, Spring 1982), pp. 95–103, cf. J. A. Sharpe, 'Domestic Homicide in Early Modern England', *The Historical Journal*, xxiv (1981), pp. 29–48.

Index

Past and Present Publications

General Editor: T. H. ASTON, *Corpus Christi College, Oxford*

* Also issued as a paperback
† Co-published with the Maison des Sciences de l'Homme, Paris

Printed in the United Kingdom
by Lightning Source UK Ltd.
123384UK00001B/133-135/A